The province compared

Alberta and
Ontario

The Provincial Shield

Alberta and
Great Britain

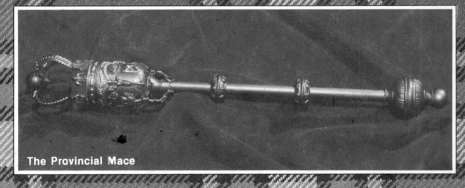

The Provincial Flower,
the wild rose

The Provincial Mace

Alberta and
California

The Provincial Bird, the horned owl

In the background,
the Provincial Tartan

THE
ATLAS
OF ALBERTA

A special project of

ALBERTA REPORT
The Weekly Newsmagazine

© 1984, Interwest Publications Ltd.

published by

Interwest Publications Ltd.

17327 - 106A Ave.
Edmonton, Alberta
T5S 1M7
(403) 484-8884

General Editor
Ted Byfield

Director of Production
Derrick Sorochan

Marketing Director
A. Gordon Salway

Research
Joanne Hatton
Michael Byfield

Art Direction
Jeanneke Sundland

Design and Layout
Tesoro DeGuzman Jr.

Typography
Robert Tomkinson

Executive Director
Richard D. McCallum

Lithography
Color Graphics Alberta Ltd.

Printing
The Jasper Printing Group Ltd.

Binding
North-West Book Company Limited

Canadian Cataloguing in Publication Data

Main entry under title:

The Atlas of Alberta

A special project of Alberta Report.
Includes index.
ISBN 0-9691852-1-9

1. Alberta - Maps. 2. Alberta - Historical
geography - Maps. 3. Cities and towns -
Alberta - Maps. 4. Alberta - Economic
conditions - Maps. I. Byfield,
Ted. II. Alberta Report.
G1165.A42 1984   912'.7123   C84-091430-X

Acknowledgements and Credits

Alberta Report gratefully acknowledges the indispensable contribution of hundreds of citizens to this project, some of whom are listed below.

Individuals

Mrs. Marguerite Ahlf, Local Historian, Edson

Ralph Allman, Alberta Energy Resources Conservation Board, Calgary

Brian Andre, Addressing Technician, County of Strathcona

Mary Andrews, Local Historian, Banff

Judy Archie, Secretary-Manager, Leduc Chamber of Commerce

John Barr, Director of Public Affairs, Syncrude Canada Ltd., Edmonton

Mrs. Edith Bedy, Local Historian, Drayton Valley

Bill Bell, Local Historian, Leduc

P. Belley, Planning Department Secretary, Town of High River

Dorothy Bergos, Manager, Drumheller Chamber of Commerce

Willy Bogdan, Kelowna, B.C., former Director of Mapping, Alberta Bureau of Surveying and Mapping

Arlene Borgstede, Local Historian, St. Albert

Courtney Breckenridge, Director of Municipal Planning, County of Parkland

Henry Bruch, Planning Department, Municipal District of Rocky View

Brenda Bryce, Secretary, Sherwood Park Chamber of Commerce

Les Canning, Engineering Assistant, Town of Peace River

Alan Cassley, Senior Project Engineer, Pipeline Department, Energy Resources Conservation Board, Calgary

B. Charchun, Land Records/Surveys Officers, Alberta Region, Indian and Northern Affairs, Edmonton

Chris Clark, Photographer, Kelowna, B.C.

Ed Clarke, President, Capital Markets West, Ponoka

Jeanette Cook, Development Clerk, Municipal District of Sturgeon

Murray Cook, Local Historian, Peace River

Jean Cote, Canadian National Railways Historian, Edmonton

Patricia Craig, Photo Library Co-ordinator, Alberta Public Affairs Bureau, Edmonton

Robert Cundy, Executive Director, Red Deer Regional Planning Commission

Michael Dawe, Archivist, Red Deer District Museum and Archives

Hugh Dempsey, Chief Curator, Glenbow Museum, Calgary

William Dewan, Director of Public Relations, Canadian National Railways, Edmonton

T.C. Dick, Signing/marking Co-ordinator, Traffic Operations Division, City of Calgary

E. Dietrich, Technician, Red Deer Regional Planning Commission

Richard Dressler, R.S.D. Canadian Geographics Ltd., Edmonton

Mary Fitl, Information Officer, Alberta Recreation and Parks

Jane Flaherty, General Manager, Jasper Chamber of Commerce

Don Foulger, Government of Canada, Energy Mines and Resources, Ottawa

Ed Fox, Energy Resources Conservation Board, Calgary

A.M. Gibeault, Town Manager, Town of Morinville

Barb Giese, Secretary, County of Parkland

R.N. Giffen, Executive Director, Edmonton Metropolitan Regional Planning Commission

R. Bruce Goodwin, Executive Director, Prairie Provinces Water Board, Regina

Wayne Gordon, City Planner, City of St. Albert

K. Gwodz, Technician, Red Deer Regional Planning Commission

Brian Haley, Long Range Planning, City of Calgary

Dr. Stan Hambley, Local Historian, Camrose

Lesly A. Hanson, Manager, Stony Plain Chamber of Commerce

Dianne Harp, Community Relations Officer, City of Fort McMurray

Patrick Hart, Cartographer, City of Fort McMurray

E.G. (Ted) Hicks, Development Officer, Town of Edson

George K. Higa, Engineering Design Supervisor, City of Lethbridge

Barb Holub, Manager, Hinton Chamber of Commerce

Rob Honsberger, former Assistant City Commissioner, City of Lloydminster

Dennis N. Hoybak, Assistant Supervisor, Alberta Recreation and Parks, Edmonton

Gary L. Hudson, Development Officer, Town of Airdrie

Hiromi Ikemura, Senior Planning Technician, City of St. Albert

Ron Jacob, Planning Department, City of Calgary

Alex Johnston, Local Historian, Lethbridge

Marilyn Kan, Local Historian, Jasper

Gerry Keefe, Project Engineer, Town of Drayton Valley

Ed Kennedy, Executive Director, Alberta Bureau of Surveying and Mapping, Edmonton

Eugene Kletke, Assistant Director, Technical Services, Alberta Bureau of Surveying and Mapping, Edmonton

Mrs. Lillian Knupp, Local Historian, High River

John Kost, Manager, Town of Ponoka

Gerry Krish, Senior Marketing Consultant, Travel Alberta, Edmonton

Juliette Lafleur, Local Historian, St. Paul

Donelda Laing, Manager, Spruce Grove Chamber of Commerce

Clair Lamarre, Information Officer, Parks Canada, Calgary

Debbie Landis, Grande Prairie Chamber of Commerce

Maurice Landry, Director of Development & Engineering, Town of Brooks

Omer Lavallee, Historian, Canadian Pacific Railway, Montreal, Que.

Pat Lengyel, Secretary-Manager, Stettler and District Chamber of Commerce

Jean Lillie, Secretary-Treasurer, Vegreville District Chamber of Commerce

Colette Longhe, Tourism Assistant, Camrose Chamber of Commerce

Esther Lunan, Local Historian, Spruce Grove

D. Macdonald, Municipal Planning Director, Edmonton Metropolitan Regional Planning Commission

Perry Mah, Photographer, Edmonton

Jack Marsh, Mapping Branch, Alberta Energy and Natural Resources, Edmonton

Brian McFarlane, Area Supervisor, Energy Resources Conservation Board, Edmonton

Brian Miller, Public Affairs, Alberta Economic Development, Edmonton

Cheryl Mocan, Communications Co-ordinator, Calgary Transit

Arthur W. Murdoch, Assistant Provincial Archivist, Archives of Ontario, Toronto

Gunter Narquardt, Government of Canada, Energy Mines and Resources, Ottawa

Les Newman, Economics, Energy Resources Conservation Board, Calgary

Dave Oliphant, Manager, Medicine Hat Chamber of Commerce

Earl Olson, Director of Public Affairs, Canadian Pacific Railway, Calgary

Jim Orydsuk, Planning Department, City of Edmonton

Gill Oslund, Snell & Oslund Surveys (1979) Ltd., Red Deer

Sharon Pearce, Director of Communications, Alberta Bureau of Surveying and Mapping, Edmonton

Don Pearson, Gas Department, Energy Resources Conservation Board, Calgary

Kathryn A. Persson, Communications Co-ordinator, Heritage Park Society, Calgary

Lynda Pierce, Manager, Lloydminster Chamber of Commerce

Ken Pinoski, Development Officer, County of Leduc

Marguerite Playle, Local Historian, Drumheller

Linda Plumer, Secretary, Brooks Chamber of Commerce

Robert Popow, President, Lacombe Chamber of Commerce

Art Potvin, Alberta Agriculture, Irrigation Division, Lethbridge

Bruce Randall, Business Development Officer, City of St. Albert

Alex Rennie, Public Affairs, Canadian National Railways, Edmonton

Gordon Riddell, Planning Services Division, Alberta Municipal Affairs, Edmonton

I. Robinson, Executive Director, Calgary Regional Planning Commission

C.F. Schile, Local Government Administrator, Town of Taber

Fred Schulz, Alberta Transportation, Edmonton

Rita Sigvaldason, Secretary, Crowsnest Pass Chamber of Commerce

Mike Skakum, Regional Publishing and Printing Co-ordinator, Parks Canada, Calgary

Wayne Sorenson, Construction Programming Branch, Alberta Transportation, Edmonton

N. Sveinson, President, Innisfail Chamber of Commerce

G. Thomas, Chief Draftsman, Calgary Regional Planning Commission

W.H. Thrall, Director, Lands Membership and Estates, Indian and Northern Affairs Canada, Edmonton

Tom Tinkler, Creative Services, Alberta Public Affairs Bureau, Edmonton

John Trefanenko, St. Paul Chamber of Commerce

Henry Unrau, Local Historian, Sherwood Park

Bill Vander Meer, Engineering Department, City of Edmonton

Beckie Vogel, Office Supervisor, Banff Chamber of Commerce

Carl Von Einsiedel, Northern Pipeline Agency, Calgary

Robert J. Walker, Proofreader, Edmonton

Thomas Walls, Alberta Recreation and Parks, Edmonton

Marvin Weiss, Assistant Director, Provincial Mapping, Alberta Bureau of Surveying and Mapping, Edmonton

Ronald Whistance-Smith, Curator, University of Alberta Map Collection, Edmonton

I.L.E. White, Administrative Supervisor, Traffic Planning Section, City of Edmonton

Ken Williams, Regional Information Adviser, Indian and Northern Affairs Canada, Edmonton

Tom Willock, Director, Medicine Hat Museum and Art Gallery

Dr. L.J. (Roy) Wilson, Instructor, Medicine Hat College

W.L. Winger, Municipal Manager, Town of Whitecourt

Lorill Wingrave, Secretary-Manager, Wetaskiwin Chamber of Commerce

Mrs. C.R. Wood, Local Historian, Stony Plain

Libby Young, Local Historian, Lloydminster

Organizations

Anglican Church of Canada, Calgary Diocese

Anglican Church of Canada, Edmonton Diocese

Catholic Archdiocese of Calgary

Catholic Archdiocese of Edmonton

The Chambers of Commerce of Airdrie, Banff, Brooks, Calgary, Camrose, Municipality of Crowsnest Pass, Drumheller, Edmonton, Edson, Fort McMurray, Fort Saskatchewan, Grande Prairie, High River, Hinton, Innisfail, Jasper, Lacombe, Leduc, Lethbridge, Lloydminster, Medicine Hat, Morinville, Peace River, Ponoka, Red Deer, Sherwood Park, Spruce Grove, St. Albert, St. Paul, Stettler, Stony Plain, Taber, Vegreville, Wetaskiwin, Whitecourt

Council of Edmonton Lutheran Churches

Lutheran Information Services, Calgary

Old Strathcona Foundation Association, Edmonton

United Church of Canada, Alberta Conference Office

Yellowhead Highway Association, Edmonton

Companies

Alberta Government Telephones

Canada Post Corporation

Dome Petroleum Limited, Calgary

Edmonton Telephones

Imperial Oil Ltd., Edmonton and Calgary

Interprovincial Pipe Line Limited, Edmonton

Mohawk Oil Co. Ltd., Edmonton

Petro-Canada, Calgary

Shell Canada Ltd., Edmonton and Calgary

Texaco Canada Inc., Edmonton and Calgary

Trans Mountain Pipe Line Co. Ltd., Edmonton

Turbo Resources Ltd., Edmonton and Calgary

Government Departments

Town of Airdrie

Alberta Bureau of Surveying and Mapping

Alberta Chief Electoral Office

Alberta Energy & Natural Resources, Surveys and Mapping Branch

Alberta Environment, Water Resources Management Services

Alberta Map Sales Office

Alberta Municipal Affairs

Town of Banff

Battle River Regional Planning Commission, Wetaskiwin

Town of Brooks

City of Calgary

City of Calgary Archives

City of Calgary Election Office

Calgary Public School Board

Calgary Separate School Board

City of Camrose

Municipality of Crowsnest Pass

Town of Drayton Valley

City of Drumheller

City of Edmonton

City of Edmonton Archives

City of Edmonton Election Office

City of Edmonton Planning Department, Maps and Publications

Edmonton Public School Board

Edmonton Separate School Board

Town of Edson

Energy Resources Conservation Board, Calgary

City of Fort McMurray

Town of Fort Saskatchewan

Fort Saskatchewan Library

Town of Fort Saskatchewan Planning Department

Government of Canada, Energy, Mines & Resources

City of Grande Prairie

Town of High River

Town of Innisfail

Town of Jasper

Town of Lacombe

City of Leduc

City of Lethbridge

City of Lloydminster

City of Medicine Hat

Town of Morinville

Old Man River Regional Planning Commission, Lethbridge

Palliser Regional Planning Commission, Hanna

Parks Canada

Town of Peace River

Peace River Regional Planning Commission, Grande Prairie

Town of Ponoka

Provincial Archives, Edmonton

City of Red Deer

Sherwood Park Information Centre

South East Alberta Regional Planning Commission, Medicine Hat

Town of Spruce Grove

City of St. Albert

Town of St. Paul

Town of Stettler

Town of Stony Plain

Town of Taber

Travel Alberta

University of Alberta

University of Alberta, Map Collection

University of Calgary

Town of Vegreville

City of Wetaskiwin

Wetaskiwin Library

Town of Whitecourt

Yellowhead Regional Planning Commission, Onoway

Atlas Staff

Artists

Kelly Ann Akins
Don Brown
Alison Cleary
Tesoro DeGuzman
Nancy Herridge
Gordon Hudson
Kathleen Marta
Samuel Motyka
Ross Reid
Derrick Sorochan
Linda A. Taylor
Richie Velthius

Researchers and Proofreaders

Keith Bennett
Victor Beranek
Cynthia Bezrucki
Bill Brommit
Mike Byfield
Ted Byfield
Thomas M. Byfield
Virginia Byfield
Terry Gibbons
Joanne Hatton
Jane Hennig
J. Stephen Hopkins
Ann Hopkins
Gillian Neelands
Dave Pernarowski
A. Gordon Salway
Gordon Scott
Wendy Tang

Production

Bart Brusse
Vincent Byfield
Terry Garth
John Gee
Richard McCallum
Jeanneke Sundland
Robert Tomkinson

Outside Production Assistance

Aube Typographics Ltd., Edmonton
BJM and Associates, Edmonton
Color Graphics Alberta Ltd., Edmonton
EFT Systems, Edmonton
Geo Graphica Consulting Ltd., Edmonton
Graphic Enterprises, Edmonton
North-West Book Company Ltd., Surrey, B.C.
North West Survey Group, Edmonton
R.N. Graphics Ltd., Edmonton
Riley's Reproduction & Printing Ltd., Edmonton
The Jasper Printing Group Ltd., Edmonton

Bibliography

Government of Canada, Department of Energy, Mines and Resources, The National Atlas of Canada, Ottawa, 1971.

Crowsnest Pass Historical Society, Crowsnest and its People. Coleman, 1980.

Ed Gould, All Hell For A Basement. Medicine Hat, City of Medicine Hat, 1981.

James G. MacGregor, A History of Alberta. Edmonton, Hurtig Publishers, 1972.

Eric J. and Patricia M. Holmgren, Place Names of Alberta. Saskatoon, Western Producer Prairie Books, 1976.

Hazel Hart, The History of Hinton. Hinton, 1980.

United News, Metro Calgary Plus. Ottawa Pathfinder Urban Atlas, 1981.

W.F. Lothian, A History of Canada's National Parks, 1976.

How the atlas came about

That a magazine should produce an atlas is an idea that can make no claim to originality. In 1982 the *Reader's Digest* of Canada published a remarkably detailed Atlas of Canada. Prior to that, *Time* magazine came out with a competent Atlas of the World. Even an atlas of Alberta is not new. The University of Alberta turned out a fine volume in 1969. But the university, being an academic institution, produced what was in essence an academic atlas depicting the geophysics of the province, vital to research and learning, but not immediately useful to Albertans in their everyday lives. If a provincial news magazine is to produce a provincial atlas, I, its publisher, decided, it must be something like the news itself—pertinent to people's immediate needs, up-to-date, for many people indispensable. Great idea, said *Alberta Report*'s editors, but did I have the faintest idea of what I was undertaking? The answer after nearly two years finding out: No.

The atlas as we conceived it must be divided into three parts. First, there must be an historical section presenting maps of the province as it developed from its origins in the fur trade until now.

Second, and by far the most problematic, there must be what we considered a "bread and butter" section, showing detailed street maps of 39 Alberta cities and towns, locating every school, church, park, hospital, hotel or motel, shopping centre, bank, liquor store, post office, police station, grain elevator, all-night restaurant or service station, estate development, showing all streets and avenues and how they are numbered and which ones are one-way, showing details of the downtowns of both major cities, with every building over three storeys clearly identified, showing where the business, industrial and residential sections lie, showing railways and through highways, bridges, points of interest, in fact anything anyone would need to navigate with confidence through every urban area in Alberta.

Third, there must be a resource section, depicting the province's natural assets in a way most useful to the reader: national and provincial parks showing such things as hiking trails and campgrounds; a map showing the over 500 lakes and rivers of Alberta and how they drain to the ocean; maps of all the major oil and gas fields with detail on the size of each reserve, which company drilled the discovery well and when; similar maps of the oil and gas pipelines; maps showing the many passes through the Rocky Mountains, all but four of which have never been developed; instructional maps on such things as how to read an Alberta survey description; and finally, of course, maps showing the location of agricultural producing areas, where the various grains are grown, where livestock is raised.

Before undertaking such a project, *AR* initially consulted Edward A. Kennedy, executive director of the Alberta Bureau of Surveying and Mapping. The first and the third sections, he said, were well within the range of feasibility; the second would represent a massive undertaking since this much detail on the cities and towns had never to his knowledge been assembled. However, for the best advice on how to do it he directed us to Willy Bogdan, former director of mapping of the Alberta Bureau of Surveying and Mapping, now retired in Kelowna.

Mr. Bogdan's enthusiasm for the project was immediate. He flew to Edmonton and set out a method of producing the essential municipal maps for the second section. But we needed a determined man to run the project, he said, one who would not rest until it was finished. We found such a man on our own staff. Artist Derrick Sorochan joined the project as its production director in July of 1982 and supervised the preparation of almost every map in the book. He was assisted throughout the project by Linda A. Taylor. The artistic concepts are those of *AR* art director Jeanneke Sundland. Artist Tesoro DeGuzman Jr. laid out the pages and created the cover design.

What we lacked was what cartographers call "field information." It was all very well to announce we would include every church, but where were all the churches located? Where were the all-night service stations? Where precisely were all the hotels and banks? We pondered a half dozen ways of having the information gathered for us and found that nothing worked, but to go out and get it ourselves. This of course, entailed a street-by-street survey of every municipality in Alberta with a population over 4,900. Who could be found for this?

The answer came in two people. Victor Beranek, recently arrived from Poland where he had run a driving school, was a man with a gift for accuracy and a need for a job. Thomas Byfield, then 17, who has been a member of the Byfield family since he was about four weeks old, had inherited from his Indian forebears an uncanny sense of direction and location. Together over the period of about nine months they tracked the province—an odd team, the stocky young Indian, notebook and work maps in hand, the erect and dignified European pointing out data that the maps must contain. Meanwhile, as their information began pouring back to the tiny room at *AR*'s head offices, Mr.

Clockwise from upper right: Production Manager Sorochan, the Survey and Mapping Bureau's Kennedy, field workers Byfield and Beranek, cartographer Bogdan, artist Taylor.

Sorochan had hired another three staff artists to work it into the blank maps the province had provided and three more people to check each location, first against the field work, then against such sources as telephone books and city directories. Slowly all the municipal maps that appear in this volume took shape.

But even then, was the information really correct? To provide yet another check on it, *AR* circulation manager Keith Bennett sent the completed maps to chambers of commerce throughout Alberta. Map checkers were hired at Edmonton and Calgary to go over all the streets again. Downtown maps were checked by Miss Taylor and by *AR* staffers at Calgary. Even taxicab companies were consulted to see if their drivers could find errors. And from all these sources little errors continued to be found. Streets that had been slated for development were not yet there. This bank branch had closed and another opened. The problem is, of course, that a map is a static thing and a city is never static. It constantly changes.

In the meantime, Ronald Whistance-Smith, director of the University of Alberta's map collection, had with the Glenbow Foundation and the Canadian Pacific Railway helped us to assemble the collection of maps in the historical section. The Energy Resources Conservation Board, Parks Canada, various agencies of the provincial government, and Donald Brown, a professional cartographer, had provided the maps appearing in the resource section.

By the fall of 1983 we concluded that the work was as accurate as we could make it, and the time had come to bring the job to a conclusion. We are grateful for the help of hundreds of people, some of whom are identified on page 3. Whether the work is a success, however, only you, the reader, can decide.

Ted Byfield
Publisher
Alberta Report

How to use the atlas

How to find:

- **A church, school, hotel, point of interest, or named street or avenue in Edmonton;**
  Turn to the Edmonton general index on pages 34 and 35. Find the sought-for subject in the appropriate list. Turn to the denoted page. Check the square indicated by the grid numbers for the subject. Churches are indicated thus ♠, schools thus △, hotels thus □, points of interest thus ✳. (Example: To find the Riviera Hotel in Edmonton, look under hotels on page 34. The Riviera is listed as 13,C4,50. Turn to page 50. Look in square C4 for [13].)

- **A specific building in downtown Edmonton;**
  Turn to page 47. Look it up in the list of downtown buildings. Search the square indicated by the grid numbers for the building you're looking for whose name will be spelled out on the map. (Nearly all buildings over three storeys are shown.)

- **A specific building at the University of Alberta;**
  Turn to page 48. Look it up in the list of university buildings. Search the square indicated by the grid numbers for the building you're looking for whose name will be spelled out on the map.

- **A church, school, hotel, point of interest or named street or avenue in Calgary;**
  Turn to the Calgary general index on pages 72 and 73. Find the sought-for subject in the appropriate list. Turn to the denoted page. Check the square indicated by the grid numbers for the subject. Churches are indicated thus ♠, schools thus △, hotels thus □, points of interest thus ✳. (Example: To find the Highlander Motor Hotel in Calgary, look under hotels on page 73. The Highlander is listed as 18, E2, 79. Turn to page 79. Look in square E2 for [18].)

- **A specific building in downtown Calgary;**
  Turn to pages 82 and 83. Look it up on the list of downtown buildings. Search the square indicated by the grid numbers for the building you're looking for whose name will be spelled out on the map. (Nearly all buildings over three storeys are shown.)

- **A specific building at the University of Calgary;**
  Turn to page 81. Look it up in the list of university buildings. Search the square indicated by the grid numbers for the building you're looking for whose name will be spelled out on the map.

- **A church, school, hotel or point of interest in any Alberta city or town over 4,900 population other than Calgary or Edmonton;**
  See the Municipal Map Index below. Turn to the map of the city or town. The symbols and grid numbers for the churches, schools, hotels and points of interest are given in the legend beside the map. (Indexes are also provided for the named streets and avenues of the city of St. Albert, and Sherwood Park.)

- **The location and population of any town in Alberta;**
  Turn to pages 26 and 27. Look up the name of the town in the gazetteer. Turn to the page and grid numbers indicated. Search the given square for the town. Its population is carried behind its name in the gazetteer.

- **A given neighbourhood in Calgary or Edmonton;**
  The names of the neighbourhood subdivisions of Edmonton are carried on the map on page 33. Those in Calgary are on page 71.

- **The location of an Alberta Indian reserve or Metis settlement;**
  The Indian reserves are on page 131, the Metis settlements on page 135.

- **A county or municipal district in Alberta;**
  Counties and municipal districts are listed by number on page 25, and shown on the accompanying map. The population and county seat is also shown.

- **The distance between Alberta centres:**
  A road distance table in miles and kilometres is given on the outside endsheet inside the back cover.

- **The identification of a school, church, hotel, or point of interest that you see on a map:**
  Check the legend that accompanies each map or the general legend at right for the meaning of the symbol. The number will identify the specific building.

General legend

Banks:
- ● Bank of Montreal
- ● Bank of Nova Scotia
- ● Canadian Imperial Bank of Commerce
- ● Credit Union
- ● Royal Bank
- ● Toronto Dominion Bank
- ● Treasury Branch
- **B** Bus Depot
- Campground
- ◯ Chamber of Commerce
- ♠ Church
- City Hall/Town Office
- County Office
- Court House
- Day Care - Drop in
- Golf Course
- Grain Elevator
- Health Unit
- **H** Hospital
- □ Hotel/Inn/Motel
- **?** Information Booth
- **L** Library
- Liquor Store
- ✳ Point of Interest
- Police Station/R.C.M.P. Station
- Post Office
- Provincial Legislature - Edmonton only
- ▲ Recreation Facilities: Community Centre Skating Rink Swimming Pool
- Restaurant - 24 hour only
- △ School
- **G** Service Station - 24 hour only
- **S** Shopping Centre
- Train Station
- **W** Water Tower
- Light Rapid Transit System- Above ground / Below ground
- ▬ Highway
- ▬ Dangerous Goods Route
- Commercial Area
- Residential Area
- Industrial Area
- Park, school or playground
- Undeveloped/Partially Developed Area
- Parking Lots
  Edmonton and Calgary city centre, University of Alberta and the University of Calgary maps only.

Ave. - Avenue   Pl. - Place
Blvd. - Boulevard   Rd. - Road
Cl. - Close   St. - Street
Ct. - Court   Sq. - Square
Cres. - Crescent   Tr. - Trail
Dr. - Drive

Index of municipal maps

Table of Contents

The Resources of Alberta

The map of Alberta is never complete

by Ronald Whistance-Smith

If our civilization did not already possess the idea of the map, someone would surely invent it—and quickly. It is so basic a tool in understanding one's surroundings, and so rapidly conveys this understanding to others. But in fact it was invented a very long time ago. Five-thousand-year-old maps on clay tablets, both regional and "world," have been found in the Tigris-Euphrates region, and other early ones on Italian cave walls, on the bottom of Egyptian coffins, and on various pieces of bone. In the South Pacific, pre-literate Marshall Islanders created maps from the centre ribs of palm leaves lashed together with fibre cord. The ribs form a pattern representing the waves as deflected by islands, with the islands themselves denoted by shells or coral fastened to the ribs. A trained native navigator reads the pattern of main swells set up by the Trade Winds and the secondary cross swells resulting from deflection. Animal skins were much used in Europe, both before and after the invention of paper. Many early navigational charts drawn on sheepskin or parchment were able to withstand the rigours of sea travel.

Indian map makers in northwestern North America also used animal skin (deer, beaver and bear); these, and native guides, were of no small help to the first European arrivals in constructing their own maps of the continent's vast interior. The newcomers had rudimentary compasses to assist them in establishing direction, and they estimated distances between points on the basis of the time it took to travel between them. Indian map makers, apparently lacking the compass, nevertheless seem to have had a remarkable ability to portray in proper perspective the territory over which they roamed.

Henry Kelsey was the first European, so far as we know, to reach what we call Alberta. A Hudson's Bay Company employee, he was sent into the western interior in 1684 to convince the plains Indians that they should bring their furs to the English on Hudson Bay rather than to the French around Lake Superior. Explorer Kelsey produced no map of his journey (though so far as we know he made it back to his post without getting lost), but his reports convinced his superiors of the need for mapping the interior.

Courtesy of the Provincial Archives of Alberta

Dominion land surveyors in western Canada, late 1800s or early 1900s

The first maps to show reasonable estimates of the longitude of the west coast of North America had appeared in the mid-16th century, but many continued to depict a greatly exaggerated western extension north of the Spanish explorations. Some cartographers showed the inlet of the Strait of Juan de Fuca leading to a great inland sea, sometimes extending this body of water well into present-day Alberta and labelling it the "Great Sea of the West" or "Mer de l'Ouest." Others, not so sure, simply wrote (in French or English) "It be not known whether this be land or water."

Such maps were being published right up until the 1760s. Though accurate latitudinal information, which required just the basic survey equipment of the time—a sextant or quadrant—was fairly common by then, establishment of longitude was much more difficult. In 1789, however, a talented Hudson's Bay Company surveyor named Philip Turnor set out for the Lake Athabasca country, accompanied by an apprentice named Peter Fidler. Another HBC apprentice, one David Thompson, was to have gone too. But he broke his leg while hauling firewood at the post, an injury which was to plague him through many of his later illustrious years as the premier mapper of the West. (See article, page 10.) During this trip, in 1791, Turnor established the longitude of Fort Chipewyan, to calculate the distance between this post and Hudson's Bay. The following year, Captain George Vancouver established the longitude of Nootka Sound and other parts of the west coast, thereby enabling distance calculations between the interior and the coast.

Meanwhile intrepid voyagers had been filling in many of the details. The Chevalier de La Verendrye as early as 1729-30 had been collecting maps and information both from the Indians and the French coureurs de bois, which were combined at Quebec into a map extending from Lake of the Woods as far west as the Rockies. La Verendrye and his sons in 1731 embarked westward from Lake Nipigon, north of Lake Superior, to found new fur trade posts and gather still more information. They did not reach Alberta, but one son, Pierre, had a group of Indians produce a map of the country west of the Red River, showing lakes, rivers and heights of land; another La Verendrye son, Francois, is credited with the discovery of the Saskatchewan River in 1749.

For its part, the Hudson's Bay Company, seeking to combat the French incursion, in 1754 sent Anthony Henday into the interior. His job was to persuade the Indians to bring their furs to the English on the Bay rather than to the French around Lake Superior. The HBC, although it realized the need for maps in its fur trade operations, was not so committed to exploration and survey in general as some thought it should be. Other expeditions were only carried out under pressure from the government hydrographer in London. In

any event, Henday in this instance reached what we now call Rocky Mountain House, and the information he brought back would have found its way on to HBC maps. So did data from the diaries kept by the factors of all the scattered trading posts. So indeed did the discoveries recorded and published by competing Montreal fur traders like the La Verendryes, like Connecticut Yankee trader Peter Pond who made maps of western Canada between 1785 and 1790 (some of them produced for prominent Americans like the president of Harvard University to support Pond's arguments for increased U.S. involvement in the area), and like former HBC apprentice David Thompson after he was appointed "Surveyor and Map Maker" by the rival company in 1797.

Official HBC map maker Aaron Arrowsmith in London published his first map of North America, the British territories and the northern U.S., in four sheets in 1795. By 1802 he was able to issue an enlarged, six-sheet edition including the rest of the U.S. Succeeding editions of the Arrowsmith map—about a score of them between 1795 and 1850—incorporated not only the work of HBC and North West Company explorers but copied information from the maps of the American Lewis and Clark expedition and that of Zebulon Pike. Nevertheless in the late 1850s, when governments began the work of evaluating Rupert's Land for possible purchase from the Hudson's Bay Company, David Thompson's map of the country that stretches from Hudson Bay to the Fraser River in the north, and from Sault Ste. Marie to the mouth of the Columbia in the south, was considered the best available. (It is said in fact that as late as 1915 many maps published by the Canadian government, by railways and other agencies, were based on the cartographic work performed by David Thompson one hundred years earlier.) The survey which next entered present-day Alberta, to evaluate the country in terms of suitability for settlement, was the famous expedition led by Captain John Palliser. The observations of its medical doctor, geologist and naturalist, Dr. James Hector, delineated the "fertile belt" on the northern fringe of the more arid prairie and the three steppes of the western interior, and led to the definition of the "Palliser Triangle" in southwestern Saskatchewan and southeastern Alberta. Dr. Hector is also credited with discovery of the Kicking Horse Pass; indeed it was he who was kicked in the head there by his horse.

The maps prepared by the British War Office from field sketches by Captain Palliser, Dr. Hector and expedition botanist Eugene Borgeau set the stage for more detailed Alberta surveys some 25 years later, when settlement began to warrant them. By then, the surveyors had been the direct cause of the first of the two Riel Rebellions, the one at Red River in 1869, sparked when advance survey parties arrived on the Metis lands. The full western survey of a square township grid pattern actually began on the prairies in Manitoba in 1871, four years after Confederation and a year after the transfer of Rupert's Land to Canada. By the early 1880s township maps at a scale of one inch to one-half mile (1:31,680) began to appear. The more refined instruments by then available resulted in maps which, if they lost much of the old romance and beauty, gained much more in detail and accuracy.

The first of the Alberta township maps was of the Edmonton area, published in 1891. More were gradually produced, always of the settled areas, in two series of sectional maps, one at a scale of one inch to three miles, the other at one inch to six miles. They indicated relief by a series of short pen strokes called hachures, by form lines, and later by contours (lines joining points of equal height above sea level). The first attempt to provide systematic map coverage of Canada, they continued in circulation until the early 1950s when a federal 4" = 1 mile series, based on aerial photos, covered the prairies.

Since the frontier of settlement is still advancing in Alberta, new townships are always being surveyed and new roads built. Besides, old surveys are continually being checked and the geodetic network, the base to which all surveys are tied, is constantly being refined. The modern surveyor has electronic measuring equipment, satellites which can tell him his exact position on the earth regardless of weather, calculators to speed his conclusions, and computers which will store myriad information and then produce from it a map of a given area on a given scale. The computer, using data received from satellites, can indeed be called upon to show relative soil moisture patterns, vegetation types, diseased vegetation, crop patterns, cloud patterns, or any other patterns.

Map making has come a long, long way—but the satellite maps still serve the same purpose as the palm frond wave patterns, or the clay tablets of the Euphrates, or the Cree deerhide depiction . . . They help us form an image of our surroundings; they help us find our way; and they satisfy a need to know.

Ronald Whistance-Smith is curator of the University of Alberta Map Collection

The earliest maps

The earliest maps of that section of the world's surface that would one day become known as Alberta were produced by fur traders who had to first penetrate and then cross the province's northern regions in their search for a river passage across the continent. Before there was an Edmonton therefore, and long before there was a Calgary, a fur station had been established at Fort Chipewyan in the province's northeastern sector, a key point on a trade route that was soon to be channelling fur east and goods west along the rivers that border the Canadian Shield. The two maps on this page are among the earliest on which recognizable geographic features of modern Alberta begin to appear.

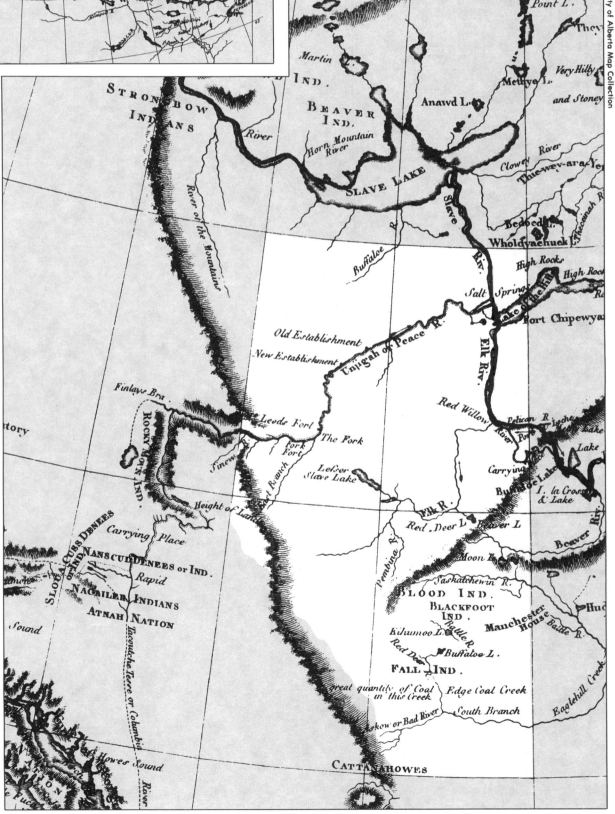

The map above was prepared by Peter Pond, an American fur trader who had moved into Montreal shortly after the British captured it from the French. Like others who would follow through the centuries, he was a born promoter of western possibilities, and Pond's original version of this map he is said to have scrawled in a Quebec bar as he drummed up investment capital for his fur trade ventures in the Athabasca region.

Pond, however, was leaning largely on hearsay from the Indians as the map demonstrates. He believed, for instance, that a river drained great Slave westward to the Pacific. He called it "Cooks or Slave River," and it was said to plunge over a waterfall that is "the largest in the world."

He told his plans to a Dr. P. Dodd-ridge, who relayed them to a friend in London, adding: "Another man, by the name of M'Kenzie, was left by Pond at Slave Lake with orders to go down the (Cook's) River, and from thence to Unalaska, and so to Kamchatka, and thence to England, through Russia, &c. If he meets with no accident, you may have him with you next year . . ."

This was the limit of Pond's achievements and his subsequent involvement in two murders forced the Nor'Westers to discredit him. But the "M'Kenzie" mentioned was, of course, Sir Alexander Mackenzie who followed "Cook's River" to its actual mouth on the Arctic Ocean and, since it wasn't the Pacific, termed it "the River of Disappointment." Today it bears his name. In a subsequent voyage up the Peace and over into the upper reaches of the Fraser he did find a route to the Pacific.

His travels bequeathed to posterity the map at the right, a portion of his full rendering of northern North America as it was known at that time. Modern Alberta is shown in outline. Certain observations of Alberta have already been made—the coal deposits in the southwest have been noted; the Red Deer, Battle, Beaver and Peace Rivers have been named, as have both branches of the Saskatchewan. The Athabasca he calls the Elk, and Lake Athabasca "the Lake of the Hills."

David Thompson's amazing map

The first comprehensive map to include all of the area of the future Alberta was produced in 1813 and 1814 by the veteran fur trader and surveyor David Thompson. Its accuracy and scope were so impressive that they amaze geographers to this day. Much of the work was in fact done by Thompson, his wife and their numerous children travelling across a wilderness by foot, dogsled and canoe.

Thompson, born to poverty in London, England in 1770, attended the famous Grey Coat School for orphaned children, then apprenticed with the Hudson's Bay Company. He served 14 years on the shores of Hudson Bay and on the Saskatchewan River. But the HBC's arch-rivals, the North West Company of Montreal, gave him the opportunity he cherished—to combine surveying and fur trading.

In the succeeding 15 years, from 1797 to 1812, he travelled more than 50,000 miles throughout what is now the Canadian West and American Northwest from his headquarters at Rocky Mountain House, Alberta. He crossed, recrossed and crossed again the Rockies through Howse and Athabasca Passes. He was the first white man to traverse the Columbia from source to mouth, and he established Canadian fur trading posts as he went. He mapped the headwaters of the Missouri, the Churchill, Lake Athabasca, both the Saskatchewans and many of their tributaries. Accompanying him on many of these journeys was his Metis wife, Charlotte Small, and some of their seven sons and six daughters.

All their findings he incorporated into one map of northwestern North America which at a dramatic meeting was unveiled before the partners of the North West Company at its annual meeting at Fort William, now Thunder Bay, Ontario.

The map in its entirety is reprinted below. It resides today in the Archives of Ontario at Toronto. It covers, of course, most of Western Canada, and the map bearings of its thousands of lakes and rivers were so accurate that they remained the basis of much Canadian map making right into the early 20th century.

The Alberta portion of the map is in "blow up" on page 11, and from it you can see exactly what Thompson did and did not know. The Peace and Athabasca Rivers are carried in detail because these were, of course, the highways of the fur trade. The Clearwater is shown entering the Athabasca from the east (at what is now Fort McMurray) with Lac la Loche and what is now called Peter Pond Lake precisely located on the Saskatchewan side of the border. These were principal trade routes of the time. The North Saskatchewan, the Battle, the Red Deer and the Bow are also in position, as is Lesser Slave Lake and the Lesser Slave River which connects it to the Athabasca.

However, there are curious, if understandable, omissions. For example, a gap is shown in the Rockies between the headwater of the Athabasca near modern Jasper and that of the Peace, indicating Thompson's admission that he didn't know what was in there.

In 1812 Thompson left the West for good and moved to Terrebonne near Montreal. His career in the East, however, was a gradual slide into oblivion that ended sadly. He then spent 10 years surveying the international boundary between Quebec and what is now Manitoba. He died in obscurity near Montreal in 1857, nearly blind and in dire poverty. This was due to two facts. His great map had never been published, and much of

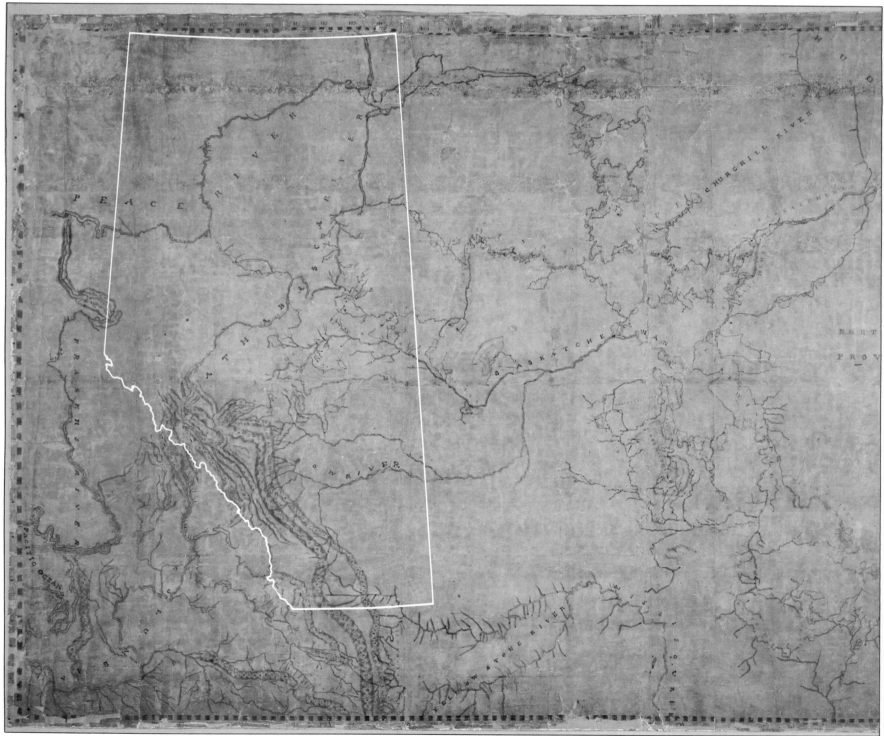

Courtesy of the Archives of Ontario

his work had been copied by an HBC map maker named Aaron Arrowsmith who gained great reputation from it and did not credit it to Thompson. Only years later, when the geologist J.B. Tyrrell of the Geological Survey of Canada discovered the Thompson map, was the magnitude of his achievement realized

As Tyrrell and other historians reviewed Thompson's work, they saw that he was one of the great geographers, not just of Canada but of the world. When he came to Canada in 1784 its map was blank from Lake Winnipeg to the Pacific. When his work in the West was done, much of it had been filled in. It seemed impossible, yet one man, his wife and children had plotted with accuracy the main routes of travel through 1,700,000 square miles of North America.

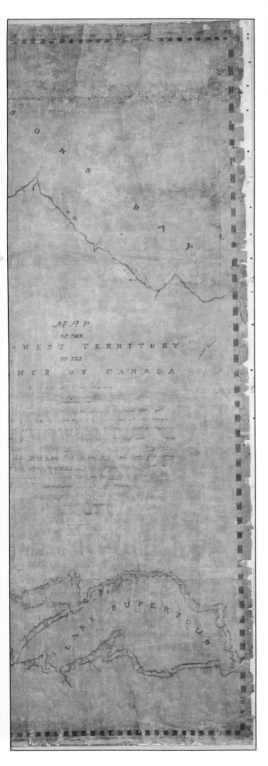

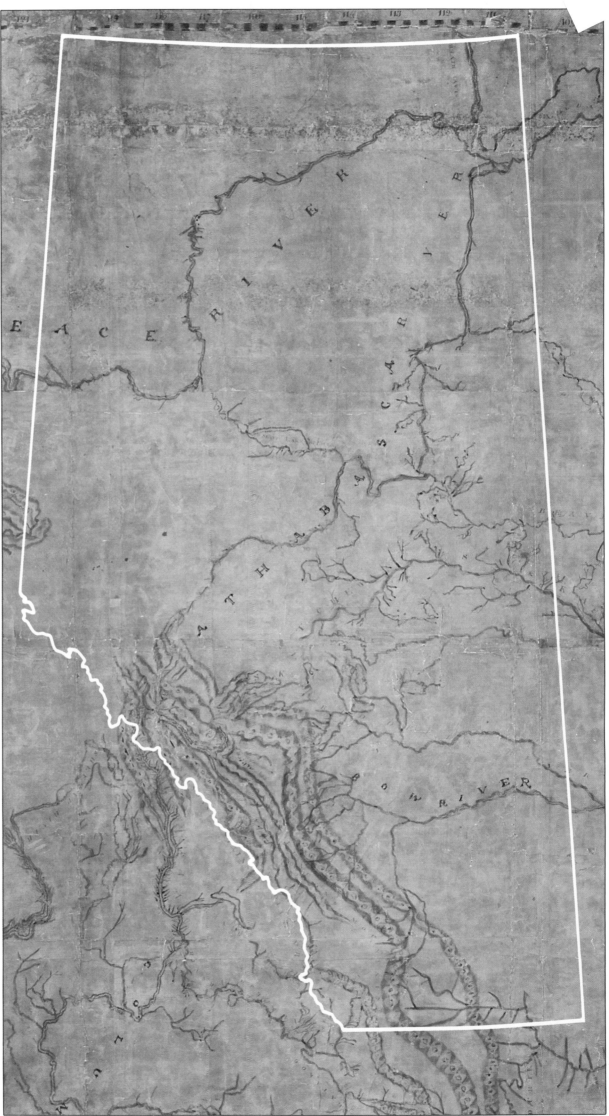

The forts of Alberta

The first white establishments in the province were the forts of the fur trade, and its earliest maps would have shown heavy development in the far north and centre, almost nothing in the south.

Note, for instance, that the posts with the earliest dates were established in the Lake Athabasca area, beginning with "Pond's Fort" of 1778, the first recorded development in the province. Others followed in the next decade along the Athabasca and Peace Rivers.

But by then development was also occurring along the North Saskatchewan. Fort Edmonton and Fort Augustus had appeared by 1795, and Rocky Mountain House by 1799. The name "Terre Blanche," bestowed on North Saskatchewan forts at that period, survives today as "Whitemud," the name of a creek at Edmonton and also a freeway.

But development at Calgary had scarcely started. The only trace on the Bow was Peigan Post of 1832, three to four decades after Edmonton had started. Calgary's day would come later with the arrival of the Canadian Pacific which at first sent it soaring ahead of Edmonton.

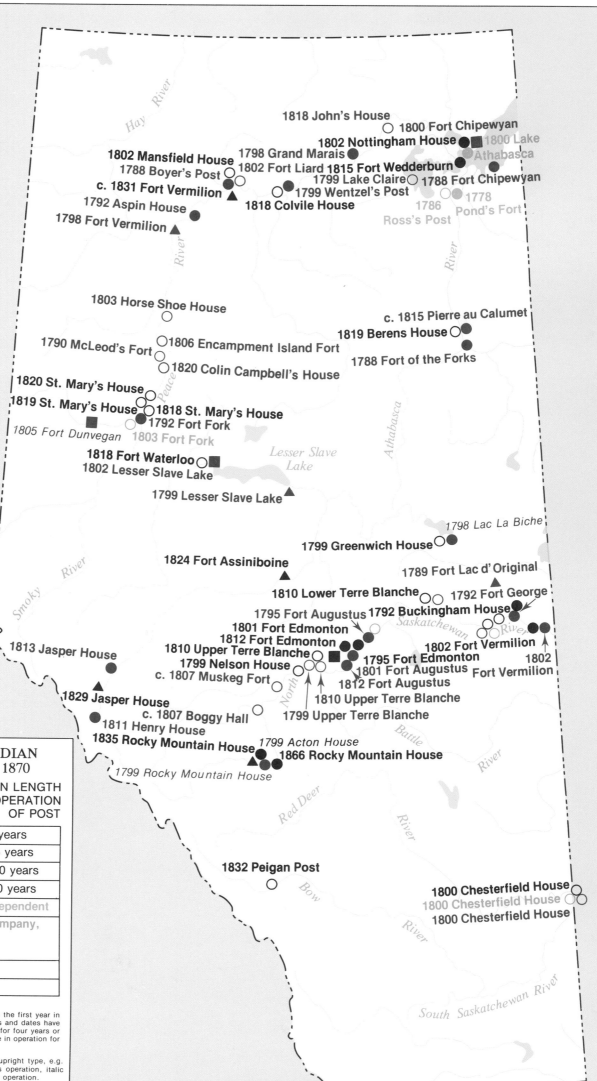

Adapted by Geo Graphica Consulting Ltd. from records in the University of Alberta Map Collection.

POSTS OF THE CANADIAN
FUR TRADE, 1600 to 1870

FIRST KNOWN OWNER OF POST*				KNOWN LENGTH OF OPERATION OF POST
○	○	○	○	1 to 3 years
●	●	●	●	4 to 15 years
▲	▲	–	▲	16 to 50 years
■	■	–	■	Over 50 years
			Canadian Independent	
			New North West Company, also known as the XY Company	
		North West Company		
Hudson's Bay Company				

c. (circa) = about

The date applied to a post on the map indicates the first year in which it is known to have been operated. Names and dates have been applied to all posts that were in operation for four years or more, and where space allows, to those that were in operation for less than four years.

* Change of ownership is not shown. Names in upright type, e.g. **1835 Rocky Mountain House** signify continuous operation, italic type, e.g. *1799 Acton House* signifies intermittent operation.

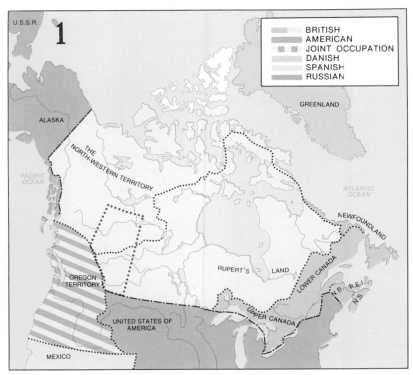

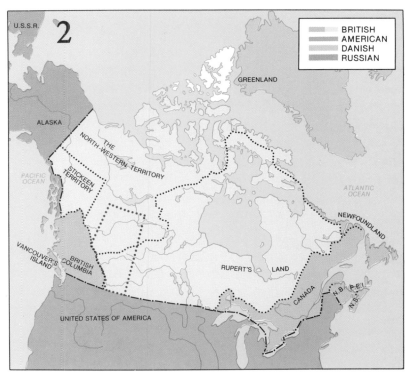

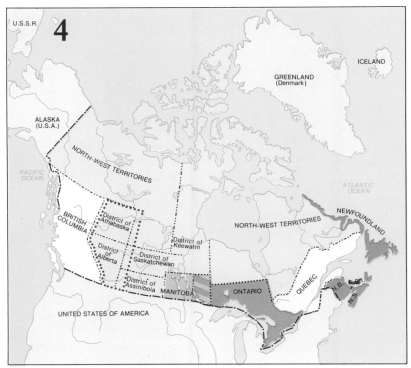

Boundaries of the past

1 (1825)

In its earliest recorded history, the territory that was to become Alberta was claimed by the Hudson's Bay Company of London and the North West Company of Montreal. In 1820 the companies merged, conferring the whole region on the HBC. However, a U.S.-British treaty created the Oregon territory, jointly possessed by both, and a sliver of the territory lay within modern Alberta.

2 (1862)

The colony of British Columbia together with the adjoining Stickeen Territory begins to fashion what will one day approximate Alberta's western boundary.

3 (1876)

Canada has now been a dominion for nine years and British Columbia a province for five. Alberta's future western boundary has now taken form.

4 (1882)

Alberta has now been divided into two districts within the territories, Athabaska in the north and Alberta in the south. The eastern boundary, however, follows a line between the 111th and 112th meridian, not the 110th as it does today.

5 (1895)

The northern District of Athabaska has by now been expanded to include much of northern Saskatchewan. One proposal subsequently rejected would have combined Athabaska, Alberta, Saskatchewan and Assiniboia into a single province. The Laurier government decided, however, it would become too powerful, and the present map emerged instead.

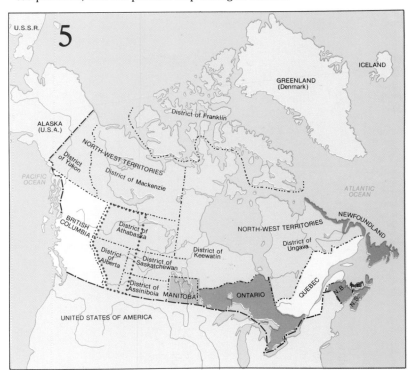

The map that would have changed the Canadian West

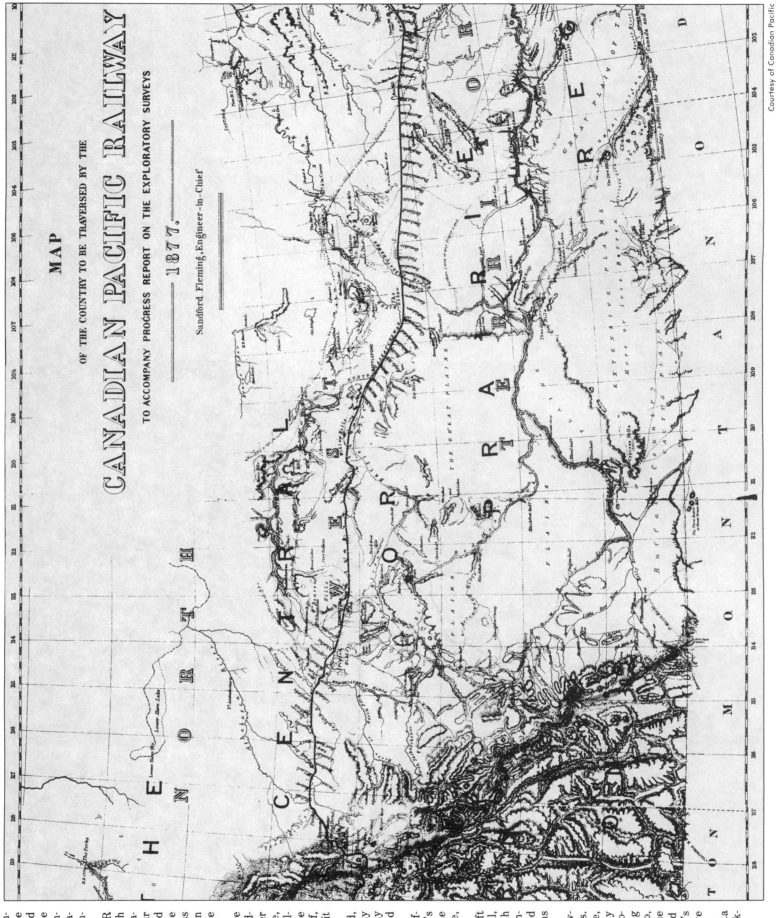

CANADIAN PACIFIC RAILWAY

MAP

OF THE COUNTRY TO BE TRAVERSED BY THE

TO ACCOMPANY PROGRESS REPORT ON THE EXPLORATORY SURVEYS

——— 1877. ———

Sandford Fleming, Engineer-in-Chief

Courtesy of Canadian Pacific

This unusual map of western Canada would have changed its future face entirely if the vision it depicts had ever been fulfilled. It is, in fact, the proposal made by Sir Sandford Fleming for the future route of the Canadian Pacific through the West. Fleming was CP's engineer-in-chief.

Fleming's plan was to take the CPR northwest out of Winnipeg through what would one day become Saskatoon and the already established fur trade station at Edmonton. He would then have carried it through the relatively accessible Yellowhead Pass to the valley of the North Thompson River in British Columbia and thence to Vancouver.

Fleming proposed names for future towns along his route west of Edmonton, one being Ponoka, another Lacombe. Both of these, of course, would wind up instead on the Calgary-Edmonton rail line that was to be built later. As for Calgary itself, Fleming doesn't bother to even put it on his map.

If Fleming's plan had been followed, Alberta today would likely boast only one large centre, Edmonton, the way most provinces do, and Calgary would have remained a small town.

But history was to unfold very differently. The CPR rejected Fleming's route, choosing instead to run the railway through the southern prairie, creating both Regina and Calgary.

In the meantime the change left Edmonton with no railway at all, except the branch line that ran north from Calgary. Embittered Edmontonians cursed the CPR and watched Calgary mushroom to proportions much beyond their community's.

Two further developments, however, restored Edmonton's fortunes. After Alberta became a province, Edmonton was made the capital city and a year later the site of the provincial university. Then in the ensuing few years it hosted not one, but two, transcontinental railway systems, the Canadian Northern and the Grand Trunk Pacific. Both took Fleming's route to the Yellowhead and survive today as the Canadian National.

From that time to this both Alberta centres have raced one another neck-and-neck in their growth.

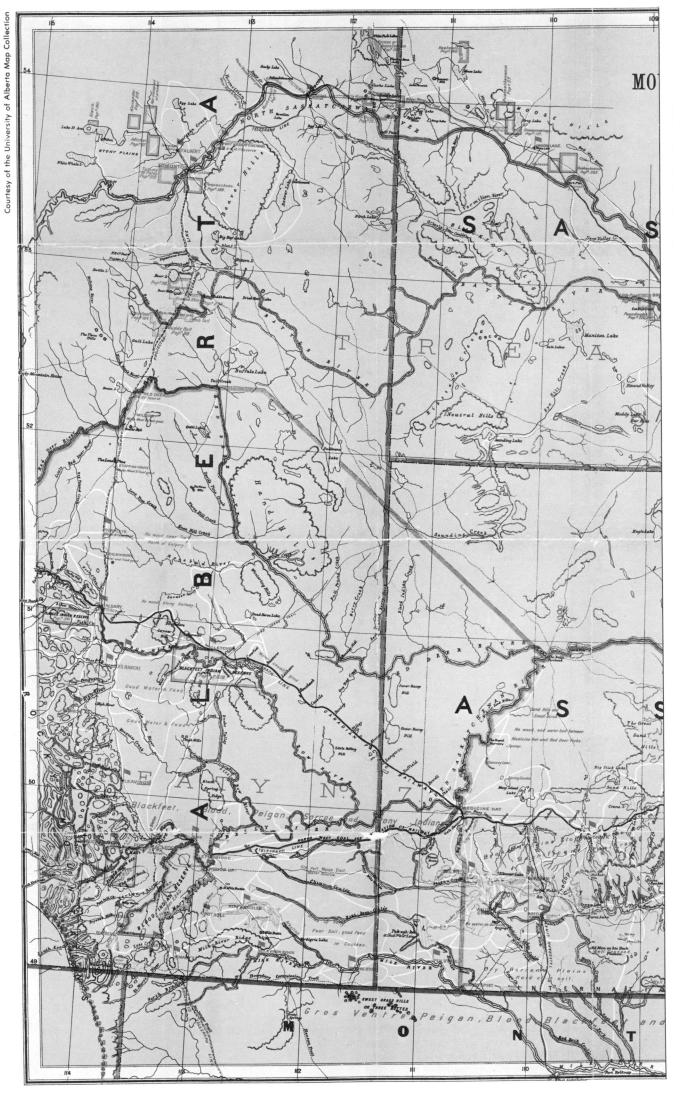

The first roads

The patrol routes of the Royal North West Mounted Police provided Alberta, and Saskatchewan too, with many of its first fixed overland routes, some of which would one day become highways—still patrolled by the Mounties.

The Mounties had come out in 1874, their 300 red coats moving westward across the prairie from Dufferin, now Emerson, on the Manitoba-Minnesota border. They established their main base at Fort Macleod and quickly brought to a halt the whisky trade that had been established by American traders at Fort Whoop Up which defiantly flew the U.S. flag on Canadian territory.

But their biggest task followed when they moved the Indians who had lived for centuries on the open prairie into the reserves provided for them under treaty.

Shown here is an excerpt from a NWMP map made during the territorial period. The reserves had been established, but serious agricultural settlement had not yet begun. The future Province of Alberta would embrace the Territory of Alberta shown here, plus a slice of the Territories of Saskatchewan and Assiniboia. The Saskatchewan-Alberta boundary will run down the 110th Meridian. (It could be taken for a "10" on the map since the meridian line itself runs through the second "1".)

The NWMP posts are identified with red flags. Dotted lines may be discerned running out from them and between them, from Fort Macleod to Calgary, for instance, from Calgary to Edmonton, and from Edmonton to Battleford down both sides of the North Saskatchewan. Portions of these will become highways. Other trails, now long lost, cover enormous distances. The Lord Lorne Trail, for example, runs from Fort Macleod to Battleford, and a whole system of trails radiates from something called the "Bull's Forehead" at the junction of the Red Deer and South Saskatchewan Rivers, one to Edmonton, one to Battleford, one south to the CPR mainline.

On the Calgary-Edmonton trail, site of the projected telegraph line, only Red Deer has so far appeared as a name recognizable today. North of Calgary we find Dickinson's, Scarlet's, Stopping House, Miller's, Muddy Bull (near Morningside) with an unidentified NWMP post between the future Wetaskiwin and Bigstone Creek.

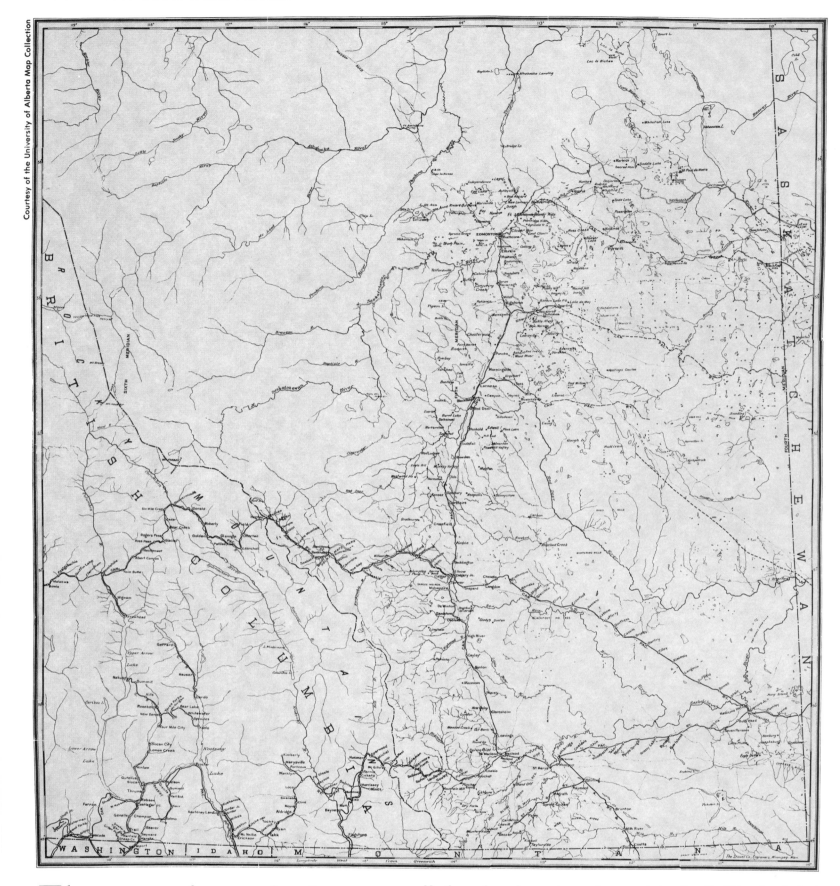

The province is born

When the province of Alberta was born in 1905, Stovel Press of Winnipeg issued one of the first published maps of it to help settlers discover where the townships lay. In this version of the Stovel map, we have removed the grid pattern of township lines, in order to show more clearly the development of the new province.

It can be seen immediately, for instance, that settlement was almost entirely restricted to three Canadian Pacific Railway lines. They were (and are): 1. The main line, by then about 20 years old, entering the province east

of Medicine Hat, running northwest to Calgary, then weaving through the Kicking Horse Pass to Golden, B.C., Revelstoke and eventually Vancouver. 2. The Crowsnest line, striking west from Dunmore Junction east of Medicine Hat, to Lethbridge, Macleod, the Crowsnest Pass and eventually Creston and Trail. 3. The line north from Macleod through Calgary, previously the Calgary and Edmonton Railway, with Edmonton in resentful isolation at its northern terminus.

Coming west towards Edmonton, however, is the projected Canadian

Northern, shown here only as a broken line, which will soon give the northern city its "own" railway. Shortly thereafter, another line will appear in Edmonton from the southeast called the Grand Trunk Pacific. It will bring into existence a whole new string of towns, including Wainwright, which have not yet made their appearance. Two more CP lines are projected to come west, one to Wetaskiwin and the other to Lacombe, and the westernmost fragments of them have already been constructed.

It is also noteworthy that no fewer than five American lines have pushed into Alberta and British Columbia.

Other disclosures on the map: The Yellowhead Pass is shown in approxi-

mate location. It will be taken by both the Canadian Northern and Grand Trunk Pacific. Later, of course, these will be combined in the Canadian National. But in 1905 the great CN mountain centre of Jasper still bears its old fur trade name, Henry House. In south central Alberta, Drumheller has not yet appeared, though "Rosebud Creek" already exists near that city's future location. And a little to the northwest a shortcut trail can be seen east of the rail line between Carstairs and Innisfail. Like all the other roads that tie the little settlements to the railway, it is mud and largely impassable in wet weather. One day, however, this will become the route of No. 2, our most-travelled superhighway.

The settlements take root

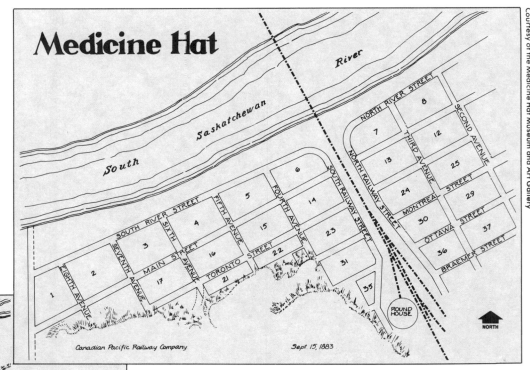

Medicine Hat in 1883

This map was the original survey map of the new townsite prepared by the Canada Land Company, a subsidiary of the CPR which owned the land. Although the map was completed in 1883, lots were not offered for sale until 1885 because of a dispute with the federal government over the location of the Blackfoot Indian reserve. The delay in offering the lots for sale to those who were already living in the community caused a great deal of concern and mistrust of the railway. As a division point of the CPR, Medicine Hat was dominated by the company and was administered by trustees with the Canada Land Company at Winnipeg until 1894 when residents finally decided to declare Medicine Hat a village. The new status introduced local taxation for improvements which the trustees had been reluctant to provide.

Red Deer in 1890

This was the first map of the Red Deer townsite and was prepared by G.B. Bemister, a Dominion Land Surveyor. He produced the map for Osler, Hammond and Nanton, land agents in Winnipeg for the Calgary and Edmonton Railway Company. The railway had planned to put the town further north but the Reverend Leonard Gaetz, a rancher, offered the railway half of his property in exchange for locating the town at this site. The railway was built by the C. and E. Railway Company but leased on completion to the CPR. This was a fairly common practice and allowed land grant advantages to the giant railway company which had already exhausted its own grants from the federal government.

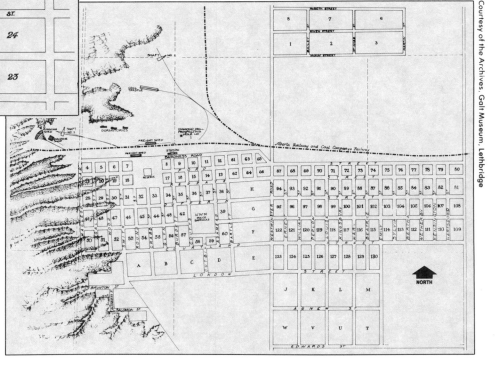

Lethbridge in 1890

This 1890 map shows the Alberta Railway and Coal Company Railway which ran from what was originally called the Coal Banks (now Lethbridge) to Dunmore east of Medicine Hat. This narrow gauge railway was built in 1885 to move coal for the CPR. It was dubbed "The Turkey Trail" because of its small cars and their rocking motion as they travelled down the track. The line was extended in 1890 to Coutts and into Great Falls, Montana. By 1892, it had performed so profitably that it was leased by the CPR. Five years later, the CPR bought the original line from Dunmore to Lethbridge and converted it to a standard gauge. Coal production continued to play a part in the Lethbridge economy until 1965.

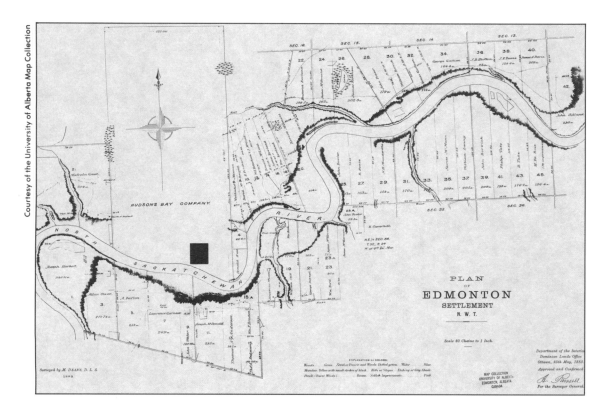

Edmonton
The settlement and the emerging city

The map above was made for the Dominion Lands Office of the Department of the Interior in 1882, 10 years before the incorporation of the Town of Edmonton and 17 years before the incorporation of its sister, the Town of Strathcona, on the south bank of the North Saskatchewan River. The Hudson's Bay Company fort appears as a black square on the river bank in the reserve of land which the company held onto after parting with most of what was to become the West to the Dominion of Canada in 1870.

Already some of the outlines of modern Edmonton are evident. Malcolm Groat's estate overlooks the Groat Ravine at the left while the long narrow river lots to the east of the HBC reserve define the future 92nd to 99th Streets. Commonwealth Stadium today stands atop the upper reaches of what was then called "Rat Creek Ravine." (A more elegant age would later rename it Kinnaird Ravine.)

The map at the right was made at the peak of a boom in 1911, the last year of the "twin cities" before they were merged into modern Edmonton. By now the skeletal form of the present city has taken shape. The Grand Trunk Pacific Railway has created the Calder yards and the Canadian Northern the downtown yards. Both companies will be merged within 10 years into the Canadian National.

The street number system has appeared, though it begins with "First Street" (now 101st) downtown and the numbers build westward. East of First, the old name system still obtains. The southern portion of the HBC reserve has already been developed, and the northern will one day become the Edmonton Municipal Airport.

The restored Fort Edmonton

Below is a map of Fort Edmonton Park, west of the Quesnell Bridge, where the city's past is recreated at three periods—1885, 1905 and 1920.

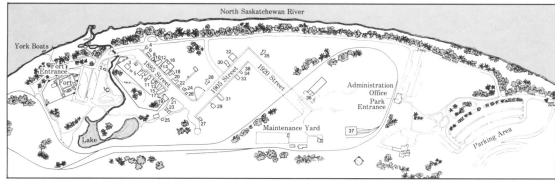

1. Wind Mill
2. The Trading Post Souvenir Shop

1885 Street

3. The Ottewell Homestead
4. Bellerose School
5. Bulletin Building
6. James McDonald's Carpenter Shop
7. Hutchings & Riley's Harness Shop & Kernohan's Millinery
8. Raymer's Jewellery
9. McDougall Church

10. Byrnes' Shoe Shop
11. Lauder's Bake Shop
12. Ross Brothers' Hardware
13. Lauder's Bakery
14. Secord Complex
15. Daly's Drugstore & Dr. Wilson's Office
16. J.A. McDougall's General Store
17. Kelly's Saloon
18. Sanderson and Looby's Blacksmith Shop
19. McCauley's Livery Stable
20. Jasper House Hotel
21. Peter Erasmus House

22. N.W.M.P. Complex
23. Egge's Stopping House
24. Kenneth McDonald House
25. Egge's Barn and Bunkhouse (Public Washroom)
26. Dominion Land Office

1905 Street

27. Henderson Farm
28. St. Anthony's Church
29. Rutherford House
30. Ernest Brown Studio
31. Masonic Hall
32. Fire Hall Civic Centre

33. Post Office (under construction)
34. Bank of Montreal (under construction)

1920 Street

35. Anglican Church of St. Michael's and All Angels (future project)
36. Mellon Farm
37. Streetcar Barn
38. Ukrainian Bookstore

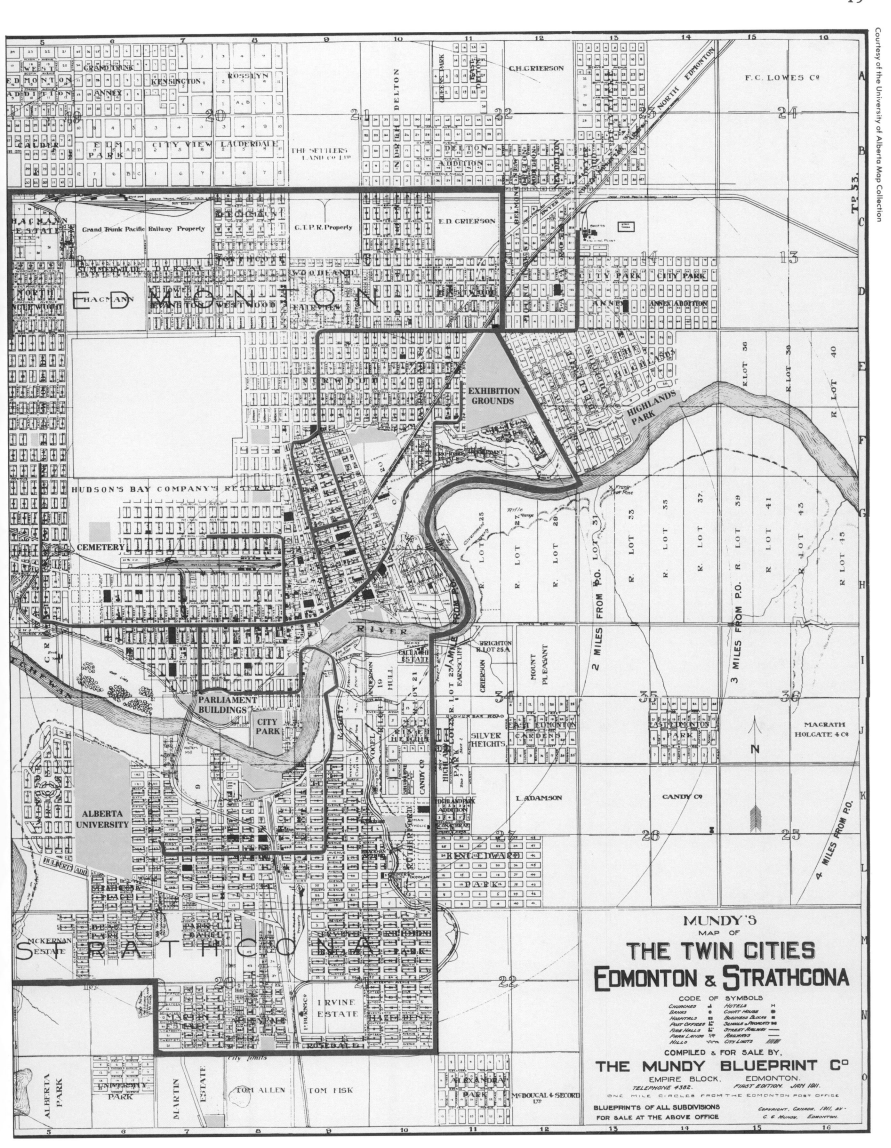

MUNDY'S
MAP OF
THE TWIN CITIES
EDMONTON & STRATHCONA

CODE OF SYMBOLS

COMPILED & FOR SALE BY,
THE MUNDY BLUEPRINT Cº
EMPIRE BLOCK, EDMONTON.
TELEPHONE 4382.   FIRST EDITION. JAN 1911.
ONE MILE CIRCLES FROM THE EDMONTON POST OFFICE

BLUEPRINTS OF ALL SUBDIVISIONS
FOR SALE AT THE ABOVE OFFICE

COPYRIGHT, CANADA, 1911, BY
C. G. MUNDY, EDMONTON.

Calgary

On the brink of two booms

The maps on these two pages portray the city of Calgary as it verged on the two booms that would bring it to its modern status of world oil and financial centre. The map on page 20 did not intend to depict a settlement at all, rather Township 24 in Range 1 west of the Fifth Meridian where the Canadian Pacific was slated to make two crossings of the Bow River, only the first of which is shown. Already, however, the area had several residents, most of them Northwest Mounted Police veterans with names like Denny, Walker, Butlin, Barwis and Van Courtlandt, whose residences are shown. So, too, are those of former Metis buffalo hunters like Faillan, Amouse, Mayett and McGillis.

The essentials of the future city's central geography were already in place. The downtown area would one day arise in the triangle of land bounded by the CP line, the bend of the Bow and its confluence with the Elbow where the NWMP fort and the Hudson's Bay Company post were located.

In the ensuing winter squatters would establish a tent town on the east bank of the Elbow in Section 14, where the CPR was expected to lay out the townsite. The following year the railway surprised them by putting it in Section 15 instead. The lines bounding these sections would one day become some of Calgary's main streets as the lower map shows. Of the various trails shown on the map with dotted lines, only the "McLeod" (now spelled Macleod) survives as a reality so designated on modern maps of the city. The trail in Section 7, however, would one day become the Richmond Road. In the three decades that followed immediately after this map was made, the development of Alberta agriculture was to turn the "township" into a city. Hence this map shows Calgary verging on its first great boom.

The map on page 21, a transit route system publication made in 1955, shows it verging on its second. By then the shape of the modern city was already clear, but the vast expansion that would accompany the oil hey-day of the '60s and '70s had not yet occurred. Hence the Glenmore reservoir was built appreciably outside the developed area in the southwest. There has been no development beyond Nose Creek to the east, and Ogden and Thorncliffe respectively marked the limits of south and north urban growth. The airstrips built during the Second World War at Currie Barracks were beyond the city's urban border and Bowness was a distinct community well beyond the limits of the map. The population of this Calgary of

1955 was about 175,000, less than a third of the population of the early 1980s. Such was the impact of the oil boom that was to come.

The two booms are the high-water marks of both Calgary and Alberta economic development. For Calgary there was a third, though less significant than the two. In 1890 and '91 the new Calgary and Edmonton Railway made Calgary the jumpoff point for the Alberta north, though this one was shortlived and faded within a year until the first big boom began at the century's turn.

Real estate built in that boom, which reached its zenith between 1909 and the crash in 1913, was never fully occupied, say the city's historians, for nearly 30 years.

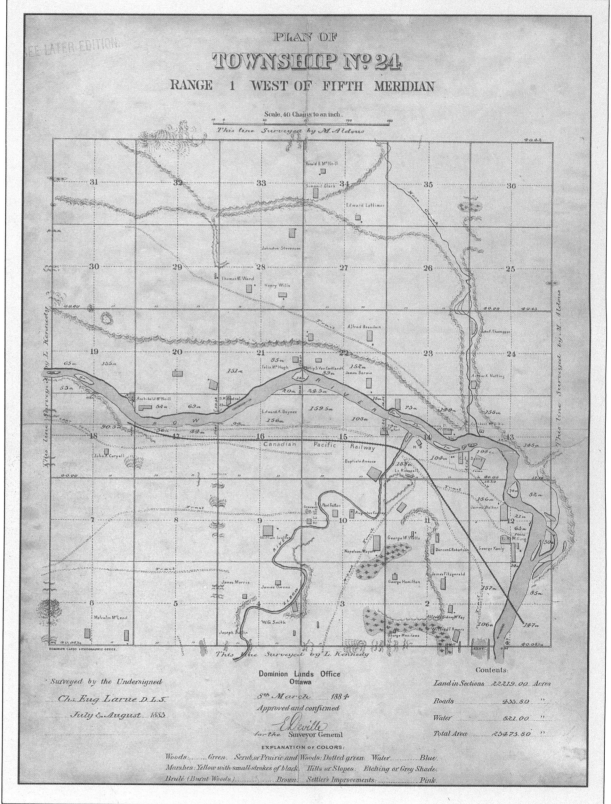

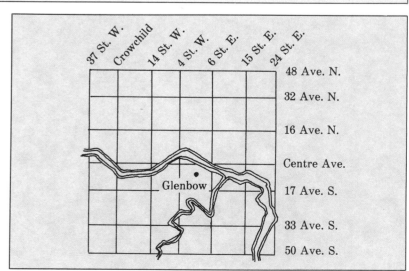

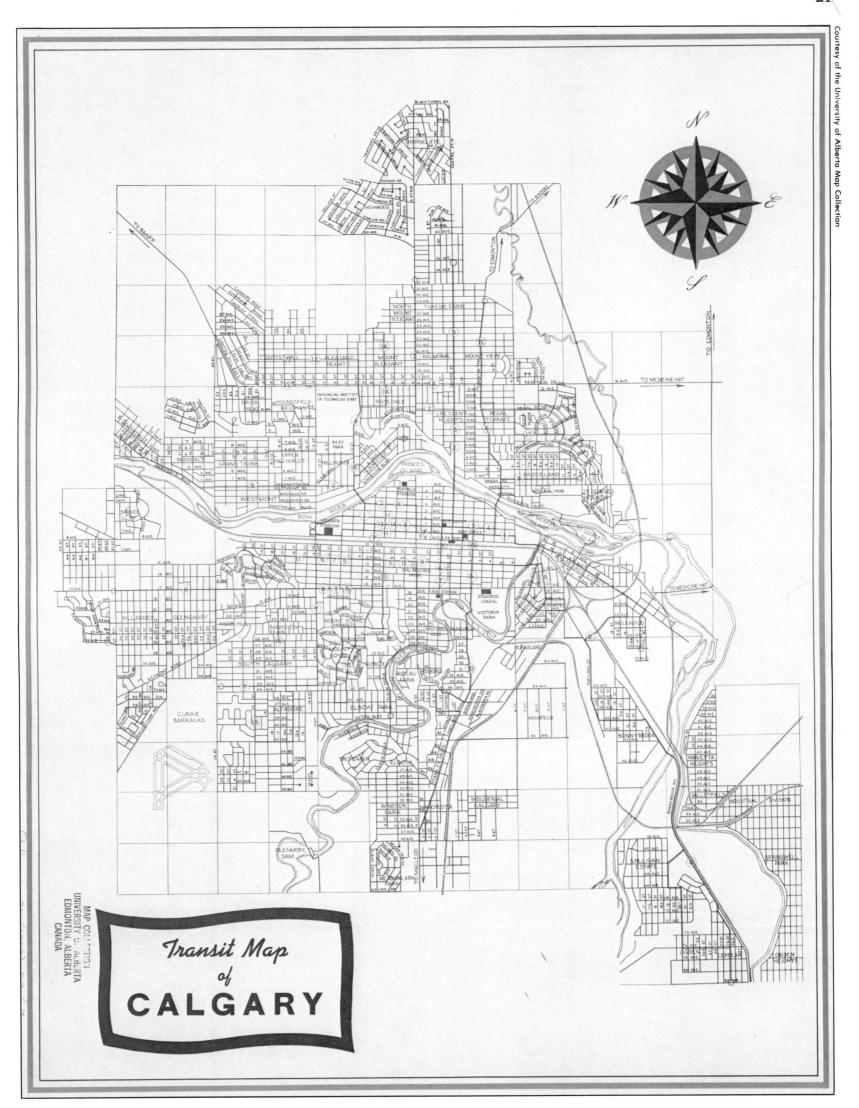

Transit Map
of
CALGARY

The coal mine map of Edmonton

If fur and pemmican were Edmonton's first industry, coal became its second. Fort Edmonton blacksmiths used it for their forges and settlers gopher-holed for it in the North Saskatchewan riverbank. Commercial operations began in 1880. The engineer who drew this map said mining was concentrated in three districts: Big Island, Rabbit Hill and in the city between Groat ravine and Clover Bar. Mines ranged in size from those that produced virtually nothing (prospects) to the Black Diamond mine that produced 3,125,950 tons. When operations closed in 1970, the total number of recorded mines had reached 153. For architects and engineers of downtown high-rises the location of the mines is of vital interest.

0	1		2	3	Miles
0	1	2	3	4	5	Kilometres

Source: Atlas: Coal-workings
of the Edmonton Area
Richard S. Taylor
(1971)

MANNING FWY

137 AVE

97 ST

CONVENTION CENTRE

(1931-1945)

(1920-1937)

(1899-1934)

(1904-1934)

(1883-1897)

118 AVE

(1906-1909)

(1917-1940)

(1908-1930)

170 ST

CHATEAU LACOMBE

(1931-1951)

JASPER

(1905-1952)

16

(1905-1911)

REFINERY ROW

RIVER

(1932-1950)

SASKATCHEWAN

109 ST

104 ST

(1907-1944)

(1933-1945)

WHITEMUD FWY

(1908-1921)

CROSS-SECTION: SEE BELOW

(1952-1970)

WHITEMUD FWY

NORTH

RAINBOW VALLEY
CAMPGROUND

2

NORTH

(1923-1940)

(1948-1956)

PRODUCTION DATES INDICATED

UNDERGROUND WORKINGS . . . .

(1928-1934)

SMALL MINES OR PROSPECTS . . . . ⚒

STRIP MINES . . . .

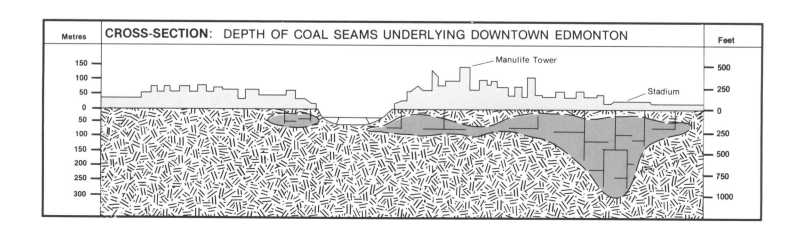

CROSS-SECTION: DEPTH OF COAL SEAMS UNDERLYING DOWNTOWN EDMONTON

Metres		Feet
150	Manulife Tower	500
100		
50		250
0	Stadium	0
50		
100		250
150		500
200		750
250		
300		1000

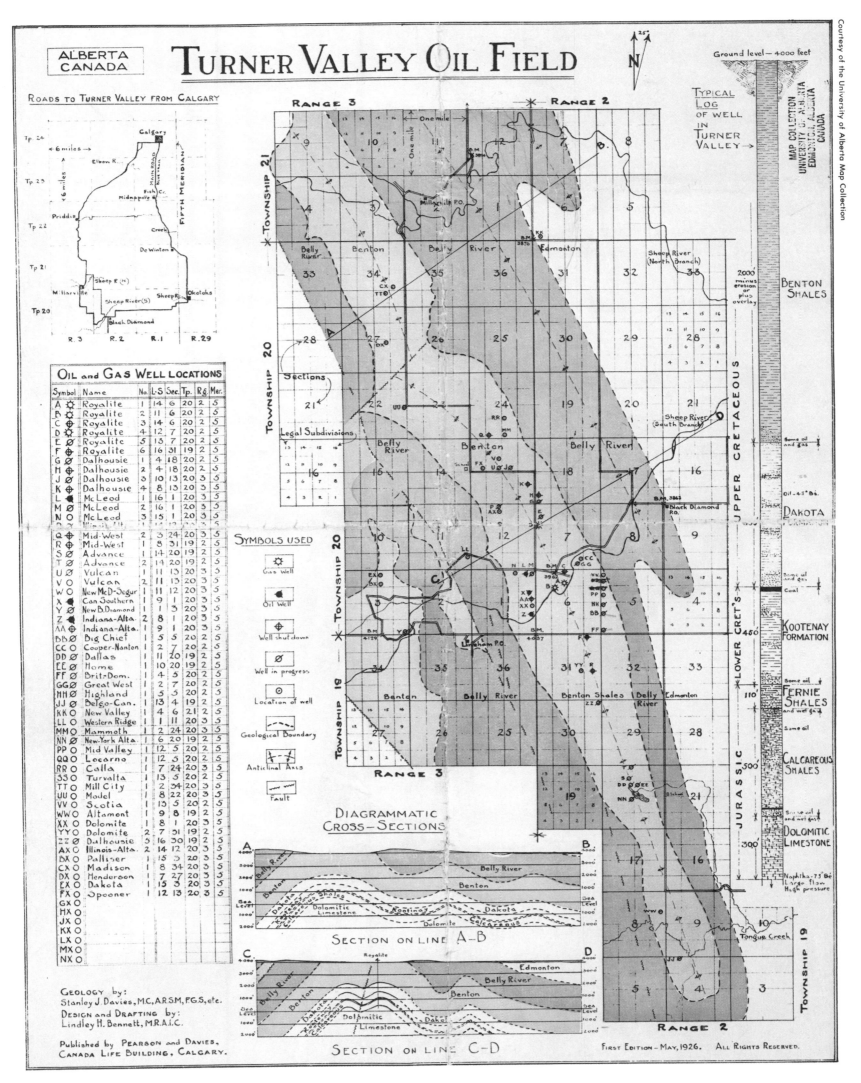

The first great oil strike

The Turner Valley was never to become a major Alberta field but the oil strike there in 1914 prefigured the great discoveries that would one day follow to the north.

As a by-product of oil, Turner Valley produced gas in such quantities that, so the story goes, the burn-off flares made it possible to read a newspaper at night in downtown Calgary, 30 miles away.

Calgary's proximity to Turner Valley had another permanent implication for Alberta's geography. Though the great oil finds of the future would lie around Edmonton, the head offices of the companies remained in Calgary, making it the administrative centre of the industry. Of the companies listed on this map, few survive today.

ALBERTA
the province

Alberta is a frontier land, geographically isolated from the world's major population belts. The province's western border, formed by the 120th meridian and the crest of the Rocky Mountains, bars easy access to the Pacific basin. Other Alberta boundaries—the 60th parallel to the north, the 110th meridian in the east and the 49th parallel on the south—nearly all face towards North America's vast, relatively empty Great Plains, which sweep from the Arctic Ocean to the Gulf of Mexico.

The province's 255,000 square miles (660,411 square kilometres) are inhabited by 2.3 million people. In area the province surpasses the combined total of Great Britain, Denmark and West Germany, nations occupying similar latitudes in Europe. Soviet Siberia and a small northerly tip of China are the only Asian lands parallelling Alberta.

Topographically the province divides naturally into northern, central and southern regions. The northern is dominated by coniferous forests of spruce and pine, interspersed with occasional tracts of open prairie. The area is drained northward by the Athabasca and Peace Rivers, all tributary to the Mackenzie River system. These waters flow ultimately to the Arctic Ocean. The centre is a pleasant parkland and rolling plain dotted with groves of timber. The treeless plains of the south extend from the Red Deer River to the border with Montana. Nearly all the south and centre lies in the drainage basin of the Saskatchewan Rivers.

Along the range of the Alberta Rockies, 26 peaks rise over 10,000 feet (3,048 metres), the highest being Mount Columbia in the southwest at 12,294 feet (3,747 metres).

The provincial climate is dry and sunny. The south receives 2,000 to 2,200 hours of sunlight annually, more than any other part of Canada.

Precipitation can vary greatly but averages 13.8 inches (35 cm.) a year in the north, 17.7 inches (45 cm.) at Edmonton, slightly over 11.8 inches (30 cm.) around Calgary, and 19.7 inches (50 cm.) or more in much of the foothills.

Drought is a danger; Medicine Hat in the southeast has received as little as 6.7 inches (17 cm.) of moisture a year. Hailstorms occasionally damage crops across Alberta. The frost-free period ranges from 110 days at Lethbridge in the deep south to just 65 days high in the north.

Throughout Alberta temperatures vary dramatically, from southern highs over 100° F (38° C) to record lows under −76° F. (−60° C.) in the Peace River valley bottom. Warm winds, known as chinooks, periodically break through the Rockies barrier and flood the south, including Calgary, with warm Pacific air. A chinook can raise the temperature by as much as 68° F. (38° C.) within two hours. Due to these dry airflows, the far south can enjoy highs above freezing on 50% or more of winter days. All over the province low humidity mitigates the cold's impact.

About one in 10 Canadians lives in Alberta. The 1981 national census showed 77% of Alberta's population residing in urban centres, with well over half the total in the Calgary and Edmonton areas. In 1983 Calgary registered 620,692 inhabitants, Edmonton 560,085. Between 1971 and 1981 the provincial population jumped over 37%, but with the onset of economic recession in the early 1980s, Alberta began to experience a significant emigration, as it had in the decades preceding 1950.

Albertans tend to be young. One-third of the population is under 21; another third is 21 to 35. Contrary to a common misconception, native-born Albertans are not a minority in their own province; in 1981 two out of three Alberta residents had been born here. One out of five came from outside Canada.

The province's road network amounted to 93,208 miles (150,000 km.) in 1982, with 6,649 miles (10,700 km.) of paved highway. Over 1.9 million vehicles were registered by 1981. The railways' main trackage totalled 6,711 miles (10,800 kilometres). Regular flights within the province and around the world were available from nine air carriers. Alberta had licensed 63 airports, including two internationals. The province has 10 daily newspapers, nine television stations, 31 AM radio stations and 12 FM stations.

The province is governed by a 79-member legislative assembly. The 1983-1984 provincial budget planned expenditures of $9.68 billion. The Alberta Heritage Trust Fund, made up of a portion of resource revenues, stood at $13.3 billion at the end of September 1983.

The provincial government owns the telephone system throughout the province except in Edmonton, where the city operates its own system. The Alberta government also operates its own consumer banks through 130 Treasury Branches.

There are three conventional universities in the province: University of Alberta in Edmonton, University of Calgary and the University of Lethbridge. The first two offer a full range of programs at the undergraduate and graduate levels while the University of Lethbridge specializes in undergraduate programs and teacher education. Athabasca University offers degree courses through correspondence. There are 10 public junior colleges and several private ones in the province providing diplomas and university transfer programs.

In 1981, Statistics Canada reported that 9.6% of Albertans held university degrees, the highest proportion in Canada. Just over 40% had education beyond the secondary level.

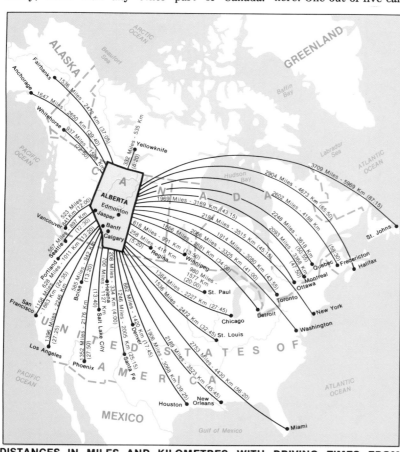

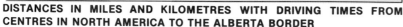

DISTANCES IN MILES AND KILOMETRES WITH DRIVING TIMES FROM CENTRES IN NORTH AMERICA TO THE ALBERTA BORDER

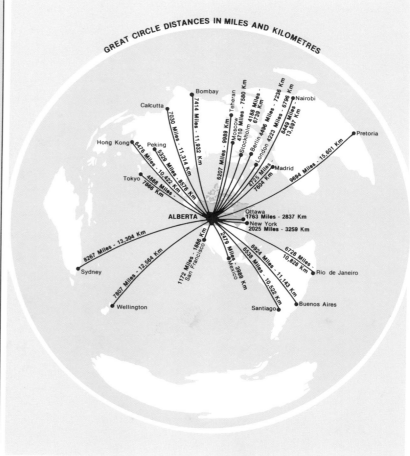

The rural municipalities

Counties

NO.	NAME	SEAT OF GOVERNMENT	POPULATION
1.	Grande Prairie	Grande Prairie	12,078
2.	Vulcan	Vulcan	3,715
3.	Ponoka	Ponoka	7,536
4.	Newell	Brooks	6,199
5.	Warner	Warner	3,460
6.	Stettler	Stettler	5,092
7.	Thorhild	Thorhild	3,323
8.	Forty Mile	Foremost	3,451
9.	Beaver	Ryley	5,347
10.	Wetaskiwin	Wetaskiwin	9,026
11.	Barrhead	Barrhead	5,517
12.	Athabasca	Athabasca	5,974
13.	Smoky Lake	Smoky Lake	2,910
14.	Lacombe	Lacombe	8,783
16.	Wheatland	Strathmore	5,513
17.	Mountain View	Didsbury	8,832
18.	Paintearth	Castor	2,495
19.	St. Paul	St. Paul	6,101
20.	Strathcona	Sherwood Park	48,024
21.	Two Hills	Two Hills	3,380
22.	Camrose	Camrose	7,564
23.	Red Deer	Red Deer	13,664
24.	Vermilion River	Kitscoty	7,533
25.	Leduc	Leduc	13,258
26.	Lethbridge	Lethbridge	8,779
27.	Minburn	Vegreville	4,041
28.	Lac Ste. Anne	Sangudo	7,614
29.	Flagstaff	Sedgewick	4,507
30.	Lamont	Lamont	4,687
31.	Parkland	Stony Plain	23,626
		Total	252,029

Municipal Districts (M.D.)

NO.	NAME	SEAT OF GOVERNMENT	POPULATION
6	Cardston	Cardston	4,292
9	Pincher Creek	Pincher Creek	2,970
14	Taber	Taber	5,637
26	Willow Creek	Claresholm	4,534
31	Foothills	High River	9,725
34	Acadia	Acadia Valley	604
44	Rocky View	Calgary	17,362
47	Starland	Morrin	2,068
48	Kneehill	Three Hills	5,761
52	Provost	Provost	2,611
61	Wainwright	Wainwright	3,837
87	Bonnyville	Bonnyville	9,407
90	Sturgeon	Morinville	13,682
92	Westlock	Westlock	7,059
130	Smoky River	Falher	2,858
133	Spirit River	Spirit River	891
135	Peace	Berwyn	1,520
136	Fairview	Fairview	1,889
		Total	96,707

Improvement Districts (I.D.)

NO.	SEAT OF GOVERNMENT	POPULATION
1	Medicine Hat	4,703
4	Waterton National Park*	176
5	Kananaskis Country**	122
6	Canmore	382
7	Drumheller	1,258
8	Canmore	1,268
9	Banff National Park	6,949
10	Rocky Mountain House	9,201
12	Jasper National Park*	3,970
13	Elk Island National Park*	36
14	Edson	8,119
15	Whitecourt	2,670
16	Valleyview	5,350
17	Slave Lake (East) High Prairie (Central) Peace River (North)	11,699
18	Lac la Biche (South) Fort McMurray (North)	9,605
19	Spirit River	1,757
20	Spirit River	3,000
21	Peace River	2,936
22	Peace River	4,250
23	High Level	5,837
24	Wood Buffalo National Park *	188
	Total	83,476

* Administered by Parks Canada
** Administered by Alberta Parks and Recreation

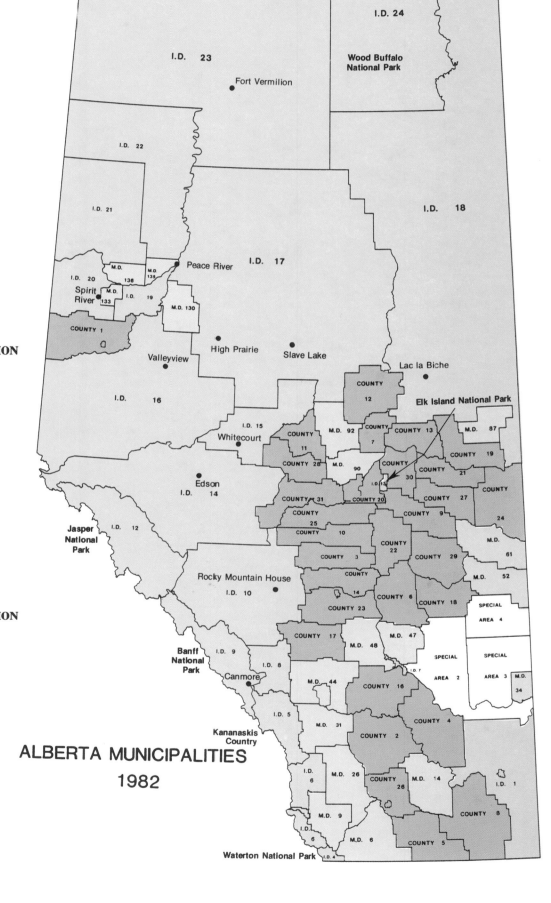

ALBERTA MUNICIPALITIES
1982

Alphabetical list of cities, towns and villages in Alberta. Population figure follows, according to 1983 census, then the location on the map, then the page number. Population given only where it exceeds 50.

A

Abee		B4, 29
Acadia Valley	136	C2, 31
Acme	492	A2, 31
Aden		C4, 31
Aetna		B4, 31
Airdrie	10 431	A2, 31
Alberta Beach	510	A4, 29
Alcomdale	50	A4, 29
Alcurve		C4, 29
Alder Flats	94	A1, 31
Aldersyde	89	A3, 31
Alhambra	58	A2, 31
Alix	837	A2, 31
Alliance	208	B1, 31
Alpen Siding		B4, 29
Alsike		A1, 31
Altario	50	C2, 31
Amisk	212	C1, 31
Andrew	569	B4, 29
Anzac	138	B2, 29
Ardenode		A3, 31
Ardmore	238	C4, 29
Ardrossan	126	A1, 31
		A4, 29
Armena		B1, 31
Arrowwood	165	B3, 31
Ashmont	119	B4, 29
Athabasca	1862	A3, 29
Atikameg		C2, 28
Atmore		B3, 29

B

Balzac		A2, 31
Banff	3410	C3, 30
Barnwell	359	B4, 31
Barons	323	B3, 31
Barrhead	3736	A4, 29
Bashaw	875	B1, 31
Bassano	1200	B3, 31
Bawlf	351	B1, 31
Bay Tree		A2, 28
Beach Corner		A1, 31
		A4, 29
Bear Canyon		A2, 28
Beaumont	3202	A1, 31
		A4, 29
Beauvallon		B4, 29
Beaver Crossing		C3, 29
Beaverdam		C4, 29
Beaverlodge	1937	A3, 28
Beaver Mines		A4, 31
Beiseker	648	A2, 31
Bellis	55	B4, 29
Benalto	72	A2, 31
Bentley	825	A1, 31
Berrymoor		A1, 31
		A4, 29
Berwyn	674	B2, 28
Bezanson	65	B3, 28
Big Coulee		A3, 29
Big Stone		C2, 31
Big Valley	360	B2, 31
Bindloss		C3, 31
Bittern Lake	153	B1, 31
Black Diamond	1545	A3, 31
Blackfalds	1488	A2, 31
Blackfoot	208	C1, 31
		C4, 29
Blackie	343	A3, 31
Bloomsbury		A4, 29
Blueberry Mountain		A2, 28
Blue Ridge	195	C4, 28
Bluesky	135	B2, 28
Bluffton	112	A1, 31
Bodo		C2, 31
Bon Accord	1425	A4, 29
Bonanza		A2, 28
Bonnyville	4664	C4, 29
Botha	172	B2, 31
Bow City		B3, 31
Bowden	1021	A2, 31
Bow Island	1499	C3, 31
Boyle	679	B3, 29
Boyne Lake		B4, 29
Bragg Creek	384	A3, 31
Brant		A3, 31
Breton	548	A1, 31
Breynat		B3, 29
Brocket		A4, 31
Brooks	9421	B3, 31
Brosseau		B4, 29
Brownfield		B2, 31
		C2, 31
Brownvale	148	B2, 28
Bruce	93	B1, 31
Bruderheim	1238	B4, 29
Brule		B1, 30
		B4, 28
Buck Creek		A1, 31
Buck Lake	169	A1, 31
Buffalo		C3, 31
Buffalo Head Prairie		C1, 28
		C4, 27
Buffalo Lake		A3, 28
Buford		A1, 31
Burdett	250	C4, 31
Burmis	88	A4, 31
Busby	73	A4, 29
Byemoor		B2, 31

C

Cadogan	80	C1, 31
Cadomin	129	B1, 30
Cadotte Lake	135	C2, 28
Calahoo	143	A4, 29
Calais		B3, 28
Calgary	620 692	A3, 31
Calling Lake		A3, 29
Calmar	1118	A1, 31
		A4, 29
Cambria		B2, 31
Camp Creek		A4, 29
Camrose	12 809	B1, 31
Canmore	3745	C3, 30
Canyon Creek	138	C3, 28
Carbon	438	B2, 31
Carcajou		B1, 28
		B4, 27
Cardston	3267	B4, 31
Carmangay	281	B3, 31
Carnwood		A1, 31
Caroline	431	A2, 31
Carrot Creek		C1, 30
		C4, 28
Carseland	117	A3, 31
Carstairs	1725	A2, 31
Carvel		A4, 29
Carway		B4, 31
Caslan		B3, 29
Castor	1123	B2, 31
Cayley	232	A3, 31
Cereal	252	C2, 31
Cessford		B3, 31
Champion	380	B3, 31
Chancellor		B3, 31
Chard		C2, 29
Chateh		B3, 26
Chauvin	335	C1, 31
Cheadle		A3, 31
Cherhill	71	A4, 29
Cherry Grove		C3, 29
Cherry Point		A2, 28
Chief Mountain		A4, 31
Chinook		C2, 31
Chinook Valley		B2, 28
Chipewyan Lake	147	A2, 29
Chipman	281	B4, 29
Chisholm	60	A3, 29
Clairmont	599	B3, 28
Clandonald	136	C1, 31
		C4, 29
Claresholm	3493	A3, 31
Cleardale		A2, 28
Cline River		C2, 30
Clive	364	A1, 31
Cluny	111	B3, 31
Clyde	376	A4, 29
Coaldale	4671	B4, 31
Coalhurst	1119	B4, 31
Cochrane	4044	A3, 31
Codesa		B2, 28
Cold Lake	2245	C3, 29
Colinton	126	A3, 29
College Heights	332	A1, 31
Compeer		C2, 31
Condor	52	A2, 31
Conklin	133	B3, 29
Conrich		A3, 31
Consort	632	C2, 31
Cooking Lake	237	A1, 31
		A4, 29
Coronado		A4, 29
Coronation	1268	B2, 31
Countess		B3, 31
Coutts	400	B4, 31
Cowley	304	A4, 31
Craigmyle	52	B2, 31
Cranford		B4, 31
Cremona	410	A2, 31
Crestomere		A1, 31
Crooked Creek		B3, 28
Crossfield	1358	A2, 31
Crowsnest Pass, Municipality of	7577	A4, 31
Bellevue		
Blairmore		
Coleman		
Frank		
Hillcrest Mines		
Cynthia	56	C1, 30
		C4 28
Czar	184	C1, 31

D

Dalemead		A3, 31
Dapp		A4, 29
Darwell		A1, 31
		A4, 29
Daysland	700	B1, 31
Deadwood		B2, 28
DeBolt		B3, 28
Delacour		A3, 31
Del Bonita		B4, 31
Delburne	555	A2, 31
Delia	239	B2, 31
Demmitt		A3, 28
Derwent	142	C4, 29
Deville		B1, 31
		B4, 29
Devon	3931	A1, 31
		A4, 29
Dewberry	181	C4, 29
De Winton	75	A3, 31
Diamond City	73	B4, 31
Dickson		A2, 31
Didsbury	3235	A2, 31
Dixonville	56	B2, 28
Dogpound		A2, 31
Donalda	266	B1, 31
Donatville		B3, 29
Donnelly	382	B3, 28
Dorothy		B2, 31
Drayton Valley	4867	A1, 31
Driftpile		C3, 28
Drumheller	6671	B2, 31
Duchess	429	B3, 31
Duffield	83	A1, 31
		A4, 29
Dunmore	89	C3, 31
Dunvegan		B2, 28
Duvernay		B4, 29

E

Eaglesham	207	B2, 28
East Coulee	261	B2, 31
Eckville	842	A2, 31
Edberg	150	B1, 31
Edgerton	389	C1, 31
Edmonton	560 085	A4, 29
		A1, 31
Edmonton Beach	329	A1, 31
		A4, 29
Edson	7329	C1, 30
		C4, 28
Edwand		B4, 29
Egremont	57	A4, 29
Elk Point	1057	C4, 29
Elkwater	101	C4, 31
Ellscott		B3, 29
Elmworth		A3, 28
Elnora	278	B2, 31
Embarras Portage		E3, 27
Empress	254	C3, 31
Enchant	53	B3, 31
Endiang		B2, 31
Enilda	164	C3, 28
Ensign		A3, 31
Entrance	81	B1, 30
		B4, 28
Entwistle	468	A1, 31
		A4, 29
Erskine	234	B2, 31
Esther		C2, 31
Etzikom	69	C4, 31
Eureka River		B2, 28
Evansburg	784	C1, 30
		C4, 28
Exshaw	389	C3, 30

F

Fabyan	63	C1,31
Fairview	2869	B2, 28
Falher	1204	B2, 28
Fallis		A1, 31
		A4, 29
Falun		A1, 31
Faust	298	C3, 28
Fawcett	129	A3, 29
Fawcett Lake		A3, 29
Fenn		B2, 31
Ferintosh	155	B1, 31
Finnegan		B2, 31
Fisher Home		A1, 31
Fitzgerald		E1, 27
Flatbush		A3, 29
Fleet		B2, 31
Foisy		B4, 29
Foremost	576	C4, 31
Forestburg	955	B1, 31
Fork Lake		B3, 29
Fort Assiniboine	217	A3, 29
Fort Chipewyan	1179	F3, 27
Fort Kent	111	C4, 29
Fort MacKay	166	B1, 29
Fort Macleod	3139	B4, 31
Fort McMurray	34 494	B2, 29
Fort Saskatchewan	12 474	A4, 29
Fort Vermilion	729	C3, 27
Fox Creek	1978	C4, 28
Fox Lake		D3, 27
Franchere		C4, 29
Freedom		A4, 29
Frog Lake		C4, 29

G

Gadsby	56	B2, 31
Gainford		A1, 31
		A4, 29
Galahad	175	B1, 31
Garden Creek	160	D3, 27
Gem		B3, 31
Ghost Lake		A2, 31
Gibbons	2592	A4, 29
Gift Lake	432	C2, 28
Girouxville	325	B2, 28
Gleichen	381	B3, 31
Glendon	455	B4, 29
Glenevis		A3, 29
Glenwood	266	A4, 31
Goodfare		A3, 28
Goodfish Lake		B4, 29
Goodridge		B4, 29
Gordondale		A2, 28
Granada		C1, 30
		C4, 28
Grand Centre	3119	C3, 29
Grande Cache	4624	A4, 28
Grande Prairie	24 076	B3, 28
Granum	399	A4, 31
Grassland	61	B3, 29
Grassy Lake	211	B4, 31
Green Court	84	C4, 28
Grimshaw	2488	B2, 28
Grouard		C3, 28
Grouard Mission	213	C3, 28
Grovedale		B3, 28
Gull Lake	80	A1, 31
Gunn	223	A4, 29
Gurneyville		C4, 29
Guy	56	B3, 28
Gwynne	67	A1, 31

H

Habay		B2, 26
Hairy Hill	72	B4, 29
Halkirk	156	B2, 31
Hamlin		B4, 29
Hanna	2996	B2, 31
Hardisty	680	C1, 31
Hartell		A3, 31
Hay Camp		E1, 27
Hay Lakes	318	B1, 31
Haynes		A2, 31
Hays	75	B3, 31
Hayter		C1, 31
Hazeldine		C4, 29
Heath		C1, 31
Heinsburg	80	C4, 29
Heisler	212	B1. 31
Hemaruka		C2, 31
Hespero		A2, 31
High Level	2673	B3, 26
High Prairie	2580	C3, 28
High River	5049	A3, 31
Highridge		A4, 29
Highvale		A1, 31
		A4, 29
Hilda	80	C3, 31
Hilliard	55	B4, 29
Hill Spring	220	A4, 31
Hines Creek	529	B2, 28
Hinton	8825	B1, 30
		B4, 28
Hoadley		A1, 31
Hobbema	56	A1, 31
Holden	430	B1, 31
		B4, 29
Hondo		A3, 29
Hoselaw		C4, 29
Hotchkiss		B2, 28
Huallen		A3, 28
Hughenden	251	C1, 31
Hussar	179	B3, 31
Huxley	53	B2, 31
Hylo		B3, 29
Hythe	681	A3, 28

I

Iddesleigh		C3, 31
Imperial Mills	105	B3, 29
Indian Cabins		B1, 27
Innisfail	5444	A2, 31
Innisfree	255	B1, 31
		B4, 29
Irma	474	C1, 31
Iron River		C3, 29
Iron Springs	56	B3, 31
Irricana	726	A2, 31
Irvine	360	C3, 31
Island Lake		A3, 29
Islay	119	C1, 31
		C4, 29
Itaska Beach		A1, 31

J

James River Bridge		A2, 31
Jarvie	75	A4, 29
Jasper	3404	B1, 30
Jean Cote	59	B2, 28
Jenner		C3, 31
John D'or Prairie		C3, 27
Josephburg	150	B4, 29
Joussard	270	C3, 28

K

Kananaskis		C3, 30
Kapasiwin		A4, 29
		A1, 31
Kathleen		C3, 28
Kathyrn		A2, 31
Kavanagh	61	A1, 31
Keg River		B1, 28
		B4, 26
Kelsey		B1, 31
Keoma		A2, 31
Kikino	160	B3, 29
Killam	1005	B1, 31
Kingman	74	B1, 31
Kinsella	68	B1. 31
Kinuso	285	C3, 28
Kipp		B4, 31
Kirkcaldy		B3, 31
Kirriemuir		C2, 31
Kitscoty	545	C1, 31
		C3, 29

L

Lac La Biche	2069	B3, 29
Lac la Nonne		A4, 29
Lacombe	5954	A1, 31
La Corey		C3, 29
La Crete		C1, 28
		C3, 27
Lafond		B4, 29
La Glace	136	A3, 28
Lake Isle		A1, 31
		A4, 29
Lake Louise	140	C2, 30
Lamont	1673	B4, 29
Langdon	141	A3, 31
Lavoy	134	B1, 31
		B4, 29
Leavitt	70	A4, 31
Leduc	12 471	A1, 31
		A4, 29
Leedale		A1, 31
Legal	1042	A4, 29
Leslieville	132	A2, 31
Lethbridge	58 086	B4, 31
Lindale		A1, 31
		A4, 29
Lindbergh		C4, 29
Lindbrook		B1, 31
		B4, 29
Linden	461	A2, 31
Lisburn		A4, 29
Little Buffalo	203	C2, 28
Little Smoky		B3, 28
Lloydminster	15 231	C1, 31
		C4, 29
Lodgepole	130	C1, 30
Lomond	204	B3, 31
Lone Pine		C4, 28
Longview	291	A3, 31
Looma		A1, 31
		A3, 29
Loon Lake	178	C2, 28
Lougheed	261	B1, 31
Lousana		B2, 31
Lundbreck	142	A4, 31
Lyalta		A3, 31
Lymburn		A3, 28

M

MacKay		C1, 30
		C4, 28
Madden		A2, 31
Magrath	1576	B4, 31
Maleb		C4, 31
Mallaig	339	B4, 29
Ma-Me-O Beach	82	A1, 31
Manning	1262	B2, 28
Mannville	788	C1, 31
		C4, 29
Manola	52	A4, 29
Manyberries	60	C4, 31
Mariana Lake		B2, 29
Marie-Reine	55	B2, 28
Markerville		A2, 31
Marlboro	165	C1, 30
		C4, 28
Marwayne	500	C1, 31
		C4, 29
Mayerthorpe	1475	C4, 28
McLaughlin		C1, 31
McLennan	1176	C3, 28
McRae		B4, 29
Meadowview		A4, 29
Meander River		B2, 26
Meanook		A3, 29
Mearns		A4, 29
Medicine Hat	41 493	C3, 31
Medley	5500	C3, 29
Meeting Creek		B1, 31
Menaik		A1, 31
Metiskow	99	C1, 31
Mewatha Beach		B3, 29
Michichi		B2, 31
Michigan Centre		A1, 31
Mildred Lake		B1, 29
Milk River	894	B4, 31
Millarville		A3, 31
Millet	1087	A1, 31
Millicent		B3, 31
Milo	117	B3, 31
Minburn	146	B1, 31
		B4, 29
Mirror	552	B1, 31
Mission Beach		A1, 31
Monarch	183	B4, 31
Monitor	65	C2, 31
Morecambe		B4, 29
Morinville	5109	A4, 29
Morley		A3, 31
Morningside	53	A1, 31
Morrin	245	B2, 31
Mossleigh	55	A3, 31
Mountain View	61	A4, 31
Mulhurst	104	A1, 31
Mundare	655	B1, 31
		B4, 29
Munson	148	B2, 31
Musidora		B4, 29
Muskeg River	61	B4, 28
Myrnam	397	B4, 29

N

Nacmine	333	B2, 31

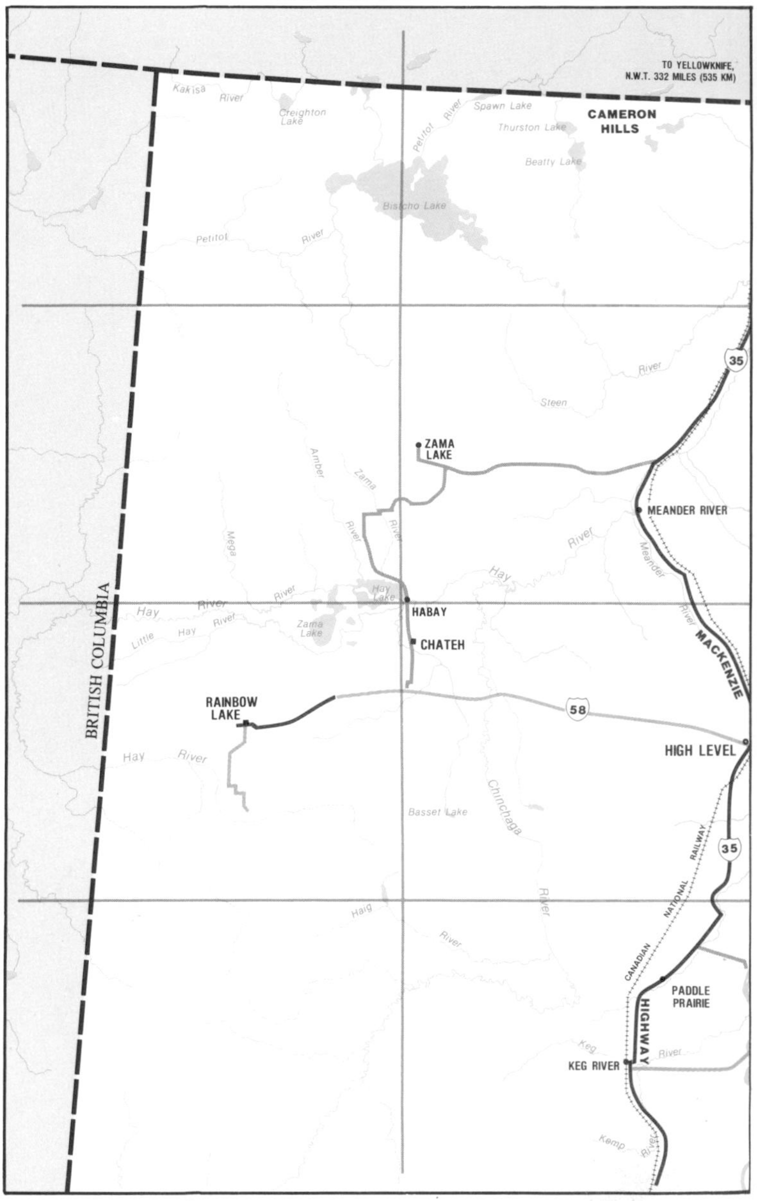

A Adjoining Map, Page 28 B

ROAD CLASSIFICATIONS
- Primary Highways (Paved)
- Secondary Roads (Paved)
- Improved (Gravelled)
- Improved (Gravelled and partially oiled)
- Unimproved

HIGHWAY MARKERS
- 2 Primary Highway
- Yellowhead Highway
- Crowsnest Highway
- Trans-Canada Highway
- 2 12 Secondary Roads

POPULATION SYMBOLS
- Under 250
- 250 to 1,000
- 1,000 to 2,500
- 2,500 to 5,000
- 5,000 to 10,000
- 10,000 to 25,000
- 25,000 to 50,000
- 50,000 and over

Map labels: TO HAY RIVER, N.W.T. 109 MILES (176 KM) — NORTHWEST TERRITORIES — FORT SMITH — RAPIDS OF THE DROWNED — MOUNTAIN RAPIDS, PELICAN RAPIDS, CASSETTE RAPIDS — FITZGERALD — INDIAN CABINS — STEEN RIVER — WARDEN STATION — HAY CAMP — CARIBOU MOUNTAINS — WOOD BUFFALO NATIONAL PARK — ROAD — WINTER ROAD — DEMICHARGE RAPIDS — Lake Athabasca — GARDEN CREEK — Lake Claire — FORT CHIPEWYAN — ROCKY LANE — JEAN D'OR PRAIRIE — FOX LAKE — FORT VERMILION — LA CRETE — EMBARRAS PORTAGE — SASKATCHEWAN — BUFFALO HEAD PRAIRIE — CARCAJOU — BUFFALO HEAD HILLS — BIRCH MOUNTAINS — FERRY

Inset map: FORT McMURRAY — GRANDE PRAIRIE — EDMONTON — RED DEER — CALGARY — MEDICINE HAT — LETHBRIDGE

Adjoining Map, Page 29

Adjoining Map, Page 26

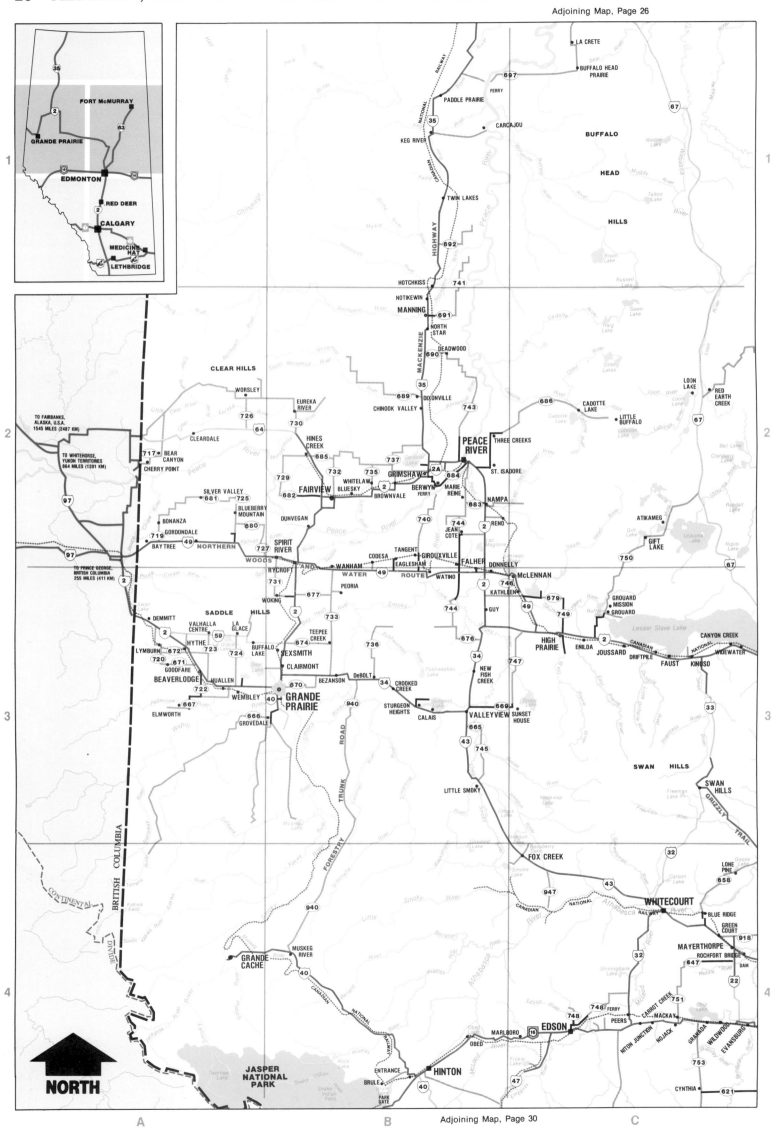

NORTH

Adjoining Map, Page 30

Miles 10   0   10   20   30   40.   50

Kilometres 10   0   10   20   30   40   50   60   70

Adjoining Map, Page 27

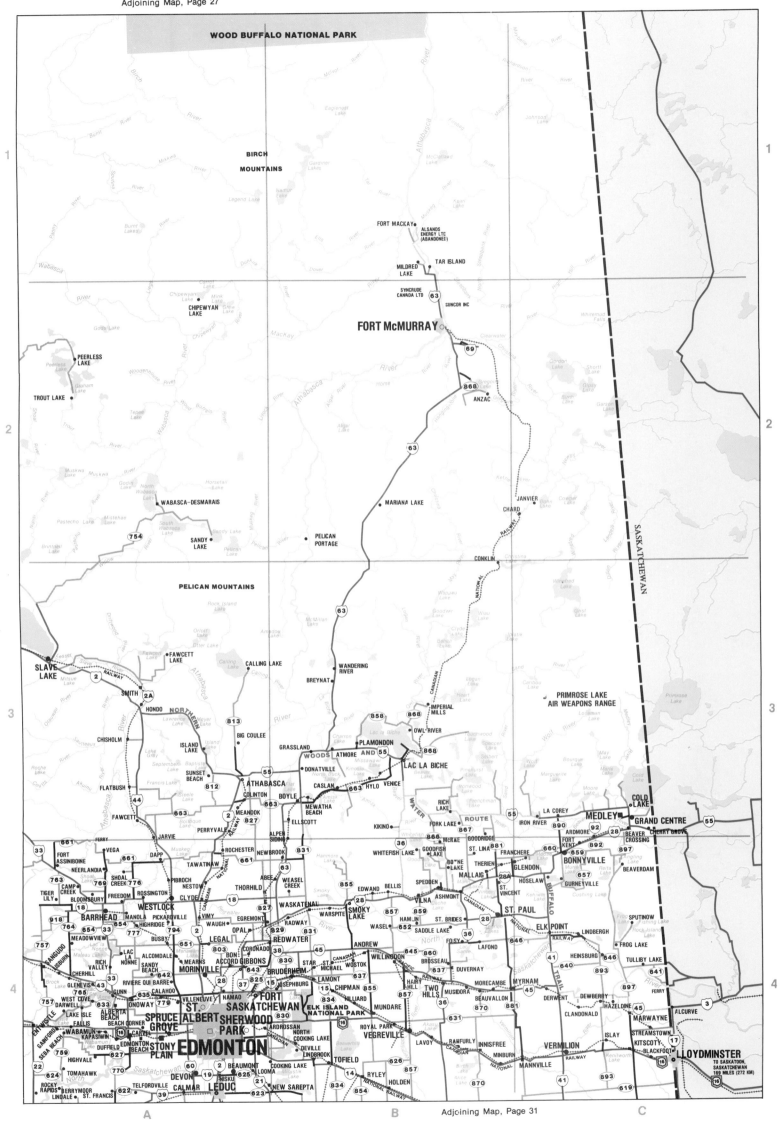

Adjoining Map, Page 31

Adjoining Map, Page 28

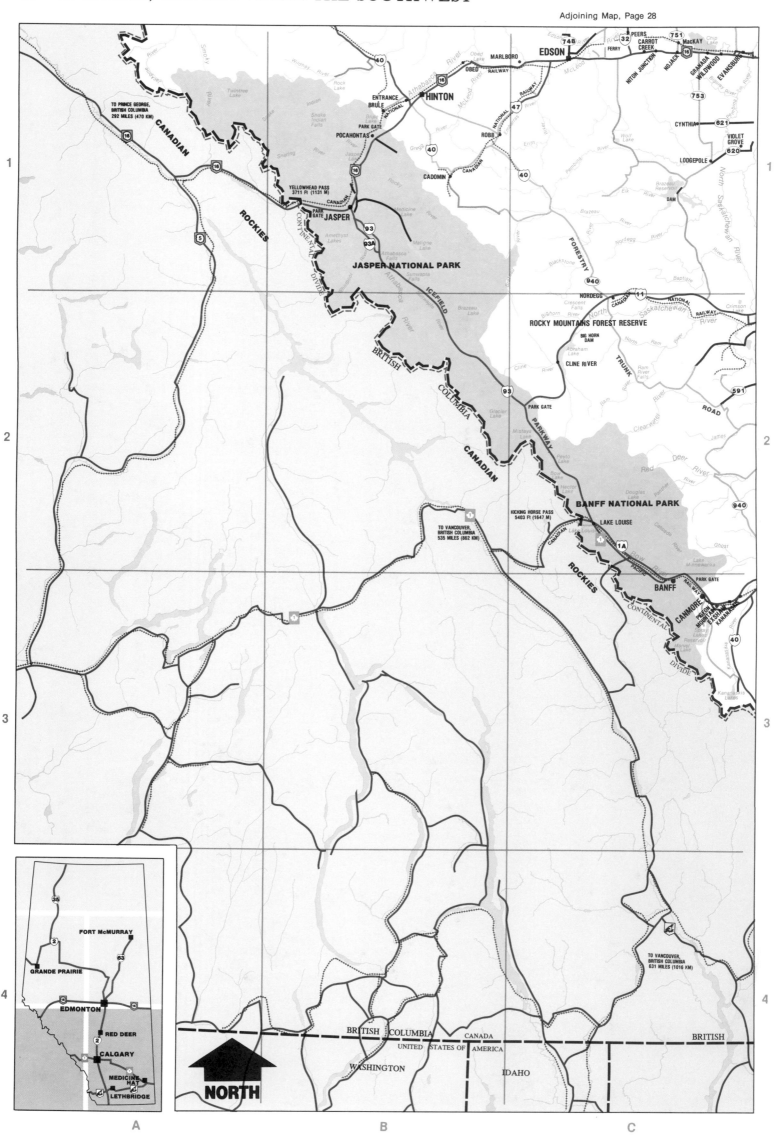

NORTH

Adjoining Map, Page 29

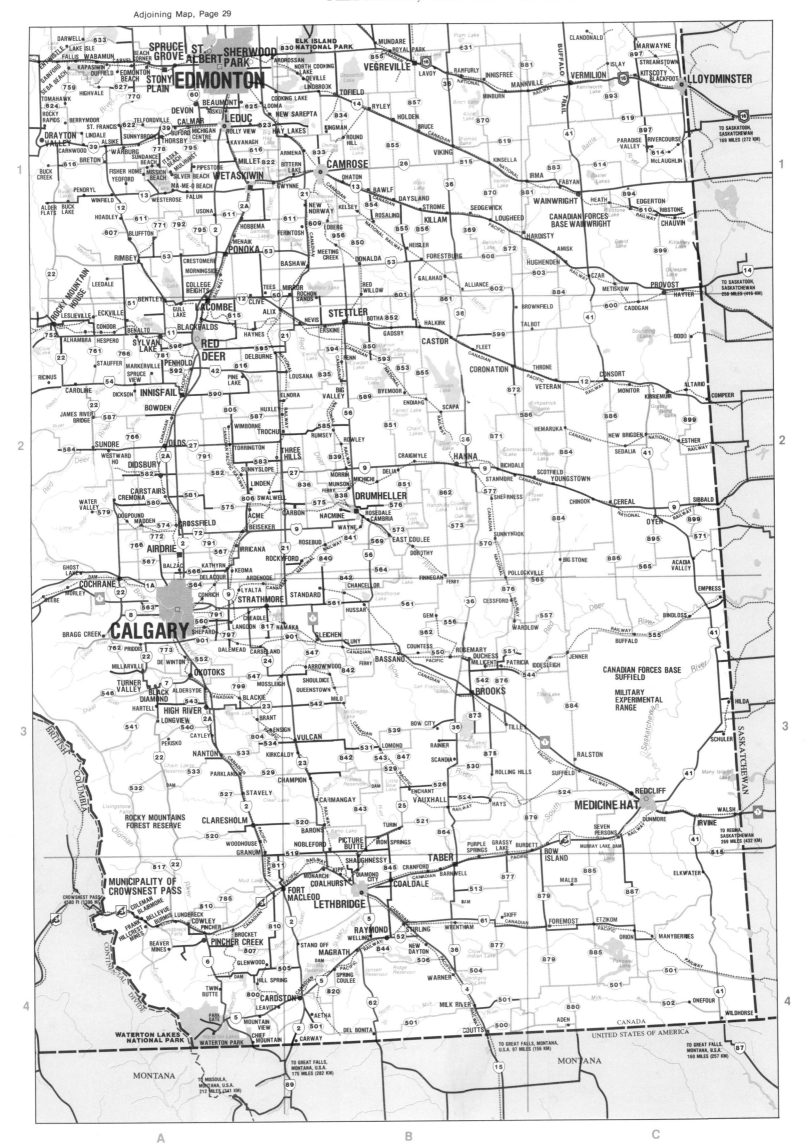

EDMONTON
the capital city

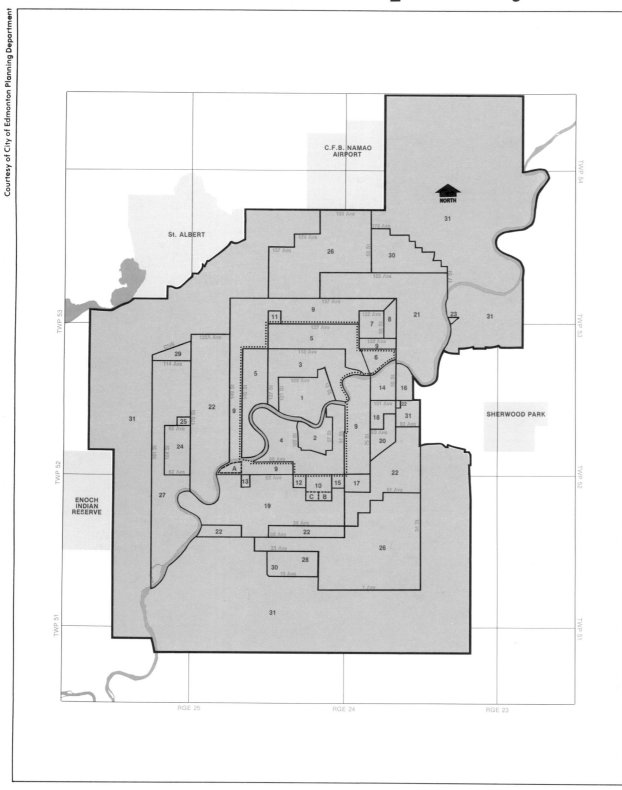

Population: 560,085.

Location: On Highways 2 and 16, 183 miles (294 km.) north of Calgary on the North Saskatchewan River.

Street System: Since early in the 20th century, Edmonton streets have been numbered. Avenues run east and west from First Avenue in the south to 259 Avenue in the north with even house numbers on the north side. Streets run north and south from First Street in the east to 231 Street in the west with even house numbers on the west side. 101 Street runs roughly through the centre of the city, as does 101 Avenue which has been allowed to retain its original name, Jasper Avenue. If a street name carries a letter after the number (i.e. 106A Avenue), this means it is an extra street in the system (i.e., between 106 and 107 Avenue).

An Edmonton address on a numbered street can be found easily. No. 9180 149 Street, for instance, is between 91 Avenue and 92 Avenue on the west side of 149 Street. No. 17303 106A Avenue is located between 173 and 174 Street on the south side of 106A Avenue. The number system can also apply to named streets. For instance, 10632 Jasper Avenue would lie between 106 and 107 Street.

In 1982, with the annexation of vast outlying areas, a new street system was designed for Edmonton which will eventually see the whole area divided into four quadrants. First Street is to be renamed Meridian Street and First Avenue Quadrant Avenue so that nearly the whole of the existing city will lie within the northwest quadrant. Streets already developed on the city's far eastern and southern outskirts (east of Meridian Street, and south of Quadrant Avenue) are being numbered according to the four-quadrant system of the future.

History: Edmonton was originally Fort Edmonton, a site selected by the Hudson's Bay Company in 1795. Trader John Tomison named the fort after the site of a British estate owned by Sir James Winterlake, then deputy governor of the company. Edmonton became a town in 1892 and a city in 1904. The following year the Canadian Northern Railway reached the city and in 1906 Edmonton was declared the capital of the new province of Alberta.

How the capital grew
Annexations since the incorporation of the town of Edmonton in 1892

1 1892 Incorporation of Town of Edmonton, Hudson's Bay Reserve to River Lot 14 - 3.4 sq. mi.

2 1899 Incorporation of Town of Strathcona, River Lot 9 to River Lot 17 - 1.56 sq. mi.

3 1904 Incorporation of City of Edmonton, Groat Estate/Inglewood to Parkdale/Riverdale - 3.75 sq. mi.

4 1907 Incorporation of City of Strathcona, Windsor Park/Belgravia to Bonnie Doon/Hazeldean - 5.94 sq. mi.

5 1908 Buena Vista to Westmount, North Inglewood to Eastwood/Virginia Park - 7.5 sq. mi.

6 1911 Highlands - 1 sq. mi.

••• 1912 Amalgamation of City of Edmonton and City of Strathcona

7 1912 Belmont Park - 1 sq. mi.

8 1912 Kennedale - .59 sq. mi.

9 1913 Dominion Industrial to Quesnell Heights/Brander Gardens to Parkallen, Bonaventure to Belvedere, Forest Heights to Argyll - 15.02 sq. mi.

10 1914 Allendale/Duggan to Coronet/Papaschase - 1 sq. mi.

11 1917 Calder - .28 sq. mi.

A 1922 Separation of north Brander Gardens - .39 sq. mi.

B 1922 Separation of Papaschase - .14 sq. mi.

12 1947 Pleasantview - .25 sq. mi.

13 1950 Whitemud Creek - .13 sq. mi.

C 1951 Separation of part of Duggan - .17 sq. mi.

14 1954 Capilano/Fulton Place - .5 sq. mi.

15 1954 Coronet - .25 sq. mi.

16 1956 Gold Bar - 1 sq. mi.

17 1958 Davies Industrial - .70 sq. mi.

18 1959 Terrace Heights/Ottewell - .88 sq. mi.

19 1959 Terwillegar Park/Riverbend to Strathcona Industrial Park and re-annexation of A, B, C - 10.86 sq. mi.

20 1960 Ottewell to Girard Industrial - 1.2 sq. mi.

21 1961 Beverly/Clareview to Dickinsfield - 11.02 sq. mi.

22 1964 Jasper Place and Southeast Industrial - 16.92 sq. mi.

23 1967 Clover Bar Power Plant - .06 sq. mi.

24 1969 Springfield/Callingwood - 2.03 sq. mi.

25 1970 Springfield - north - .13 sq. mi.

26 1971 Castle Downs/Lake District and Mill Woods - 23.55 sq. mi.

27 1972 West Jasper Place - 10.07 sq. mi.

28 1974 Kaskitayo - 1.22 sq. mi.

29 1976 Northwest Industrial - .84 sq. mi.

30 1980 Pilot Sound and Twin Brooks - 4.41 sq. mi.

31 1982 Edmonton Northwest/Yellowhead to Heritage Valleys/The Meadows to Ranchlands/Northeast - 142.66 sq. mi.

Edmonton locales

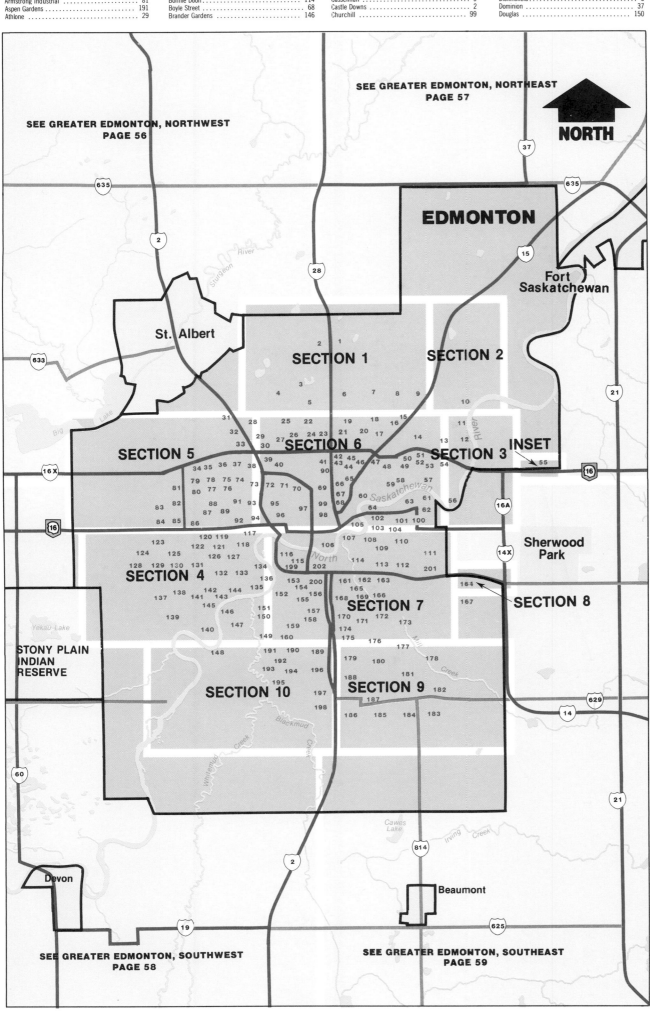

SEE GREATER EDMONTON, NORTHWEST PAGE 56

SEE GREATER EDMONTON, NORTHEAST PAGE 57

SEE GREATER EDMONTON, SOUTHWEST PAGE 58

SEE GREATER EDMONTON, SOUTHEAST PAGE 59

NORTH

EDMONTON

Fort Saskatchewan

St. Albert

Sherwood Park

STONY PLAIN INDIAN RESERVE

Devon

Beaumont

SECTION 1
SECTION 2
SECTION 3
INSET
SECTION 4
SECTION 5
SECTION 6
SECTION 7
SECTION 8
SECTION 9
SECTION 10

Named Streets*

Nearly all streets and avenues in Edmonton are numbered. The following are named. The index gives the grid references, followed by the page number.

Churches

Churches listed are those holding title to a building. Index gives symbol number ⚑, followed by grid references, followed by page number. No symbol numbers are given for downtown and university maps (pages 47 and 48) because the name is spelled out on the map.

Hotels

Index gives symbol number ☐, followed by grid references, followed by page number. No symbol numbers are given for downtown and university maps (pages 47 and 48) because the name is spelled out on the map.

Points of Interest

Index gives symbol number ✱, followed by grid references, followed by page number. No symbol numbers are given for downtown and university maps (pages 47 and 48) because the name is spelled out on the map.

*Abbreviations: Ave.—Avenue; Blvd.—Boulevard; Cir.—Circle; Ct.—Court; Cres.—Cresent; Dr.—Drive; Fwy.—Freeway; Pl.—Place; Pt.—Point; Rd.—Road; St.—Street; Tr.—Trail.

Schools

Each is identified by symbol number ⌂, followed by grid references, followed by page number. No symbol numbers are given for downtown and university maps (pages 47 and 48) because the name is spelled out on the map.

School	Sym	Grid	Pg
Abbott Elementary School	10	A2	39
Afton Elementary School	11	D2	41
Alberta School for the Deaf	44	B3	50
Aldergrove Elementary School	21	C2	40
Alex Taylor Elementary School	88	D4	45
Allendale Elementary and Junior High School	46	B3	50
Anne Fitzgerald Catholic Elementary School	4	B1	39
Annunciation Catholic Elementary School	12	D1	41
Archbishop Macdonald Catholic High School	12	F4	43
Archbishop O'Leary Catholic High School	19	D1	45
Argyll Elementary School (Closed June 1983)	38	D3	51
Athlone Elementary School	4	A1	44
Austin O'Brien Catholic Senior High School	5	E1	51
Avalon Junior High School	49	B4	50
Avonmore Elementary and Junior High School	41	D3	51
Balwin Junior High School	24	E1	45
Bannerman Elementary School	2	B4	38
Baturyn Elementary School	1	C2	36
Beacon Heights Elementary School	46	F2	45
Beacon Heights Elementary School	8	A2	39
Belgravia Elementary School	26	A3	50
Bellevue Elementary School	62	E3	45
Belmead Elementary School	9	C2	40
Belmont Elementary School	3	A1	39
Belvedere Elementary School	27	F1	45
Bennett School (Closed June 1972)	2	D1	51
Beverly Heights Elementary School (Closed June 1981)	12	A3	39
Beverly Heights Elementary School (Closed June 1981)	67	F3	45
Bishop Savaryn Catholic Elementary School	6	C3	36
Bonnie Doon Composite High School	22	D2	51
Braemar Elementary School	11	E1	51
Brander Gardens Elementary School	40	E4	41
Brightview Elementary School	15	E4	43
Britannia Junior High School	19	E4	43
Brookside Elementary School	41	F4	41
Caernarvon Elementary School	8	B4	36
Calder Elementary School	8	B1	44
Callingwood Elementary School	33	D3	41
Canora Elementary School (Closed June 1973)	16	E4	43
Capilano Elementary School	95	F4	45
Cardinal Leger Catholic Junior High School	14	D4	37
Caritas High School (Private) (Located in Father Lacombe Catholic Elementary School)	12	C1	44
Carter McGee Catholic Elementary School	3	E1	55
Centennial Elementary School	38	D4	41
Centennial Montessori School (Private)	15	B2	50
Clara Tyner Elementary School	10	E1	51
Continuing Education Centre	84	C4	44
Coralwood Seventh-Day Adventist Junior Academy (Private)	33	A2	44
Coronation Elementary School	11	F4	43
Coronation Elementary School	68	A3	44
Covenant Community Training Centre (Private) (Located in The Peoples' Church)	57	C3	44
Crawford Plains Elementary School	27	D3	53
Crestwood Elementary and Junior High School	7	F1	41
Cromdale Elementary School	61	D3	45
D. S. MacKenzie Elementary and Junior High School	7	F1	55
Dan Knott Junior High School	17	B3	53
Delton Elementary School	39	D2	45
Delwood Elementary School	21	E1	45
Dickinsfield Junior High School	23	D4	37
Donnan Elementary and Junior High School	39	D2	51
Dovercourt Elementary School	2	F2	43
Dovercourt Elementary School	32	A2	44
Duggan Elementary School	13	F1	55
Dunluce Community School	4	B3	36
East Edmonton Christian School (Private)	15	A3	39
Eastglen Composite High School	63	E3	45
Eastwood Elementary and Junior High School	41	D2	45
Ecole Primaire Catholique Frere Antone	12	B2	53
Edith Rogers Junior High School	3	B1	52
Edmonton Academy (Located in St. John's Catholic School)	76	B4	44
Edmonton Christian Academy (Private) (Located in Fundamental Baptist Church)	78	B4	44
Edmonton Hebrew Elementary School (Private) (Located in Talmud Torah Elementary School)	74	A4	44
Ekota Elementary School	20	B3	53
Elizabeth Seton Catholic Elementary and Junior High School	2	A1	39
Ellerslie Junior High School	28	B4	53
Ellerslie Primary School	29	B4	53
Elmwood Elementary School	25	D2	41
Elves Memorial Child Development Centre	14	F4	43
Evansdale Elementary School	9	D4	37
Evelyn Unger School for Language and Learning Development (Private)	20	E4	43
Evelyn Unger School for Language and Learning Development (Private)	37	D3	51
Excelsior Elementary and Junior High Education Academy (Private) (Located in King Edward Elementary and Junior High School)	18	C2	50
F. R. Haythorne County School	1	Inset	52
Father Lacombe Catholic Elementary School	11	C1	44
Father Leo Green Catholic Elementary School	15	E4	37
Forest Heights Elementary School	91	E4	45
Fulton Place Elementary School	92	F4	45
Garneau Elementary and Junior High School	14	B2	50
Glendale Elementary School	3	D1	41
Glengarry Elementary School	15	D1	45
Glenora Elementary School	72	A4	44
Gold Bar Elementary School	96	F4	45
Good Shepherd Catholic School (Closed June 1982)	37	C4	40
Grace Martin Elementary School	5	B1	52
Grandin Catholic Elementary School	1	B1	50
Grandview Heights Elementary and Junior High School	42	A3	50
Greenfield Elementary School	11	E1	55
Greenview Elementary School	8	C1	53
Grovenor Elementary School	23	F4	43
H. A. Gray Elementary School	37	C2	44
H. E. Benault Catholic Elementary and Junior High School	24	D2	41
Hardisty Junior High School	93	F4	45
Harry Ainlay Composite High School	5	E1	55
Hazeldean Elementary School	36	C3	50
High Park Elementary School	5	E3	43
Highlands Junior High School	65	F3	45
Hillcrest Junior High School	26	D2	41
Hillview Elementary School	10	C2	53
Holy Cross Catholic Elementary and Junior High School	21	F4	43
Holy Family Catholic Junior High School	26	D3	53
Holyrood Elementary School	8	D1	51
Homesteader Elementary School	30	F1	45
Homesteader Elementary School	5	A1	39
Idylwylde Elementary School	23	D2	51
Inglewood Elementary School	49	B3	44
J. A. Fife Elementary School	10	E3	37
J. H. Picard Catholic Junior and Senior High School	19	C2	50
J. J. Bowlen Catholic Elementary and Junior High School	18	E4	37
J. Percy Page Composite High School	15	B2	53
James Gibbons Elementary School	2	E2	41
Jasper Place Composite High School	14	D2	41
John Barnett Elementary School	11	E4	37
John Paul I Catholic Elementary School	9	C1	53
Kameyosek Elementary School	13	B2	53
Katherine Therrien Catholic Elementary School	7	B3	36
Keheewin Elementary School	17	F3	55
Kenilworth Junior High School	24	E2	51
Kensington Elementary School	6	B1	44
Kildare Elementary School	25	E4	37
Killarney Junior High School	16	D1	45
King Edward Elementary and Junior High School	17	C2	50
Kirkness Elementary School	3	B3	38
L. Y. Cairns Vocational School	54	B4	50
Lansdowne Elementary School	47	A4	50
LaPerle Elementary School	8	C1	40
Lauderdale Elementary School	13	C1	44
Laurier Heights Elementary School	30	F2	41
Laurier Heights Junior High School	29	F2	41
Lawton Junior High School	13	A3	39
Lee Ridge Elementary School	7	B1	53
Lendrum Elementary School	50	B4	50
Londonderry Junior High School	16	E4	37
Lorelei Heights Elementary and Junior High School	5	C3	36
Louis St. Laurent Catholic Junior High School	4	E1	55
Lynnwood Elementary School	28	E2	41
M. E. Lazerte Composite High School	17	E4	37
Malcolm Tweedie Elementary School	2	B1	52
Malmo Elementary School	48	A4	50
Mayfield Elementary School	14	F4	43
McArthur Elementary School	1	A1	44
McArthur Elementary School	29	A4	36
McCauley Elementary and Junior High School	86	D4	45
McDougall Elementary and Junior High School	82	C3	44
McKay Avenue School (Closed June 1983)	—	B3	47
McKee Elementary School	52	B4	50
McKernan Elementary and Junior High School	27	B2	50
McLeod Elementary School	12	F4	37
McNally Composite High School	90	E4	45
McQueen Elementary School	9	F3	43
Meadowlark Christian School (Our Lady of Lourdes Catholic School) (Private)	18	E4	43
Meadowlark Elementary School	15	E2	41
Mee-Yan-Noh Elementary School	17	D1	45
Menisa Elementary School	19	B3	53
Meyokumin Elementary School	21	C3	53
Meyonohk Elementary School	14	B2	52
Mill Creek Elementary School	32	C2	50
Millwoods Christian School (Private)	1	B1	52
Montrose Elementary School	43	F2	45
Mount Carmel Catholic Elementary and Junior High School	30	B2	50
Mount Pleasant Elementary School	53	B4	50
Mount Royal Elementary School	66	F3	45
Newton Elementary School	44	F2	45
North Edmonton Christian Elementary and Junior High School (Private)	29	F1	45
North Edmonton Elementary School	25	E1	45
Northmount Elementary School	24	D4	37
Norwood Elementary School	58	D3	45
Notre Dame Catholic Elementary School	16	E2	41
Old Scona Academic High School	16	B2	50
Oliver Elementary School	77	B4	44
Ormsby Elementary School	35	C3	40
Ottewell Junior High School	9	E1	51
Our Lady of Fatima Catholic Elementary School	4	E1	41
Our Lady of Peace Catholic Elementary and Junior High School	6	E3	43
Our Lady of the Prairies Catholic Elementary School	36	D3	40
Our Lady of Victories Catholic Elementary School	27	E2	41
Overlanders Elementary School	7	B2	39
Parkallen Elementary School	43	B3	50
Paradale Elementary and Junior High School	59	D3	45
Parkview Elementary and Junior High School	17	F2	41
Patricia Heights Elementary School	31	D3	41
Pollard Meadows Elementary School	25	D3	53
Prince Charles Elementary School	36	B2	44
Prince Rupert Elementary School	54	B3	44
Princeton Elementary School	23	E1	45
Queen Alexandra Elementary School	29	B2	50
Queen Elizabeth Composite High School	14	D1	45
Queen Mary Park Elementary School	79	B3	44
R. J. Scott Elementary School	14	A3	39
Richard Secord Elementary School	2	E1	55
Rideau Park Elementary School	6	F1	55
Rio Terrace Elementary School	32	E3	41
Ritchie Junior High School	33	C3	50
Riverbend Junior High School	42	E4	41
Riverdale Elementary School	89	C4	45
Ross Sheppard Composite High School	4	F3	43
Ross Sheppard Composite High School	50	A3	44
Rosslyn Junior High School	9	B1	44
Rundle Elementary School	17	A3	39
Rutherford Elementary School	20	D2	51
Sacred Heart Catholic Elementary and Junior High School	85	C4	44
St. Agnes Catholic School (Closed June 1981)	45	B3	50
St. Alphonsus Catholic Elementary School	60	D3	45
St. Andrew Catholic Elementary School	53	A3	44
St. Angela Catholic Elementary School	2	A1	44
St. Anne Catholic Elementary School	22	D4	37
St. Augustine Catholic Elementary School	12	F1	55
St. Basil Catholic Elementary and Junior High School	55	C3	44
St. Bede Catholic Elementary School	19	A4	39
St. Benedict Catholic Elementary School	10	C2	40
St. Bernadette Catholic Elementary School	9	A2	39
St. Bonaventure Catholic Elementary and Junior High School	1	B4	38
St. Boniface Catholic Elementary and Junior High School	1	E1	55
St. Brendan Catholic Elementary and Junior High School	12	E1	51
St. Catherine Catholic Elementary and Junior High School	80	C3	44
St. Cecilia Catholic Junior High School	18	D1	45
St. Charles Catholic Elementary School	2	C2	36
St. Clare Catholic Elementary and Junior High School	42	E2	45
St. Clement Catholic Elementary and Junior High School	18	B3	53
St. Dominic Catholic Elementary and Junior High School	19	F4	37
St. Edmund Catholic Elementary and Junior High School	7	B1	44
St. Elizabeth Catholic Elementary School	6	B3	53
St. Francis of Assisi Catholic Elementary and Junior High School	26	E1	45
St. Francis Xavier Catholic Senior High School	13	D1	41
St. Gabriel Catholic Elementary and Junior High School	94	F4	45
St. Gerard Catholic Elementary School	40	D2	45
St. Gregory Catholic School (Closed June 1977)	13	F4	43
St. Hilda Catholic Elementary and Junior High School	4	B1	53
St. James Catholic Elementary and Junior High School	40	D2	51
St. Jerome Catholic Elementary and Junior High School	18	A3	39
St. John's Catholic School (Closed June 1983)	75	B4	44
St. Joseph Catholic Senior High School	81	C4	44
St. Justin Catholic Elementary School	22	D2	41
St. Kevin Catholic Elementary and Junior High School	3	D1	51
St. Leo Catholic Elementary and Junior High School	45	F2	45
St. Lucy Catholic Elementary School	3	B3	36
St. Margaret Catholic School (Closed June 1983)	35	C3	50
St. Maria Goretti Catholic Elementary and Junior High	6	A1	39
St. Mark Catholic Elementary and Junior High School	48	A3	44
St. Martha Catholic Elementary and Junior High School	34	C3	40
St. Martin Catholic Elementary and Junior High School	51	B4	50
St. Mary Catholic Junior High School	34	C3	50
St. Mary's Salesian Private Junior High School	27	F4	37
St. Matthew Catholic Elementary School	20	D1	45
St. Michael Catholic Elementary School	87	D4	45
St. Monica Catholic Elementary School	43	E4	41
St. Nicholas Catholic Elementary and Junior High School	16	A3	39
St. Patrick Catholic Elementary School	38	C2	44
St. Paul's Catholic Elementary School	6	F1	41
St. Peter's Catholic School for Autistic Children	28	B3	50
St. Philip Catholic Elementary School	13	D4	37
St. Pius X Catholic Elementary and Junior High School	35	A2	44
St. Richard Catholic Elementary School	22	C3	53
St. Rita Catholic Elementary School	31	A2	44
St. Rita Catholic Elementary School	1	F2	43
St. Rose Catholic Junior High School	20	F2	41
St. Sophia Catholic Elementary School	11	B2	39
St. Stanislaus Catholic Elementary School	10	E1	55
St. Teresa Catholic Elementary School	16	E2	55
St. Thomas Catholic Elementary School	21	C2	51
St. Thomas More Catholic Junior High School	2	D1	41
St. Timothy Catholic Elementary School	21	B4	36
St. Vincent Catholic Elementary School	17	F4	43
St. Vincent Catholic Elementary and Junior High School	70	A4	44
St. Vladimir Catholic Elementary School	22	E1	45
St. William Catholic Elementary School	28	F1	45
St. William Catholic Elementary School	14	F4	37
Sakaw Elementary School	23	C3	53
Satoo Elementary School	16	B3	52
Scott Robertson Elementary School	10	C1	44
Sherbrooke Elementary and Junior High School	34	A2	44
Sherwood Elementary School	5	F1	41
Sifton Elementary School	3	A1	44
Sir John Thompson Catholic Junior High School	8	A1	53
Spruce Avenue Elementary and Junior High School	56	C3	44
Steele Heights Elementary and Junior High School	20	F4	37
Steinhauer Elementary School	15	F2	55
Stratford Junior High School	19	E2	41
Strathcona Composite High School	31	B3	50
Strathearn Elementary School	7	D1	51
Strathearn Junior High School (Closed June 1983)	6	D1	51
Sweetgrass Elementary School	14	E2	55
Talmud Torah Elementary School	73	A4	44
Tempo Private School	39	E4	41
Terrace Heights Elementary School	4	E1	51
Thorncliffe Elementary School	23	D2	41
Tipaskan Elementary School	11	B2	52
Vernon Barford Junior High School	8	D1	55
Victoria Composite High School	83	C4	44
Virginia Park Elementary School	64	E3	45
W. P. Wagner High School	55	D3	51
Waverley Elementary School	25	E2	51
Weinlos Elementary School	24	C2	52
Wellington Junior High School	5	A1	44
West Edmonton Christian High School (Private)	10	F4	43
West Edmonton Christian School (Private)	8	F3	43
Westbrook Elementary School	9	E1	55
Westglen Elementary School	69	A4	44
Westlawn Junior High School	1	D1	41
Westminster Junior High School	22	F4	43
Westminster Junior High School	71	A4	44
Westmount Junior High School	52	A3	44
Westview Village Primary School	25	A4	42
Windsor Park Elementary School	13	A2	50
Winnifred Stewart School for the Mentally Retarded	51	A3	44
Winterburn Elementary and Junior High School	18	A2	54
Woodcroft Elementary School	47	A3	44
Woodcroft Elementary School	3	F3	43
York Elementary School	26	F4	37
Youngstown Elementary School	24	E4	43

Edmonton's ward boundaries and phone exchange areas

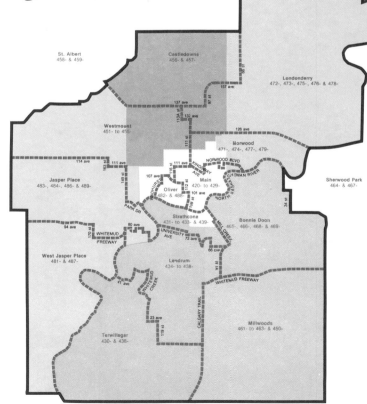

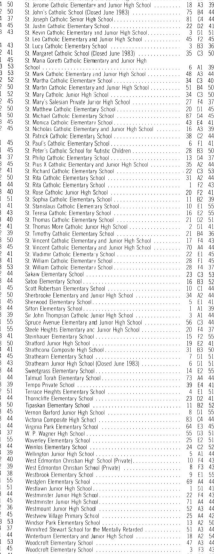

Phone exchanges

As illustrated on the accompanying map, Edmonton is divided into phone exchange districts, each with precise geographic boundaries. One or more three-digit prefixes (e.g. 428-) is assigned to each exchange. If an individual moves or a business changes its location, the original phone number can be retained at no extra charge to the subscriber as long as the new address lies within the same exchange district.

The only prefix shared between two districts is 438. Numbers higher than 438-6000 belong to the Terwillegar exchange, those below to Lendrum.

■■ Phone exchange boundaries

Ward boundaries

The city of Edmonton is divided into six wards. Residents of each ward elect two aldermen to city council. The mayor is elected at large by all city residents. Municipal elections are held every three years.

- Ward 1
- Ward 2
- Ward 3
- Ward 4
- Ward 5
- Ward 6

NORTH

Miles
Kilometres

A   B   C

⛪ CHURCHES
1. Castle Downs Pentecostal Church C2
2. Castle Downs United Church (Meetings in Dunluce Community School) B3
3. St. Charles Roman Catholic Church .. B3
4. Castle Downs Baptist Church C3
5. All Saints Lutheran Church B4
6. First Church of the Nazarene D4
7. McClure United Church (Meetings in M. E. Lazerte Composite High School) .. E4
8. Reformed Church in America E4
9. St. Dominic Roman Catholic Church .. E4
10. Steele Heights Baptist Church F3
11. Emmaus Lutheran Church F4
12. Exaltation of the Holy Cross Ukrainian Catholic Church B4

✳ POINTS OF INTEREST
1. Canadian Airborne Forces Museum ... C4

⌂ SCHOOLS
1. Baturyn Elementary School C2
2. St. Charles Catholic Elementary School C2
3. St. Lucy Catholic Elementary School ... B3
4. Dunluce Community School B3
5. Lorelei Heights Elementary and Junior High School C3
6. Bishop Savaryn Catholic Elementary School C3
7. Katherine Therrien Catholic Elementary School B3
8. Caernarvon Elementary School B4
9. Evansdale Elementary School D4
10. J. A. Fife Elementary School E3
11. John Barnett Elementary School E4
12. McLeod Elementary School F4
13. St. Philip Catholic Elementary School D4
14. Cardinal Leger Catholic Junior High School D4
15. Father Leo Green Catholic Elementary School E4
16. Londonderry Junior High School E4
17. M. E. Lazerte Composite High School E4
18. J. J. Bowlen Catholic Elementary and Junior High School E4
19. St. Dominic Catholic Elementary and Junior High School F4
20. Steele Heights Elementary and Junior High School F4
21. St. Timothy Catholic Elementary School B4
22. St. Anne Catholic Elementary School ... D4
23. Dickinsfield Junior High School D4
24. Northmount Elementary School D4
25. Kildare Elementary School E4
26. York Elementary School F4
27. St. Mary's Salesian Private Junior High School F4
28. St. William Catholic Elementary School F4
29. McArthur Elementary School A4

For explanation of symbols, see General Legend on page 5

Adjoining Map, Page 38

Adjoining Map, Page 45

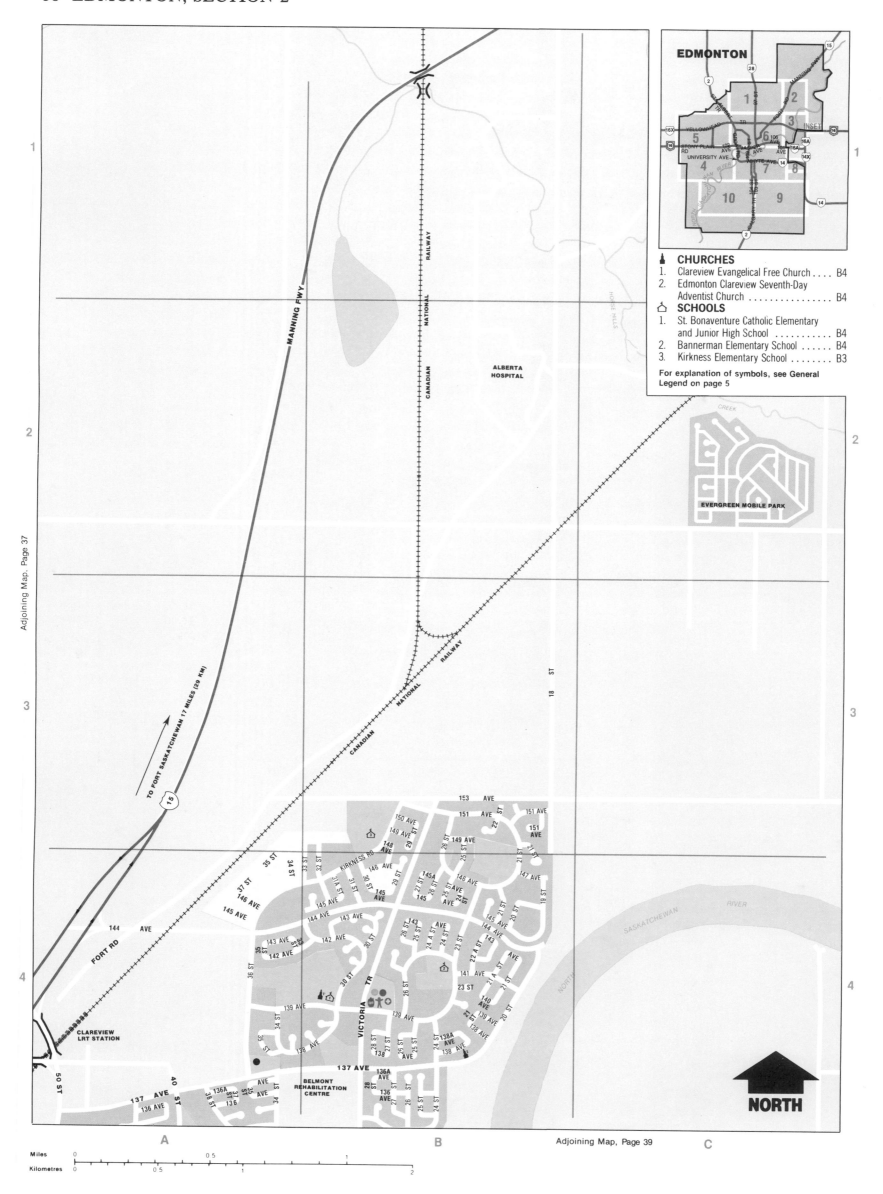

EDMONTON

Adjoining Map, Page 37

CHURCHES
1. Clareview Evangelical Free Church B4
2. Edmonton Clareview Seventh-Day
   Adventist Church B4

SCHOOLS
1. St. Bonaventure Catholic Elementary
   and Junior High School B4
2. Bannerman Elementary School B4
3. Kirkness Elementary School B3

For explanation of symbols, see General
Legend on page 5

ALBERTA
HOSPITAL

EVERGREEN MOBILE PARK

MANNING FWY

CANADIAN NATIONAL RAILWAY

TO FORT SASKATCHEWAN 17 MILES (29 KM)

15

CANADIAN NATIONAL RAILWAY

18 ST

153 AVE
151 AVE
151 AVE
150 AVE
149 AVE
149 AVE
148 AVE
KIRKNESS RD
146 AVE
146 AVE
147 AVE
145 AVE
145A
145
145
35 ST
34 ST
33 ST
32 ST
27 ST
29 ST
28 ST
26 ST
25 ST
22 ST
21 ST
19 ST
20 ST
27 ST
146 AVE
145 AVE
145 AVE
144 AVE
143 AVE
143 AVE
142 AVE
144 AVE
143 AVE
142 AVE
143 AVE
143 AVE
144 AVE
141 AVE
140 AVE
139 AVE
139 AVE
138 AVE
138A AVE
137 AVE
136A AVE
136 AVE
FORT RD
144 AVE
CLAREVIEW
LRT STATION
50 ST
40 ST
137 AVE
136 AVE
38A ST
35 ST
34 ST
136 AVE
BELMONT
REHABILITATION
CENTRE
VICTORIA TR
36 ST
35 ST
34 ST
30 ST
26 ST
28 ST
27 ST
25 ST
24 ST
23 ST

HORSE HILLS

CREEK

NORTH SASKATCHEWAN RIVER

NORTH

Adjoining Map, Page 39

Miles   0   0.5   1
Kilometres 0   0.5   1   2

A   B   C
1   2   3   4

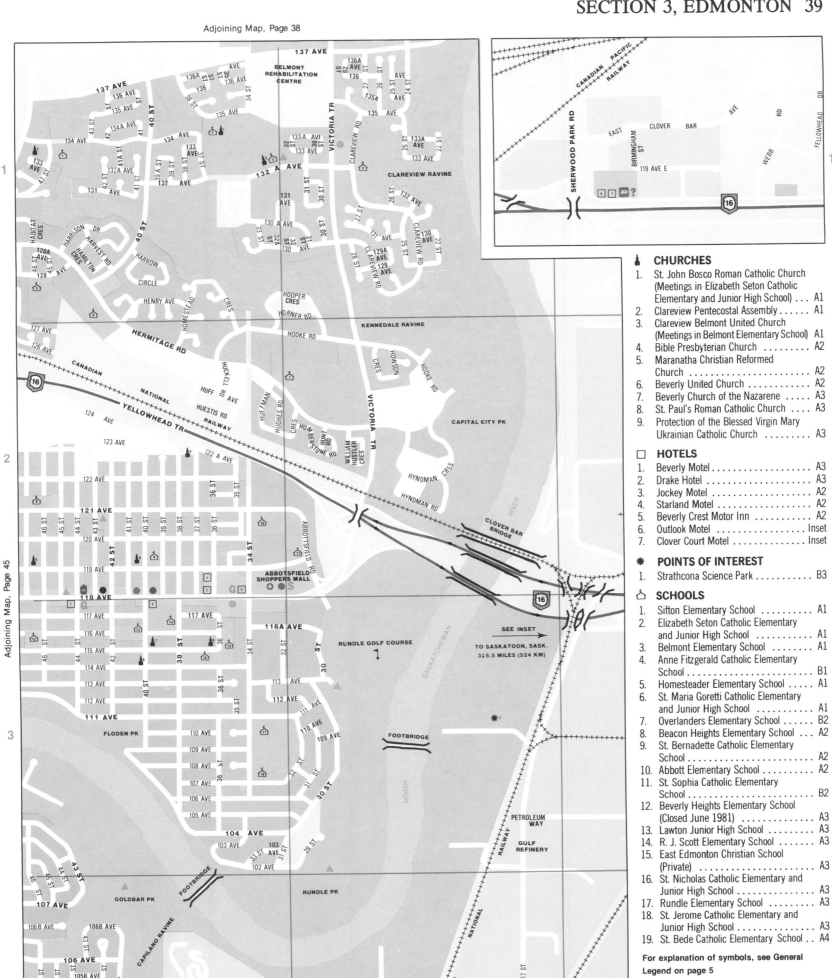

Adjoining Map, Page 38

Adjoining Map, Page 45

Adjoining Map, Page 51

♠ CHURCHES

1. St. John Bosco Roman Catholic Church
   (Meetings in Elizabeth Seton Catholic
   Elementary and Junior High School) . . . A1
2. Clareview Pentecostal Assembly A1
3. Clareview Belmont United Church
   (Meetings in Belmont Elementary School) A1
4. Bible Presbyterian Church A2
5. Maranatha Christian Reformed
   Church A2
6. Beverly United Church A2
7. Beverly Church of the Nazarene A3
8. St. Paul's Roman Catholic Church A3
9. Protection of the Blessed Virgin Mary
   Ukrainian Catholic Church A3

☐ HOTELS

1. Beverly Motel A3
2. Drake Hotel A3
3. Jockey Motel A2
4. Starland Motel A2
5. Beverly Crest Motor Inn A2
6. Outlook Motel . . . . Inset
7. Clover Court Motel . . . . Inset

✳ POINTS OF INTEREST

1. Strathcona Science Park B3

⌂ SCHOOLS

1. Sifton Elementary School A1
2. Elizabeth Seton Catholic Elementary
   and Junior High School A1
3. Belmont Elementary School A1
4. Anne Fitzgerald Catholic Elementary
   School B1
5. Homesteader Elementary School A1
6. St. Maria Goretti Catholic Elementary
   and Junior High School A1
7. Overlanders Elementary School B2
8. Beacon Heights Elementary School . . . A2
9. St. Bernadette Catholic Elementary
   School A2
10. Abbott Elementary School A2
11. St. Sophia Catholic Elementary
    School B2
12. Beverly Heights Elementary School
    (Closed June 1981) A3
13. Lawton Junior High School A3
14. R. J. Scott Elementary School A3
15. East Edmonton Christian School
    (Private) A3
16. St. Nicholas Catholic Elementary and
    Junior High School A3
17. Rundle Elementary School A3
18. St. Jerome Catholic Elementary and
    Junior High School A3
19. St. Bede Catholic Elementary School . . A4

**For explanation of symbols, see General
Legend on page 5**

Adjoining Map, Page 42

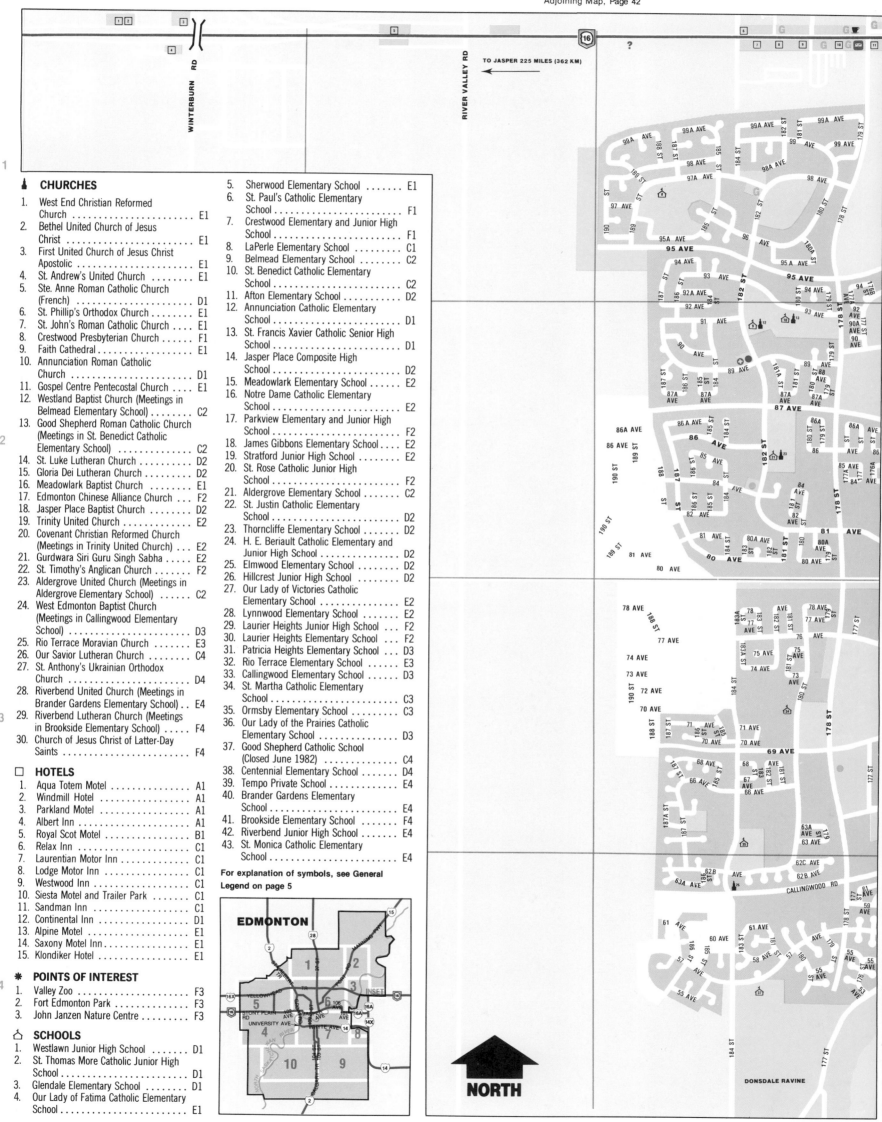

♦ CHURCHES

1. West End Christian Reformed Church E1
2. Bethel United Church of Jesus Christ E1
3. First United Church of Jesus Christ Apostolic E1
4. St. Andrew's United Church E1
5. Ste. Anne Roman Catholic Church (French) D1
6. St. Phillip's Orthodox Church E1
7. St. John's Roman Catholic Church ... E1
8. Crestwood Presbyterian Church F1
9. Faith Cathedral E1
10. Annunciation Roman Catholic Church D1
11. Gospel Centre Pentecostal Church E1
12. Westland Baptist Church (Meetings in Belmead Elementary School) C2
13. Good Shepherd Roman Catholic Church (Meetings in St. Benedict Catholic Elementary School) C2
14. St. Luke Lutheran Church D2
15. Gloria Dei Lutheran Church D2
16. Meadowlark Baptist Church E1
17. Edmonton Chinese Alliance Church ... F2
18. Jasper Place Baptist Church D2
19. Trinity United Church E2
20. Covenant Christian Reformed Church (Meetings in Trinity United Church) ... E2
21. Gurdwara Siri Guru Singh Sabha E2
22. St. Timothy's Anglican Church F2
23. Aldergrove United Church (Meetings in Aldergrove Elementary School) C2
24. West Edmonton Baptist Church (Meetings in Callingwood Elementary School) D3
25. Rio Terrace Moravian Church E3
26. Our Savior Lutheran Church C4
27. St. Anthony's Ukrainian Orthodox Church D4
28. Riverbend United Church (Meetings in Brander Gardens Elementary School) .. E4
29. Riverbend Lutheran Church (Meetings in Brookside Elementary School) F4
30. Church of Jesus Christ of Latter-Day Saints F4

☐ HOTELS

1. Aqua Totem Motel A1
2. Windmill Hotel A1
3. Parkland Motel A1
4. Albert Inn A1
5. Royal Scot Motel B1
6. Relax Inn C1
7. Laurentian Motor Inn C1
8. Lodge Motor Inn C1
9. Westwood Inn C1
10. Siesta Motel and Trailer Park C1
11. Sandman Inn C1
12. Continental Inn D1
13. Alpine Motel E1
14. Saxony Motel Inn E1
15. Klondiker Hotel E1

✱ POINTS OF INTEREST

1. Valley Zoo F3
2. Fort Edmonton Park F3
3. John Janzen Nature Centre F3

⌂ SCHOOLS

1. Westlawn Junior High School D1
2. St. Thomas More Catholic Junior High School D1
3. Glendale Elementary School D1
4. Our Lady of Fatima Catholic Elementary School E1

5. Sherwood Elementary School E1
6. St. Paul's Catholic Elementary School F1
7. Crestwood Elementary and Junior High School F1
8. LaPerle Elementary School C1
9. Belmead Elementary School C2
10. St. Benedict Catholic Elementary School C2
11. Afton Elementary School D2
12. Annunciation Catholic Elementary School D1
13. St. Francis Xavier Catholic Senior High School D1
14. Jasper Place Composite High School D2
15. Meadowlark Elementary School E2
16. Notre Dame Catholic Elementary School E2
17. Parkview Elementary and Junior High School F2
18. James Gibbons Elementary School ... E2
19. Stratford Junior High School E2
20. St. Rose Catholic Junior High School F2
21. Aldergrove Elementary School C2
22. St. Justin Catholic Elementary School D2
23. Thorncliffe Elementary School D2
24. H. E. Beriault Catholic Elementary and Junior High School D2
25. Elmwood Elementary School D2
26. Hillcrest Junior High School D2
27. Our Lady of Victories Catholic Elementary School E2
28. Lynnwood Elementary School E2
29. Laurier Heights Junior High School ... F2
30. Laurier Heights Elementary School ... F2
31. Patricia Heights Elementary School ... D3
32. Rio Terrace Elementary School E3
33. Callingwood Elementary School D3
34. St. Martha Catholic Elementary School C3
35. Ormsby Elementary School C3
36. Our Lady of the Prairies Catholic Elementary School D3
37. Good Shepherd Catholic School (Closed June 1982) C4
38. Centennial Elementary School D4
39. Tempo Private School E4
40. Brander Gardens Elementary School E4
41. Brookside Elementary School F4
42. Riverbend Junior High School E4
43. St. Monica Catholic Elementary School E4

For explanation of symbols, see General Legend on page 5

EDMONTON

NORTH

Adjoining Map, Page 54

Miles
0   0.5   1
Kilometres
0   0.5   1   2

A   B   C

Adjoining Map, Page 43

STONY PLAIN RD 16A

GRANT MacEWAN COMMUNITY COLLEGE

MAYFAIR GOLF AND COUNTRY CLUB

WILLIAM HAWRELAK PK

MacKINNON RAVINE

McKENZIE RAVINE

SUMMIT DR

SUMMIT POINT

RAVINE DR

ST. GEORGE'S CRES

RIVERSIDE

RIVERSIDE CRES

McKENZIE DR

PARK DR

CO-OP SHOPPING CENTRE

WEST EDMONTON MALL

MEADOWLARK RD

MEADOWLARK PARK SHOPPING CENTRE

BUENA VISTA RD

BUENA VISTA PK

VALLEY VIEW DR

VALLEYVIEW POINT

VALLEY VIEW CRES

VALLEY VIEW CRES

WHITEMUD DR

VALLEY ZOO

LAURIER PK

LAURIER DR

QUESNELL CRES

QUESNELL RD

QUESNELL CRES

WESTRIDGE RD

WESTRIDGE CRES

PATRICIA CRES

PATRICIA DR

PATRICIA RAVINE

WOLF WILLOW RD

WALSH CRES

WOLF WILLOW

WOLF WILLOW RD

WAKINA DR

WANYANDI RD

WALKER RD

WOLF WILLOW RD

WOLF WILLOW RAVINE

QUESNELL BRIDGE

FORT EDMONTON PARK RD

FORT EDMONTON PK

WHITEMUD RD

KELLOR RD

FOX DR

WHITEMUD PK

GRANDVIEW DR

BRANDER DR

WHITEMUD DR

RIVERBEND RD

UNIVERSITY OF ALBERTA EXPERIMENTAL FARM

NORTH SASKATCHEWAN RIVER

EDMONTON GOLF AND COUNTRY CLUB

COUNTRY CLUB RD

GARIEPY CRES

LESSARD DR

LANSDOWNE DR

RAINBOW VALLEY CAMPGROUNDS

Adjoining Map, Page 50

Adjoining Map, Page 55

D   E   F

1   2   3   4

⛪ CHURCHES

1. Westmount Presbyterian Church F3
2. Jehovah's Witnesses Kingdom Hall (Mayfield Congregation) F3
3. Church of Jesus Christ of Latter-Day Saints F3
4. St. James United Church F4
5. Third Christian Reformed Church (Meetings in St. James United Church) F4
6. St. Barnabas Anglican Church E4
7. Ebenezer United Church E4
8. Edmonton Bethel Seventh-Day Adventist Church (Meetings in Ebenezer United Church) E4
9. Holy Spirit Roman Catholic Church ... E4
10. Ukrainian Catholic Church of the Assumption of the Blessed Virgin Mary E4
11. Assembly of God Christian Fellowship E4
12. Missionary Church F4
13. St. Herman's Orthodox Church F4
14. Jasper Place Church of God E4
15. St. Paul's Anglican Church F4

☐ HOTELS

1. Royal Nite Inn F1
2. Bonaventure Motor Hotel F2
3. Edmonton Yellowhead Motor Inn F2
4. Aladdin Motel E3
5. Royal Western Motel E3
6. Aurora Motel F3
7. New West Hotel F3
8. Mayfield Inn E4
9. Algonquin Motor Lodge D4
10. Aqua Totem Motel A4
11. Windmill Motel A4
12. Parkland Motel A4
13. Albert Inn A4
14. Royal Scot Motel B4
15. Relax Inn C4
16. Laurentian Motor Inn C4
17. Lodge Motor Inn D4
18. Westwood Inn D4
19. Siesta Motel and Trailer Park D4
20. Sandman Inn D4
21. Continental Inn E4
22. Alpine Motel E4
23. Saxony Motel Inn E4
24. Klondiker Hotel E4

✸ POINTS OF INTEREST

1. City of Edmonton Planetarium and Space Sciences Centre F3

⌂ SCHOOLS

1. St. Rita Catholic Elementary School ... F2
2. Dovercourt Elementary School F2
3. Woodcroft Elementary School F3
4. Ross Sheppard Composite High School F3
5. High Park Elementary School E3
6. Our Lady of Peace Catholic Elementary and Junior High E3
7. Mayfield Elementary School E4
8. West Edmonton Christian School (Private) F3
9. McQueen Elementary School F3
10. West Edmonton Christian High School (Private) F4
11. Coronation Elementary School F4
12. Archbishop Macdonald Catholic High School F4
13. St. Gregory Catholic School (Closed June 1977) F4
14. Elves Memorial Child Development Centre F4
15. Brightview Elementary School E4
16. Canora Elementary School (Closed June 1973) E4
17. St. Vincent Catholic Elementary and Junior High School F4
18. Meadowlark Christian School (Our Lady of Lourdes Catholic School) (Private) E4
19. Britannia Junior High School E4
20. Evelyn Unger School for Language and Learning Development (Private) E4
21. Holy Cross Catholic Elementary and Junior High School F4
22. Westminster Junior High School F4
23. Grovenor Elementary School F4
24. Youngstown Elementary School E4
25. Westview Village Primary School A4

For explanation of symbols, see General Legend on page 5

EDMONTON

RING ROAD

KIRK LAKE

122 AVE
121 AVE
190 ST

16X

184 ST

182 ST

114 AVE
112 AVE
111 AVE
109 AVE
108 AVE
107 AVE

CANADIAN NATIONAL RAILWAY

DEPT. OF NATIONAL DEFENCE

WESTVIEW VILLAGE

HILLVIEW RD
WINTERBURN RD
211 ST
207 ST
RIVER VALLEY RD

105 ST

NORTH ⬆

TO SPRUCE GROVE
TO STONY PLAIN
← TO JASPER 225 MILES (362 KM)
TO VANCOUVER 762 MILES (1226 KM)
16

A   B   Adjoining Map, Page 40   C

Miles 0 ... 0.5 ... 1
Kilometres 0 ... 0.5 ... 1 ... 2

Adjoining Map, Page 44

Adjoining Map, Page 36

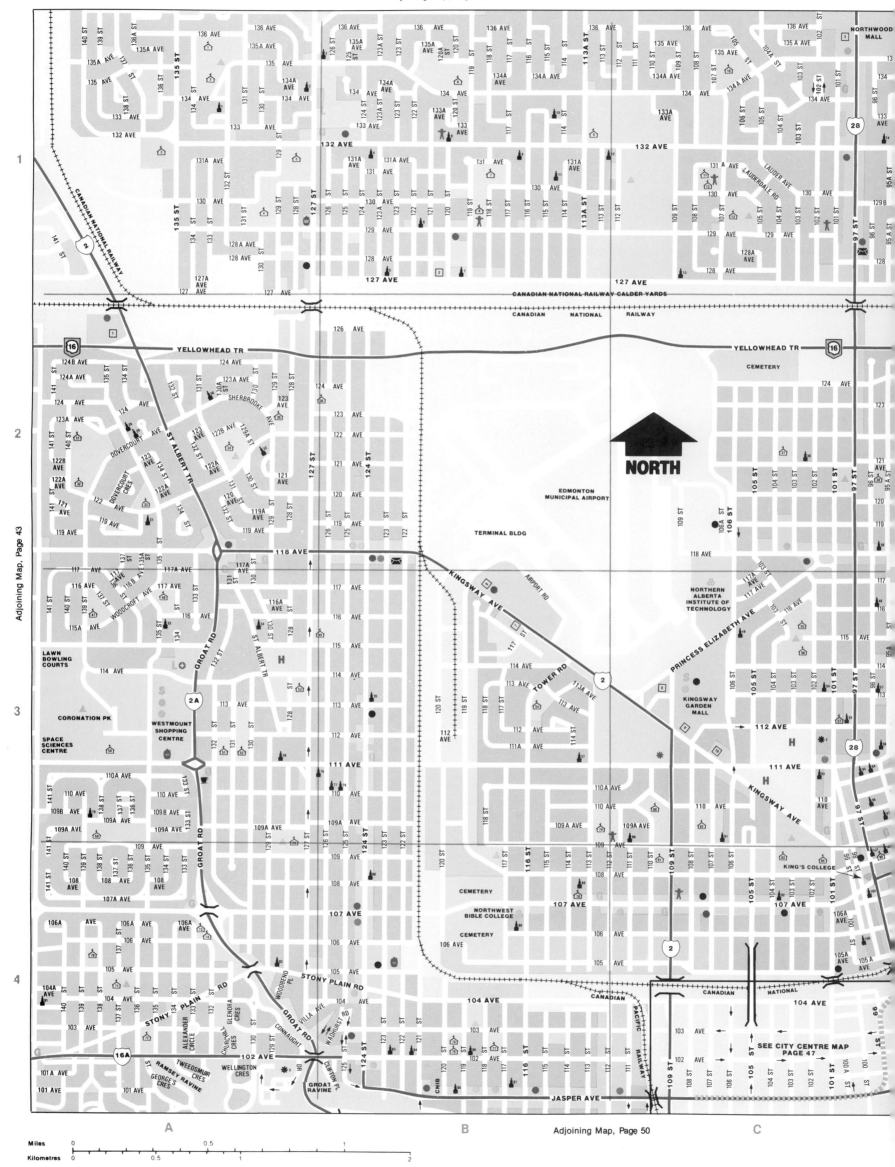

Adjoining Map, Page 43

NORTH

EDMONTON
MUNICIPAL AIRPORT

TERMINAL BLDG

CANADIAN NATIONAL RAILWAY CALDER YARDS

CANADIAN NATIONAL RAILWAY

YELLOWHEAD TR

CEMETERY

CANADIAN NATIONAL RAILWAY

KINGSWAY AVE

AIRPORT RD

NORTHERN
ALBERTA
INSTITUTE OF
TECHNOLOGY

KINGSWAY
GARDEN
MALL

PRINCESS ELIZABETH AVE

KINGSWAY AVE

KING'S COLLEGE

NORTHWEST
BIBLE COLLEGE

CEMETERY

CEMETERY

TOWER RD

LAWN
BOWLING
COURTS

CORONATION PK

SPACE
SCIENCES
CENTRE

WESTMOUNT
SHOPPING
CENTRE

GROAT RD

ST ALBERT TR

SHERBROOKE AVE

DOVERCOURT CRES

WOODCROFT AVE

STONY PLAIN RD

GROAT RD

STONY PLAIN RD

ALEXANDER CIRCLE

CHURCHILL CRES

GLENORA CRES

WOODBEND PL

VILLA AVE

CONNAUGHT

WADHURST RD

CLIFTON PL

WELLINGTON CRES

RAMSEY RAVINE

TWEEDSMUIR CRES

GEORGE'S CRES

GROAT RAVINE

JASPER AVE

CANADIAN NATIONAL

CANADIAN PACIFIC RAILWAY

SEE CITY CENTRE MAP
PAGE 47

NORTHWOOD MALL

LAUDERDALE RD

Adjoining Map, Page 50

Adjoining Map, Page 37

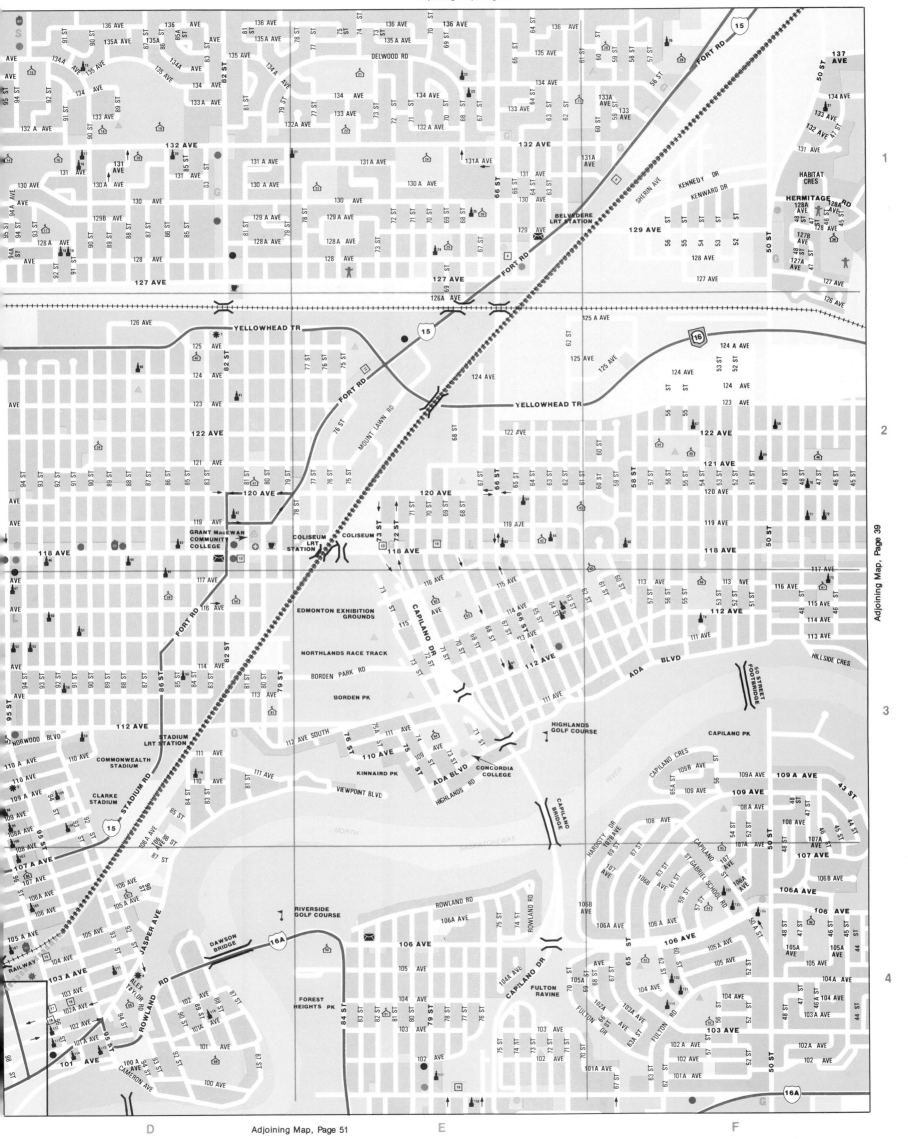

Adjoining Map, Page 39

Adjoining Map, Page 51

EDMONTON, LEGEND FOR SECTION 6

(Map on pages 44 and 45)

CHURCHES

1. St. Angela Roman Catholic Church A1
2. Exaltation of the Holy Cross Ukrainian Catholic Church B1
3. Good Shepherd Anglican Church A1
4. Chalmers United Church B1
5. Endtime Message Tabernacle B1
6. St. Michael's Ukrainian Orthodox Church B1
7. St. Vladimir's Ukrainian Catholic Church B1
8. Zion Baptist Church B1
9. St. Edmund Roman Catholic Church B1
10. Reorganized Church of Jesus Christ of Latter-Day Saints B1
11. Glad Tidings Christian Reformed Church B1
12. Al Rachid Mosque B1
13. Jehovah's Witnesses Kingdom Hall (Rosslyn Congregation) C1
14. Northgate Baptist Church C1
15. Pilgrim United Church D1
16. Killarney Pentecostal Church D1
17. Romanian Orthodox Church D1
18. Church of the Holy City (Swedenborgian) D1
19. Church of the New Jerusalem (Meetings in Church of the Holy City - Swedenborgian) D1
20. St. Matthew's Roman Catholic Church D1
21. Christ the King Lutheran Church E1
22. Delwood Road Baptist Church E1
23. Jehovah's Witnesses Kingdom Hall (Balwin Congregation) E1
24. Russian Church of St. Vladimir E1
25. St. Francis of Assisi Roman Catholic Church (Meetings in Francis of Assisi Catholic Elementary and Junior High School) E1
26. Trinity Christian Reformed Church F1
27. Clareview Pentecostal Assembly F1
28. Dovercourt Baptist Church A2
29. Edmonton Chinese Baptist Church (Meetings in Dovercourt Baptist Church) A2
30. St. Pius X Roman Catholic Church A2
31. Kirk United Church A2
32. Canadian Reformed Church Providence A2
33. Mount Zion Lutheran Church A3
34. Inglewood Church of Christ A3
35. Westminster United Church B3
36. St. Andrew's Roman Catholic Church A3
37. Fellowship Baptist Church B3
38. Westwood Baptist Church C2
39. St. Patrick's Roman Catholic Church C2
40. Baptist Church of Emmanuel D2
41. Ukrainian Evangelical Baptist Church D2
42. Buchanan Eastwood United Church D2
43. St. Alphonsus Roman Catholic Church D2
44. St. Andrew's Presbyterian Church D2
45. Calvin Hungarian Presbyterian Church D3
46. St. Faith's Anglican Church D2
47. Salvation Army - Northside Corps D3
48. Norwood United Church C3
49. Holy Rosary Roman Catholic Church (Polish) C3
50. Edmonton Four Square Gospel Church D3
51. Slavic Church of Evangelical Christians of Edmonton D3
52. Bethel Gospel Chapel D3
53. Shiloh Baptist Church D3
54. Chinese Pentecostal Church C3
55. Peoples' Church C3
56. Jehovah's Witnesses Kingdom Hall C3
57. St. George's Ukrainian Catholic Cathedral C3
58. Standard Church of America D3
59. Santa Maria Goretti Roman Catholic Church (Italian) D3
60. Free Methodist Church Parkdale D3
61. St. Mary's Anglican Church E3
62. Highlands United Church E3
63. St. Elias Ukrainian Greek Orthodox Church E2
64. Ukrainian Catholic Church of the Holy Eucharist E2
65. St. Clare Roman Catholic Church E2
66. All Saints Orthodox Church F2
67. Newton Church of God F2
68. Beverly Alliance Church F2
69. Jehovah's Witnesses Kingdom Hall (Highlands Congregation) F2
70. Community Christian Church F2
71. Beverley Four Square Gospel Church F2
72. Maranatha Christian Reformed Church F2
73. Bethlehem Lutheran Church F3
74. Highlands Baptist Church F3
75. Bethel Christian Reformed Church (Meetings in Highlands United Church) E3
76. St. Peter's Anglican Church B3
77. Unitarian Church of Edmonton B3
78. Metropolitan Community Church of Edmonton (Meetings in the Unitarian Church of Edmonton) B3
79. Westmount Presbyterian Church A3
80. Beulah Alliance Church B4
81. Missionary Church A4
82. Victory Baptist Church A4
83. Robertson-Wesley United Church B4
84. Christ Church (Anglican) B4
85. Beth Shalom Synagogue B4
86. Beth Israel Synagogue B4
87. Faith Mennonite Church B4
88. Central Pentecostal Tabernacle B4
89. Fundamental Baptist Church B4
90. Central United Church C3
91. St. John's Greek Orthodox Cathedral C3
92. Full Gospel Seventh Avenue Apostolic Church C4
93. Edmonton Central Seventh-Day Adventist Church C3
94. Norwood Seventh-Day Adventist Church C3
95. St. Peter's Lutheran Church C3
96. First Christian Reformed Church C3
97. Holy Trinity Canadian Orthodox Church C3
98. St. Stephen's Anglican Church D3
99. Ansgar Lutheran Church D3
100. Sacred Heart Roman Catholic Church D3
101. St. Josaphat's Ukrainian Greek Catholic Church C4
102. Immaculate Conception Roman Catholic Church (French) C4
103. St. John's Evangelical Lutheran Church D4
104. St. Emeric Roman Catholic Church (Hungarian) C4
105. Second Christian Reformed Church D4
106. Nativity of Mary (Croatian) Roman Catholic Church C4
107. Ukrainian Pentecostal Temple D4
108. Edmonton Chinese Baptist Church D3
109. Central Lutheran Church D3
110. Our Lady of Fatima Portuguese Catholic Church D3
111. Spiritualist Centre of Edmonton D4
112. House of Refuge Mission D4
113. Chinese United Church D4
114. Russian Orthodox Cathedral of St. Barbara D4
115. St. Boniface Roman Catholic Church (German) D4
116. Rundle United Church D4
117. St. Stephen's United Church E4
118. St. Michael the Archangel Roman Catholic Church E4
119. Grace United Church F4
120. Spanish Pentecostal Church F4
121. St. Augustine's Anglican Church F4
122. Hope Lutheran Church F4
123. Edmonton South Seventh-Day Adventist Church F4
124. Roman Catholic Church of the Resurrection F4

HOTELS

1. Bonaventure Motor Hotel A2
2. Dover Hotel B1
3. Rosslyn Motor Inn C1
4. Transit Hotel E1
5. Hotel Londonderry F1
6. Edmonton Inn B3
7. Chateau Louis Motor Inn B3
8. City Centre Inn C3
9. Kingsway Inn C3
10. Pan-American Motel C3
11. Sands Motor Hotel E2
12. Cromdale Hotel D2
13. The Forum Inn E2
14. East Glen Motor Inn E2
15. York Hotel D4
16. New Gateway Hotel D4
17. Empire Hotel D4
18. Royal Hotel D4
19. Patricia Motel E4

POINTS OF INTEREST

1. Antique Motorcycle Museum D2
2. City of Edmonton Archives C3
3. Ukrainian Museum of Canada D3
4. Canadian Aviation Hall of Fame D4
5. Government House, Provincial Museum and Archives of Alberta A4

SCHOOLS

1. McArthur Elementary School A1
2. St. Angela Catholic Elementary School A1
3. Sir John Thompson Catholic Junior High School A1
4. Athlone Elementary School A1
5. Wellington Junior High School A1
6. Kensington Elementary School B1
7. St. Edmund Catholic Elementary and Junior High School B1
8. Calder Elementary School B1
9. Rosslyn Junior High School B1
10. Scott Robertson Elementary School C1
11. Father Lacombe Catholic Elementary School C1
12. Caritas High School (Private) (Located in Father Lacombe Catholic Elementary School) C1
13. Lauderdale Elementary School C1
14. Queen Elizabeth Composite High School D1
15. Glengarry Elementary School D1
16. Killarney Junior High School D1
17. Mee-Yan-Noh Elementary School D1
18. St. Cecilia Catholic Junior High School D1
19. Archbishop O'Leary Catholic High School D1
20. St. Matthew Catholic Elementary School D1
21. Delwood Elementary School E1
22. St. Vladimir Catholic Elementary School E1
23. Princeton Elementary School E1
24. Balwin Junior High School E1
25. North Edmonton Elementary School E1
26. St. Francis of Assisi Catholic Elementary and Junior High School E1
27. Belvedere Elementary School F1
28. St. William Catholic Elementary School F1
29. North Edmonton Christian Elementary and Junior High School (Private) F1
30. Homesteader Elementary School F1
31. St. Rita Catholic Elementary School A2
32. Dovercourt Elementary School A2
33. Coralwood Seventh-Day Adventist Junior Academy (Private) A2
34. Sherbrooke Elementary and Junior High School A2
35. St. Pius X Catholic Elementary and Junior High School A2
36. Prince Charles Elementary School B2
37. H. A. Gray Elementary School C2
38. St. Patrick Catholic Elementary School C2
39. Delton Elementary School D2
40. St. Gerard Catholic Elementary School D2
41. Eastwood Elementary and Junior High School D2
42. St. Clare Catholic Elementary and Junior High School E2
43. Montrose Elementary School F2
44. Newton Elementary School F2
45. St. Leo Catholic Elementary and Junior High School F2
46. Beacon Heights Elementary School F2
47. Woodcroft Elementary School A3
48. St. Mark Catholic Elementary and Junior High School A3
49. Inglewood Elementary School B3
50. Ross Sheppard Composite High School A3
51. Winnifred Stewart School for the Mentally Retarded A3
52. Westmount Junior High School A3
53. St. Andrew Catholic Elementary School A3
54. Prince Rupert Elementary School B3
55. St. Basil Catholic Elementary and Junior High School C3
56. Spruce Avenue Elementary and Junior High School C3
57. Covenant Community Training Centre (Private) (Located in The Peoples' Church) C3
58. Norwood Elementary School D3
59. Parkdale Elementary and Junior High School D3
60. St. Alphonsus Catholic Elementary School D3
61. Cromdale Elementary School D3
62. Bellevue Elementary School E3
63. Eastglen Composite High School E3
64. Virginia Park Elementary School E3
65. Highlands Junior High School F3
66. Mount Royal Elementary School F3
67. Beverly Heights Elementary School (Closed June 1981) F3
68. Coronation Elementary School A3
69. Westglen Elementary School A4
70. St. Vincent Catholic Elementary and Junior High School A4
71. Westminster Junior High School A4
72. Glenora Elementary School A4
73. Talmud Torah Elementary School A4
74. Edmonton Hebrew Elementary School (Private) (Located in Talmud Torah Elementary School) A4
75. St. John's Catholic School (Closed June 1983) B4
76. Edmonton Academy (Private) (Meetings in St. John's Catholic School) B4
77. Oliver Elementary School B4
78. Edmonton Christian Academy (Private) (Located in Fundamental Baptist Church) B4
79. Queen Mary Park Elementary School B3
80. St. Catherine Catholic Elementary and Junior High School C3
81. St. Joseph Catholic Senior High School C4
82. McDougall Elementary and Junior High School C3
83. Victoria Composite High School C4
84. Continuing Education Centre C4
85. Sacred Heart Catholic Elementary and Junior High School C4
86. McCauley Elementary and Junior High School D4
87. St. Michael Catholic Elementary School D4
88. Alex Taylor Elementary School D4
89. Riverdale Elementary School D4
90. McNally Composite High School E4
91. Forest Heights Elementary School E4
92. Fulton Place Elementary School F4
93. Hardisty Junior High School F4
94. St. Gabriel Catholic Elementary and Junior High School F4
95. Capilano Elementary School F4
96. Gold Bar Elementary School F4

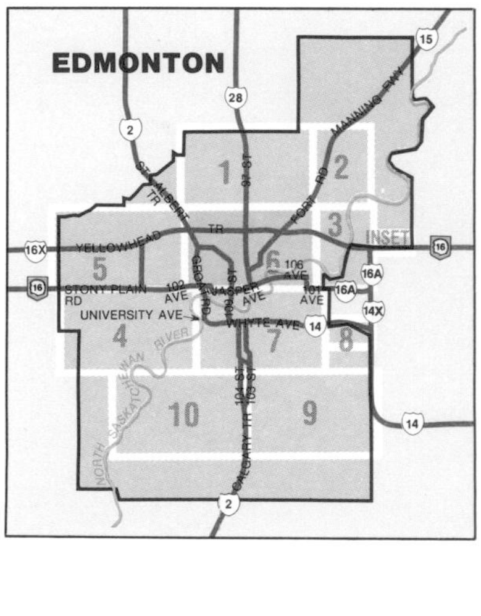

For explanation of symbols, see General Legend on page 5

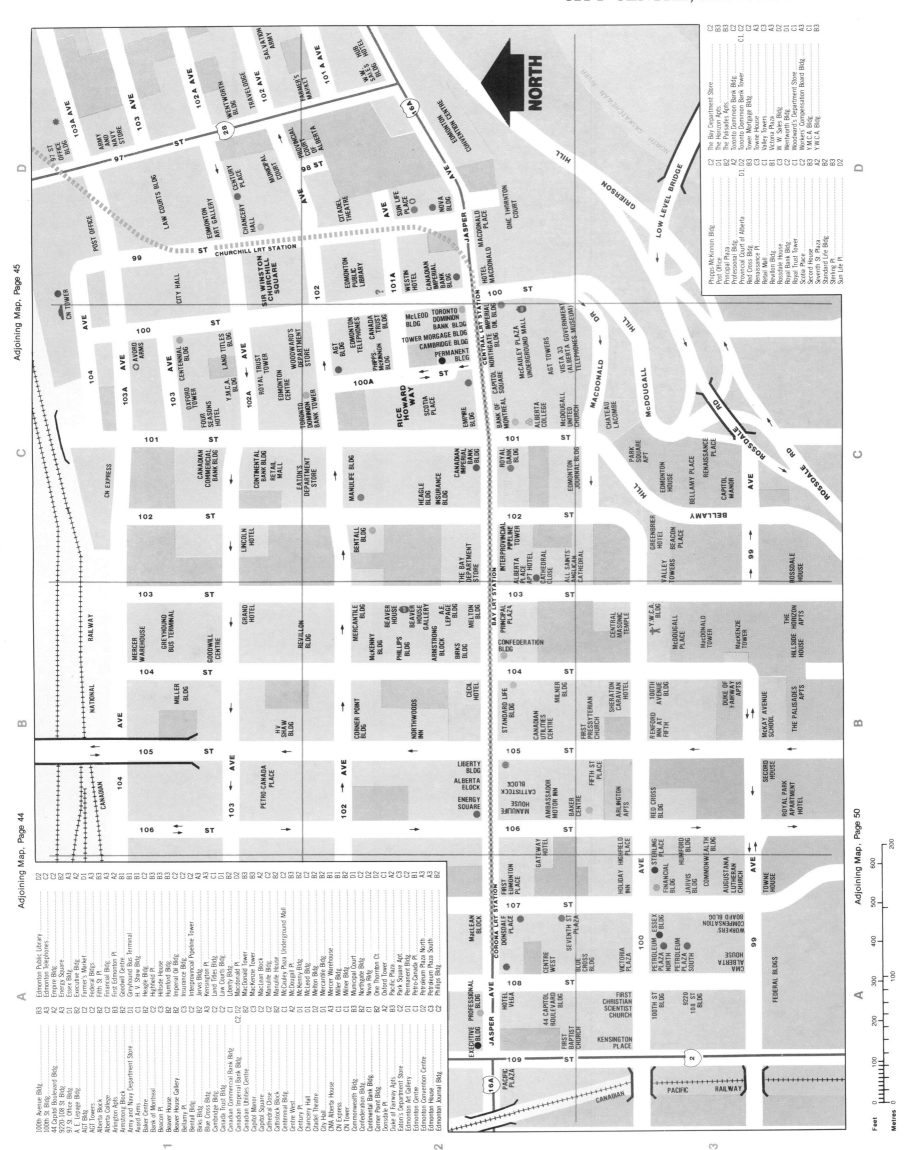

Adjoining Map, Page 45

Adjoining Map, Page 44

Adjoining Map, Page 50

NORTH

Adjoining Map, Page 50

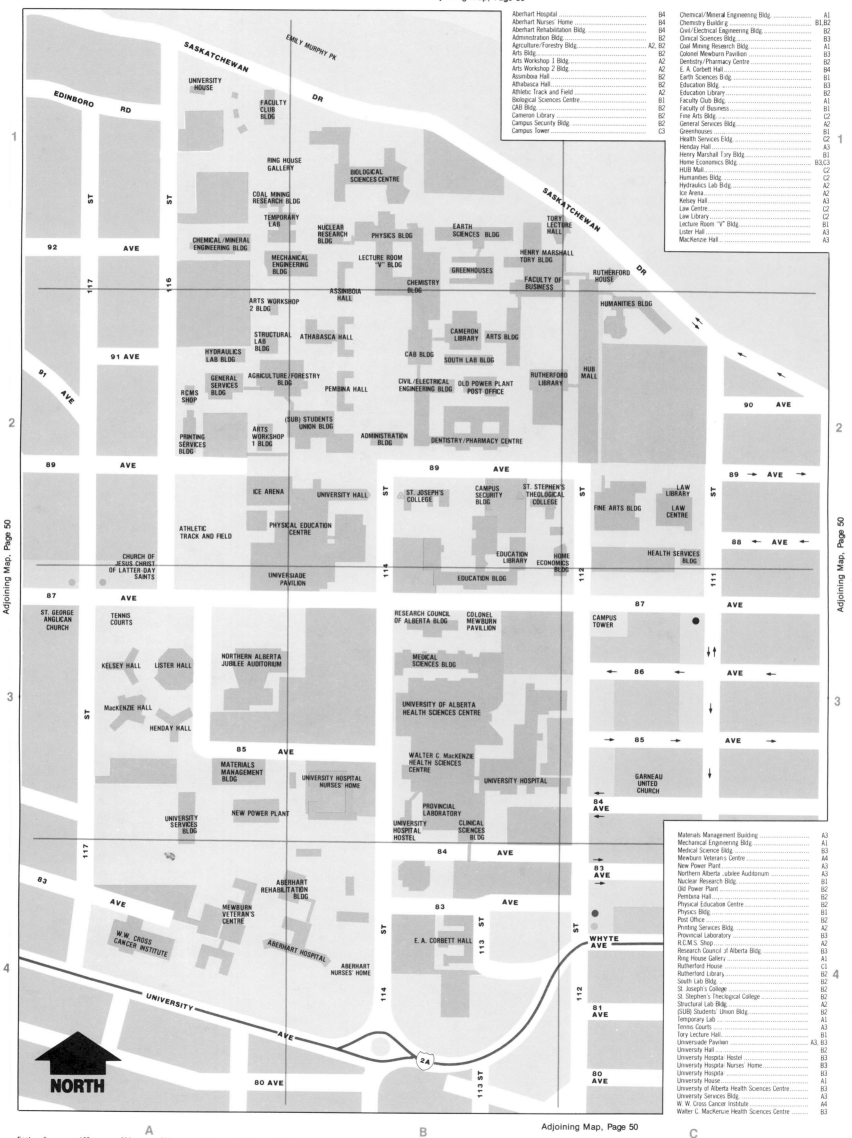

Adjoining Map, Page 50

Adjoining Map, Page 50

Adjoining Map, Page 50

⚑ CHURCHES

1. St. George's Greek Orthodox Church B1
2. St. Joseph's Roman Catholic Cathedral B1
3. Grace Lutheran Church B1
4. St. Joachim Roman Catholic Church (French) B1
5. St. Michael the Archangel Roman Catholic Church E1
6. Eastminster Presbyterian Church E1
7. St. Andrew's Ukrainian Greek Orthodox Church E1
8. Braemar Baptist Church E1
9. Bethel Lutheran Church E1
10. St. Nicholas Ukrainian Catholic Church E1
11. Holyrood Mennonite Church D1
12. St. Luke's Anglican Church D1
13. Strathearn United Church D1
14. Assumption Roman Catholic Church .. D1
15. Central Baptist Church D1
16. Mission of the Ressurection Anglican Catholic Church (Meetings in Braemar Elementary School) E1
17. Ottewell United Church E1
18. Ottewell Christian Reformed Church E1
19. Salvation Army - Edmonton Temple ... E1
20. First Church of God D1
21. Church of Jesus Christ of Latter-Day Saints D2
22. New Apostolic Church D1
23. Knox Metropolitan United Church B2
24. Church of Jesus Christ of Latter-Day Saints B2
25. St. Anthony's Roman Catholic Church B2
26. Strathcona Presbyterian Church B2
27. Bible Life Assembly B2
28. Church of Scientology C2
29. Strathcona Baptist Church C2
30. Knox Evangelical Free Church C2
31. Edmonton Korean Baptist Church C2
32. German Church of God C2
33. Holy Trinity Anglican Church C2
34. Trinity Lutheran Church C2
35. Southside Pentecostal Assembly C2
36. Edmonton Korean Alliance Church.... C2
37. Moravian Church C2
38. Bonnie Doon Baptist Church D2
39. St. Thomas D'Aquin Roman Catholic Church (French) D2
40. Edmonton German Church of God D2
41. Evangelical Covenant Church D2
42. Ascension Lutheran Church D2
43. Evangel Pentecostal Assembly D2
44. Idylwylde Free Methodist Church E2
45. German Bethel Baptist Church D2
46. Avonmore United Church D2
47. McKernan Christian Church B2
48. St. Paul's United Church A2
49. Vietnamese Alliance Church A3
50. First Mennonite Church B2
51. McKernan Baptist Church B2
52. Calvary Lutheran Church B2
53. Sharon Gospel Chapel............ B2
54. Evangelical Fellowship Church...... B2
55. Jehovah's Witnesses Kingdom Hall ... C2
56. German Zion Baptist Church C2
57. Immaculate Heart Roman Catholic Church C2
58. Redeemer Lutheran Church C3
59. Ritchie United Church C3
60. Bible Baptist Church............. D2
61. St. Paul's Lutheran Church D2
62. St. Matthew's Evangelical Lutheran Church D2
63. King Edward Park Church of Christ ... D2
64. St. David's Anglican Church D2
65. St. James Roman Catholic Church ... D2
66. Calvary Baptist Church C3
67. Edmonton Faith Temple B3
68. St. Basil's Ukrainian Catholic Church B3
69. Salvation Army - Parkallen Corps ... B3
70. St. Agnes Roman Catholic Church B3
71. Pleasantview United Church B3
72. Apostolic Christian Church B3
73. Richmond Park Evangelical Church ... D3
74. Reorganised Church of Jesus Christ of Latter-Day Saints D3
75. Cross of Christ Lutheran Chapel for the Deaf A3
76. Lendrum Mennonite Brethren Church B4
77. The Church of St. John the Evangelist (Anglican) B4
78. Lansdowne Baptist Church A4
79. Holy Spirit Lutheran Church B4
80. McLaurin Memorial Baptist Church ... B4
81. Emmanuel Lutheran Brethren Church B4
82. Edmonton Korean Seventh-Day Adventist Church (Meetings in Emmanuel Lutheran Brethren Church) B4
83. Campus Crusade for Christ C4

▢ HOTELS

1. Tower on the Park Apartment Hotel ... B1
2. Hillside Plaza Apartment Hotel B1
3. Venture Inn B1
4. Rex Motor Inn E1
5. Capilano Motor Inn F2
6. Renford Inn on Whyte B2
7. Strathcona Hotel C2
8. Commercial Hotel C2
9. Park Hotel C2
10. Highway Motor Inn F2
11. Regency Inn E3
12. Roadrunner Motel C3
13. Riviera Hotel C4
14. Southbend Motel C4
15. Van Winkle Motor Inn C4
16. Southgate Motor Inn C4
17. Relax Inn C4
18. Terrace Inn C4

✳ POINTS OF INTEREST

1. Muttart Conservatory C1
2. John Walter Historic Site B1

⌂ SCHOOLS

1. Grandin Catholic Elementary School .. B1
2. Bennett School (Closed June 1972) ... D1
3. St. Kevin Catholic Elementary and Junior High School D1
4. Terrace Heights Elementary School ... E1
5. Austin O'Brien Catholic Senior High School E1
6. Strathearn Junior High School (Closed June 1983) D1
7. Strathearn Elementary School D1
8. Holyrood Elementary School D1
9. Ottewell Junior High School E1
10. Clara Tyner Elementary School E1
11. Braemar Elementary School E1
12. St. Brendan Catholic Elementary and Junior High School E1
13. Windsor Park Elementary School A2
14. Garneau Elementary and Junior High School B2
15. Centennial Montessori School (Private) B2
16. Old Scona Academic High School B2
17. King Edward Elementary and Junior High School C2
18. Excelsior Elementary and Junior High Education Academy (Private) (Located in King Edward Elementary and Junior High School) C2
19. J. H. Picard Catholic Junior and Senior High School C2
20. Rutherford Elementary School D2
21. St. Thomas Catholic Elementary School D2
22. Bonnie Doon Composite High School D2
23. Idylwylde Elementary School D2
24. Kenilworth Junior High School E2
25. Waverley Elementary School E2
26. Belgravia Elementary School A3
27. McKernan Elementary and Junior High School B2
28. St. Peter's Catholic School for Autistic Children B2
29. Queen Alexandra Elementary School B2
30. Mount Carmel Catholic Elementary and Junior High School B2
31. Strathcona Composite High School ... B3
32. Mill Creek Elementary School C2
33. Ritchie Junior High School C3
34. St. Mary Catholic Junior High School C3
35. St. Margaret Catholic School (Closed June 1983) C3
36. Hazeldean Elementary School C3
37. Evelyn Unger School for Language and Learning Development (Private) D3
38. Argyll Elementary School (Closed June 1983) D2
39. Donnan Elementary and Junior High School D2
40. St. James Catholic Elementary and Junior High School D2
41. Avonmore Elementary and Junior High School D3
42. Grandview Heights Elementary and Junior High School A3
43. Parkallen Elementary School B3
44. Alberta School for the Deaf B3
45. St. Agnes Catholic School (Closed June 1981) B3
46. Allendale Elementary and Junior High School B3
47. Lansdowne Elementary School A4
48. Malmo Elementary School A4
49. Avalon Junior High School B4
50. Lendrum Elementary School B4
51. St. Martin Catholic Elementary and Junior High School B4
52. McKee Elementary School B4
53. Mount Pleasant Elementary School ... B4
54. L. Y. Cairns Vocational School B4
55. W. P. Wagner High School.......... D3

For explanation of symbols, see General Legend on page 5

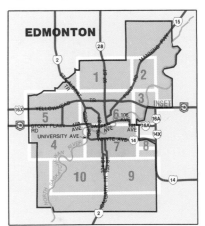

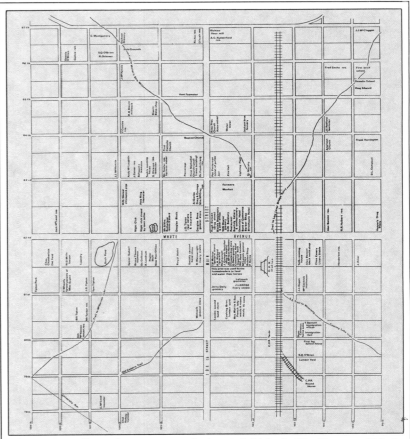

This map outlines the area now designated historic Strathcona which is governed by development regulations aimed at preserving its character. The buildings, trails and so forth within the area date to the years immediately preceding the First World War.

Old Strathcona: the past preserved

In 1891 the Calgary-Edmonton Railway reached the North Saskatchewan River. There on the south bank a new community formed at the railhead, originally known as South Edmonton. The name was changed to Strathcona in tribute to the famed CPR financier when the town was incorporated in 1899.

Edmontonians, that is the people north of the river, watched in disgust as their new rival prospered, achieving a population of 3,500 and city status by 1907. Making matters worse the same year, the province's first university was sited in Strathcona.

However, the two cities amalgamated in 1912 and, in one sense anyway, Strathcona has outlived Edmonton. As high-rises obliterated downtown Edmonton's original identity and the oil boom swept away most of the architectural heritage of both cities, concerned citizens formed the Old Strathcona Foundation to save the Main Street atmosphere of the "south side."

Since 1976 the foundation has helped formulate strict guidelines that govern all development within the core of Strathcona and restores historic properties. This map identifies many of the sites ordered preserved.

Legend for Edmonton, Section 7 appears on page 49

Adjoining Map, Page 52

NORTH

Miles
Kilometres

Adjoining Map, Page 51

EDMONTON SECTION 9

♠ CHURCHES

1. Millbourne Alliance Church B1
2. Calvary Temple B1
3. Edmonton Gospel Temple B1
4. Millwoods Presbyterian Church
   (Meetings in Lee Ridge Elementary
   School) B1
5. Hillview Baptist Church C2
6. South Woods United Congregation
   (Meetings in Hillview Elementary
   School) C2
7. Lee Ridge Baptist Church D2
8. Millwoods Mennonite Brethren
   Church D2
9. Abundant Life Chapel A2
10. St. Theresa's Roman Catholic
    Church B2
11. Millwoods Evangelical Free Church
    (Meetings in Grant MacEwan
    Community College) B2
12. Millwoods Pentecostal Assembly C2
13. Jehovah's Witnesses Kingdom Hall
    (Woodvale Congregation) C2
14. Holy Trinity Roman Catholic Church . . . B2
15. Lord of Life Lutheran Church B2
16. St. Patrick's Anglican Church (Meetings
    in Meyonohk Elementary School) B2
17. Millwoods Moravian Church D2
18. St. Clement's Roman Catholic Chapel
    (Meetings in St. Clement Catholic
    Elementary and Junior High
    School) B3
19. Hillview United Church (First Millwoods
    Congregation) (Meetings in Sakaw

Elementary School) C3
20. St. Paul's Evangelical Lutheran
    Church C4

☐ HOTELS

1. Relax Inn A1
2. Terrace Inn A1
3. Convention Inn A1
4. Derrick Motel A1
5. Trailway Motor Inn Motel A1
6. South Centre Motel A1

⌂ SCHOOLS

1. Millwoods Christian School (Private) . . . B1
2. Malcolm Tweedle Elementary
   School B1
3. Edith Rogers Junior High School B1
4. St. Hilda Catholic Elementary and
   Junior High School B1
5. Grace Martin Elementary School B1
6. St. Elizabeth Catholic Elementary
   School B1
7. Lee Ridge Elementary School B1
8. Greenview Elementary School C1
9. John Paul I Catholic Elementary
   School C1
10. Hillview Elementary School C2
11. Tipaskan Elementary School B2
12. Ecole Primaire Catholique Frere
    Antoine B2
13. Kameyosek Elementary School B2
14. Meyonohk Elementary School B2
15. J. Percy Page Composite High School . . B2
16. Satoo Elementary School B3
17. Dan Knott Junior High School B3
18. St. Clement Catholic Elementary and
    Junior High School B3
19. Menisa Elementary School B3
20. Ekota Elementary School B3
21. Meyokumin Elementary School C3
22. St. Richard Catholic Elementary
    School C3
23. Sakaw Elementary School C3
24. Weinlos Elementary School C2
25. Pollard Meadows Elementary
    School D3
26. Holy Family Catholic Junior High
    School D3
27. Crawford Plains Elementary School . . . D3
28. Ellerslie Junior High School B4
29. Ellerslie Primary School B4

EDMONTON SECTION 8 (INSET)

⌂ SCHOOLS

1. F. R. Haythorne County School . . . . . Inset

**For explanation of symbols, see General
Legend on page 5**

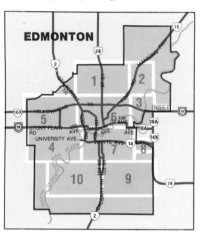

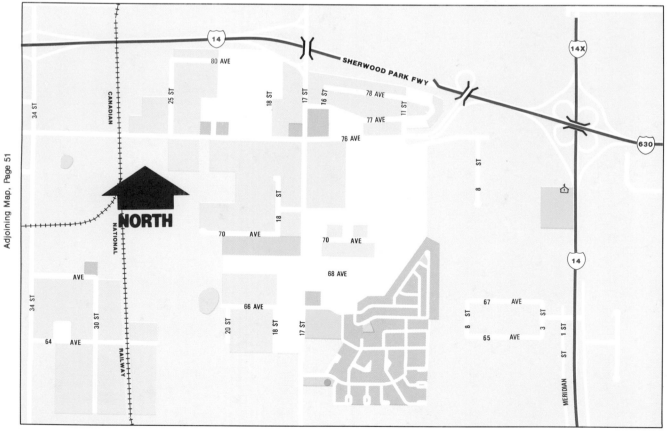

Adjoining Map, Page 55

Adjoining Map, Page 51

Adjoining Map, Page 53

A

Miles

Kilometres

NORTH

1

2

3

4

B

C

D

E

NORTH

Adjoining Map, Page 41
Adjoining Map, Page 50
Adjoining Map, Page 52

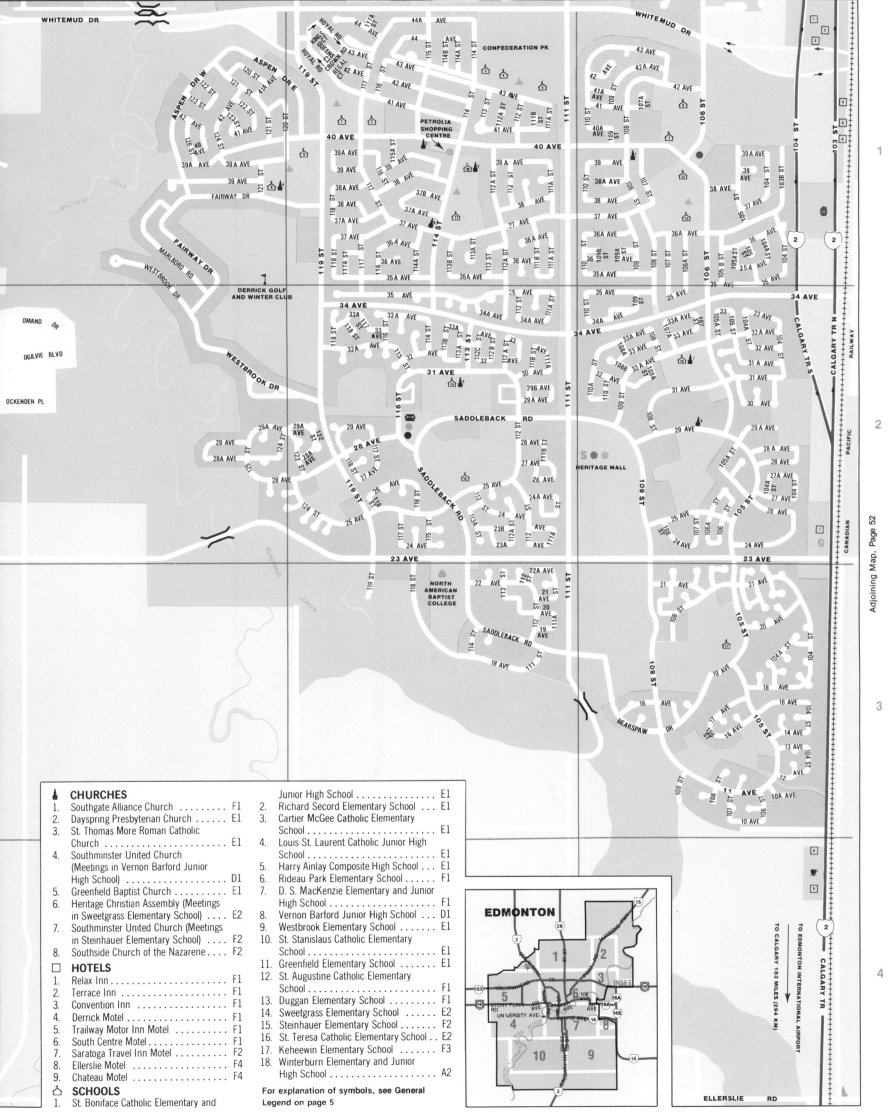

CHURCHES

1. Southgate Alliance Church F1
2. Dayspring Presbyterian Church E1
3. St. Thomas More Roman Catholic Church E1
4. Southminster United Church (Meetings in Vernon Barford Junior High School) D1
5. Greenfield Baptist Church E1
6. Heritage Christian Assembly (Meetings in Sweetgrass Elementary School) E2
7. Southminster United Church (Meetings in Steinhauer Elementary School) F2
8. Southside Church of the Nazarene F2

HOTELS

1. Relax Inn F1
2. Terrace Inn F1
3. Convention Inn F1
4. Derrick Motel F1
5. Trailway Motor Inn Motel F1
6. South Centre Motel F1
7. Saratoga Travel Inn Motel F2
8. Ellerslie Motel F4
9. Chateau Motel F4

SCHOOLS

1. St. Boniface Catholic Elementary and Junior High School E1
2. Richard Secord Elementary School . . . E1
3. Cartier McGee Catholic Elementary School E1
4. Louis St. Laurent Catholic Junior High School E1
5. Harry Ainlay Composite High School . . . E1
6. Rideau Park Elementary School F1
7. D. S. MacKenzie Elementary and Junior High School F1
8. Vernon Barford Junior High School . . . D1
9. Westbrook Elementary School E1
10. St. Stanislaus Catholic Elementary School E1
11. Greenfield Elementary School E1
12. St. Augustine Catholic Elementary School F1
13. Duggan Elementary School F1
14. Sweetgrass Elementary School E2
15. Steinhauer Elementary School F2
16. St. Teresa Catholic Elementary School . . E2
17. Keheewin Elementary School F3
18. Winterburn Elementary and Junior High School A2

For explanation of symbols, see General Legend on page 5

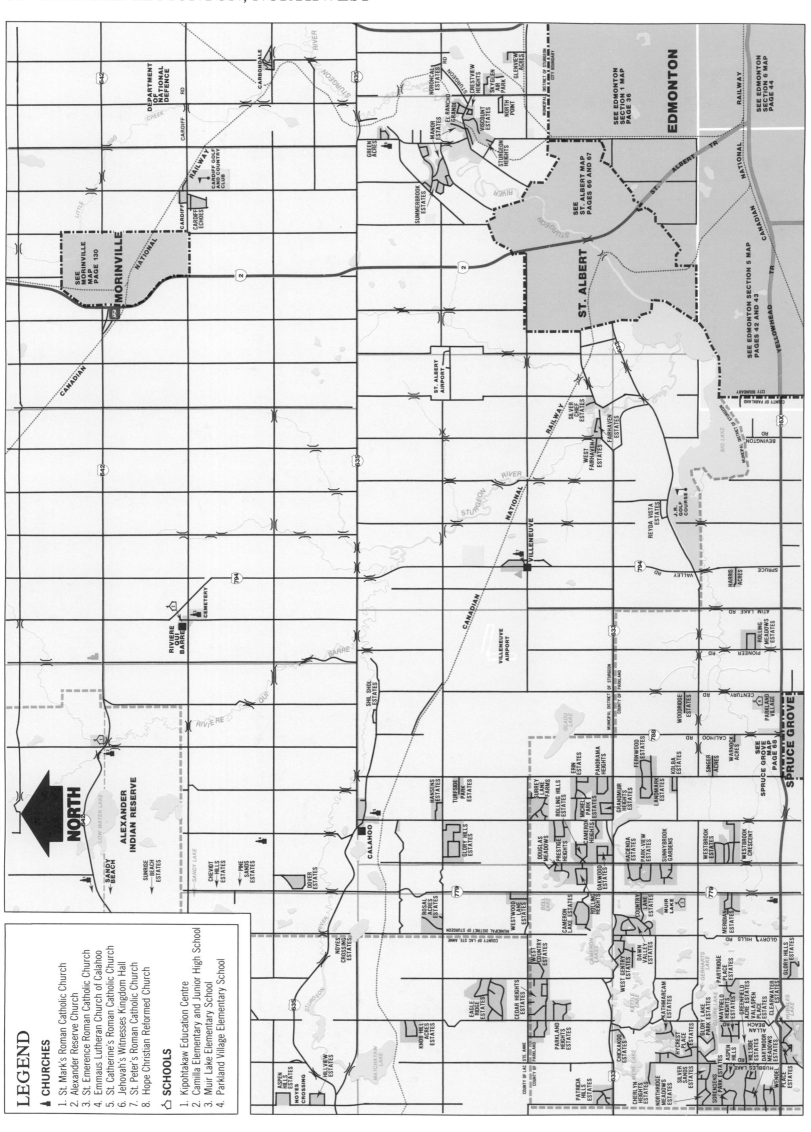

LEGEND

CHURCHES

1. St. Mark's Roman Catholic Church
2. Alexander Reserve Church
3. St. Emerence Roman Catholic Church
4. Emmaus Lutheran Church of Calahoo
5. St. Catherine's Roman Catholic Church
6. Jehovah's Witnesses Kingdom Hall
7. St. Peter's Roman Catholic Church
8. Hope Christian Reformed Church

SCHOOLS

1. Kipohtakaw Education Centre
2. Camilla Elementary and Junior High School
3. Muir Lake Elementary School
4. Parkland Village Elementary School

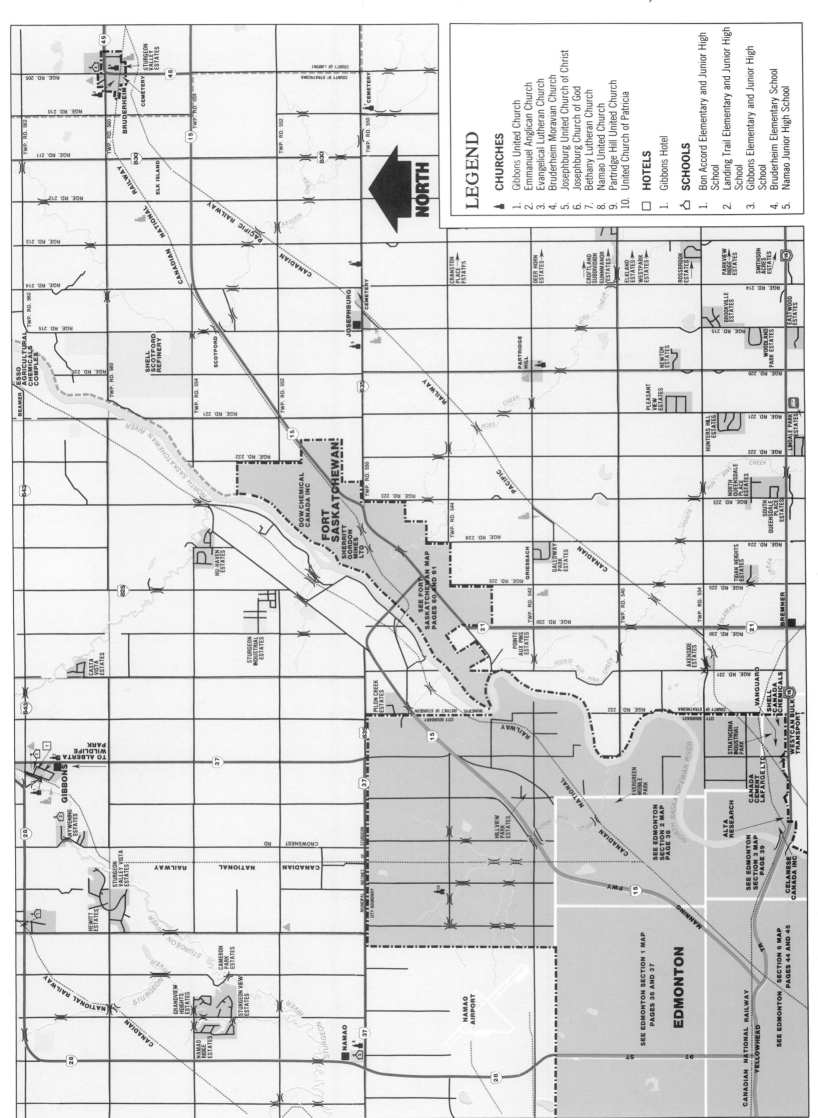

NORTH

EDMONTON

FORT SASKATCHEWAN

GIBBONS

NAMAO

Miles
Kilometres

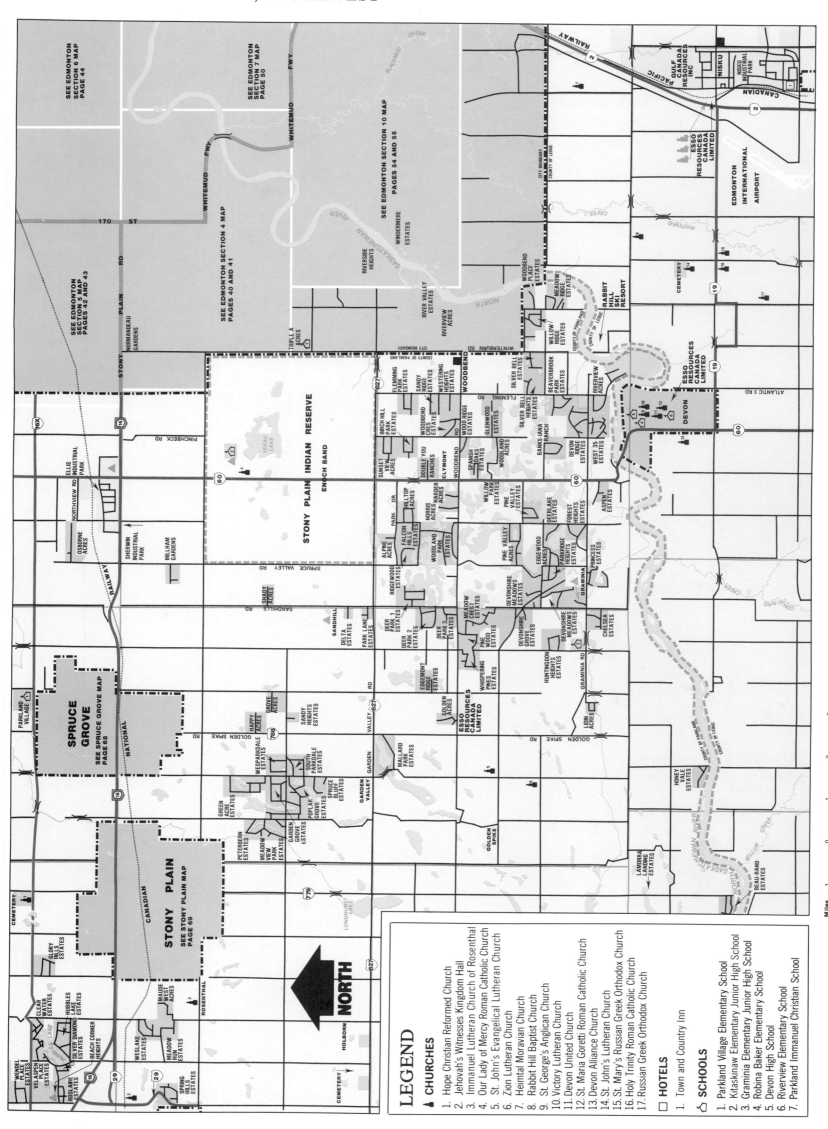

SPRUCE GROVE
SEE SPRUCE GROVE MAP PAGE 68

STONY PLAIN
SEE STONY PLAIN MAP PAGE 69

STONY PLAIN INDIAN RESERVE
ENOCH BAND

EDMONTON INTERNATIONAL AIRPORT

NORTH

LEGEND

♣ CHURCHES

1. Hope Christian Reformed Church
2. Jehovah's Witnesses Kingdom Hall
3. Immanuel Lutheran Church of Rosenthal
4. Our Lady of Mercy Roman Catholic Church
5. St. John's Evangelical Lutheran Church
6. Zion Lutheran Church
7. Heimtal Moravian Church
8. Rabbit Hill Baptist Church
9. St. George's Anglican Church
10. Victory Lutheran Church
11. Devon United Church
12. St. Maria Goretti Roman Catholic Church
13. Devon Alliance Church
14. St. John's Lutheran Church
15. St. Mary's Russian Greek Orthodox Church
16. Holy Trinity Roman Catholic Church
17. Russian Greek Orthodox Church

☐ HOTELS

1. Town and Country Inn

⌂ SCHOOLS

1. Parkland Village Elementary School
2. Kitaskinaw Elementary Junior High School
3. Graminia Elementary Junior High School
4. Robina Baker Elementary School
5. Devon High School
6. Riverview Elementary School
7. Parkland Immanuel Christian School

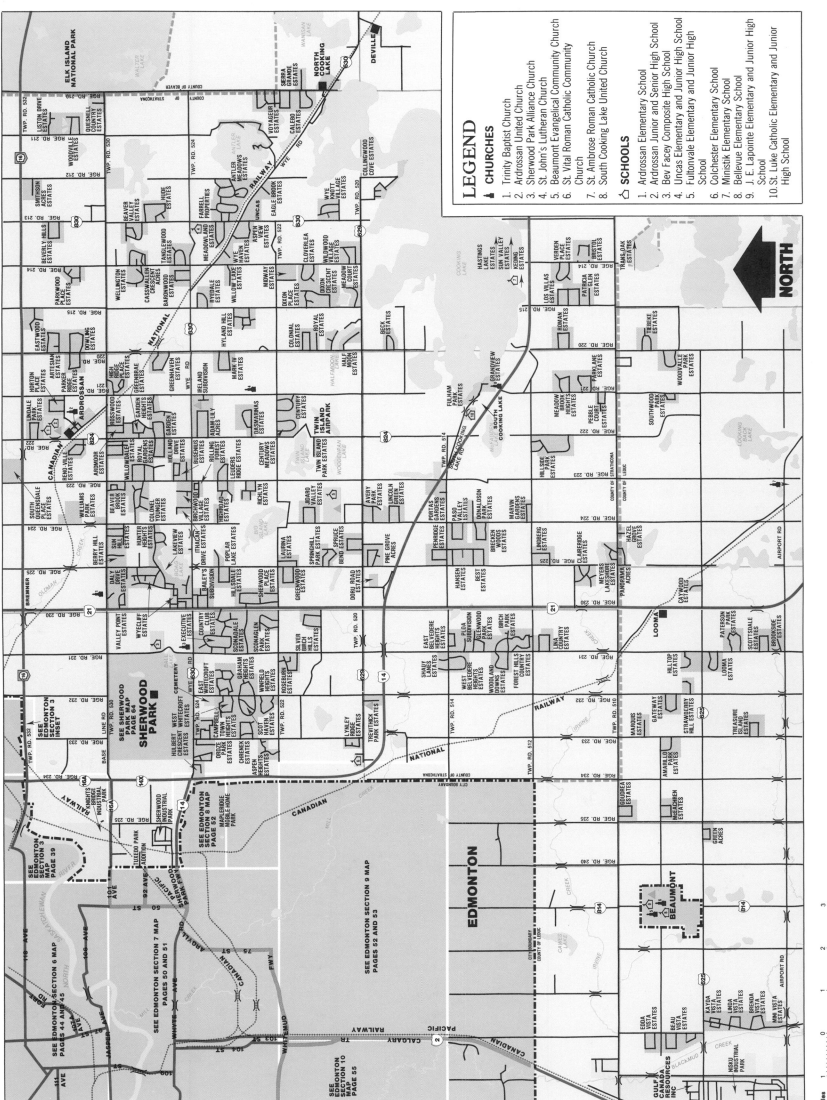

LEGEND

CHURCHES

1. Trinity Baptist Church
2. Ardrossan United Church
3. Sherwood Park Alliance Church
4. St. John's Lutheran Church
5. Beaumont Evangelical Community Church
6. St. Vital Roman Catholic Community Church
7. St. Ambrose Roman Catholic Church
8. South Cooking Lake United Church

SCHOOLS

1. Ardrossan Elementary School
2. Ardrossan Junior and Senior High School
3. Bev Facey Composite High School
4. Uncas Elementary and Junior High School
5. Fultonvale Elementary and Junior High School
6. Colchester Elementary School
7. Ministik Elementary School
8. Bellevue Elementary School
9. J. E. Lapointe Elementary and Junior High School
10. St. Luke Catholic Elementary and Junior High School

Fort Saskatchewan

Population: 12,474.

Location: On Highways 15 and 21 on the North Saskatchewan River, 17 miles (27 km.) northeast of Edmonton.

Street System: Streets run north and south, from 79 Street in the west to 115 Street in the east, with odd numbers on the east side of the streets. Avenues run east and west, from 83 Avenue in the south to 103 Avenue in the north, with odd numbers on the south side of the avenues.

Transportation Facilities: There is no passenger rail service. One bus runs daily to and from Edmonton with access to other centres from there. Courtesy Taxi provides service to Edmonton LRT stations. No inter-city courier service is available.

History: The North West Mounted Police set up a fort, initially called Sturgeon Creek Post, at this site in 1875. The name was later changed to Fort Saskatchewan. It was incorporated as a village in 1899 and as a town in 1904.

LEGEND

⚑ CHURCHES
1. Fort Saskatchewan Catholic Church
2. First United Church of Christ
3. St. George's Anglican Church
4. Church of The Nazarene
5. Christ Lutheran Church
6. Fort Saskatchewan Alliance Church
7. Jehovah's Witnesses Kingdom Hall

☐ HOTELS
1. Brant Hotel
2. Fort Hotel
3. Fort Motel

✳ POINTS OF INTEREST
1. Fort Saskatchewan Museum and Historic Site

⌂ SCHOOLS
1. Park Elementary School
2. Fort Saskatchewan Elementary School
3. Our Lady of the Angels Catholic School
4. James Mowatt Elementary School
5. Pope John XXIII Catholic Elementary School
6. Fort Saskatchewan High School
7. Fort Saskatchewan Junior High School
8. Win Ferguson School
9. Rudolph Hennig Elementary School
10. Fort Saskatchewan Christian School (Private)
11. Fort Saskatchewan Catholic High School

For explanation of symbols, see General Legend on page 5

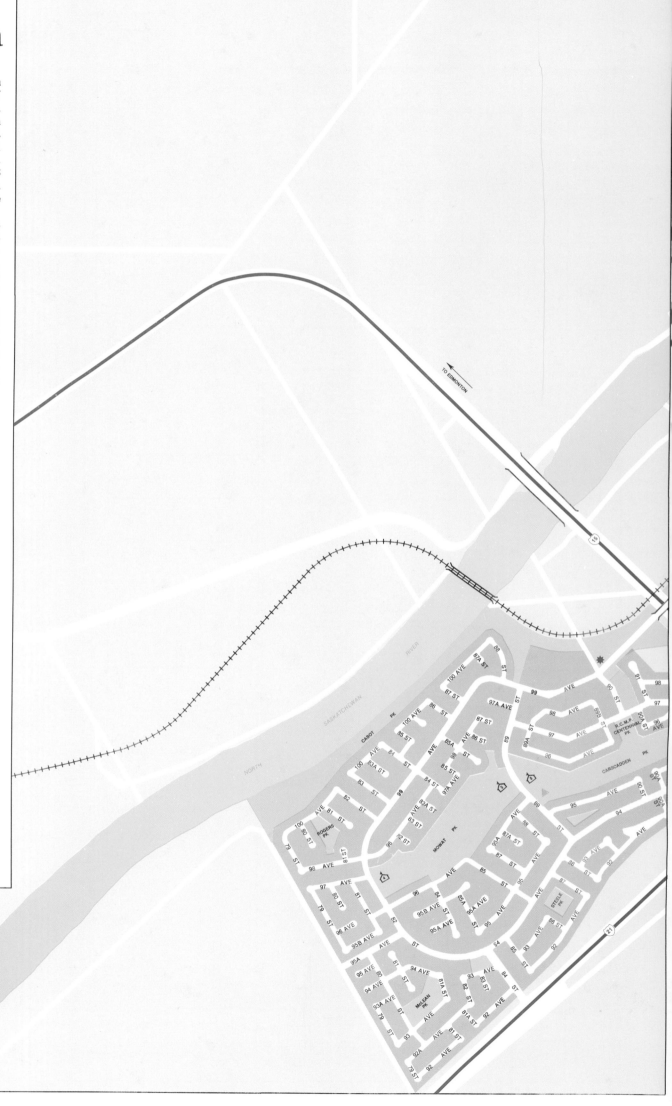

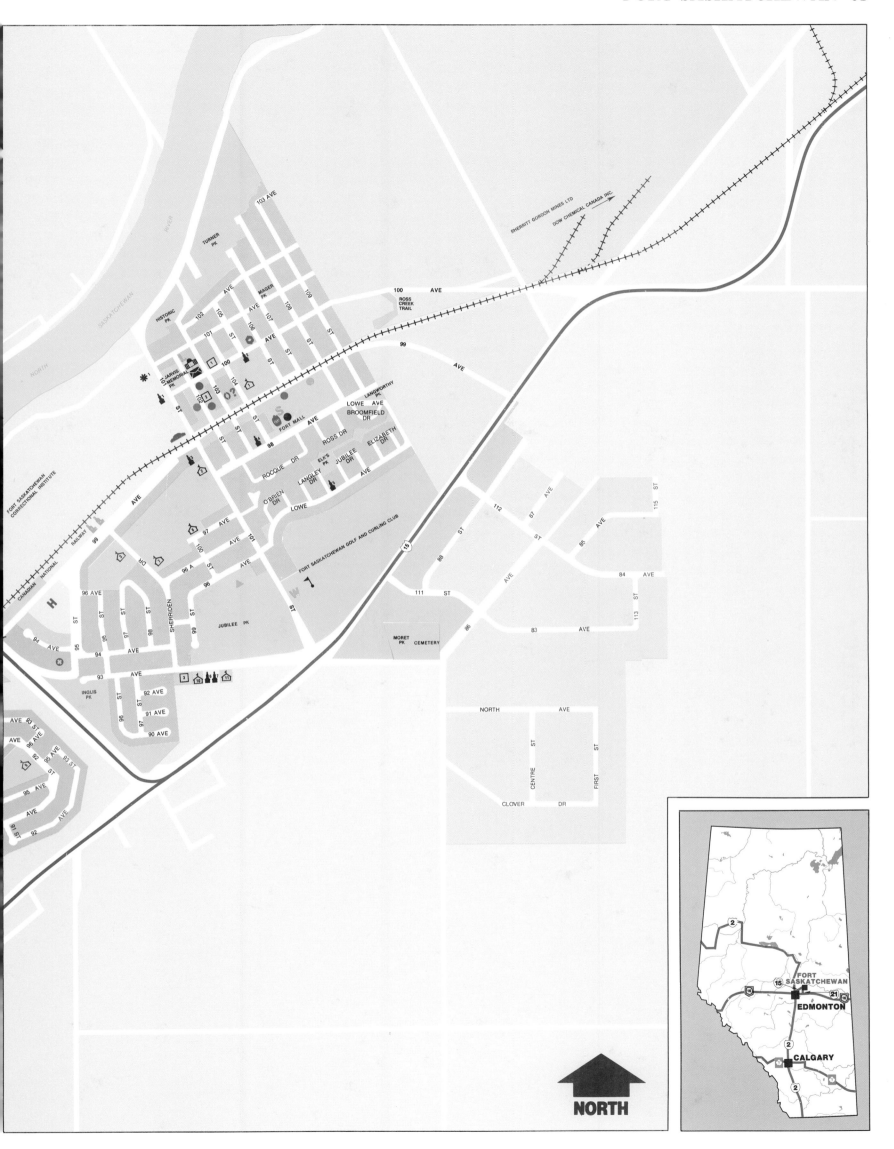

NORTH

Leduc

Population: 12,471.

Location: On Highway 2, 21 miles (34 km.) south of Edmonton and 162 miles (261 km.) north of Calgary at junction of Highway 39.

Street System: Streets run north and south, from 36 Street in the east to 54 Street in the west with odd numbers on the east side of the streets. Avenues run east and west, from 33 Avenue in the south to 70 Avenue in the north. Odd numbers are on the south side of the avenues.

Transportation Facilities: Leduc is on the CP Rail line but has no passenger rail service. Five buses run daily to Ed-

monton and three to Calgary. Couriers from Edmonton will pick up and deliver in Leduc. Scheduled air service is available from Edmonton International Airport, 3 miles (5 km.) north on Highway 2.

History: Leduc began as a termination point of the telegraph line from Winnipeg in 1876. R.T. Telford, a former member of the Northwest Mounted Police, homesteaded at Leduc in 1892 and the settlement was incorporated as a village in 1899. Leduc was named after Father Hippolyte Leduc, an Oblate priest. Leduc was incorporated as a city in 1983.

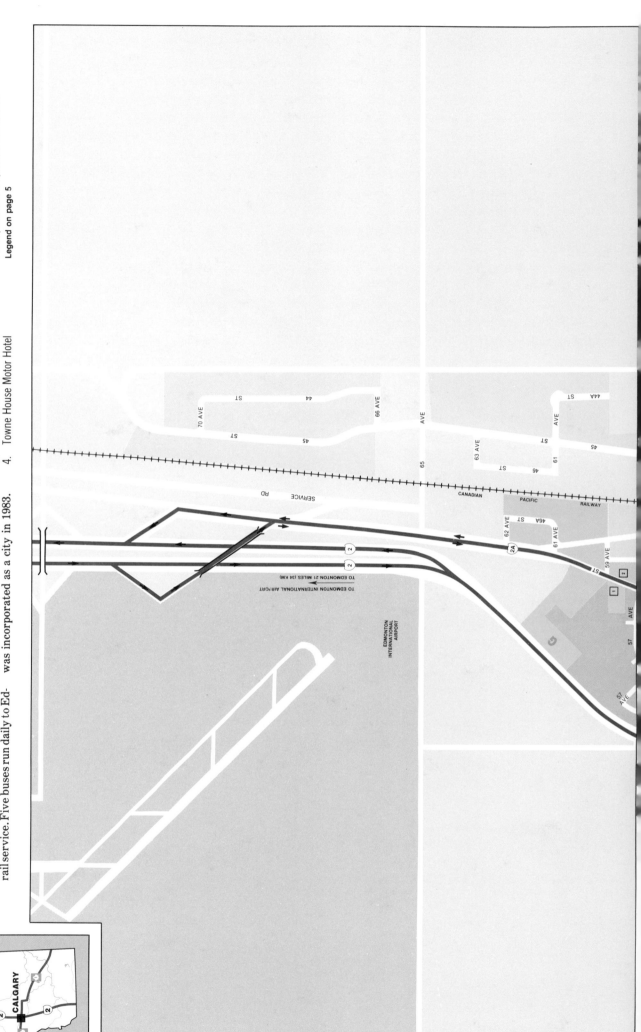

NORTH

TO DRAYTON VALLEY 65 MILES (105 KM)

TO WETASKIWIN 21 MILES (34 KM)

TO CALGARY 162 MILES (261 KM)

LEDUC GOLF AND COUNTRY CLUB

CANADIAN PACIFIC RAILWAY

Feet
Metres

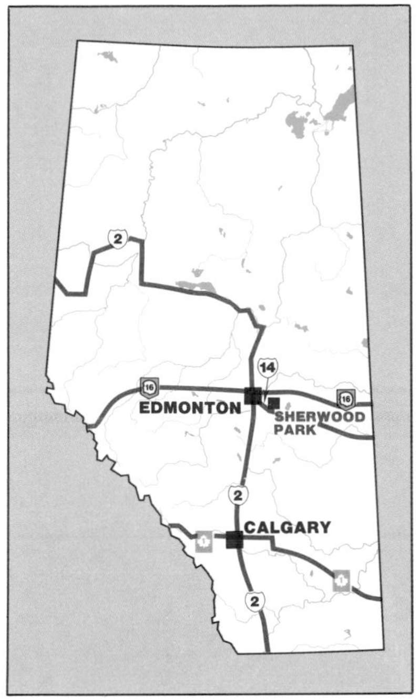

Sherwood Park

Population: 30,251.

Location: Sherwood Park is a hamlet, 9 miles (15 km.) east of Edmonton and 185 miles (298 km.) northeast of Calgary.

Transportation: Local bus service to Edmonton runs every half-hour daily, to the University of Alberta, twice daily. There is no passenger rail service. Local and inter-city courier service is available.

History: Sherwood Park was planned as a bedroom community to Edmonton by a local landowner, John Campbell, in the early 1950s. The name Sherwood Park was given to what was to be the first phase of Campbelltown. The first resident of Sherwood Park moved in on New Year's Eve, 1955.

LEGEND

CHURCHES

1. Our Lady of Perpetual Help Roman Catholic Church
2. Sherwood Park Pentecostal Assembly
3. Church of Jesus Christ of Latter-Day Saints
4. Salisbury United Church
5. Seventh-Day Adventist Church
6. Sherwood Park Baptist Church
7. Victory Baptist Church
8. St. Thomas Anglican Church
9. Church of the Nazarene
10. Sherwood Faith Centre
11. Mt. Olivet Lutheran Church
12. Sherwood Park United Church
13. Sherwood Park Alliance Church

HOTELS

1. Sherwood Park Motor Inn

SCHOOLS

1. Madonna Catholic Elementary School
2. Clover Bar Junior High School
3. Mills Haven Elementary School
4. Jean Vanier Catholic Elementary School
5. Glen Allen Elementary School
6. Archbishop Jordan Catholic High School
7. Wes Hosford Elementary School
8. Woodbridge Farms Elementary School
9. Westboro Elementary School
10. Broadmoor Junior High School
11. Salisbury Composite High School
12. Father Kenneth Kearns Catholic Elementary School
13. St. Theresa Catholic Elementary School
14. Pine Street Elementary School
15. Brentwood Elementary School
16. Sherwood Heights Junior High School
17. Our Lady of Perpetual Help Catholic Elementary and Junior High School
18. Campbelltown Elementary School
19. Robin Hood School (For the Mentally and Physically Handicapped)
20. Strathcona Christian Academy
21. Bev Facey High School

For explanation of symbols, see General Legend on page 5

Street Index
Sherwood Park

Acacia Ct. ... B2,B3
Adamson Cres. ... A3
Alder Ave. ... B3,C3
Alder Ct. ... C3
Alderwood Cres. ... C3
Applewood Rd. ... C3
Arbutus Ct. ... C3
Ash St. ... B3
Athabascan Ave. ... A1
Avondale Ct. ... D2
Baseline Rd. ... A1,B1,C1,D1
Beauvista Dr. ... B1,B2
Birch Ave. ... B3
Birch Cres. ... B3
Blackfoot Rd. ... A1
Bluebird Cres. ... C2
Bluebird Ct. ... C2
Bonnyville Ct. ... B2
Bonnyville Dr. ... B2
Braeside Cres. ... B2
Braeside Ter. ... B2
Brentwood Blvd. ... C2,C3
Broadmoor Blvd. ... A1,A2,A3
Broadmoor Dr. ... B2
Caragana Ct. ... C3
Caragana Ave. ... C3
Cardinal Pl. ... C3
Cedar St. ... B3
Chippewa Rd. ... A1
Circlewood Dr. ... C3
Conifer St. ... B2,B3
Cottonwood Ave. ... B3,C3
Crane Rd. ... C3
Cree Rd. ... A1
Curlew Cres. ... C2,C3
Cypress Ave. ... B2,B3
Dogwood Ct. ... B3
Eagle Ct. ... C2
Eagle Dr. ... C2,C3
Elm Ct. ... B3
Evergreen St. ... B3
Fairview Ct. ... B2
Falcon Dr. ... C3
Fir St. ... A3,B3
Flamingo Dr. ... C2
Gainsboro Ct. ... D2
Gainsboro Pl. ... D2
Gainsboro Rd. ... D2
Galaxy Way ... C1
Gale Ave. ... C1
Galen Cres. ... D2
Galen Pl. ... D2
Galloway Ave. ... D1
Galloway Bay ... D1
Galloway Ct. ... D1
Galloway Dr. ... C1,D1
Galloway Pl. ... D1
Galloway Rd. ... C1
Galloway St. ... C1
Galloway Ter. ... D1
Galveston Ave. ... C2
Garden Cres. ... D2
Garfield Cres. ... C1
Garland Ct. ... D2
Garland Cres. ... D2
Garland Ter. ... D2
Garnet Ave. ... C1
Garnet Cres. ... C1
Garnet Rd. ... C1
Garrison Cres. ... C1
Gatewood Blvd. ... C1
Gatewood Pl. ... C1
Georgian Ct. ... C2
Georgian Pl. ... C2
Georgian Ter. ... D1
Georgian Way ... C1,C2,D1,D2
Gilby St. ... D1
Gillies Rd. ... A2
Gillingham Cres. ... C1
Gilmore Ave. ... C1
Glacier Cres. ... C1
Glamorgan Dr. ... C1,D1
Glenbrook Blvd. ... C1
Glen Allen Blvd. ... D1,D2,D3
Glencoe Blvd. ... D1
Glengarry Cres. ... D1
Glenmore Ave. ... B2
Glenridge Pl. ... C1
Glenridge Rd. ... C1
Glenwood Dr. ... C3
Gloucester Ave. ... D2
Graham Ct. ... C1
Graham Pl. ... C1
Graham Rd. ... C1
Granada Blvd. ... C2
Grant Ave. ... C1
Granville Cres. ... D1
Gravenhurst Cres. ... C1,D1
Greengrove Ave. ... D1,D2
Greengrove Cres. ... D1,D2
Greenwood Way ... C3
Greystone Ct. ... D1
Greystone Cres. ... D1
Greystone Pl. ... D1
Greystone Ter. ... D1
Groveland Ave. ... D1,D2
Groveland Pl. ... D2
Groveland Rd. ... D1,D2
Guilford St. ... C1
Hawkins Cres. ... A3
Hawthorne St. ... B3
Haythorne Cres. ... A2
Haythorne Pl. ... A2
Haythorne Rd. ... A2
Hazel St. ... C2,C3
Heron Rd. ... C2,C3
Highwood Pl. ... C3
Holly Ave. ... C3
Hummingbird Ct. ... C2
Hummingbird Rd. ... C2
Ivy Ct. ... C3
Ivy Cres. ... B3,C3
Jay Ct. ... C2
Juniper Ave. ... B3
Kaska Rd. ... A1
Keith Rd. ... A3
Kingfisher Bay ... C2
Kingfisher Ct. ... C2
Kingfisher Rd. ... C2
Larch Ct. ... B3
Lark St. ... C3
Larwood Pl. ... C3
Lueders Cres. ... A2
Lueders Ct. ... A2
Madison Ave. ... B1,C1
Main Blvd. ... B1,C1
Main Pl. ... B1
Main Ter. ... B1
Malvern Bay ... B1
Malvern Ct. ... B1
Malvern Dr. ... B1
Malvern Pl. ... B1
Malvern Ter. ... B1
Manchester Dr. ... B1
Manor Ct. ... B1
Manor Dr. ... B1
Manor Pl. ... B1
Manor Ter. ... B1
Maple Ct. ... B2
Mardale Cres. ... C1
Markham Cres. ... B1
Marion Dr. ... B1,C1
Marion Pl. ... B1
Market St. ... B1
Maywood Rd. ... C3
McDermid Dr. ... A2
Meadowbrook Rd. ... B1,C1
Meadowood Cres. ... C3
Medhurst Cres. ... B1
Melrose Cres. ... B1
Melrose Pl. ... B1
Menlo Cres. ... B1
Meridian Rd. ... C1
Merryvale Cres. ... C1
Merrywood Cres. ... C1
Milburn Cres. ... A1
Milburn Pl. ... B1
Milford Cres. ... B1
Millers Rd. ... B1
Mission St. ... B1
Mony Penny Cres. ... A2
Moreland Cres. ... B1
Moreland Rd. ... B1
Moyer Dr. ... A2,A3
Nottingham Dr. ... A2
Oak St. ... B2,B3
Ordze Rd. ... A3
Oriole Cres. ... C2
Oriole Dr. ... C2
Parker Dr. ... A2
Parker Man. ... A2
Parker Pl. ... A2
Parker Ter. ... A2
Peacock Dr. ... C2
Penguin Cres. ... D2
Pine St. ... B2,B3,C2,C3
Poinciana Ct. ... C3
Privet Ct. ... C2
Raven Dr. ... C2
Redwood Ct. ... B3
Robin St. ... C3
Rosewood Dr. ... C3
Rosewood Pl. ... C3
Sage Ct. ... C3
Sage Cres. ... C3
Sandpiper Ct. ... C2
Sandpiper Dr. ... C2
Seneca Rd. ... A1
Sherwood Dr. ... B2,C1,C2
Sioux Rd. ... A1
Spruce Ave. ... B3
Starling Dr. ... C2
Strathcona Dr. ... A2,A3
Strathcona Pl. ... A2
Sunset Pl. ... B2
Swallow Ave. ... C2,D2
Sycamore St. ... B3
Tamarack Ave. ... B3
Vantage Lane ... A3
Ventnor Pl. ... A3
Victoria Ct. ... A3
Victoria Man. ... A3
Victoria Way ... A3
Village Downs ... A3
Village Ct. ... B2
Village Dr. ... A3
Village Estate ... A3
Village Gr. ... A3
Village Lane ... A3
Village Mews ... A3
Village Pl. ... A3
Village Rd. ... A2,B2
Village Sq. ... A3
Village Ter. ... A3
Virginia Cres. ... A3
Viscount Cres. ... A3
Vista Ct. ... A3
Vista Dr. ... A3
Vista Man. ... A3
Wellington Lane ... A1
Wells Point Lane ... A1
Willow St. ... B3
Wilson Cres. ... A2
Woodbine Ct. ... A2
Woodbine Rd. ... A2
Woodbridge Way ... A1,A2
Woodfield Dr. ... A2
Woodfield Pl. ... A2
Woodlake Ct. ... A2
Woodlake Man. ... A2
Woodlake Pl. ... A2
Woodlake Rd. ... A1,A2
Woodstock Dr. ... A1,A2
Woodstock Ter. ... A2
Wren Cres. ... C2,C3
Wye Rd. ... A3,B3,C3,D3
Yew Ct. ... C3

Street Index
St. Albert
(Map on p. 66 and 67)

Abbey Cres. ... D3
Abel Pl. ... D3
Acorn Cres. ... E3
Addison Cres. ... D3
Adrian Pl. ... D3
Afton Cres. ... D3
Akins Dr. ... D3,E3
Alan Pl. ... D3
Alcott Cres. ... D3
Alder Pl. ... D3
Alderwood Blvd. ... D3
Allison Pl. ... D3
Alpine Blvd. ... D3,E3
Alpine Pl. ... D3
Amber Cres. ... D2,D3
Amherst Cres. ... E3
Andrew Cres. ... E2
Anita Cres. ... E3
Annette Cres. ... D3
Apple Pl. ... D3
Arbor Cres. ... E3
Arlington Dr. ... D3,D4
Ash Cres. ... D3
Ash Pl. ... D3
Aspen Cres. ... D2,E2
Attwood Dr. ... D3
Austin Cres. ... E3
Balmoral Dr. ... C3
Banting Pl. ... D2
Beacon Cres. ... C2
Beaverbrook Cres. ... C2
Bellerose Dr. ... B2,C1
Bellevue Cres. ... C2
Belmont Dr. ... C2,C3
Bennett Pl. ... C2
Bernard Dr. ... C2
Berrymore Dr. ... C2
Birch Dr. ... C2
Bishop St. ... C2
Bocock Pl. ... C2
Boudreau Rd. ... C1,C2,D2,E2
Bradburn Cres. ... C2,D2
Brandon St. ... C2,C3
Brentwood Pl. ... C2
Broadview Cres. ... C2
Brunswick Cres. ... C2,D2
Burnham Ave. ... C2
Burnham Pl. ... C2
Burns St. ... C2
Butterfield Cres. ... C1
Calder Pl. ... E2,F2
Campbell Rd. ... E2,E3
Carnegie Dr. ... E2
Carriage Way ... E2
Carswell St. ... E2
Chatelain Dr. ... F2
Chevigny St. ... E2
Chisholm Ave. ... E2,F2
Corriveau Ave. ... E2,F2
Cunningham Rd. ... C3
Dalhousie St. ... A1
Danforth Cres. ... A1
Dawson Dr. ... B1,B2
Dayton Cres. ... A1
Deerbourne Dr. ... B1
Delbrook Blvd. ... B1
Dion Pl. ... B1
Dorchester Dr. ... A1
Dufferin St. ... A1
Duncan Ct. ... A1
Dunsmuir Ct. ... A1
Durham Ave. ... A1
Edmonton St. ... B3
Fairchild Dr. ... C2,D2
Fairfax Cres. ... C3,D3
Fairholm Pl. ... C2
Fair Oaks Dr. ... D2,D3
Fairview Blvd. ... C2,C3
Falcon Cres. ... C3
Fallhaven Pl. ... D3
Falstaff Ave. ... D3
Farmstead Ave. ... C3
Fawcett Cres. ... D3
Fenwick Cres. ... D3
Fermont St. ... D3
Fernwood Cres. ... D2
Finch Cres. ... D2,D3
Flagstone Cres. ... D2
Fleetwood Cres. ... D2
Flint Cres. ... D2
Forest Dr. ... C3,D2,D3
Franklin Pl. ... C2
Gainsborough Ave. ... B4
Galarneau Pl. ... C4
Galaxy Pl. ... C4
Garcia Pl. ... C4
Garden Cres. ... B4
Gareth Pl. ... C4
Garfield Pl. ... C4
Garland Pl. ... B3
Garnett Dr. ... C4
Garraway Pl. ... C4
Gate Ave. ... C4
Gatewood Ave. ... B4
Gaylord Pl. ... B3
Geneva Cres. ... B4
Georgia Pl. ... B4
Gervais Rd. ... C4
Gilchrist Pl. ... C3
Gillian Cres. ... B4
Gilmore Cres. ... B3
Giroux Rd. ... A1,B1
Glacier Pl. ... B4
Gladstone Cres. ... B4
Glen Meadow Cres. ... C3
Glenhaven Cres. ... B3,B4
Glenmore Cres. ... B3
Glenview Cres. ... B3
Glenwood Cres. ... B4
Gloucester Dr. ... C4
Goodridge Dr. ... C4
Gordon Cres. ... C4
Gould Pl. ... B4
Graham Ave. ... B4
Granada Pl. ... B4
Grandin Pl. ... B3,C3
Grandin Rd. ... C2,C3
Grandora Cres. ... C4
Grandville Ave. ... B4
Grandville Pl. ... B3,B4
Grange Dr. ... C4
Granite Ave. ... C4
Grantham Pl. ... B4
Green Grove Dr. ... B3,C3
Green Lees Pl. ... C4
Greenbrier Cres. ... B4
Greenhill St. ... C4
Greenview Cres. ... B3,C3
Greenwich Cres. ... B4
Greenwood Pl. ... B3
Greer Cres. ... B4
Grenfell Ave. ... B4
Gresham Blvd. ... B3
Gretna Pl. ... B4
Greystone Pl. ... B4
Grosvenor Blvd. ... B3,B4
Herbert Rd. ... C4,D3,D2,E2
Inglewood Dr. ... B1,C1
Labelle Cres. ... A1,B1
Lachambre Pl. ... B1
Lafonde Cres. ... A2
Laird Pl. ... B1
Lamartine Cres. ... A2
Lambert Cres. ... B2
Lamoureux Pl. ... B1
Lancaster Cres. ... A2
Langholm Dr. ... B1
Langley Ave. ... A2
Larch Way ... B1
Larkspur Cres. ... A2
Larose Dr. ... A1,A2
Larson Ave. ... A1
Latimer Pl. ... B1
Laurier Cres. ... B2
Lauriston Pl. ... B1
Laval Dr. ... B1
Lavoie Pl. ... B1
Lawrence Cres. ... A1,A2
Laydon Dr. ... A2
Leblanc Pl. ... B1
Leddy Ave. ... B1
Lemay Pl. ... B1
Lennox Dr. ... B1
Leon Pl. ... A2,B2
Lepine Pl. ... B1
Lester Cres. ... A2
Levasseur Rd. ... A4,B4,C4
Lexington Dr. ... B1
Liberton Dr. ... B1
Lincoln Cres. ... B1
Lindbergh Cres. ... A1,A2
Linwood Cres. ... B1
Livingstone Cres. ... A1,B1
Lloyd Pl. ... A1,B1
Lockhart Dr. ... A1
Lodgepole Cres. ... A1
Lombard Cres. ... B2
Longview Cres. ... A1,A2
Lorne Cres. ... B1
Lorraine Cres. ... A1
Louisbourg Pl. ... B1
Lovatt Pl. ... B1
Loyola Pl. ... B1
Lucerne Cres. ... A1
Madison Ave. ... B2
Madonna Dr. ... B2
Malmo Ave. ... A2,B2
Maple Dr. ... B2
Marchand Pl. ... A2,B2
Marion Cres. ... B2
McKenney Ave. ... A2,B2
Meadowview Dr. ... A3
Michener Pl. ... B2
Milburn Cres. ... A2
Mill Dr. ... B2
Mission Ave. ... A2,A3,B2,B3
Montcalm Cres. ... A2,B2
Mont Clare Pl. ... B2
Morgan Cres. ... A2
Mount Royal Dr. ... B2
Muir Dr. ... B2
Mural Cres. ... B2
Murray Cres. ... A2
Page Dr. ... E2
Patterson Cres. ... E2
Pembina Pl. ... E2
Pembroke Cres. ... E2
Perron St. ... B2,B3
Perrault Pl. ... E2
Pine Grove Pl. ... E2
Pineridge Cres. ... E2
Pineview Dr. ... E2
Poirier Ave. ... E2
Portland Pl. ... E2
Princeton Cres. ... E2
Rayborn Ave. ... A4
Remos St. ... B3
Renault Cres. ... A4
Riel Dr. ... A3,A4
River Crest Cres. ... B2
Rowland Cres. ... A4
Sable Cres. ... C3
Salina Dr. ... C3
Salisbury Ave. ... C3
Savoy Pl. ... C4
Scarboro Pl. ... C3
Seymore Cres. ... C3
Sheridan Dr. ... C3
Sir Winston Churchill Ave. ... A4,B3,C2,C3,D2
Sonora Dr. ... C3
Sorrel Cres. ... C3
Springfield Cres. ... C3,D3
Spruce Cres. ... C3
Stanley Dr. ... D3
Sterling St. ... C3
Sturgeon Rd. ... C1,C2,D1
Sunnyside Cres. ... C3
Sunset Blvd. ... C3
Swallow Cres. ... C3
Sycamore Ave. ... C3
Sylvan Dr. ... C3
St. Albert Rd. ... B1,B2,C3,C4,D4
St. Anne St. ... B2,B3
St. Michael St. ... B3
St. Thomas St. ... B3
St. Vital Ave. ... B2
Tache St. ... B3
Wagner Pl. ... D1
Wakefield Blvd. ... C1
Wakefield Pl. ... C1
Walden Cres. ... D1
Walnut Pl. ... C1
Washington Pl. ... C1
Waterford Pl. ... D1
Waverly Dr. ... D1
Weatherby Pl. ... C1
Wedgewood Pl. ... D2
Welland Cres. ... D1
Wentworth Cres. ... D1
Westview Pl. ... D2
Westwood Dr. ... C1,C2,D1
Wheatstone Cres. ... D1
Whitby Pl. ... D1
Whitehall Cres. ... C1,D1
White Oak Pl. ... D2
Whitman Pl. ... D1
Willowbrook Cres. ... D1,D2
Wimbleton Cres. ... D1
Windermere Cres. ... D1,D2
Windsor Cres. ... C1,C2,D1
Wingate Pl. ... C1
Willoughby Dr. ... D1
Wolcott Pl. ... D1
Woodcrest Ave. ... D2
Woodlands Rd. ... D1,D2
Woodstock Pl. ... D1
Wordsworth Pl. ... D1
Wycliffe Pl. ... D1

St. Albert

Population: 35,032.

Location: On Highway 2 at the northwest boundary of the City of Edmonton.

Street System: The city is divided into 11 residential and three industrial subdivisions. Each subdivision is named and the streets within each begin with the same letter as the subdivision name. For example, all the streets in Grandin begin with "G." The numbering system on the closed bays and crescents varies with the subdivisions.

Transportation Facilities: There is no passenger rail service. The city has daily transit bus service, except Sundays, into Edmonton. Greyhound also maintains service between St. Albert, Edmonton and other centres. The city of St. Albert operates a handibus for the handicapped. Inter-city courier service is available. There is no scheduled air service, but there is a private airport.

History: The area was first settled in 1861 by Father Albert Lacombe and 20 Metis families in a community called Mission Hill, claimed to be the oldest settlement not associated with a fort in Alberta. That community was wiped out by disease but resettled in 1880, again mostly by Metis families. In 1885, Bishop Vital-Julien Grandin of the St. Albert diocese organized a home guard to fight, if need be, for the federal cause in the Riel Rebellion. The majority of the guard were Metis and one of their leaders was Felix Dumont, nephew of Riel's lieutenant, Gabriel Dumont. St. Albert was incorporated as a village in 1899, as a town in 1904, and as a city in 1977.

LEGEND

♦ CHURCHES
1. Sturgeon Valley Baptist Church
2. Christ Community Church
3. St. Albert Roman Catholic Parish
4. Grace Full Gospel Assembly Church
5. Braeside Presbyterian Church
6. St. Albert Alliance Church
7. First Baptist Church
8. St. Albert Evangelical Lutheran Church
9. St. Albert United Church
10. Presbyterian Reformed Church
11. St. Peter's Evangelical Lutheran Church
12. Elim Pentecostal Church
13. Christian Reformed Church
14. Community Church of The Nazarene
15. St. Matthew Anglican Church
    (Meetings in Newman Theological College)

□ HOTELS
1. Bruin Inn
2. Sleep Inn
3. St. Albert Motor Inn

✳ POINTS OF INTEREST
1. Father Lacombe Chapel
2. St. Albert Museum and Cultural Centre

⌂ SCHOOLS
1. William D. Cutts Elementary and Junior High School
2. Bertha Kennedy Catholic Community Core School
3. Keenooshyo Elementary School
4. Neil M. Ross Catholic Elementary and Junior High School
5. Ronald Harvey Elementary School
6. St. Albert Catholic High School

For location of named streets, see page 65

7. Father Jan Catholic Elementary School
8. Sir Alexander MacKenzie
   Elementary School
9. Vincent J. Maloney Catholic
   Junior High School
10. Lorne Akins Junior High School
11. Paul Kane High School
12. Elmer S. Gish Junior High School
13. Leo Nickerson Elementary School
14. Vital Grandin Catholic
    Elementary School
15. Sir George Simpson Junior High School
16. Robert Rundle Elementary School
17. Wild Rose Elementary School
18. Albert Lacombe Catholic
    Elementary School

For explanation of symbols, see General
Legend on page 5

Feet 0   500   1,000   1,500   2,000

Metres 0 100 200 300 400 500 600

Spruce Grove

Population: 11,307.

Location: On Highway 16, 17 miles (28 km.) west of Edmonton.

Transportation Facilities: There are two Greyhound buses daily each way between Edmonton and Spruce Grove. The town is situated on the CN main line but has no passenger rail service. Couriers from Edmonton will pick up and deliver parcels. No scheduled air service is available.

History: Spruce Grove's first residents were Scottish, English and French, in the late 1800s. In 1890, a large influx of German settlers arrived and the Canadian Northern Railway reached the area in 1908. The village was a self-sufficient agricultural centre until the late '60s and has since developed into a bedroom community for the growing city of Edmonton. The town's name refers to the spruce groves which were in the area prior to the settlement, some of which remain.

LEGEND

♣ CHURCHES
1. Parkland Baptist Church
2. Spruce Grove Alliance Church
3. Spruce Grove Community Church
4. Peace Lutheran Church
5. St. Joseph's Catholic Church
6. St. Andrew's United Church
7. St. Matthew's Lutheran Church
8. Church of Jesus Christ of Latter-Day Saints

☐ HOTELS
1. Grove Motor Inn
2. Cossack Inn

⌂ SCHOOLS
1. Spruce Grove Composite High School
2. St Marguerite Catholic Junior High School
3. Millgrove Elementary School
4. Woodhaven Junior High School
5. Brookwood Elementary School
6. Queen Street Elementary School
7. St. Joseph's Catholic Elementary School
8. Broxton Park Elementary and Junior High School

For explanation of symbols, see General Legend on page 5

NORTH

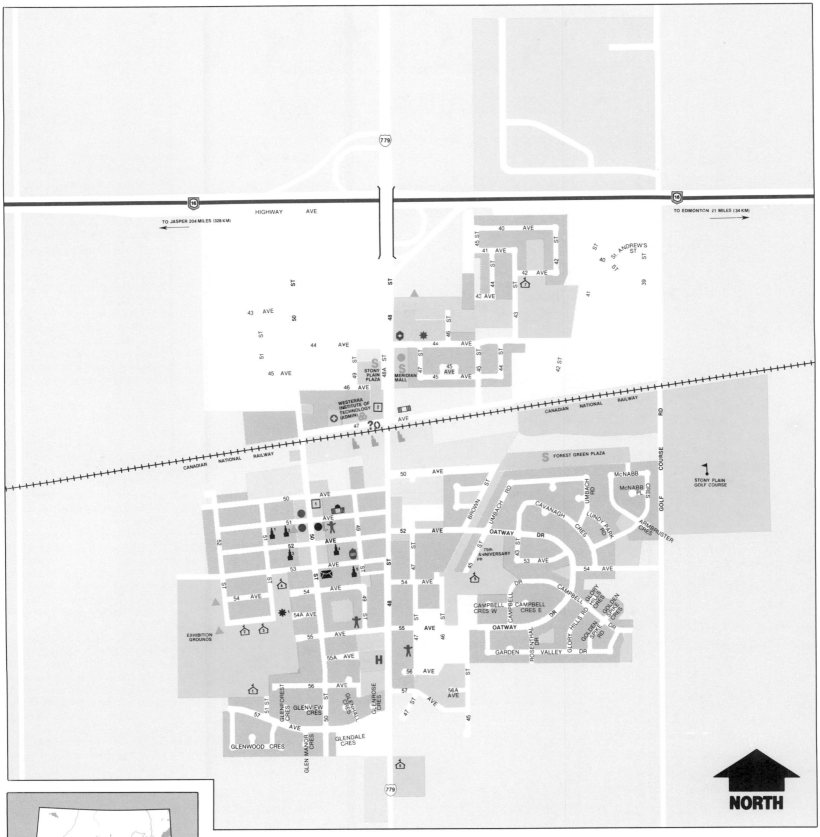

Stony Plain

Population: 5,291.

Location: On Highway 16, 21 miles (34 km.) west of Edmonton.

Street System: Streets run north and south, from 42 Street in the east to 52 Street in the west, with odd numbers on the east side of the streets. Avenues run east and west, from 40 Avenue in the north to 57 Avenue in the south, with odd numbers on the south side of the avenues.

Transportation Facilities: Stony Plain is on the CN main line but has no passenger rail service. There is Greyhound bus service to and from Edmonton twice daily each way. There is no scheduled air service but inter-city courier service is available.

History: One of Stony Plain's first settlers was John MacDonald who arrived from Ontario in 1882 and farmed until 1892 when he set up a post office and store in what became the village of Stony Plain in 1908. The town was named for the Stoney Indians who inhabited the area before the white settlers arrived. It was incorporated as a village in 1908 and as a town in 1909.

LEGEND

CHURCHES
1. St. Matthew's Lutheran Church
2. United Church of Canada
3. Good Shepherd Lutheran Church
4. Our Lady of Perpetual Help Roman Catholic Church
5. Stony Plain Alliance Church

HOTELS
1. Stony Plain Hotel
2. Stony Motor Inn

POINTS OF INTEREST
1. Multicultural Heritage Centre

SCHOOLS
1. Stony Plain Junior High School
2. Memorial High School
3. Stony Plain Elementary School
4. St. Matthew's Lutheran School
5. John Paul II Catholic Elementary and Junior High School
6. Forest Green Elementary School
7. Meridian Heights Elementary School

For explanation of symbols, see General Legend on page 5

CALGARY
the financial centre

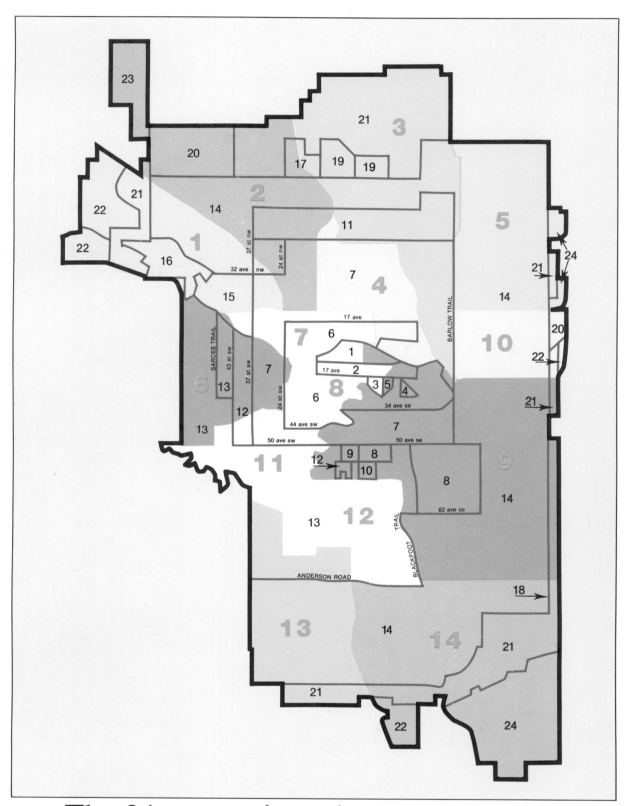

Population: 620,692.

Location: On Highways 1 and 2, 183 miles (294 km.) south of Edmonton.

Street System: Calgary is divided into four quadrants—northeast, northwest, southeast and southwest. These are defined by an east-west line and a north-south line that runs through the city. (See map on page 71 for yellow quadrant lines).

All Calgary addresses therefore carry the designation NE, NW, SE or SW to show which quadrant they're located in. The address of a numbered street reveals its location. No. 1104 14 Street SW, for instance, would be located between 11 Avenue South and 12 Avenue South on 14 Street West. Since 1104 is an even number it will be on the east side of the street. Even numbered houses on avenues are on the north side of the street.

However, an idiosyncrasy distinguishes Calgary's numbering system on avenues. Pioneer planners decided to begin numbering houses in the first block west of Centre Street with the number 101, rather than the number 1. Hence the numbers between First and Second Streets had to begin with 201 and those between Second and Third with 301. The result is confusing to non-Calgarians. Where in almost all other city street systems an address in the 500s will lie between Fifth and Sixth Streets, in the case of Calgary avenues, it will lie between Fourth and Fifth.

Calgary subdivisions developed in the last two decades have combined the number system with names. Some identity has been preserved between the name of the street and the name of the subdivision. But while Brae Place, Brabourne Mews and Brakenridge Road are all reliably in the Braeside area, Braden Crescent and Brantford Drive are at the opposite end of town. So to locate named streets, consult the Calgary general index on page 72.

History: Fort Calgary was established in 1875 by the North West Mounted Police. Colonel J.F. Macleod named it Fort Calgary after his ancestral estates in the Hebrides. Calgary was incorporated as a town in 1884 and a city in 1893.

The city of Calgary has 14 wards, each represented by one alderman on city council. The mayor is elected at large by all residents of the city. Municipal elections are held every three years.

The 24 annexations that made the city
(in colour, the 14 wards)

1 1884 Town of Calgary 2.38 sq. mi. (original townsite)
2 1893 Mount Royal and part of Mills Estates and Pearce Estates - Area not known
3 1901 Victoria Park - .14 sq. mi.
4 1903 Part of Burns Avenue - .08 sq. mi.
5 1906 Part of Grandview and Burns Avenue - .15 sq. mi.
6 1907 Hillhurst, Sunnyside, Westmount, Bridgeland, St. George Heights, Knob Hill, Bankview, South Calgary, Glencoe, Altadore, Rideau Park, Roxboro, Eriton, Burnsland and Inglewood - 9 sq. mi.

7 1910 Foothills, North Bow, part of Inglewood, part of Glamorgan/ Glenbrook and Highfield - 24 sq. mi.
8 1911 Ogden, Lynwood, Millican Estates - 4.50 sq. mi.
9 1951 Windsor Park - .25 sq. mi.
10 1952 Part of Manchester - .25 sq. mi.
11 1953 West Thorncliffe, Airport - 7.50 sq. mi.
12 1954 Part of Glenpark, part of Glamorgan/Glenbrook, part of Richmond - 1.75 sq. mi.
13 1956 Part of Richmond, Strathcona, Lakeview, part of Glenpark, Blackfoot,

Glenmore and Southland - 26.00 sq. mi.
14 1961 Varsity, Silver Springs, Dalhousie, Crowchild, Nose Hill Park, Thorncliffe, Saddle Ridge, Marlboro, Forest Lawn, Dover, Eastfield, Southeast Industrial, Riverbend, Barlow, Burnsmead, Bonavista, South Bonavista, Canyon Meadows, Livingston and Midnapore - 75.25 sq. mi.
15 1963 University Heights and Montgomery - 1.50 sq. mi.
16 1964 Bowness - 3.50 sq. mi.
17 1972 MacEwan Glen - .75 sq. mi.

18 1974 Road allowance known as 68 St. East - .17 sq. mi.
19 1975 Beddington Heights - 1.35 sq. mi.
20 1976 Hawkwood, Rundle and Abbeydale - 4.35 sq. mi.
21 1979 Beddington, Scenic Acres, Sundance and McKenzie - 25.60 sq. mi.
22 1981 Applewood, West Scenic Acres, Valley Ridge and Chapparal - 5.93 sq. mi.
23 1982 Research and Development Park - 2.59 sq. mi.
24 1983 Part of East McKenzie, part of Burlington - 7.17 sq. mi.

Calgary locales

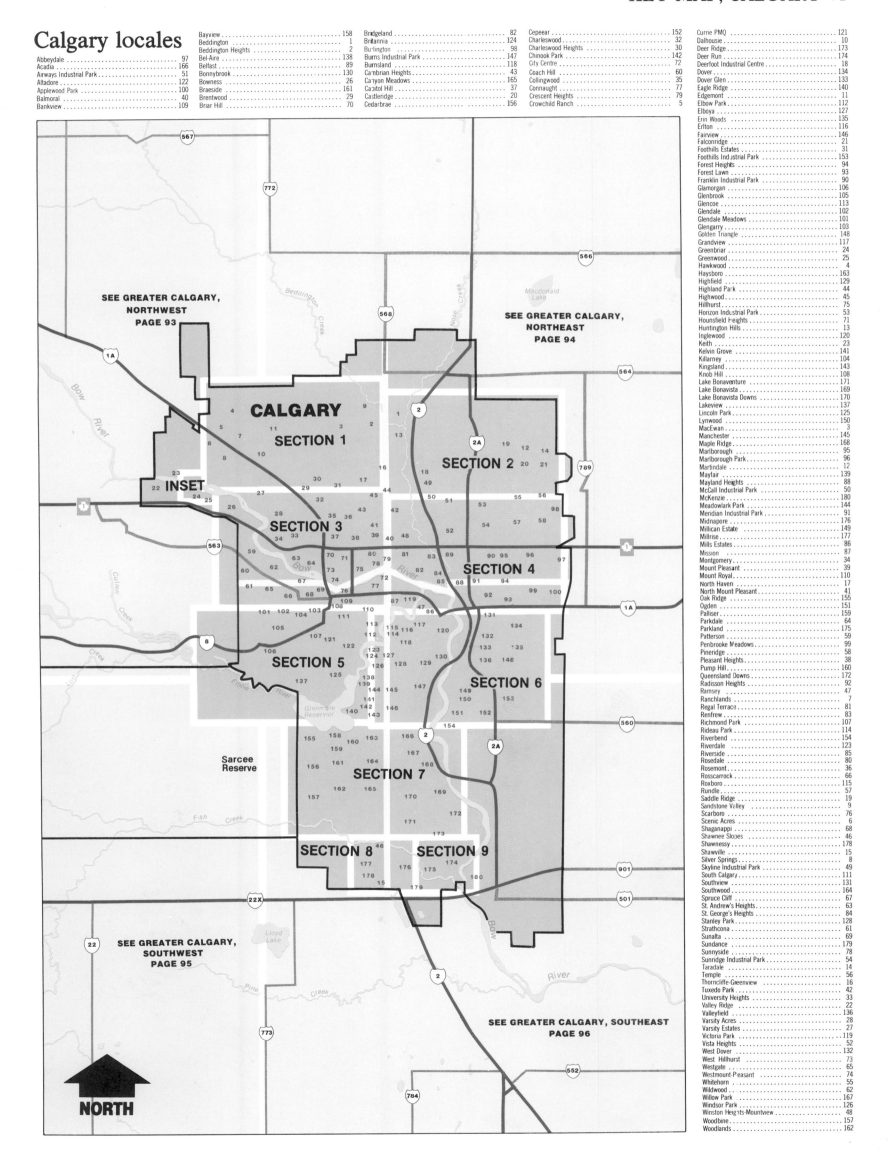

Named Streets*

Streets in older sections of Calgary are numbered; in newer sections they're often named. Index gives grid references followed by page number.

Churches

Index gives symbol number [symbol], followed by grid references, followed by page number. No symbol numbers are given for university and downtown maps (pp. 81, 82, 83) because the name is spelled out on the map.

Schools

Index gives symbol number [symbol], followed by grid references, followed by page number. No symbol numbers are given for university and downtown maps (pp. 81, 82, 83) because the name is spelled out on the map.

Hotels

Index gives symbol number [symbol], followed by grid references, followed by page number. No symbol numbers are given for university and downtown maps (pp. 81, 82, 83) because the name is spelled out on the map.

Points of Interest

Each is identified below by symbol number [symbol], followed by grid references, followed by page number. No symbol numbers are given for university and downtown maps (pp. 81, 82, 83) because the name is spelled out on the map.

8. Reorganized Church of Jesus Christ of Latter-Day Saints Ranchlands Chapel.... B3
9. Calvary Chapel Maranatha Fellowship of Calgary B2
10. St. Thomas United Church (Meetings in Dalhousie Community Hall) C3
11. Church of Jesus Christ of Latter-Day Saints B3
12. Advent Lutheran Church (Meetings in W.O. Mitchell Elementary School) B3
13. Dalhousie Mennonite Brethren Community Church C3
14. Calgary Bible Fellowship (Meetings in Silver Springs Community Centre) B3
15. Westbourne Baptist Church F3
16. Good Shepherd Moravian Community Church F3
17. Church of Jesus Christ of Latter-Day Saints F3
18. Highwood Lutheran Church F4
19. Northmount Baptist Church F4

⛪ CHURCHES

1. Ascension Catholic Parish (Meetings in St. Bede Catholic Elementary School) ... F1
2. Lutheran Triune Congregation (Meetings in Beddington Square Shopping Centre) F2
3. Beddington Pentecostal Church F2
4. Calgary Finnish Church (Meetings in Beddington Pentecostal Church) F2
5. Salvation Army - Berkshire Citadel F2
6. Westview Baptist Church A2
7. St. James Anglican Church B2

Miles
Kilometres

Adjoining Map, Page 78

20. Cambrian Heights Church of Christ...... F4
21. Christians Concerned for Life Church (Meetings in Cambrian Heights Church of Christ)................................ F4
22. Foothills Alliance Church D4
23. Hope Lutheran Church D4
24. St. Luke's Roman Catholic Church.... D4
25. Varsity Acres Presbyterian Church ... C4
26. Ambassador Baptist Church C4
27. Bowwood Gospel Chapel B4
28. Foothills United Church.................. B4
29. Assumption Roman Catholic Church .. A4
30. Shepherd of The Hills Lutheran Church A4
31. Jehovah's Witnesses Kingdom Hall (Bowness Congregation) A4
32. Bowness Baptist Church A4
33. West Calgary Full Gospel Church...... A4
34. St. Edmund's Anglican Church A4

☐ **HOTELS**
1. Crowchild Motor Inn........................ C3
2. Bowness Hotel B4
3. West Valley Motel .... Inset
4. West Wind Inn .... Inset
5. Bow Ridge Motel .... Inset

⌂ **SCHOOLS**
1. St. Bede Catholic Elementary School.... F1
2. Beddington Heights Elementary School F1
3. Dr. J. K. Mulloy Elementary School F2
4. St. Henry Catholic Elementary School F2
5. Huntington Hills Elementary Scool F3
6. St. Rita Catholic Elementary School B2
7. Ranchlands Elementary School.......... B2
8. W. O. Mitchell Elementary School...... B3
9. St. Sylvester Catholic Elementary School B3
10. Silver Springs Elementary School B3
11. West Dalhousie Elementary School C3
12. H. D. Cartwright Elementary and Junior High School.......................... C3
13. St. Dominic Catholic Elementary School C3
14. Dalhousie Elementary School C3
15. Foothills Christian Academy (Private) ... C3
16. Dr. E. W. Coffin Elementary School D3
17. Simon Fraser Junior High School D4
18. Sir Winston Churchill Senior High School D4
19. Brebeuf Catholic Elementary and Junior High School......................... D4
20. Captain John Palliser Elementary School D4
21. Colonel Sanders Elementary School F4
22. North Haven Elementary School F4
23. Dr. W. J. Collett Junior High School F4
24. Colonel Irvine Junior High School F4
25. Highwood Elementary School F4
26. Senator Patrick Burns Junior High School E4
27. St. Luke Catholic Bilingual Elementary School D4
28. Brentwood Elementary School D4
29. Varsity Acres Elementary School C4
30. St. Vincent de Paul Catholic Elementary and Junior High School..... C4
31. Marion Carson Elementary School C4
32. F. E. Osborne Junior High School C4
33. Thomas B. Riley Junior High School B4
34. Bowcroft Elementary School B4
35. Bowness Junior and Senior High School A4
36. Belvedere-Parkway Elementary School A4

For explanation of symbols, see General Legend on page 5

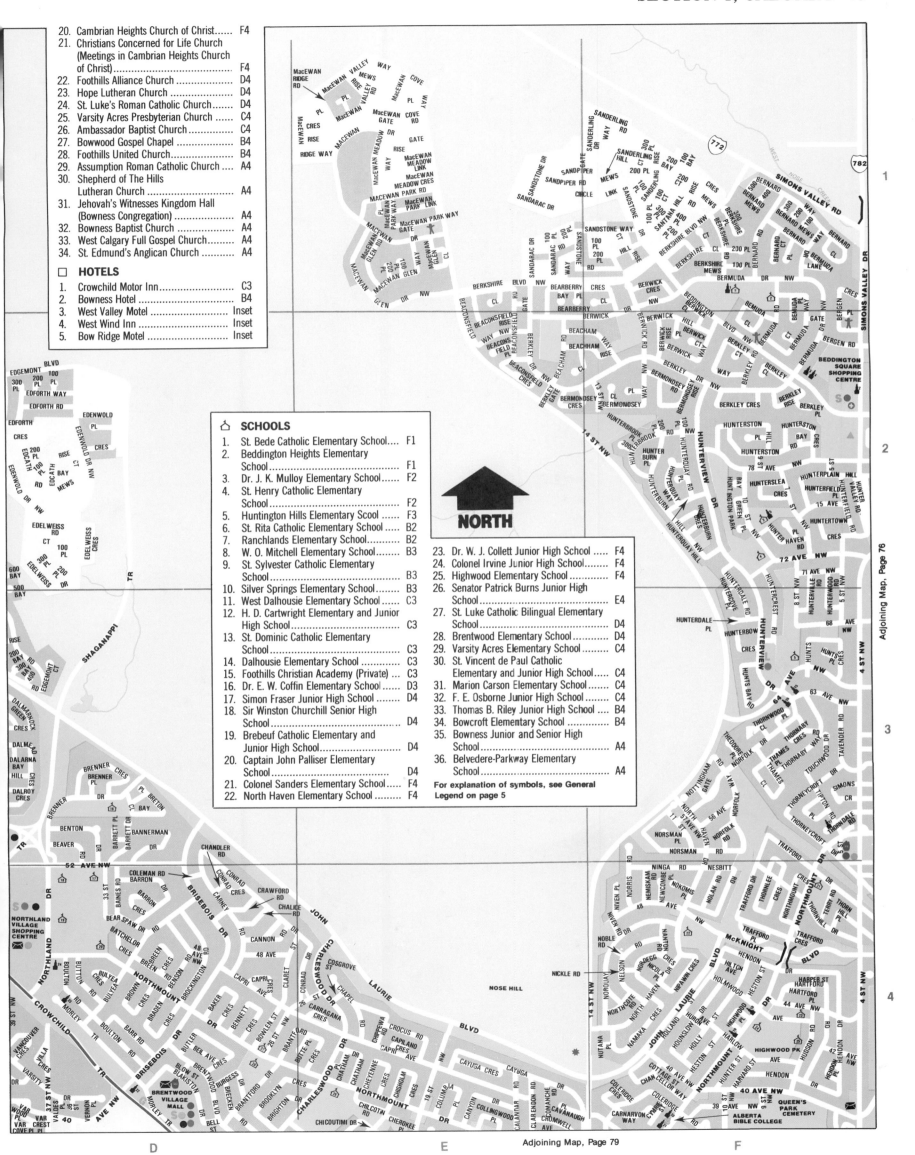

NORTH

Adjoining Map, Page 76

D   E   F

Adjoining Map, Page 75

Adjoining Map, Page 84

CHURCHES

1. Lutheran Triune Congregation (Meetings in Beddington Square Shopping Centre).................A2
2. Beddington Pentecostal Church A2
3. Calgary Finnish Church (Meetings in Beddington Pentecostal Church).........A2
4. Calgary Chinese Alliance Church A2
5. Huntington Alliance Church (Meetings in Alex Munroe Elementary School) A2
6. Symons Valley United Church (Meetings in St. Helena Catholic Junior High School).......................A3
7. Thornhill Baptist Church A3
8. Corpus Christi Roman Catholic Church A3
9. Spanish Evangelical Church (Meetings in Centre Street Evangelical Church A4
10. Centre Street Evangelical Church A4
11. Highland Mennonite Brethren Church A4
12. Calgary Evangelical Bible Church (Meetings in Colonel J. Fred Scott Elementary School) E4
13. St. Thomas More Roman Catholic Church E4
14. St. George's Anglican Church E4
15. Full Gospel Tabernacle..................E4
16. New Hope Community Church (Meetings in Falconridge Elementary School) F4

HOTELS

1. Chateau Airport C2
2. Port O'Call Inn.......................C4
3. Airliner Inn A4

SCHOOLS

1. Alex Munroe Elementary School A2
2. St. Hubert Catholic Elementary School A2
3. John G. Diefenbaker Junior and Senior High School.......................A3
4. Sir John A. MacDonald Elementary and Junior High School.......................A3
5. St. Helena Catholic Junior High School A3
6. Catherine Nichols Gunn Elementary School A3
7. Corpus Christi Catholic Elementary School A3
8. Thorncliffe Elementary School A3
9. Colonel Sanders Elementary School A4
10. Greenview Elementary School A4
11. James Fowler Senior High School........A4
12. Buchanan Elementary School A4
13. St. Wilfrid Catholic Elementary School E4
14. Colonel J. Fred Scott Elementary School E4
15. Guy Weadick Elementary School E4
16. Heritage Private Christian School (Located in Full Gospel Tabernacle) E4
17. Falconridge Elementary School F4
18. John XXIII Catholic Elementary and Junior High School........................F3

For explanation of symbols, see General Legend on page 5

CALGARY

Adjoining Map, Page 85

Miles | 0 | 0.5 | 1
Kilometres | 0 | 0.5 | 1

NORTH

Adjoining Map, Page 86

CALGARY

| Miles | 0 | 0.5 | 1 |
| Kilometres | 0 | 0.5 | 1 | 2 |

Adjoining Map, Page 75

Adjoining Map, Page 76

Adjoining Map, Page 84

Adjoining Map, Page 87

Adjoining Map, Page 88

(Map on pages 78 and 79),

⛪ CHURCHES

1. Shepherd of The Hills Lutheran Church A1
2. Assumption Roman Catholic Church A1
3. Foothills United Church A1
4. Bowwood Gospel Chapel B1
5. Maranatha Christian Reformed Church B1
6. Calgary Community Church B1
7. Faith Tabernacle B1
8. Western Baptist Church C2
9. Foothills Mennonite Church C2
10. Queen of Peace Polish Catholic Church D2
11. Foothills Lutheran Church D1
12. Brentview Baptist Church D1
13. Church of Jesus Christ of Latter-Day Saints - Bow Valley Chapel D1
14. St. Pius X Roman Catholic Church D1
15. Christian Science Church (Third Church) E1
16. St. Cyprian's Anglican Church E1
17. Canadian Martyrs Roman Catholic Church E1
18. Cambrian Heights Church of Christ E1
19. Christians Concerned for Life Church (Meetings in Cambrian Heights Church of Christ) E1
20. Cambrian Heights Baptist Church E1
21. Chinese Baptist Church (Meetings in Cambrian Heights Baptist Church) E1
22. St. Giles Presbyterian Church F2
23. Full Gospel Church Queens Park F1
24. St. Gabriel's Anglican Church F1
25. Danish Lutheran Church F1
26. Northminster United Church F1
27. Highland Mennonite Brethren Church F1
28. St. Bernard's Roman Catholic Church ... C2
29. St. Andrew's Anglican Church D2
30. Parkdale United Church D3
31. I Am Temple D3
32. Parkdale Missionary Church D3
33. Jehovah's Witnesses Kingdom Hall (Hillhurst Congregation) D3
34. Gospel Hall (West Hillhurst) D3
35. Evangelical Covenant Church D3
36. Hillhurst Church of Christ D3
37. Central Church, Seventh-Day Adventist E2
38. Faith Lutheran Church E2
39. Chinese Evangelical Free Church E2
40. Pleasant Heights United Church F2
41. St. Joseph's Roman Catholic Church F2
42. St. Michael and All Angels Anglican Church F2
43. Unitarian Church of Calgary F2
44. Metropolitan Community Church (Meetings in The Unitarian Church of Calgary) F2
45. Church of God (Seventh-Day) F1
46. Rosedale United Church F2
47. Crescent Heights Baptist Church F2
48. Church of Jesus Christ of Latter-Day Saints-Crescent Road Chapel F3
49. St. Boniface Roman Catholic Church (German) E3
50. Salvation Army - Westmount Corps E3
51. Calgary First Spiritualist Church E3
52. St. Barnabas' Anglican Church E3
53. Hillhurst United Church E3
54. First Church of the Nazarene F4
55. Hungarian Calvin Presbyterian Church F4
56. Immanuel Assembly of God Church F4
57. The House of Israel (Shaarey Tzedec Congregation) F4
58. St. Mary's Roman Catholic Cathedral F4
59. St. Paul's United Church F4
60. First Baptist Church F4
61. Christian Science Church (First Church) F4
62. Wesley United Church F4
63. St. Elizabeth's Roman Catholic Church (Hungarian) F4
64. Full Gospel Church F4
65. Grace Presbyterian Church F4
66. St. Stephen's Anglican Church E4
67. Sacred Heart Roman Catholic Church E4
68. Jehovah's Witnesses Kingdom Hall (Scarboro Congregation) E4
69. Scarboro United Church E4
70. St. Matthew's United Church D4
71. St. Martin's Anglican Church D4
72. Holy Name Roman Catholic Church C4
73. St. Demetrois Greek Orthodox Community Church C3
74. Calgary Free Methodist Church C3
75. Anglican Church of The Good Shepherd C3
76. Rosscarrock Church of Christ C4
77. Seventeenth Avenue Church of the Nazarene C4
78. St. Michael's Roman Catholic Church... C3
79. Woodcliffe United Church C3
80. Strathcona Heights Alliance Church A3
81. First Lutheran Ascension Church A3
82. Valleyview Presbyterian Church A4

☐ HOTELS

1. Bowness Hotel B1
2. Roman Antony Motel B2
3. Red Carpet Inn B2
4. Holiday Motel B2
5. Traveler's Inn B2
6. Star Motel D2
7. Round-Up Motor Inn D2
8. Avondale Motel D2
9. Mount Eisenhower Motel D2
10. Travelodge Calgary North D2
11. Circle Inn Motor Motel D2
12. Capri Motel D2
13. Cascade Friendship Inns D2
14. Village Park Inn D2
15. La Concha Motel D2
16. Royal Wayne Motor Hotel D2
17. Ranger Motor Motel E2
18. Highlander Motor Hotel E2
19. Beacon Motor Inn F2
20. Westgate Motor Hotel C4
21. Westward Inn F4

✳ POINTS OF INTEREST

1. Calgary Centennial Planetarium E3

⌂ SCHOOLS

1. Bowcroft Elementary School A1
2. Thomas B. Riley Junior High School A1
3. Assumption Catholic Elementary and Junior High School A1
4. R. B. Bennett Elementary School B1
5. Jerry Potts Elementary School C1
6. Senator Patrick Burns Junior High School D1
7. Banff Trail Elementary School D1
8. William Aberhart Senior High School D1
9. Colonel Irvine Junior High School E1
10. St. Francis Catholic High School E1
11. Collingwood Elementary School E1
12. St. Margaret Catholic Elementary and Junior High School E1
13. Rosemont Elementary School E1
14. Cambrian Heights Elementary School ... E1
15. James Fowler Senior High School F1
16. Buchanan Elementary School F1
17. Terrace Road Elementary School C2
18. Montgomery Junior High School C2
19. McKay Road Elementary School C2
20. Van Horne Secondary School D2
21. University Elementary School D2
22. Chief Crowfoot Elementary School D2
23. Parkdale Elementary and Junior High School D3
24. Briar Hill Elementary School D2
25. Branton Junior High School E2
26. Foothills Special Education Academy (Private) E2
27. Capitol Hill Elementary School E2
28. King George Elementary School F2
29. St. Joseph Catholic Elementary and Junior High School F1
30. Queen's Park Elementary School F1
31. Balmoral Elementary and Junior High School D3
32. Kensington Road Elementary School F2
33. Madelaine D'Houet Bilingual Catholic Elementary and Junior High School D3
34. Queen Elizabeth Elementary School E3
35. Queen Elizabeth Junior and Senior High School E3
36. Hillhurst Elementary Community School E3
37. Rosedale Elementary and Junior High School F2
38. Crescent Heights Senior High School F2
39. St. John Catholic Elementary School E3
40. Sunnyside Elementary Community School F3
41. Wildwood Elementary School C3
42. Westgate Elementary School C4
43. Vincent Massey Junior High School C4
44. St. Michael Catholic Elementary and Junior High School C4
45. Glenmeadow Elementary School B4
46. St. Gregory Catholic Junior High School B4
47. St. Thomas Aquinas Catholic Elementary School C4
48. Glendale Elementary School C4
49. Rosscarrock Elementary School C4
50. Spruce Cliff Elementary School C3
51. Ernest Manning Senior High School C4
52. Melville Scott Junior High School C4
53. Alex Ferguson Elementary School D4
54. St. Charles Catholic Bilingual Elementary School (Closed June 1982) D4
55. Calgary French School (Private) D4
56. Knob Hill Elementary School E4
57. Dr. Gordon Townsend School (Alberta Children's Hospital) E4
58. Logos Elementary School (Sunalta School) E4
59. Sacred Heart Catholic Elementary School E4
60. Connaught Elementary Community School E4
61. Dr. Carl Safran Special Education School F4
62. Mount Royal Junior High School E4
63. Banbury Crossroads Independent Elementary School (Private) F4
64. Western Canada Senior High School F4
65. Cliff Bungalow Elementary School F4
66. St. Mary's Catholic Elementary School F4
67. St. Mary's Catholic Community School F4
68. St. Mary's Catholic Bilingual Junior and Senior High School F4

For explanation of symbols, see General Legend on page 5

Calgary's Heritage Park

Below is a map of Heritage Park, a 60-acre peninsula jutting into Glenmore Reservoir in southwest Calgary. There, western Canada's past prior to 1914, is recreated.

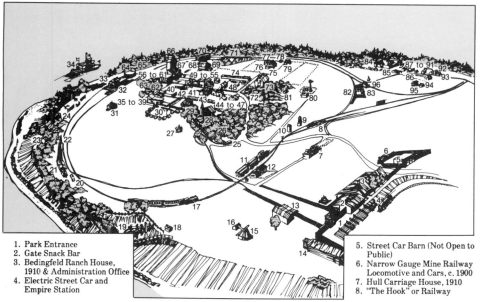

1. Park Entrance
2. Gate Snack Bar
3. Bedingfeld Ranch House, 1910 & Administration Office
4. Electric Street Car and Empire Station

5. Street Car Barn (Not Open to Public)
6. Narrow Gauge Mine Railway Locomotive and Cars, c. 1900
7. Hull Carriage House, 1910
8. "The Hook" or Railway Steam Crane, 1913
9. Railway Sand Tower, 1905
10. CPR Water Tower, 1902
11. Railway Exhibit with Historic Coaches
12. Midnapore Station, 1910
13. Curio Shop
14. Canmore Opera House, 1896
15. Bruderheim Windmill, 1910
16. Miller's Cabin, Langdon Town Hall, 1886
17. Steam Locomotive and Cars
18. Miner's Cabin, 1883
19. Water Wheel and Tunnel
20. Oil Tank Car, c. 1900
21. Dingman Discovery Well, 1913
22. Cable Tool Water Drilling Rig, 1900
23. Trapper's Cabin 1910
24. The Children's Pallisade and Playground
25. Horse Drawn Streetcar, 1882
26. Picnic Area
27. Didsbury Bandstand, 1904
28. Prince House, 1894
29. Sandstone House, 1891
30. Eugene Coste Park
31. Bowness Carousel, 1905
32. Shepard Station, 1910 and Boat Ticket Office
33. The Boat Dock Entrance
34. The S.S. Moyie
35. Vulcan Ice Cream Parlor, 1910
36. Claresholm General Store, 1904
37. Black's Jewelry Store, 1904
38. Botsford Harness Shop, 1906
39. Gledhill's Drug Store, 1908
40. Wainwright Hotel, 1906
41. Post Office and Telephone Exchange, 1908
42. Two Storey Outhouse, 1906
43. Thorpe House, 1886
44. Airdrie House, 1906
45. Rectory, 1899
46. St. Martin's Anglican Church, 1896
47. The Graveyard, 1890
48. Weedon School and Barn, 1910
49. Webster House, 1911
50. Toole Barn, 1903 (Not Open To Public)
51. Strathmore and Bow Valley Standard Print Shop, 1909
52. Baron's Pool Hall, 1910
53. Alberta Bakery, 1897
54. Flett's Blacksmith Shop, 1904
55. Nanton Livery Stable, 1910
56. Cochrane Fire Hall, 1909 and Fire Engine, 1912
57. Wing Chong Laundry, c. 1900
58. Dentist's Office, 1914
59. High River Law Office, 1909
60. Trader's Bank of Munson, 1904
61. Masonic Lodge, 1884
62. Strathmore Insurance Agent's Office, 1908
63. Atlas Lumber Yard and Office
64. Railway Round House (Not Open to Public)
65. Railway Turntable
66. Shonts Grain Elevator, 1909
67. Mannix Road Machinery, 1904
68. Ten Horse Grain Wagon Train, c. 1910
69. Gunn Barn, c. 1908
70. Train Shed (Not Open to Public)
71. Trestle Bridge (Not Open to Public)
72. Royal North West Mounted Police Barrack, 1890
73. Burns Barn, c. 1908 and Devonian Carriage Collection
74. The Machine Shed
75. Burnside Ranch House, 1904
76. The Root House
77. The Sod Shack
78. The Chicken Coop
79. Copithorne Barn, 1904 (Not Open to Public)
80. Early Colonist House Complex
81. Copithorne Barn (Not Open to Public)
82. Laggan Station, 1890
83. Bowell Station, 1896
84. Hudson's Bay Fort 1821-35
85. Walter Grant McKay Cabin, 1884
86. Gleichen School, 1886
87. Bachelor's Tent
88. Banff Curling Club House, 1898 and Photo Shop
89. North West Mounted Police Sawmill, 1875
90. Berry Creek NWMP Post, 1905
91. Homesteader's Tent
92. Drew's Saloon, 1887
93. McVittie Cabin, 1882. One of Calgary's First Houses
94. Millarville Ranchers' Hall, 1895
95. Sam Livingston's Farm, 1883
96. Indian Tipi Ring and Pole Tipi

NORTH

ST. DAVID'S UNITED CHURCH
CAPITOL HILL CRES
CASTLE RD
CROWCHILD TR NW

CAMPUS DR NW
SCURFIELD HALL OPENING 1986
SCIENCE PL NW
100 SCIENCE PL NW
200 SCIENCE PL NW
300 SCIENCE PL NW
400 SCIENCE PL NW
MATH SCIENCES BLDG
SCIENCE THEATRES BLDG
SOCIAL SCIENCES BLDG
SCIENCE "A" BLDG
SCIENCE "B" BLDG
EARTH SCIENCES BLDG
CAMPUS DR
CAMPUS GREEN NW
ARTS AND ADMINISTRATION BLDG
CAMPUS LINK NW
EDUCATION BLDG
CHURCH OF JESUS CHRIST OF LATTER-DAY SAINTS
CAMPUS GATE NW
CAMPUS DR NW
INFORMATION
POST OFFICE
FOOTHILLS ATHLETIC PK
McMAHON STADIUM
24 AVE NW

CHURCH OF JESUS CHRIST OF LATTER DAY SAINTS
PETRO-CANADA EXPLORATION RESEARCH DEVELOPMENT LABORATORY
31 ST NW
32 AVE NW
SWAN MALL WALK
LIBRARY
NORTH LIBRARY BLOCK
LIBRARY TOWER
LIBRARY PL NW
MacEWAN HALL
SCIENCE OF CALGARY HALL
CENTRE OF MacEWAN HALL
(MEETINGS IN MacEWAN HALL)
UNIVERSITY THEATRE
CALGARY HALL
REEVE THEATRE
UNIVERSITY DR
UNIVERSITY DR
USHER RD
UNIVERSITY PL NW
UNDERHILL DR NW
ULSTER RD NW
URQUHART RD

VOCATIONAL REHABILITATION RESEARCH INSTITUTE
UNIVERSITY RESEARCH PK
33 ST NW
300 ENGINEERING PL NW
200 ENGINEERING PL NW
100 ENGINEERING PL NW
ENGINEERING BLDG
ENGINEERING PL NW
NICKEL ARTS MUSEUM
MacEWAN LANE
THEATRE PL NW
COLLEGIATE RD
COLLEGIATE
DINING CENTRE
RUNDLE HALL
CASTLE HALL
BREWSTER HALL
UDELL RD NW
UPPER PL NW
UNDERHILL DR NW
UTAH DR NW
URBANA RD
UXBRIDGE RD
URALTA RD

UNIVERSITY BLVD
DINNIES BAY NW
DAYCARE BY ARRANGEMENT ONLY
PHYSICAL EDUCATION BLDG
KANANASKIS HALL
NORQUAY HALL
ATHLETIC TRACK AND FIELD
UPLANDS PL NW
UPTON PL NW
UNDERWOOD PL NW
ULYSSES ST
UNDERHILL DR
ULRICH RD NW
24 AVE NW
UNITY PL NW
UNDERHILL DR NW

37 ST NW
39 ST NW
VARMOOR PL NW
VARMOOR RD NW
JACKSON PL NW
HARRIS PL NW
VARSITY COURTS
FAMILY STUDENT HOUSING
VARLEY DR NW
LISMER GREEN NW
CASSON GREEN NW
GROUNDS DEPARTMENT
GREENHOUSE
WEATHER RESEARCH STATION
UNIVERSITY WAY
UNIVERSITY BLVD NW
32 AVE NW
TOWING COMPOUND
PHYSICAL MAINTENANCE PLANT
CAMPUS PATROL
CENTRAL HEATING BLDG

Adjoining Map, Page 78

Arts and Administration Bldg.	D2
Athletic Track and Field.	B2
Bio Science Bldg.	D1
Brewster Hall.	C2
Calgary Hall.	C2
Campus Patrol.	A2
Castle Hall.	C2
Central Heating Bldg.	B2
Dining Centre.	C2
Earth Sciences Bldg.	C1
Education Bldg.	D2
Engineering Bldg.	C1
Greenhouse.	A1
Grounds Department.	A1
Information.	D2
Kananaskis Hall.	B2
Library.	C2
Library Tower.	C2
MacEwan Hall.	C2
Math Sciences Bldg.	D1
McMahon Stadium.	D3
Nickel Arts Museum.	C1
Norquay Hall.	B2
North Library Block.	C2
Petro-Canada Exploration and Research Development Laboratory.	C1
Physical Education Bldg.	C2
Physical Maintenance.	A2
Post Office.	C2
Reeve Theatre.	C2
Residences.	B2/C2
Rundle Hall.	C2
Science "A" Bldg.	D1
Science "B" Bldg.	D1
Scurfield Hall (Opening 1986).	D2
Social Sciences Bldg.	D2
Towing Compound.	A2
University Theatre.	C2
Varsity Courts (Family Student Housing).	A1
Vocational Rehabilitation Research Institute.	C1
Weather Research Station.	A1

Feet 0 100 200 300 400 500 600
Metres 0 100 200

Adjoining Map, Page 78

Building Index

Name	Grid		Name	Grid
1st Street Plaza	E2		Gulf Canada Square	C3
4th and 4th Bldg	C2		Hanover Place	D2
505 - 8 Ave. West Bldg	C3		Harry Hays Bldg	E2
5th and 5th Bldg	C2		Heritage Place	B2
640 - 7 Ave. S.W. Bldg	B2		Hollinsworth Bldg	D3
700 - 6 Ave. S.W. Bldg	B2		Home Oil Tower	D3
706 - 7 Ave. S.W. Bldg	B2		Humford Bldg	B2
855 - 8 Ave. S.W. Bldg	B3		Husky Bldg	B3
926 - 5 Ave. S.W. Bldg	B2		I. B. M. Bldg	
999 Bldg	B3		Imperial Old Main Bldg	C2
A. G. T. Bldg	D2,E2		Indian Friendship Centre	D1
Alberta Hotel Bldg	D3		Ithacan Bldg	C2
Alberta Place	B3		Iveagh House	B2
Alberta Vocational Centre	E2,F2		J. J. Bowlen Provincial Bldg	C2
Alberta Wheat Pool Bldg	D2		La Caille	B1
Alpine Bldg	C2		Lancaster Bldg	B2
Amfac Place	B2		Lavalin Centre	B2
Amoco Canada Bldg	C2		Livingstone House	B2
Andrew Davidson Bldg	E2		London House	C2
Aquitaine Tower	B2		Lougheed Bldg	D2
Atrium I	B2		Manalta Bldg	B2
Atrium II	B2		Manulife Bldg	B3
B. P. House	C2		McDougall Place	B2
Baker House	E2		McFarlane Tower	B2
Bank of Canada Bldg	C2		Medical Centre	B3
Bank of Montreal Tower	C2,D2		Mercantile Bank Bldg	C2
Barron Bldg	C3		Merland Centre	C2
Bernco Bldg	B2		Mobil Tower	D2
Bow Bldg	A2		Monenco Place	B2
Bow Valley Square 1,2,3&4	B2		Montreal Trust Bldg	C3
Bowclaire Apts	B1		Mount Royal House	D3
Bowside Manor	D1		Natural Resources Bldg	E3
Braidie Bldg	C2		Neff Apts	B2
Briar Bldg	A3		Neilson Block	E3
Britannia Bldg	B2		New Court House	C2
Brown Clinic Bldg	B3		Ng Tower	D1
Burns Bldg	E3		Norcen Tower	B2
Cadillac Fairview Towers	D2		Northland Bank Tower	C2
Calgary Board of Education Centre Bldg	E2		Nova Tower	B3
Calgary Centre for Performing Arts	E3		Old Court House	C2
Calgary Chamber of Commerce Bldg	D2		Old Shell Bldg	A3
Calgary Convention Centre	E3		O'Neil Towers	A3
Calgary House	C2		O. I. Kwan Place	D1
Calgary International Hostel			O.I. Kwan Senior Citizens' Residence	D1
Calgary Municipal Bldg	E3		Palliser Square	D3,E3
Calgary Place	C2,D2		Panarctic Bldg	B3
Calgary Public Bldg	E3		Pan Canadian Plaza	D3
Calgary Public Library	E3		Parisian Bldg	E3
Calgary Real Estate Board	B2		Pembina Place	A3
Calgary Sun Bldg	B3		Penny Lane	C3
Calgary Tower	D3,E3		Penthouse Towers	B3
Canada Life Tower	B2		Pentland Place	B2
Canada Place	D2		Petex Bldg	C2
Canada Trust Bldg	C2, D3		Petro Chemical Bldg	B3
Canadian Fina Bldg	B3		Petro-Canada Centre	D2
Canadian Hunter Bldg	C2		Petro-Canada Towers	D2
Canadian Imperial Bank of Commerce Bldg	D3		Petroleum Club	B2
Canadian Oxy Bldg	C3		Place 800	B2
Carketen House	B2		Place Concorde	B2
Carter Place	E2		Place Nine Six	A2
Cascade Bldg	D2		Plaza 1000	A2
Catholic School Centre	E2		Plaza Bldg	C2
Centennial Bldg	B2		Police Station	D2
Centennial Shops	C3		Post Office	B2,B3,C2,C3,D2,D3,E2
Central Trust Bldg	C3		Prince's Island Place	B2
Centre Four Bldg	C3		Provincial Court and Remand Centre	E2
Century Gardens	B3		Q.R. Centre	B3
Century Square 3	B3		Regency House	C2
Century Square 2	D1		Rimbey House	B2
Century Square I	D2		Rocky Mountain Courts	E2
Chateau Towers	B2		Rocky Mountain Plaza	E2
Chevron Plaza	C2		Roslyn Bldg	C2
City Hall	E3		Royal Bank Bldg	D3
City Trust Bldg	C2		Scoba Centre	C3
Commerce Centre	A2		Selkirk House	C2
Commercial Beverage Bldg	E2		Shelbourne Bldg	C2
Compton Place	B2		Shell Centre	C2
Continental Plaza Apts			Small Claims Court House	C2
Continental Towers	A3,B3		Soma Bldg	C2
Daon Bldg	C2		Sonoma Place	B2
Devonian Gardens	D3		Standard Life Bldg	C2
Dome Tower	D3		Sun Life Plaza	D2
Eaton's Department Store	C3		Suncor Tower	C2
Eau Claire Estates	C1		Sundance Apts	B2
Eau Claire Place II			Sundial Apts	B2
Eau Claire Towers	B2		Sutton Hall	A3
Edinburgh Place	B2		Telecommunication Bldg	C2
Elveden House	B3		The 400 Club	B2
Edward's Place	F3		The Bay Department Store	D3
Energy Resources Bldg	C2		Toronto-Dominion Square	D3
Esso Plaza	D2		Trans-Canada Pipeline Tower	C3
Executive Place	B2		Tnmac House	
Fire Station	A3,E2		Veritas Bldg	C2
Foothills Place	E2		Wattco Bldg	C2
Ford Tower	C2		Westbourne Bldg	C3
Frontier Bldg	D2		Western Canada Place	B3
Glenbow Museum	E3		Western Centre	B3
Government of Canada Bldg	E2		Western Union Insurance Bldg	C2
Grain Exchange Bldg	D3		Y. M. C. A. Bldg	C2
Greyhound Bus Terminal	D2		Y. W. C. A. Bldg	D2
Greyhound Garage	D1		Yuk Sum Ng Centre	B2
Guinness House	B3			

Map Labels

Adjoining Map, Page 79 — Adjoining Map, Page 79

Feet 0 100 200 300 400 500 600 — Metres 0 100 200

MEMORIAL DR NW · LOUISE BRIDGE · BOW RIVER · EAU CLAIRE ESTATES · EAU CLAIRE AVE · LA CAILLE · BOWCLAIRE APTS · 1 AVE SW · 2 AVE SW · DOWNTOWN HELIPORT · TRINITY LUTHERAN CHURCH · YUK SUM NG CENTRE · EAU CLAIRE TOWERS · 3 AVE SW · SONOMA PLACE · LIVINGSTONE HOUSE · COMPTON PLACE · VERITAS BLDG · EAU CLAIRE PLACE II · NEFF APTS · McDOUGALL PLACE · THE 400 CLUB · McFARLANE TOWER · MERLAND CENTRE · REGENCY HOUSE · SUNCOR TOWER · 4 AVE SW · BOW BLDG · PRINCE'S ISLAND PLACE · McDOUGALL SCHOOL · PHILLIPS BLDG · PLAZA BLDG · SELKIRK HOUSE · LONDON HOUSE · CANADIAN HUNTER BLDG · 926 - 5 AVE SW BLDG · SUNDANCE APTS · HERITAGE PLACE · TRIMAC HOUSE · ENERGY RESOURCES BLDG · WATTCO BLDG · PRINCE ROYAL INN · AQUITAINE TOWER · NORTHLAND BANK TOWER · CHEVRON PLAZA · MERCANTILE BANK BLDG · 5 AVE SW · RIMBEY HOUSE · LAVALIN CENTRE · ATRIUM I · CALGARY REAL ESTATE BOARD · NORCEN TOWER · CHATEAU TOWERS · STANDARD LIFE BLDG · 5th AND 5th BLDG · FIVE TEN FIFTH BLDG · IMPERIAL OLD MAIN BLDG · EDINBURGH PLACE · CARKETEN HOUSE · ATRIUM II · PLACE 7 · CANADA LIFE TOWER · 700 6 AVE SW BLDG · SHELBOURNE BLDG · BRAIDE ITHACAN BLDG · PETEX BLDG · LUTHERAN TRIUNE CONGREGATION (MEETINGS IN CALGARY HOUSE) · CALGARY HOUSE · PLACE NINE SIX · PLACE 800 · 10 ST · 9 ST · 8 ST · 7 ST · 6 ST · 5 ST · 4 ST · 6 AVE SW · KNOX UNITED CHURCH · PLACE CONCORDE · POST OFFICE · SUNDIAL APTS · MONENCO PLACE · BERNCO BLDG · EXECUTIVE PLACE · BRITANNIA BLDG · ALPINE BLDG · FORD TOWER · SMALL CLAIMS COURT · HUMFORD BLDG · MANALTA BLDG · 706 7 AVE SW BLDG · 640 7 AVE SW BLDG · J.J. BOWLEN PROVINCIAL BLDG · CITY TRUST BLDG · OLD COURT HOUSE · NEW COURT HOUSE · COMMERCE CENTRE · PLAZA 1000 · PENTLAND PLACE · AMFAC PLACE · SANDMAN INN · CENTENNIAL BLDG · 7 AVE SW · LIGHT RAIL TRANSIT · PEMBINA PLACE · SUTTON HALL · BRIAR BLDG · O'NEIL TOWERS · PENTHOUSE TOWERS · BROWN CLINIC BLDG · NOVA TOWER · GUINNESS HOUSE · ELVEDEN HOUSE · IVEAGH HOUSE · MANULIFE HOUSE · WESTBURNE BLDG · LORD NELSON INN · MEDICAL CENTRE · CENTURY GARDENS · CANADIAN FINA BLDG · HOLIDAY INN · WESTERN UNION INSURANCE · SOMA BLDG · BARRON BLDG · TRANS CANADA PIPELINES TOWER · CENTENNIAL SHOPS · 8 AVE SW · OLD SHELL BLDG · 85-8 AVE SW BLDG · WESTERN CENTRE · Q.R. CENTRE · PANARCTIC PLAZA · POST OFFICE · PETRO CHEMICAL · HUSKY BLDG · ALBERTA PLACE · WESTERN CANADA PLACE · CANADIAN OXY BLDG · PENNY LANE · 505 8 AVE WEST BLDG · MONTREAL TRUST BLDG · CONTINENTAL TOWERS · 9 AVE SW · NORTH · FIRE STATION · CANADIAN PACIFIC RAILWAY · 999 BLDG · CALGARY SUN BLDG · 10 AVE SW · 1A

LEGEND FOR CALGARY, SECTION 4
(Map on pages 84 and 85)

♦ CHURCHES

1. Highland Mennonite Brethren Church ... A1
2. Danish Lutheran Church ... A1
3. Northminster United Church ... A1
4. Jehovah's Witnesses Kingdom Hall (Tuxedo Park Congregation) ... A1
5. North Hill Gospel Hall ... A1
6. Church of God (Seventh-Day) ... A1
7. St. Paul's Roman Catholic Church ... A1
8. Covenant of Grace Evangelical Church ... A1
9. Chalmers Presbyterian Church ... A2
10. Anglican Church of the Transfiguration ... A2
11. North Hill Church of The Nazarene ... A2
12. Unitarian Church of Calgary ... A2
13. German Church of God ... A2
14. Calgary Evangelical Bible Church (Meetings in Colonel J. Fred Scott Elementary School) ... D1
15. King of Glory Lutheran Church ... D1
16. Peace Community Christian Reformed Church (Meetings in Rundle Elementary School) ... D2
17. Rockyview Alliance Church ... F1
18. St. Paul's Lutheran Church (Meetings in Rundle Community Hall) ... E1
19. Centennial Presbyterian Church ... E1
20. Calgary Mennonite Fellowship Church ... E1
21. Evangelical Missionary Church (Meetings in Calgary Mennonite Church) ... E1
22. Pineridge Seventh-Day Adventist Church ... E1
23. Prince of Faith Lutheran Church ... E1
24. The Properties Baptist Church (Meetings in Douglas Harkness Elementary School) ... E2
25. South Calgary Mennonite Brethren Church (Meetings in St. Patrick's Catholic Elementary School) ... E2
26. Robert McClure United Church (Meetings in Pineridge Elementary School) ... E2
27. Rosedale United Church ... A2
28. Crescent Heights Baptist Church ... A2
29. Sharon Lutheran Church ... A2
30. Church of Jesus Christ of Latter-Day Saints Crescent Road Chapel ... A2
31. Ukrainian Catholic Church of Assumption ... A2
32. Russian Greek Orthodox Church of ...

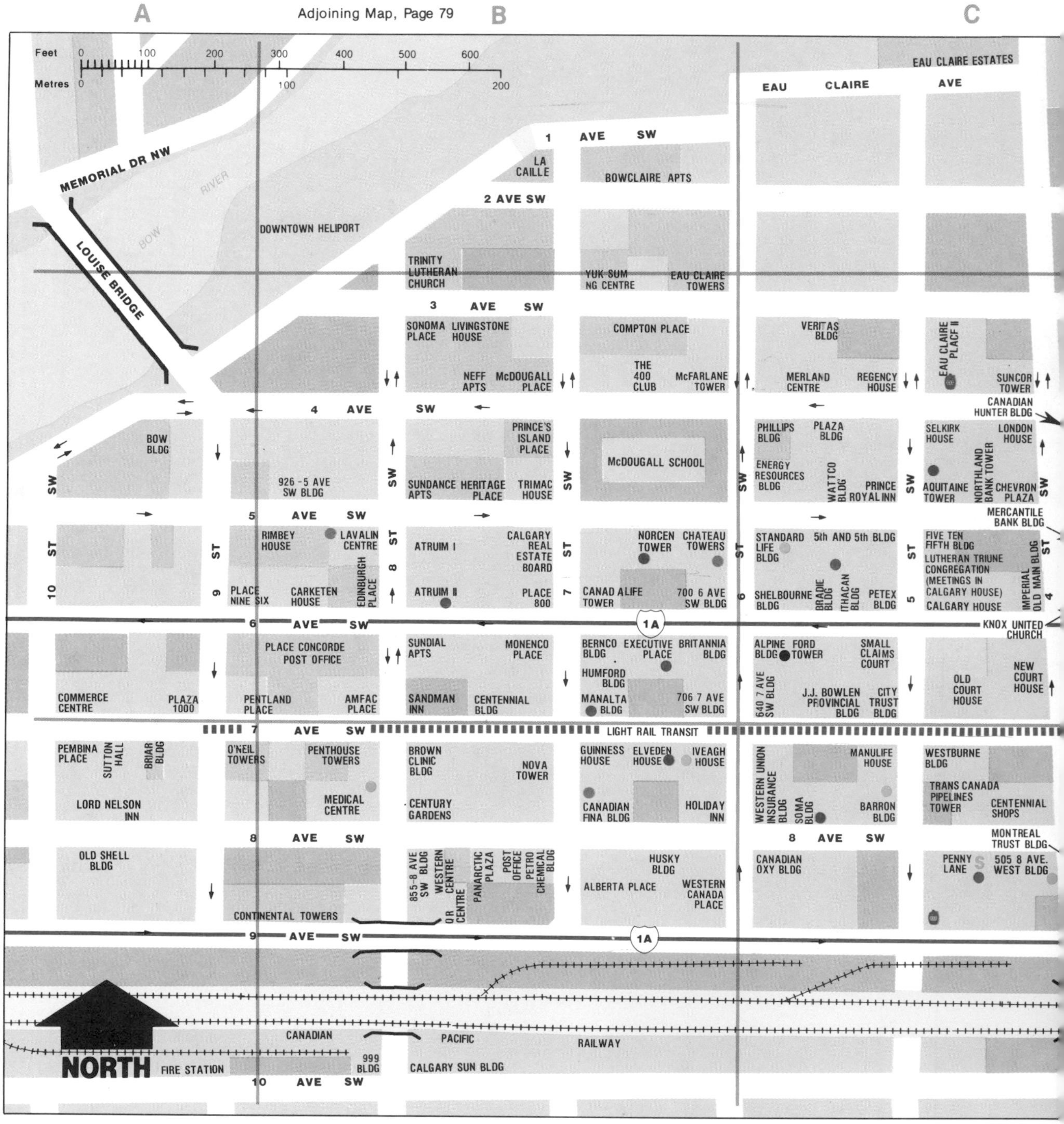

All Saints ... B2
33. Renfrew United Church ... B2
34. Temple Baptist Church ... B2
35. All Saints Anglican Church ... B2
36. Crossroads Community Gospel Church ... C2
37. St. Clement's Roman Catholic Church ... C2
38. Ascension Lutheran Church ... C2
39. First Missionary Baptist Church (Meetings in Rochell Executive Centre) ... D2
40. Marlborough Pentecostal Church ... D2
41. Grace Baptist Church ... D3
42. St. Mark's Roman Catholic Church ... E2
43. Liberty Baptist Church (Meetings in Abbeydale Elementary School) ... F3
44. Our Lady of Perpetual Help Roman Catholic Church ... A3
45. Calgary Buddhist Temple ... A3
46. St. John's Lutheran Church ... A3
47. Baptist Tabernacle ... A3
48. St. Matthew's Lutheran Church ... A3
49. Christian Fellowship Church ... B3
50. Salem Evangelical Church ... B3
51. Bridgeland Seventh-Day Adventist Church ... B3
52. Foursquare Gospel Church ... B3
53. Elim Assembly Pentecostal (German) ... B3
54. Church of Jesus Christ of Latter-Day Saints - Forest Lawn Chapel ... D3
55. Forest Heights Baptist Church ... E3
56. Prince of Peace Lutheran Church ... E3
57. Calgary East Church of The Nazarene ... E3
58. First Church of the Nazarene ... A4

59. Hungarian Calvin Presbyterian Church ... A4
60. Immanuel Assembly of God Church ... A4
61. St. Mary's Roman Catholic Cathedral ... A4
62. The House of Israel (Shaarey Tzedec Congregation) ... A4
63. Church of Jesus Christ (Apostolic) of Calgary ... A4
64. St. Ann's Roman Catholic Church ... B4
65. Jehovah's Witnesses Kingdom Hall (Grandview Congregation) ... B4
66. Standard Church of America ... B4
67. Canadian Reformed Church ... B4
68. St. Andrew's Italian Roman Catholic Church ... B4
69. St. John's Anglican Church ... B4
70. Trinity United Church ... B4
71. Temple of Praise Outreach ... B4
72. Church of Emmanuel Lutheran ... D4
73. Forest Lawn United Church ... D4
74. Salvation Army - Forest Lawn Corps ... D4
75. Truth Tabernacle United Pentecostal Church ... D4
76. Jehovah's Witnesses Kingdom Hall (Forest Lawn Congregation) ... D4
77. Forest Lawn Community Church ... D4
78. Forest Grove Mennonite Church (Meetings in Forest Lawn Senior High School) ... D4
79. Holy Trinity Roman Catholic Church ... D4
80. Evangelical Mennonite Church ... E4

☐ HOTELS

1. Hillcrest Motel ... A1
2. Sheraton Cavalier Hotel ... C1

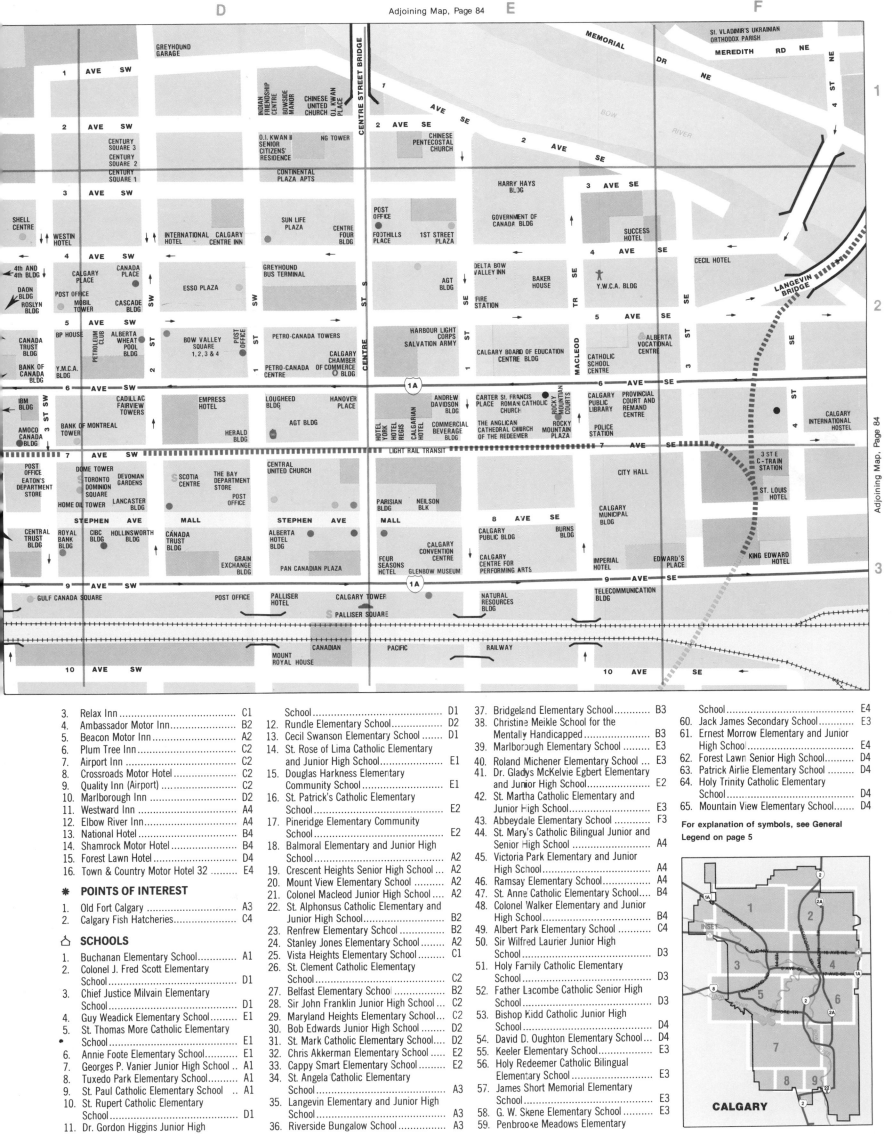

Adjoining Map, Page 84

MEMORIAL DR NE

ST. VLADIMIR'S UKRAINIAN ORTHODOX PARISH

MEREDITH RD NE

GREYHOUND GARAGE

INDIAN FRIENDSHIP CENTRE

BOWSIDE MANOR

CHINESE UNITED CHURCH

O.I. KWAN PLACE

CENTURY SQUARE 3

CENTURY SQUARE 2

CENTURY SQUARE 1

O.I. KWAN II SENIOR CITIZENS' RESIDENCE

NG TOWER

CONTINENTAL PLAZA APTS

CHINESE PENTECOSTAL CHURCH

HARRY HAYS BLDG

GOVERNMENT OF CANADA BLDG

SUCCESS HOTEL

SHELL CENTRE

WESTIN HOTEL

INTERNATIONAL HOTEL

CALGARY CENTRE INN

SUN LIFE PLAZA

CENTRE FOUR BLDG

POST OFFICE

FOOTHILLS PLACE

1ST STREET PLAZA

CECIL HOTEL

4th AND 4th BLDG

DAON BLDG

ROSLYN BLDG

CALGARY PLACE

CANADA PLACE

POST OFFICE

MOBIL TOWER

CASCADE BLDG

ESSO PLAZA

GREYHOUND BUS TERMINAL

AGT BLDG

DELTA BOW VALLEY INN

BAKER HOUSE

FIRE STATION

Y.W.C.A. BLDG

CANADA TRUST BLDG

BANK OF CANADA BLDG

BP HOUSE

Y.M.C.A. BLDG

PETROLEUM CLUB

ALBERTA WHEAT POOL BLDG

BOW VALLEY SQUARE 1, 2, 3 & 4

POST OFFICE

PETRO-CANADA TOWERS

PETRO-CANADA CENTRE

CALGARY CHAMBER OF COMMERCE BLDG

HARBOUR LIGHT CORPS SALVATION ARMY

CALGARY BOARD OF EDUCATION CENTRE BLDG

CATHOLIC SCHOOL CENTRE

ALBERTA VOCATIONAL CENTRE

IBM BLDG

AMOCO CANADA BLDG

CADILLAC FAIRVIEW TOWERS

BANK OF MONTREAL

EMPRESS HOTEL

HERALD BLDG

LOUGHEED BLDG

AGT BLDG

HANOVER PLACE

HOTEL YORK

HOTEL REGIS

CALGARIAN HOTEL

ANDREW DAVIDSON BLDG

COMMERCIAL BEVERAGE HOTEL

CARTER ST. FRANCIS PLACE

ROMAN CATHOLIC CHURCH

THE ANGLICAN CATHEDRAL CHURCH OF THE REDEEMER

ROCKY MOUNTAIN COURTS

ROCKY MOUNTAIN PLAZA

CALGARY PUBLIC LIBRARY

POLICE STATION

PROVINCIAL COURT AND REMAND CENTRE

CALGARY INTERNATIONAL HOSTEL

LIGHT RAIL TRANSIT

POST OFFICE

EATON'S DEPARTMENT STORE

DOME TOWER

TORONTO DOMINION SQUARE

HOME OIL TOWER

DEVONIAN GARDENS

LANCASTER BLDG

SCOTIA CENTRE

THE BAY DEPARTMENT STORE

POST OFFICE

CENTRAL UNITED CHURCH

PARISIAN BLDG

NEILSON BLK

CITY HALL

CALGARY MUNICIPAL BLDG

3 ST E C-TRAIN STATION

ST. LOUIS HOTEL

CENTRAL TRUST BLDG

ROYAL BANK BLDG

CIBC BLDG

HOLLINSWORTH BLDG

CANADA TRUST BLDG

GRAIN EXCHANGE BLDG

ALBERTA HOTEL BLDG

PAN CANADIAN PLAZA

STEPHEN AVE MALL

FOUR SEASONS HOTEL

CALGARY CONVENTION CENTRE

GLENBOW MUSEUM

CALGARY PUBLIC BLDG

CALGARY CENTRE FOR PERFORMING ARTS

BURNS BLDG

IMPERIAL HOTEL

EDWARD'S PLACE

KING EDWARD HOTEL

GULF CANADA SQUARE

POST OFFICE

PALLISER HOTEL

PALLISER SQUARE

CALGARY TOWER

NATURAL RESOURCES BLDG

TELECOMMUNICATION BLDG

MOUNT ROYAL HOUSE

CANADIAN PACIFIC RAILWAY

LANGEVIN BRIDGE

Adjoining Map, Page 84

For explanation of symbols, see General
Legend on page 5

CALGARY

Adjoining Map, Page 76

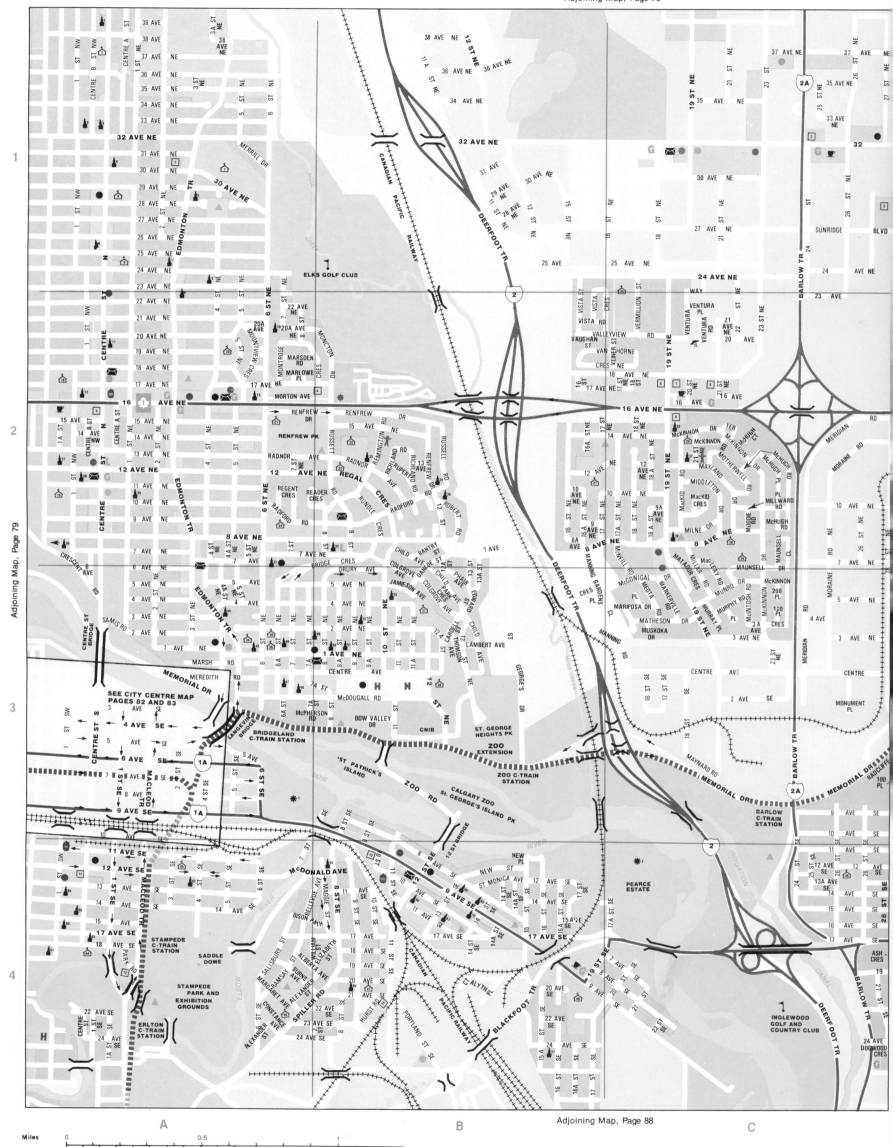

Adjoining Map, Page 79

SEE CITY CENTRE MAP
PAGES 82 AND 83

Adjoining Map, Page 88

Miles 0   0.5   1
Kilometres 0   0.5   1   2

Adjoining Map, Page 77

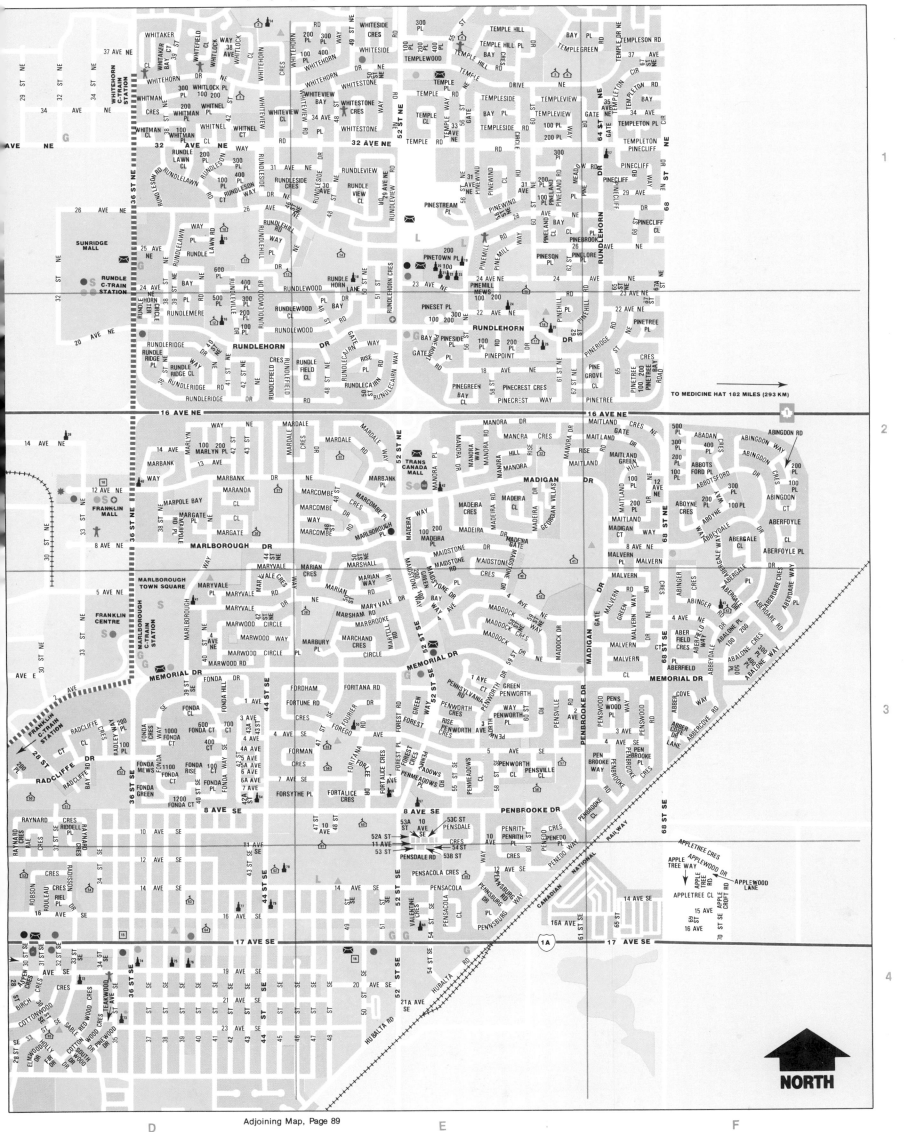

TO MEDICINE HAT 182 MILES (293 KM)

NORTH

Adjoining Map, Page 89

Adjoining Map, Page 78

⛪ CHURCHES

1. Emmanuel Christian Reformed
   Church C1
2. Bethel Baptist Church..................... C1
3. Church of God Pentecostal D1
4. Killarney Baptist Church D1
5. First Mennonite Church E1
6. Bethany Chapel.............................. E1
7. Calgary South Reformed Church E1
8. Christ Anglican Church (Elbow Park).... F1
9. Southminster United Church F1
10. West Hills Community Presbyterian
    Church (Meetings in Southminster
    United Church) F1
11. First Christian Reformed Church E1
12. St. Mark's Anglican Church.............. E1
13. South Calgary Church of The
    Nazarene E1
14. Grace Lutheran Church.................... D1
15. Knox Presbyterian Church D1
16. Christ Lutheran Church D1
17. Westminster United Church C1
18. Church of God at Glamorgan C2
19. St. Stephen's Byzantine Ukrainian
    Catholic Church C2
20. St. George's Protestant Chapel........... E2
21. Christ The King Church E2
22. Altadore Baptist Church E2
23. United Pentecostal Chapel E2
24. Riverview United Church.................. F2
25. St. Philip the Evangelist Anglican
    Church F2
26. First Evangelical Free Church F2
27. St. James Roman Catholic Church E2
28. Christian Community Church (Meetings
    in Mount Royal College D2
29. Lakeview Baptist Church D2
30. St. Laurence Anglican Church D3
31. Lakeview United Church D3
32. First Assembly (Pentecostal) Church F3
33. Beth Israel Synagogue F3
34. First Alliance Church F3
35. Salvation Army - Glenmore Temple...... F3
36. Shepherd King Lutheran Church......... F4
37. St. Peter's Anglican Church.............. F4
38. Kingsland Baptist Church F4
39. Mountainview Seventh-Day Adventist
    Church (Meetings in Kingsland Baptist
    Church) F4
40. St. Andrew's United Church F4
41. Church of Jesus Christ of Latter-Day
    Saints - Glenmore Chapel F4
42. St. Andrew's Presbyterian Church F4

✱ POINTS OF INTEREST

1. Heritage Park.................................. E4

⛪ SCHOOLS

1. St. Gregory Catholic Junior High
   School.. C1
2. St. Thomas Aquinas Catholic
   Elementary School C1
3. Glendale Elementary School.............. D1
4. Calgary Christian School (Private)........ C1
5. Glenbrook Elementary School............ C1
6. A. E. Cross Junior High School........... D1
7. Holy Name Catholic Elementary
   School.. D1
8. Killarney Elementary School D1
9. Viscount Bennett Junior and Senior
   High School................................... E1
10. Richmond Elementary School............ E1
11. St. Charles Catholic Bilingual
    Elementary School (Closed
    June 1982) E1
12. King Edward Elementary and Junior
    High School................................... E1
13. Earl Grey Elementary School F1
14. I. L. Peretz Jewish Elementary
    School.. E1
15. William Reid Elementary School.......... F1
16. Menno Simons Mennonite Elementary
    and Junior High School (Private)......... F1
17. Rideau Park Elementary and Junior
    High School................................... F1
18. Elbow Park Elementary School F1
19. Elboya Elementary and Junior High
    School.. F2
20. St. Anthony Catholic Elementary
    School.. F2

21. Baptist Leadership Training School
    (Private)....................................... E2
22. St. Raymond Catholic School (Closed
    June 1979) E2
23. Lycee Louis Pasteur, Private French
    School E2
24. Altadore Elementary School E2
25. Christian Deaf Centre (Private)
    (Located in United Pentecostal
    Chapel).. E2
26. Dr. Oakley Elementary and Junior High
    School.. E1
27. Currie Elementary School E2
28. Sir Samuel Steele Junior High School .. E2
29. Bishop Carroll Catholic High School..... E2
30. Clinton Ford Elementary School E2
31. Sir James Lougheed Elementary
    School.. D1
32. St. Andrew's Catholic Elementary
    School.. D2
33. Glamorgan Elementary School............ D2
34. Central Memorial Senior High School ... E2
35. Shaughnessy Secondary School.......... E2
36. Emily Follensbee Special Education
    School.. F2
37. Windsor Park Elementary School F2
38. St. James Catholic Elementary and
    Junior High School.......................... E3
39. Sarcee Elementary School (Closed
    June 1982) D3
40. Clem Gardner Elementary School........ D3
41. Montessori Elementary School (Private)
    (Meetings in Clem Gardner Elementary
    School) D3
42. St. Leo Catholic Elementary School..... D3
43. Bishop Pinkham Junior High School D3
44. Jennie Elliott Elementary School D3
45. Lakeview Elementary School E3
46. Bel-Aire Elementary School F3
47. Calgary Hebrew School F3
48. Glenmore Christian Academy (Private)
    (Located in First Alliance Church)........ F3
49. Milton Williams Junior High School...... F3
50. St. Augustine Catholic Elementary and
    Junior High School.......................... F3
51. Chinook Park Elementary School......... F4
52. Henry Wise Wood Senior High
    School.. F4
53. Kingsland Elementary School F4
54. Haysboro Elementary School............. F4
55. Woodman Junior High School............. F4
56. Bishop Grandin Catholic High School ... F4

**For explanation of symbols, see General
Legend on page 5**

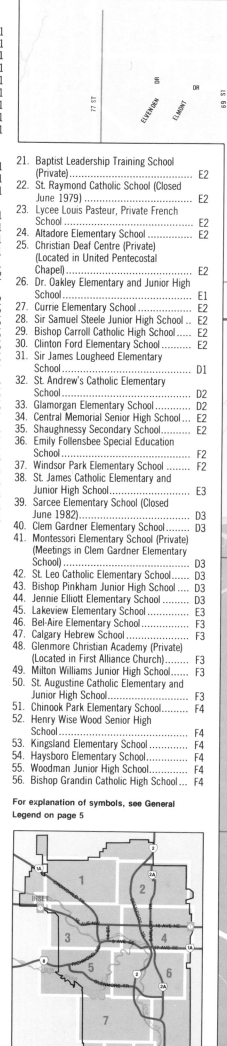

CALGARY

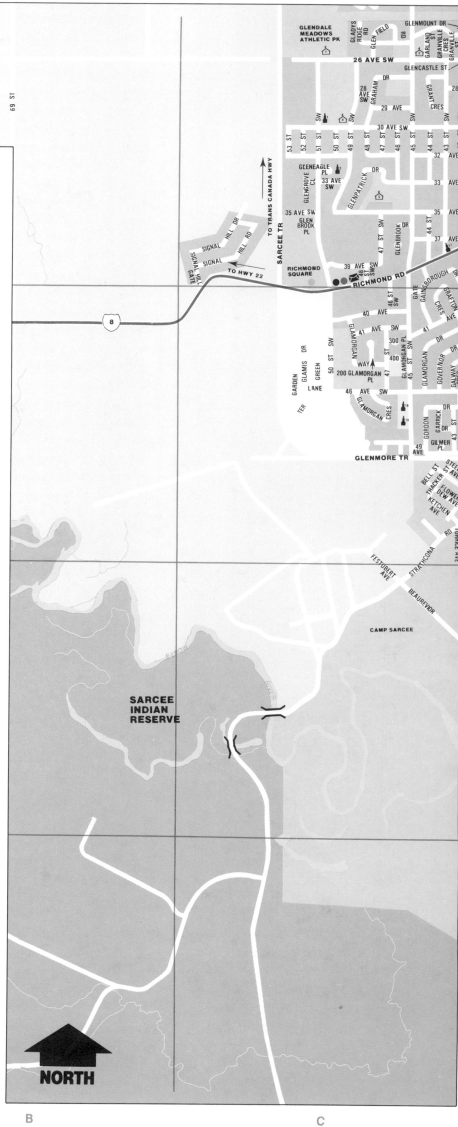

SARCEE
INDIAN
RESERVE

CAMP SARCEE

NORTH

Miles 0   0.5   1
Kilometres 0   0.5   1   2

A   B   C

Adjoining Map, Page 79

Adjoining Map, Page 88

Adjoining Map, Page 90

Adjoining Map, Page 87

STAMPEDE GROUNDS

ERLTON C-TRAIN STATION

24 AVE SE
26 AVE SE
24 AVE SW
25 AVE SW
26 AVE SW
27 AVE
28 AVE
29 AVE
30 AVE
31 AVE
34 AVE SW
37 AVE SW
38 AVE SW
38A AVE
39 AVE SW
40 AVE SW

HILLCREST AVE
ROXBORO RD
POLKBORO GLEN RD
RIDEAU RD
5A ST
5 ST
4 ST SW
3 ST
2 ST
MISSION RD
CENTRE ST
MACLEOD TR
SPILLER RD

CEMETERY
CEMETERY
CEMETERY

BRIGGS AVE
25 AVE SE
DARTMOUTH RD
HIGHFIELD RD
BLACKFOOT TR
8 ST SE
9 ST
10 ST SE
11A ST SE
34 AVE SE

BURNSLAND RD
MANCHESTER
BLACKBURN RD
BRANDON ST
CLEVELAND CRES

GULF REFINERY
BONNYBROOK RD
CANADIAN PACIFIC RAILWAY
9 AVE SE
SANCTUARY RD
24 AVE SE
26 AVE SE
28 AVE
30 AVE
34 AVE SE
16 ST
16A ST
17 ST

OGDEN RD
CANADIAN NATIONAL RAILWAY
14 ST SE
15 ST SE
36 AVE
38 AVE
41 AVE
42 AVE SE
14A ST SE
15A ST SE
16A ST SE
17A ST SE
43 AVE SE
44 AVE
47 AVE

42 AVENUE C-TRAIN STATION
41 AVE
42 AVE SE
MANHATTAN RD
MANITOBA RD
MANITOU RD
MANILLA RD
HIGHFIELD AVE PL
HASTINGS CRES
46 AVE SE
48 AVE
12 ST SE

RIVER DALE
CLIFFE AVE
PARK AVE
STANLEY PK
BRUNSWICK AVE
STANLEY DR
STANLEY CRES
44 AVE SW
45 AVE SW
46 AVE SW
47 AVE SW
48 AVE SW
49 AVE SW
50 AVE SW
51 AVE SW
52 AVE SW
53 AVE SW
54 AVE SW
55 AVE SW
56 AVE SW
57 AVE SW
58 AVE SW

51 AVE SE
53 AVE SE
58 AVE SE
BURBANK CRES
BURBANK RD
BURLEIGH CRES
BLACKFOOT TR
CANADIAN PACIFIC RAILWAY
11 ST SE

53 AVE
22 ST SE
LYNNVIEW RD
LYNNVIEW RISE
LYNNVIEW CT
BAY
LYNNBROOK GATE
LYNNBROOK
LYSANDER
LYNNVIEW CRES
LYNNWOOD
CRESTWOOD RD
LYNN RD
20A ST SE
LYNNDALE CRES
22A ST

59 AVE
60 AVE SE
62 AVE SE
64 AVE SE
5 ST SE
6 ST SE
BURBANK ROAD
DEERFOOT TR

CHINOOK SHOPPING CENTRE
CHINOOK C-TRAIN STATION
MEADOW VIEW RD SW
MACLEOD TR
KINGSMERE CRES
60 AVE
61 AVE
65 AVE
67 AVE SW
68 AVE SW
69 AVE SW

GLENMORE TR
FORGE RD
FARRELL RD
FISHER ST
FAIRMOUNT DR
FRANKLIN
FOSTER
FAWN CRES
FERNCLIFF
FYFFE
FULHAM ST
FARNHAM
FREDSON RD
FULLERTON RD
FLAVELLE RD
FROBISHER BLVD

LYSANDER
LYNNOVER RD
LYNNOVER CRES
LYTTON CRES
OGDEN CRES
OGDEN
MILLICAN RD
18 ST
18A ST SE
19 ST SE
20 ST SE
69 AVE SE
72 AVE SE
74 AVE
76 AVE
80 AVE
20A ST SE
21 ST SE
21A ST
22 ST
22A ST

71 AVE
73 AVE
HERITAGE DR
75 AVE SW
FAIRVIEW DR
FOXWELL RD
FOLEY RD
FERNE PL
FIELDING DR
FLINT
FOUNTAIN
FLEETWOOD
78 AVE SW
78 AVE SE
77 AVE
82 AVE SE
84 AVE SE
86 AVE SE

HERITAGE C-TRAIN STATION
HERITAGE DR
HADDON RD
HORTON RD
MACLEOD TR
BONAVENTURE DR
AVONBURN RD
ASHLEY CRES
ATLAS DR
ATHABASCA ST
ALLANWOOD ST
ALLSTON AVE
CHARLINGTON
AMBER RD
ABERDEEN RD
ATTICA AVE
ADDISON DR
ASHWORTH AVE
ARLINGTON PL
BAY
ALDERWOOD CL

BLACKFOOT TR
FAIRMOUNT DR
FRASER RD
RAILWAY ST
DEER GLEN DR
HERITAGE DR
70 AVE

DEERFOOT TR
BOW RIVER

GLENMORE TR WAY
RIVERSIDE RD
RIVER SIDE RD
RIVERVIEW WAY PL
RIVERGREEN CRES
RIVERVIEW CRES
RIVERVIEW CL
RIVERGREEN CRES
RIVERVALLEY DR
RIVERBROOK WAY
RIVERBIRCH RD
RIVERBIRCH CRES
RIVERBEND DR
RIVERBEND GATE
RIVERVALLEY CRES
RIVERGLEN WAY
RIVERGLEN CRES
RIVERCROFT PL
RIVER CREST DR
OLYMPIA DR
OLYMPIA CRES
RIVERCROFT
18 ST SE
20A ST SE
21A ST
22A ST
100 PL
200 PL
83 AVE
84 AVE

Adjoining Map, Page 91

Miles 0   0.5   1
Kilometres 0   0.5   1   2

A   B   C

Adjoining Map, Page 85

CHURCHES

1. Parkhill Church of Christ A1
2. Temple of Praise Outreach C1
3. St. Luke's Anglican Church D1
4. St. Philip the Evangelist Anglican Church A2
5. St. Anthony's Roman Catholic Church A2
6. Fairview Baptist Church A4
7. McDougall United Church................ A4
8. St. Bernadette's Roman Catholic Church C3
9. Ogden United Church D4
10. St. Augustine's Anglican Church......... D4
11. New Life Pentecostal Community Church C4
12. South Hill Christian Church.............. D4

HOTELS

1. Atlanta Motel A1
2. Stampeder Inn A1
3. Holiday Inn A2
4. Majestic Inn A2
5. Cambourne Motor Court A2
6. Barclay's Inn A2
7. Blackfoot Inn B3
8. Tradewinds Hotel A3
9. Travelodge Calgary South A3
10. Flamingo Motor Hotel A4
11. Glenmore Inn D4

POINTS OF INTEREST

1. Inglewood Bird Sanctuary C1

SCHOOLS

1. Erlton Elementary School (Temporarily Closed) A1
2. Rideau Park Elementary and Junior High School A1
3. Mountain View Elementary School....... D1
4. West Dover Elementary School D1
5. Holy Cross Catholic Elementary and Junior High School D1
6. Ian Bazalgette Junior High School D1
7. Valleyview Elementary School E1
8. Erin Wood Elementary School E1
9. Harold W. Riley Elementary School...... D1
10. Elboya Elementary and Junior High School A2
11. Providence Child Development Centre (Private) A2
12. Windsor Park Elementary School A2
13. Kingsland Elementary School A4
14. Le Roi Daniels Elementary School A4
15. Fairview Elementary and Junior High School A4
16. St. Matthew Catholic Elementary and Junior High School A4
17. Dr. Norman Bethune Elementary School A4
18. Acadia Elementary School B4
19. Banting-Best Elementary School C3
20. Sherwood Elementary and Junior High School C3
21. St. Bernadette Catholic Elementary School C3
22. Ogden Elementary School................ C4

For explanation of symbols, see General Legend on page 5

NORTH

CALGARY

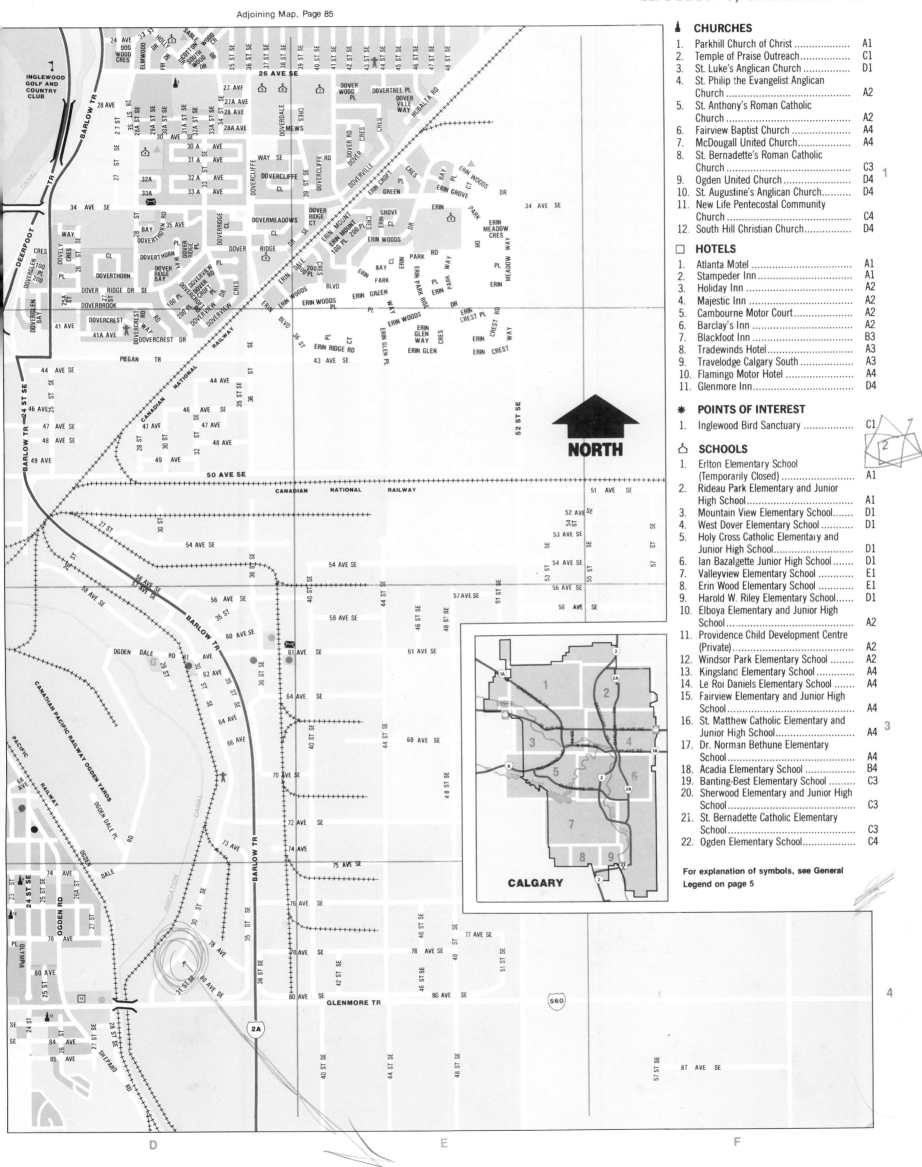

Adjoining Map, Page 87

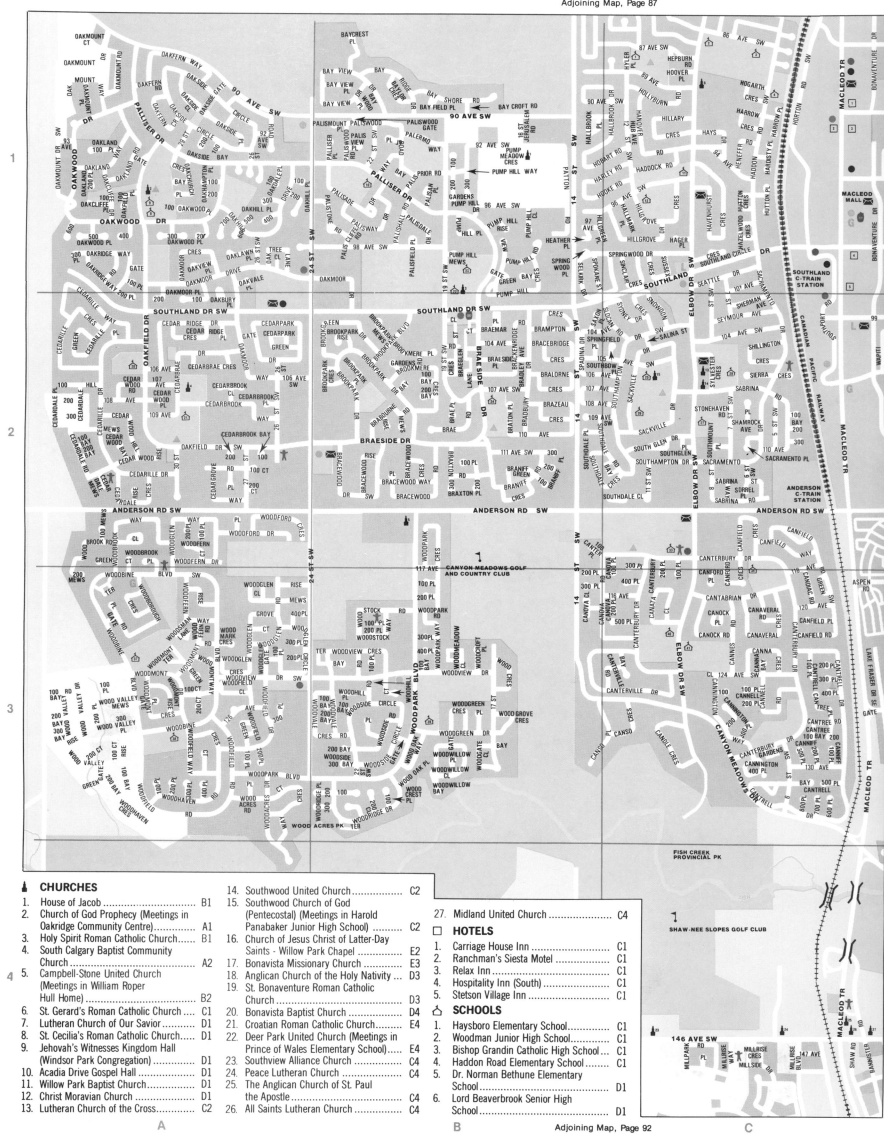

⛪ CHURCHES

1. House of Jacob B1
2. Church of God Prophecy (Meetings in Oakridge Community Centre) A1
3. Holy Spirit Roman Catholic Church...... B1
4. South Calgary Baptist Community Church A2
5. Campbell-Stone United Church (Meetings in William Roper Hull Home) B2
6. St. Gerard's Roman Catholic Church C1
7. Lutheran Church of Our Savior D1
8. St. Cecilia's Roman Catholic Church..... D1
9. Jehovah's Witnesses Kingdom Hall (Windsor Park Congregation) D1
10. Acadia Drive Gospel Hall D1
11. Willow Park Baptist Church D1
12. Christ Moravian Church D1
13. Lutheran Church of the Cross............ C2
14. Southwood United Church................. C2
15. Southwood Church of God (Pentecostal) (Meetings in Harold Panabaker Junior High School) C2
16. Church of Jesus Christ of Latter-Day Saints - Willow Park Chapel E2
17. Bonavista Missionary Church E3
18. Anglican Church of the Holy Nativity ... D3
19. St. Bonaventure Roman Catholic Church D3
20. Bonavista Baptist Church D4
21. Croatian Roman Catholic Church......... E4
22. Deer Park United Church (Meetings in Prince of Wales Elementary School)..... E4
23. Southview Alliance Church C4
24. Peace Lutheran Church C4
25. The Anglican Church of St. Paul the Apostle C4
26. All Saints Lutheran Church C4
27. Midland United Church C4

☐ HOTELS

1. Carriage House Inn C1
2. Ranchman's Siesta Motel.............. C1
3. Relax Inn C1
4. Hospitality Inn (South) C1
5. Stetson Village Inn C1

⌂ SCHOOLS

1. Haysboro Elementary School............. C1
2. Woodman Junior High School............. C1
3. Bishop Grandin Catholic High School ... C1
4. Haddon Road Elementary School C1
5. Dr. Norman Bethune Elementary School D1
6. Lord Beaverbrook Senior High School D1

Adjoining Map, Page 92

Miles 0   0.5   1

Kilometres 0   0.5   1   2

A   B   C

Adjoining Map, Page 88

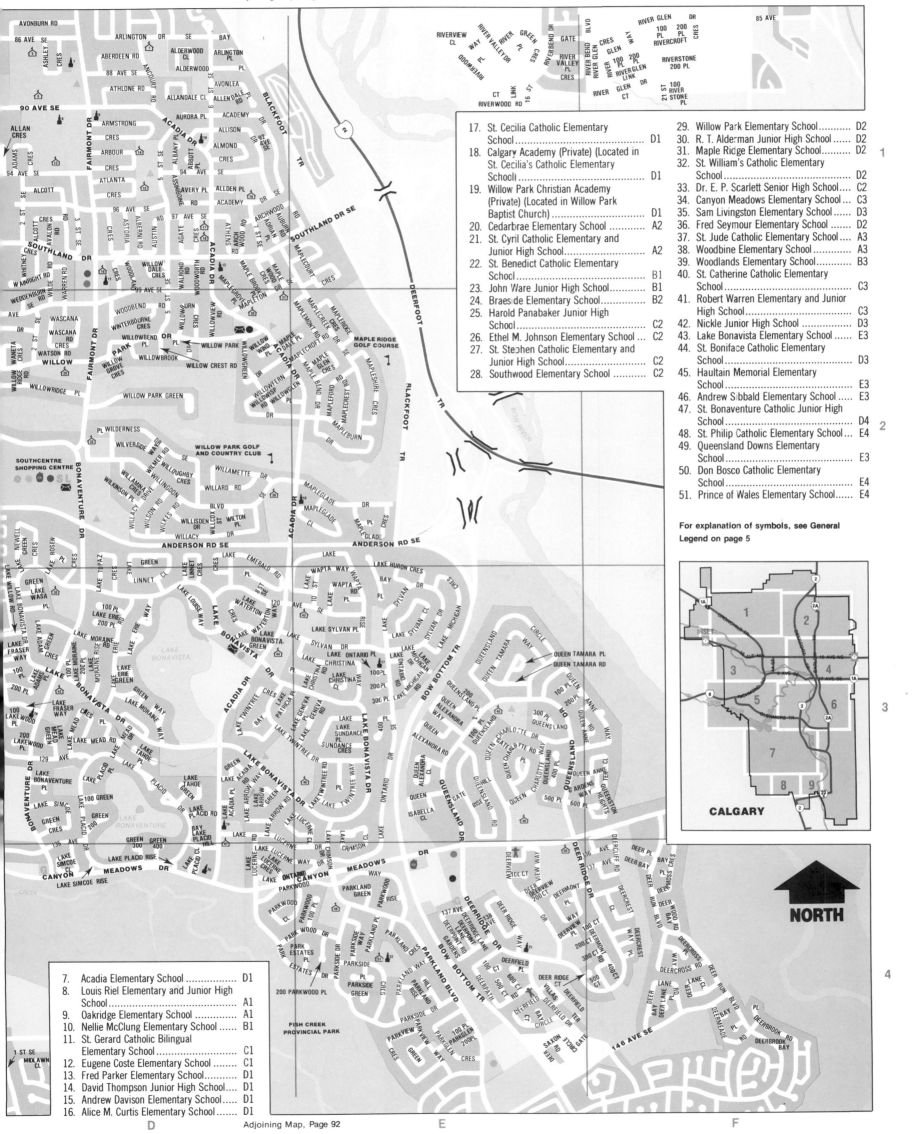

17. St. Cecilia Catholic Elementary School D1
18. Calgary Academy (Private) (Located in St. Cecilia's Catholic Elementary School) D1
19. Willow Park Christian Academy (Private) (Located in Willow Park Baptist Church) D1
20. Cedarbrae Elementary School A2
21. St. Cyril Catholic Elementary and Junior High School A2
22. St. Benedict Catholic Elementary School B1
23. John Ware Junior High School B1
24. Braeside Elementary School B2
25. Harold Panabaker Junior High School C2
26. Ethel M. Johnson Elementary School ... C2
27. St. Stephen Catholic Elementary and Junior High School C2
28. Southwood Elementary School C2

29. Willow Park Elementary School D2
30. R. T. Alderman Junior High School D2
31. Maple Ridge Elementary School D2
32. St. William's Catholic Elementary School D2
33. Dr. E. P. Scarlett Senior High School C2
34. Canyon Meadows Elementary School ... C3
35. Sam Livingston Elementary School ... D3
36. Fred Seymour Elementary School ... D2
37. St. Jude Catholic Elementary School ... A3
38. Woodbine Elementary School A3
39. Woodlands Elementary School B3
40. St. Catherine Catholic Elementary School C3
41. Robert Warren Elementary and Junior High School C3
42. Nickle Junior High School D3
43. Lake Bonavista Elementary School ... E3
44. St. Boniface Catholic Elementary School D3
45. Haultain Memorial Elementary School E3
46. Andrew Sibbald Elementary School E3
47. St. Bonaventure Catholic Junior High School D4
48. St. Philip Catholic Elementary School ... E4
49. Queensland Downs Elementary School E3
50. Don Bosco Catholic Elementary School E4
51. Prince of Wales Elementary School E4

For explanation of symbols, see General Legend on page 5

CALGARY

NORTH

7. Acadia Elementary School D1
8. Louis Riel Elementary and Junior High School A1
9. Oakridge Elementary School A1
10. Nellie McClung Elementary School ... B1
11. St. Gerard Catholic Bilingual Elementary School C1
12. Eugene Coste Elementary School C1
13. Fred Parker Elementary School D1
14. David Thompson Junior High School D1
15. Andrew Davison Elementary School D1
16. Alice M. Curtis Elementary School D1

Adjoining Map, Page 92

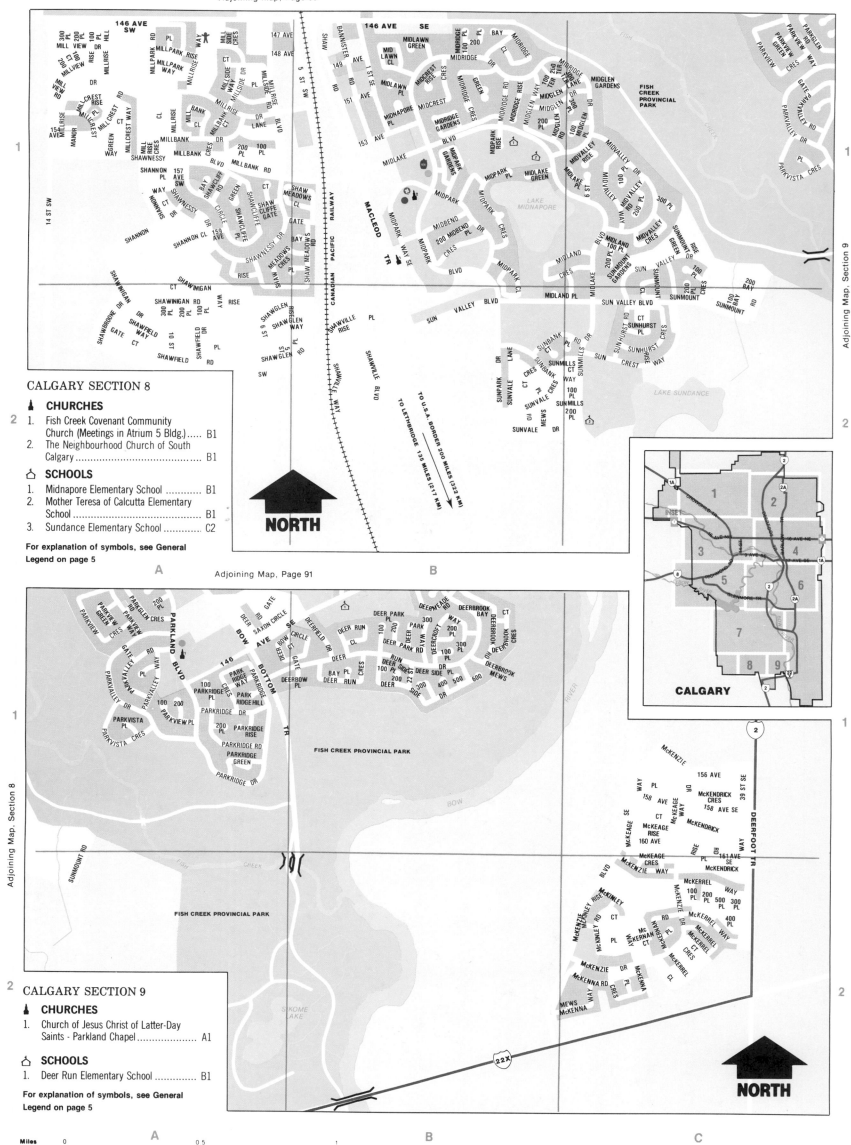

Adjoining Map, Page 91

Adjoining Map, Section 9

Adjoining Map, Section 8

CALGARY SECTION 8

♠ CHURCHES
1. Fish Creek Covenant Community Church (Meetings in Atrium 5 Bldg.) B1
2. The Neighbourhood Church of South Calgary B1

⌂ SCHOOLS
1. Midnapore Elementary School B1
2. Mother Teresa of Calcutta Elementary School B1
3. Sundance Elementary School C2

For explanation of symbols, see General Legend on page 5

NORTH

TO U.S.A. BORDER 200 MILES (322 KM)
TO LETHBRIDGE 135 MILES (217 KM)

CALGARY

CALGARY SECTION 9

♠ CHURCHES
1. Church of Jesus Christ of Latter-Day Saints - Parkland Chapel A1

⌂ SCHOOLS
1. Deer Run Elementary School B1

For explanation of symbols, see General Legend on page 5

NORTH

Miles   0   0.5   1
Kilometres 0   0.5   1   2

LEGEND

♣ CHURCHES

1. St. James Anglican Church
2. Red Deer United Church
3. Millarville Anglican Christ Church
4. Gospel Chapel
5. St. Michael's Roman Catholic Church
6. Lewis Memorial United Church
7. Pentecostal Church

☐ HOTELS

1. Black Diamond Hotel
2. Triple A Motel
3. Turner Valley Inn

⌂ SCHOOLS

1. Red Deer Lake Elementary and Junior High School
2. Millarville Elementary School
3. C. Ian McLaren Elementary and Junior High School
4. Oilfields Junior and Senior High School
5. Turner Valley Elementary and Junior High School

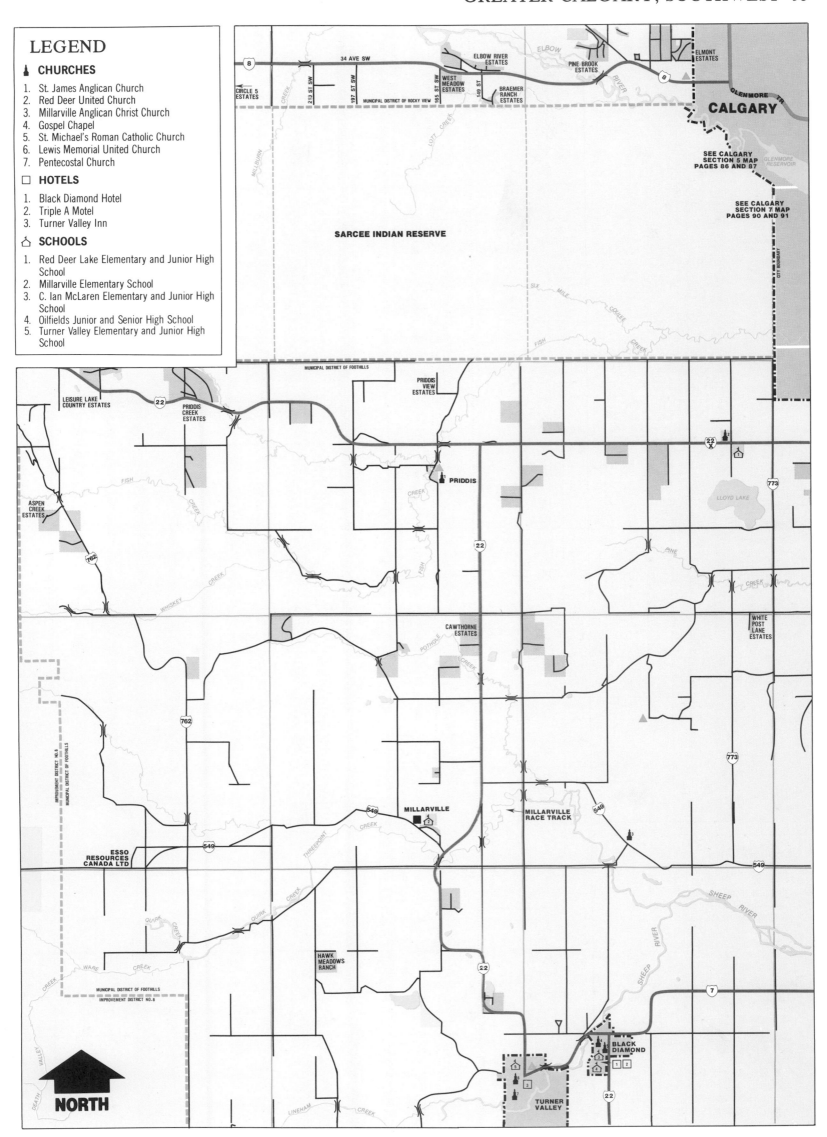

NORTH

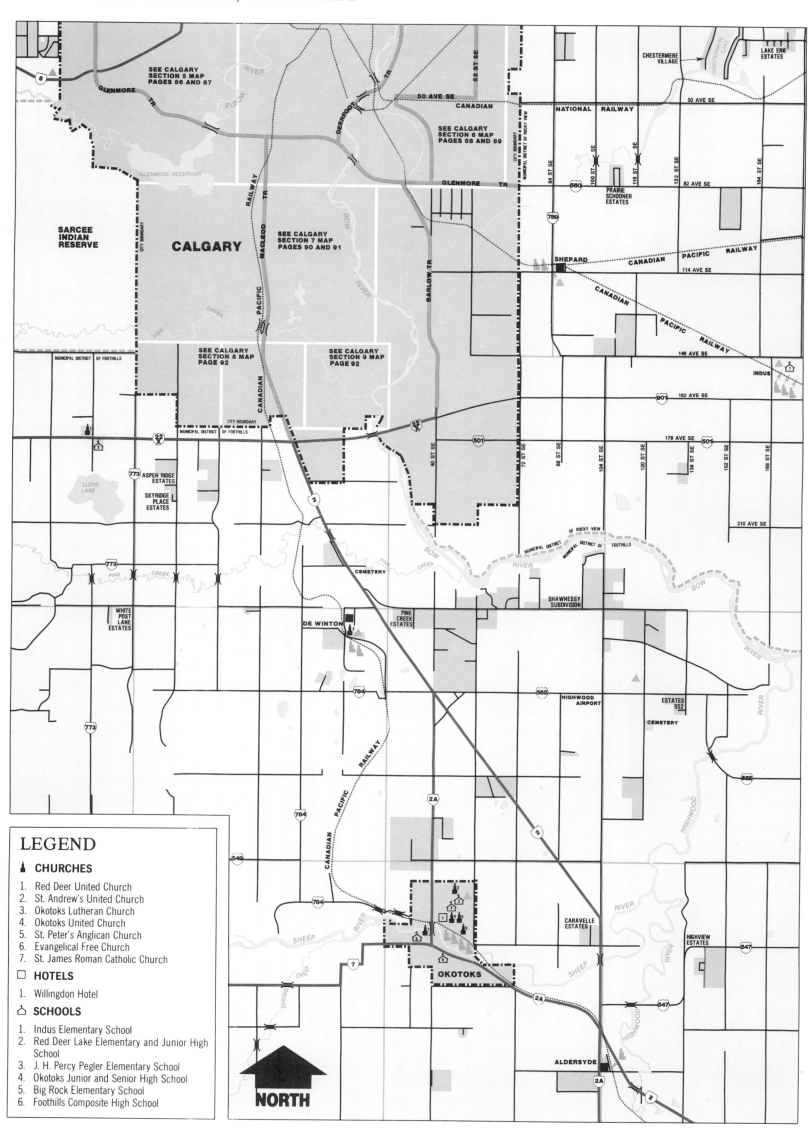

LEGEND

CHURCHES

1. Red Deer United Church
2. St. Andrew's United Church
3. Okotoks Lutheran Church
4. Okotoks United Church
5. St. Peter's Anglican Church
6. Evangelical Free Church
7. St. James Roman Catholic Church

HOTELS

1. Willingdon Hotel

SCHOOLS

1. Indus Elementary School
2. Red Deer Lake Elementary and Junior High School
3. J. H. Percy Pegler Elementary School
4. Okotoks Junior and Senior High School
5. Big Rock Elementary School
6. Foothills Composite High School

NORTH

Miles   1   0   1   2   3
Kilometres   1   0   1   2   3

Airdrie

Population: 10,431.

Location: On Highway 2, 17 miles (28 km.) north of Calgary.

Street System: In the older part of town on the west side of the highway, streets run north and south and are named. Avenues run east-west from Centre Avenue to 6 Avenue N. and from Centre Avenue to 3 Avenue S. Odd numbers are on the south side of the avenues and on the west side of the streets. In the newer areas of town streets are named.

Transportation Facilities: Airdrie is on the CP Rail line but has no passenger rail service. Cardinal Coach provides bus service to and from Calgary twice daily and Greyhound has three buses daily each way to Calgary and two to and from Edmonton. There is no scheduled air service. Inter-city courier service is available.

History: Airdrie was first settled by railway workers building the Calgary and Edmonton Railway which was completed in 1891. The community was named by William McKenzie, an engineer with the railway, after a village near his home in Glasgow, Scotland. Airdrie was incorporated in 1909, and became a town in 1974.

LEGEND

⚐ CHURCHES

1. Pentecostal Church
2. Airdrie United Church
3. Church of The Nazarene

☐ HOTELS

1. Horseman Motel
2. Airdrie Motor Inn
3. Driftwood Inn

⌂ SCHOOLS

1. George McDougall Junior High School
2. Edwards Elementary School
3. Airdrie Elementary and Junior High School
4. Muriel Clayton Elementary School
5. Bert Church High School
6. R.J. Hawkey Elementary School

For explanation of symbols, see General Legend on Page 5

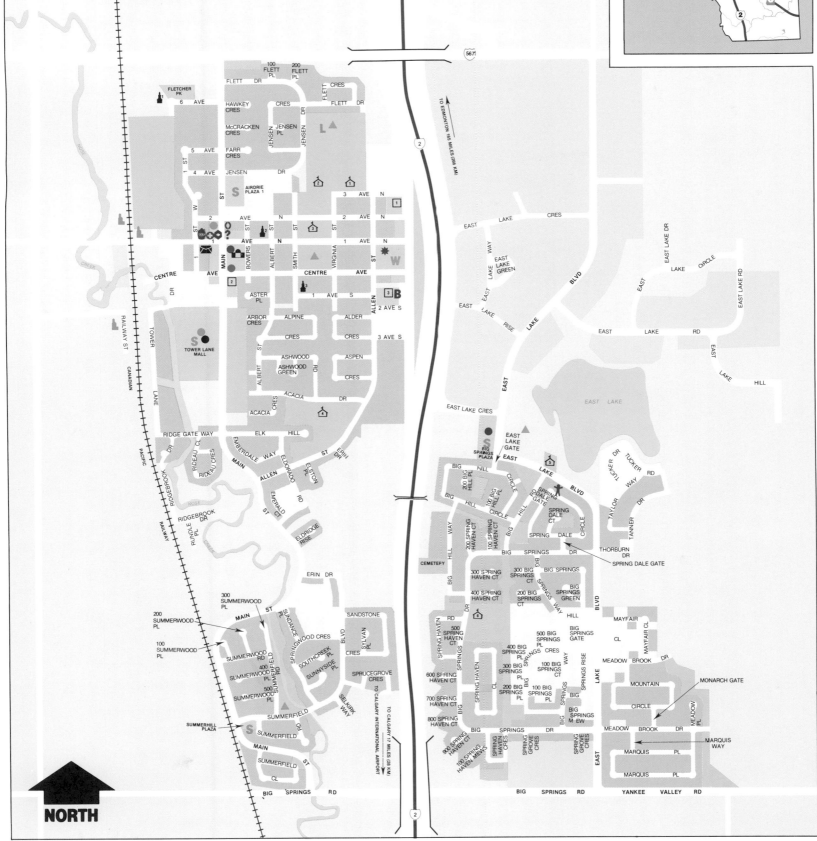

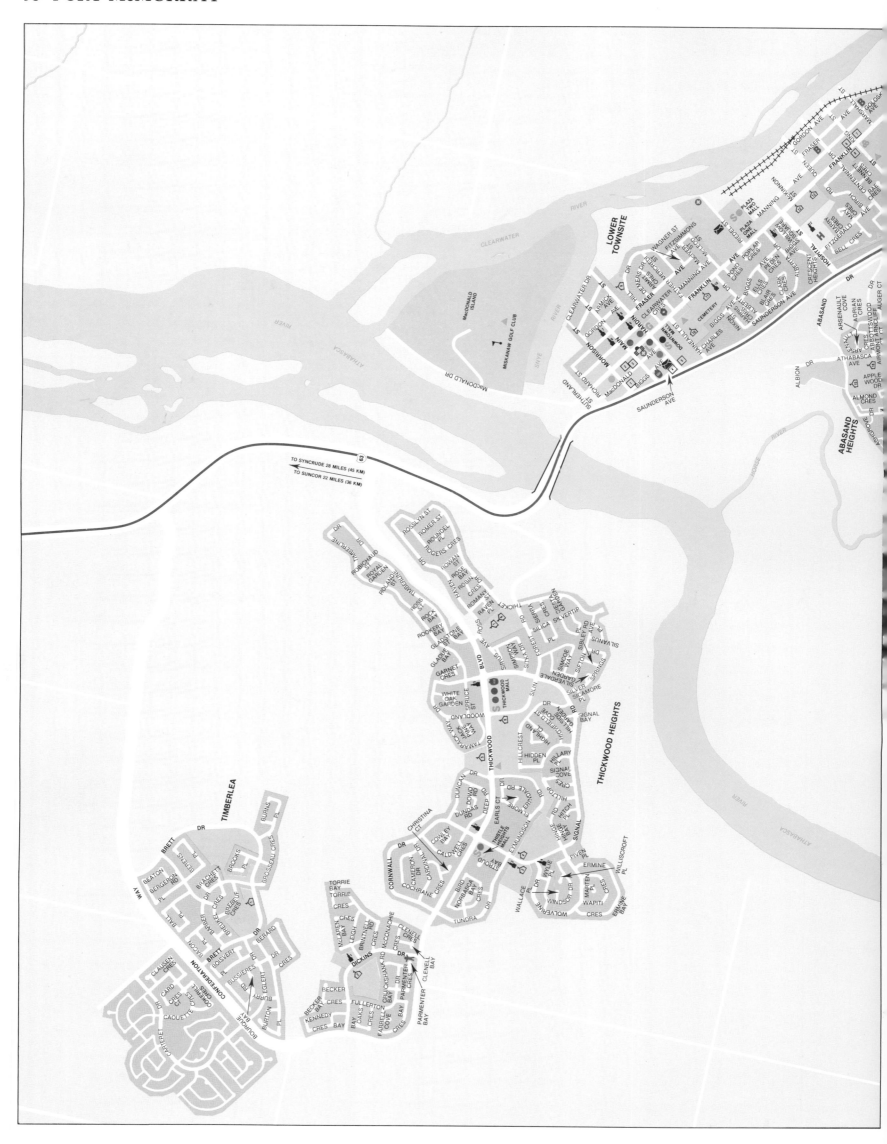

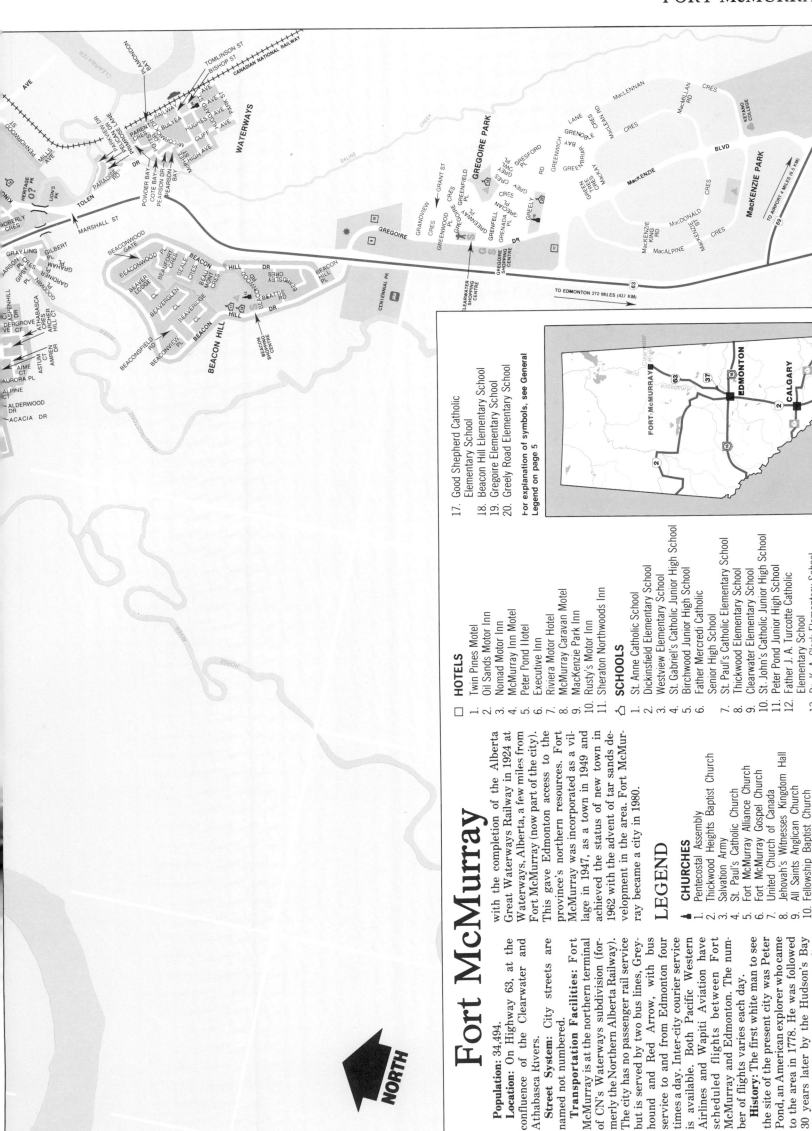

Fort McMurray

Population: 34,494.

Location: On Highway 63, at the confluence of the Clearwater and Athabasca Rivers.

Street System: City streets are named not numbered.

Transportation Facilities: Fort McMurray is at the northern terminal of CN's Waterways subdivision (formerly the Northern Alberta Railway). The city has no passenger rail service but is served by two bus lines, Greyhound and Red Arrow, with bus service to and from Edmonton four times a day. Inter-city courier service is available. Both Pacific Western Airlines and Wapiti Aviation have scheduled flights between Fort McMurray and Edmonton. The number of flights varies each day.

History: The first white man to see the site of the present city was Peter Pond, an American explorer who came to the area in 1778. He was followed 30 years later by the Hudson's Bay Company which set up a trading post. John Moberly, a Hudson's Bay factor, named the fur trading post after Chief Factor William McMurray. Development in the area was spurred with the completion of the Alberta Great Waterways Railway in 1924 at Waterways, Alberta, a few miles from Fort McMurray (now part of the city). This gave Edmonton access to the province's northern resources. Fort McMurray was incorporated as a village in 1947, as a town in 1949 and achieved the status of new town in 1962 with the advent of tar sands development in the area. Fort McMurray became a city in 1980.

LEGEND

CHURCHES

1. Pentecostal Assembly
2. Thickwood Heights Baptist Church
3. Salvation Army
4. St. Paul's Catholic Church
5. Fort McMurray Alliance Church
6. Fort McMurray Gospel Church
7. United Church of Canada
8. Jehovah's Witnesses Kingdom Hall
9. All Saints Anglican Church
10. Fellowship Baptist Church
11. Trinity Lutheran Church
12. St. John's Catholic Church
13. Christian Reformed Church
14. First United Pentecostal Church
15. Seventh-Day Adventist Church

HOTELS

1. Twin Pines Motel
2. Oil Sands Motor Inn
3. Nomad Motor Inn
4. McMurray Inn Motel
5. Peter Pond Hotel
6. Executive Inn
7. Riviera Motor Hotel
8. McMurray Caravan Motel
9. MacKenzie Park Inn
10. Rusty's Motor Inn
11. Sheraton Northwoods Inn

SCHOOLS

1. St. Anne Catholic School
2. Dickinsfield Elementary School
3. Westview Elementary School
4. St. Gabriel's Catholic Junior High School
5. Birchwood Junior High School
6. Father Mercredi Catholic Senior High School
7. St. Paul's Catholic Elementary School
8. Thickwood Elementary School
9. Clearwater Elementary School
10. St. John's Catholic Junior High School
11. Peter Pond Junior High School
12. Father J. A. Turcotte Catholic Elementary School
13. Dr. K. A. Clark Elementary School
14. Fort McMurray Composite High School
15. Frank Spragins Elementary School
16. Father Beauregard Catholic Elementary Edu Com Centre
17. Good Shepherd Catholic Elementary School
18. Beacon Hill Elementary School
19. Gregoire Elementary School
20. Greely Road Elementary School

For explanation of symbols, see General Legend on page 5

Grande Prairie

Population: 24,076.

Location: On Highway 2, 283 miles (456 km.) northwest of Edmonton.

Street System: Streets run north and south, from 89 Street in the east to 116 Street in the west, with odd numbers on the east side of the streets. Avenues run east and west, from 61 Avenue in the south to 132 Avenue in the north. Odd numbers are on the south side of the avenues.

Transportation Facilities: Grande Prairie is on the Grande Prairie subdivision of the CN, but has no passenger rail service. There are four buses daily to and from Edmonton. CP Air, Time Air and Wapiti Airlines all fly between Grande Prairie and Edmonton. Other points in Alberta served by air from Grande Prairie are Whitecourt, Grande Cache and Peace River. Inter-city courier service is available.

History: Settlers began arriving in Grande Prairie about 1908 as the area was promoted for its fertile farmland. The Canadian Northern Railway arrived in the area in 1916. The town was named by Father Emile-Jean-Marie Grouard, an Oblate, who described it as "la grande prairie." Grande Prairie was incorporated as a village in 1914, a town in 1919 and a city in 1958.

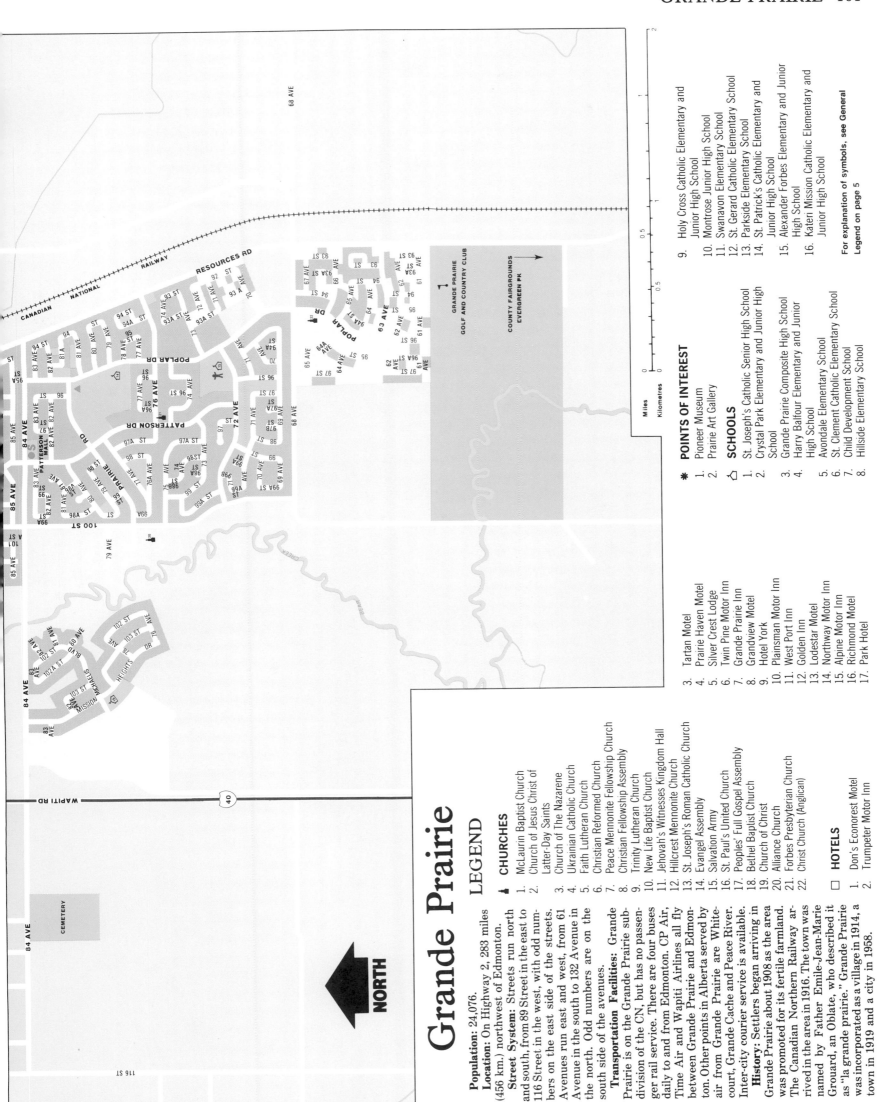

LEGEND

♠ CHURCHES

1. McLaurin Baptist Church
2. Church of Jesus Christ of Latter-Day Saints
3. Church of The Nazarene
4. Ukrainian Catholic Church
5. Faith Lutheran Church
6. Christian Reformed Church
7. Peace Mennonite Fellowship Church
8. Christian Fellowship Assembly
9. Trinity Lutheran Church
10. New Life Baptist Church
11. Jehovah's Witnesses Kingdom Hall
12. Hillcrest Mennonite Church
13. St. Joseph's Roman Catholic Church
14. Evangel Assembly
15. Salvation Army
16. St. Paul's United Church
17. Peoples' Full Gospel Assembly
18. Bethel Baptist Church
19. Church of Christ
20. Alliance Church
21. Forbes Presbyterian Church
22. Christ Church (Anglican)

☐ HOTELS

1. Don's Econorest Motel
2. Trumpeter Motor Inn
3. Tartan Motel
4. Prairie Haven Motel
5. Silver Crest Lodge
6. Twin Pine Motor Inn
7. Grande Prairie Inn
8. Grandview Motel
9. Hotel York
10. Plainsman Motor Inn
11. West Port Inn
12. Golden Inn
13. Lodestar Motel
14. Northway Motor Inn
15. Alpine Motor Inn
16. Richmond Motel
17. Park Hotel

✳ POINTS OF INTEREST

1. Pioneer Museum
2. Prairie Art Gallery

⌂ SCHOOLS

1. St. Joseph's Catholic Senior High School
2. Crystal Park Elementary and Junior High School
3. Grande Prairie Composite High School
4. Harry Balfour Elementary and Junior High School
5. Avondale Elementary School
6. St. Clement Catholic Elementary School
7. Child Development School
8. Hillside Elementary School
9. Holy Cross Catholic Elementary and Junior High School
10. Montrose Junior High School
11. Swanavon Elementary School
12. St. Gerard Catholic Elementary School
13. Parkside Elementary School
14. St. Patrick's Catholic Elementary and Junior High School
15. Alexander Forbes Elementary and Junior High School
16. Kateri Mission Catholic Elementary and Junior High School

For explanation of symbols, see General Legend on page 5

INSET A

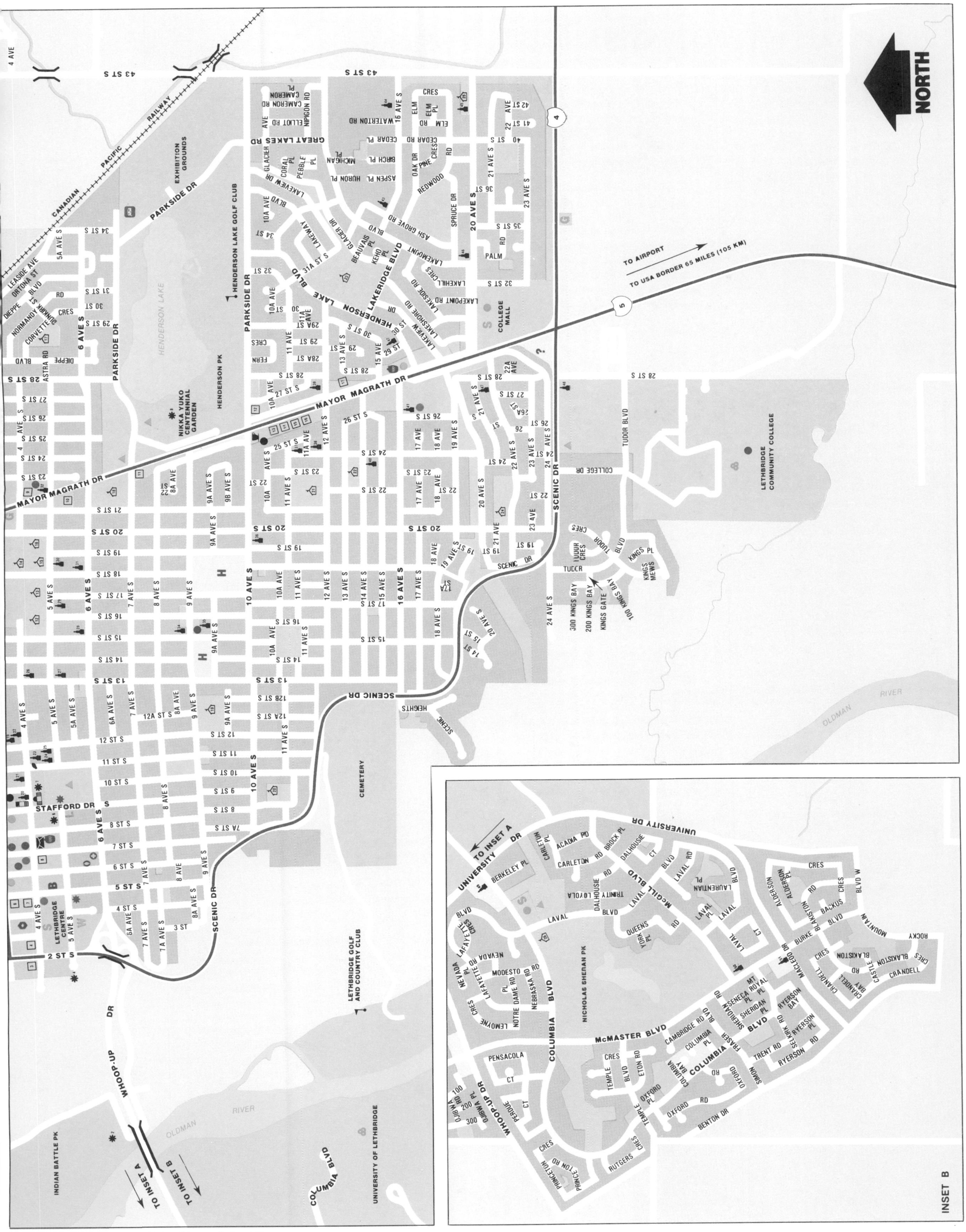

NORTH

Legend for Lethbridge appears on page 104

TO AIRPORT
TO USA BORDER 65 MILES (105 KM)

LETHBRIDGE COMMUNITY COLLEGE

COLLEGE MALL

CANADIAN PACIFIC RAILWAY

EXHIBITION GROUNDS

HENDERSON LAKE GOLF CLUB

HENDERSON LAKE

NIKKA YUKO CENTENNIAL GARDEN

HENDERSON PK

MAYOR MAGRATH DR

GREAT LAKES RD

PARKSIDE DR

HENDERSON LAKE BLVD
LAKERIDGE BLVD

SCENIC DR

CEMETERY

LETHBRIDGE GOLF AND COUNTRY CLUB

STAFFORD DR

LETHBRIDGE CENTRE

WHOOP-UP DR

INDIAN BATTLE PK

OLDMAN RIVER

UNIVERSITY OF LETHBRIDGE

COLUMBIA BLVD

To Inset A   To Inset B

INSET B

UNIVERSITY DR
TO INSET A

McMASTER BLVD
McGILL BLVD
COLUMBIA BLVD
Nicholas Sheran Pk
WHOOP-UP DR

Miles
Kilometres

TUDOR BLVD
COLLEGE DR
SCENIC DR

The irrigation districts

Over a million acres of land in southern Alberta are serviced by the province's 13 irrigation districts. Depending on rainfall and the type of crops seeded, between 75% and 90% of that land will be irrigated in a given year. Maximum water capacity of the system is two million acre-feet. The irrigation districts range in size from 3,000 acres to 300,000 acres, catering to approximately 5,900 farmers. Operation and maintenance costs are borne by the provincial government and the users. Alberta Environment pays for movement of the water from the rivers to the district and farmers pay for the service from the district to the farm gate. Capital works replacement costs in the districts are borne by the province and the water users, with the province bearing 86% of the costs and the users 14%.

The first irrigation projects in the province were built by individual settlers beginning in 1877 on small plots of land. Between 1898 and 1915 large company projects by the CPR and the coal mining Galt family were developed. In 1915, the Alberta government passed the Alberta Irrigation Districts Act which established farmer-owned and operated systems under the supervision of the provincial government. With rising costs after the Second World War, the federal and provincial governments began contributing capital and maintenance funds. It was during this period that the massive St. Mary River scheme was built. The provincial government took over the entire government portion in 1974.

It has been estimated that the irrigated area, which comprises 4% of

Alberta's crop base, generates 20% of the province's agricultural production. The system also allows producers to grow specialty crops such as grain and feed corn, dry beans and sugar beets, which are difficult to grow elsewhere on the prairies.

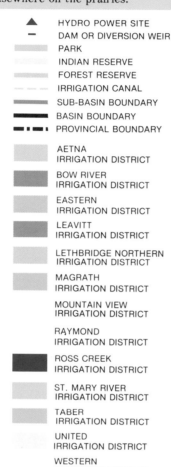

▲ HYDRO POWER SITE
— DAM OR DIVERSION WEIR
PARK
INDIAN RESERVE
FOREST RESERVE
IRRIGATION CANAL
SUB-BASIN BOUNDARY
BASIN BOUNDARY
PROVINCIAL BOUNDARY

AETNA IRRIGATION DISTRICT
BOW RIVER IRRIGATION DISTRICT
EASTERN IRRIGATION DISTRICT
LEAVITT IRRIGATION DISTRICT
LETHBRIDGE NORTHERN IRRIGATION DISTRICT
MAGRATH IRRIGATION DISTRICT
MOUNTAIN VIEW IRRIGATION DISTRICT
RAYMOND IRRIGATION DISTRICT
ROSS CREEK IRRIGATION DISTRICT
ST. MARY RIVER IRRIGATION DISTRICT
TABER IRRIGATION DISTRICT
UNITED IRRIGATION DISTRICT
WESTERN IRRIGATION DISTRICT

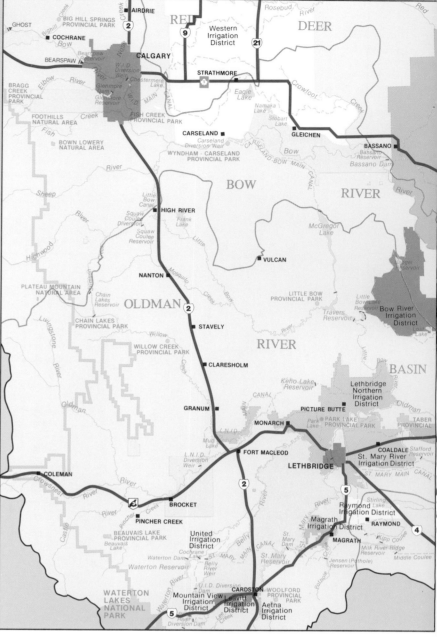

Lethbridge

(Map on pages 102 and 103)

Population: 58,086.

Location: On Highway 3, 135 miles (217 km.) southeast of Calgary and 102 miles (164 km.) west of Medicine Hat.

Street System: Streets run north and south, from 1 Street in the west to 43 Street in the east, with odd num-

bers on the east side of the streets. Avenues run east and west, from 1 Avenue to 44 Avenue north of the railway tracks and from 1 Avenue to 30 Avenue south of the tracks. Odd numbers are on the north side of the avenues.

Transportation Facilities: Lethbridge is on the CP Rail line, but has no passenger rail service. Greyhound buses run five times a day between Lethbridge and Calgary and once daily to and from Medicine Hat. Time Air has four flights daily each way between Calgary and Lethbridge and two a day between Lethbridge and Medicine Hat, once a day to and from Vancouver. Inter-city courier service is available.

History: In 1869, American traders set up shop near the present site of Lethbridge to sell whisky to the Indians. The rowdy behaviour which resulted at "Fort Whoop-up," as it was called, led to the establishment of the North West Mounted Police in 1873. Later, the area became known as the Coalbanks after Nicholas Sheran began mining coal from the banks of the Belly (now the Oldman) River. Residents began calling the community Lethbridge, after the president of the North Western Coal and Navigation Company, William Lethbridge. Lethbridge was incorporated as a town in 1891 and as a city in 1906.

LEGEND

⚓ CHURCHES

1. Park Meadow Baptist Church
2. Lethbridge Buddhist Church
3. Japanese United Church
4. Bethlen Presbyterian Church
5. Netherlands Reformed Congregation
6. Community Fellowship Church (Meetings in Wilson Junior High School)
7. Norbridge Evangelical Church in Canada
8. St. Vladimir's Ukrainian Catholic Church
9. Central Church of Christ
10. Church of Jesus Christ of Latter-Day Saints
11. St. Peter and St. Paul's Greek Catholic Church
12. Ukrainian Greek Orthodox Church
13. St. Basil's Roman Catholic Church
14. St. Mary The Virgin Anglican Church
15. First United Church
16. Bethany Baptist Church
17. First Christian Reformed Church
18. Jehovah's Witnesses Kingdom Hall
19. Lethbridge Christian Fellowship Center
20. St. Patrick's Roman Catholic Church
21. Southminster United Church
22. Christian Science Church
23. St. Augustine's Anglican Church
24. Lethbridge Mennonite Church
25. Christ-Trinity Lutheran Church
26. Salvation Army
27. Christian Tabernacle Church
28. Lethbridge Chinese Alliance Church
29. First Baptist Church
30. St. Andrew's Presbyterian Church
31. Immanuel Lutheran Church
32. Reorganized Church of Jesus Christ of Latter-Day Saints
33. Jehovah's Witnesses Kingdom Hall
34. Church of The Nazarene
35. Hebrew Congregation
36. Church of Jesus Christ of Latter-Day Saints
37. Lutheran Church of The Good Shepherd
38. Assumption of The Holy Virgin Roman Catholic Church
39. Evangelical Free Church of Lethbridge
40. McKillop United Church
41. Seventh-Day Adventist Church
42. Lakeview Mennonite Brethren Church
43. Honpa Buddhist Church
44. Church of Jesus Christ of Latter-Day Saints
45. New Hope Christian Centre
46. Glad Tidings Fellowship
47. Church of Christ
48. Church of Jesus Christ of Latter-Day Saints
49. University Drive Alliance Church
50. First Christian Reformed Church
51. Pentecostal Assembly

☐ HOTELS

1. York Hotel
2. Bridge Inn
3. Lethbridge Lodge Hotel
4. Travelodge
5. Lethbridge Hotel
6. Coal Banks Inn
7. Alec Arms Hotel
8. Marquis Hotel
9. Sandman Inn

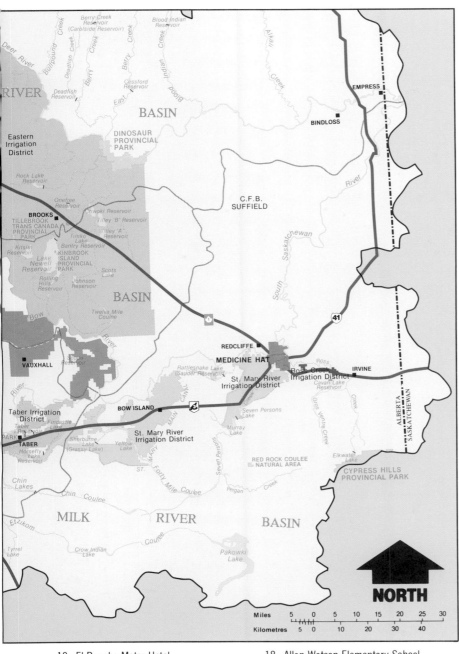

Miles 5 0 5 10 15 20 25 30

Kilometres 5 0 10 20 30 40

NORTH

10. El Rancho Motor Hotel
11. Lodge Motel
12. Park Plaza Motor Hotel
13. Bridge Town House Motel
14. Sundance Inn
15. Flagstone Motel
16. Golden West Motel
17. Heidelberg Inn

✳ POINTS OF INTEREST

1. High Level Bridge
2. Fort Whoop-Up
3. Brewery Gardens
4. Sir Alexander Galt Museum
5. Southern Alberta Art Gallery
6. Bowman Arts Centre
7. Yates Memorial Centre
8. Nikka Yuko Centennial Garden

⌂ SCHOOLS

1. Park Meadows Elementary School
2. Winston Churchill High School
3. St. Paul's Catholic Elementary School
4. Sunnyside Elementary School
5. Wilson Junior High School
6. Galbraith Elementary School
7. Senator W. A. Buchanan School
8. St. Basil's Catholic Elementary School
9. Immanuel Christian School (Private)
10. Westminster Elementary School
11. George McKillop Curriculum School
12. Hamilton Junior High School
13. Lethbridge Collegiate Institute School
14. St. Francis Catholic Junior High School
15. Catholic Central High School
16. St. Mary's Catholic Elementary School
17. General Stewart Elementary School

18. Allan Watson Elementary School
19. Fleetwood Bawden Elementary School
20. St. Patrick's Catholic Elementary School
21. Gilbert Paterson Elementary and
    Junior High School
22. Assumption Catholic Elementary School
23. Lakeview Elementary School
24. Agnes Davidson Elementary School
25. Chinook Christian Academy
26. Nicholas Sheran Elementary
    Community School

For explanation of symbols, see General Legend on page 5

Medicine Hat

(Map on pages 106 and 107)

Population: 41,167.
Location: Beside the South Saskatchewan River on the Trans-Canada Highway, 182 miles (293 km.) southeast of Calgary and 102 miles (164 km.) east of Lethbridge.
Street System: Avenues run north and south from Division Avenue, the main north-south road, to 15 Avenue W. and from Division to 22 Avenue E. Streets run east and west, from 1 Street to 22 Street north of the river and from 1 Street to 32 Street south of the river. Odd numbers are on the east

side of the avenues and the south side of the streets.
Transportation Facilities: Medicine Hat is on the CP main line with VIA passenger service once a day to and from Calgary. Greyhound buses run five times a day each way between Medicine Hat and Calgary and once daily to and from Lethbridge. Time Air has four flights a day to Calgary and two to Lethbridge. Inter- and intra-city couriers are available.
History: Medicine Hat was surveyed in 1883 by engineers for the CPR. The first settlers were men working on the building of the railway. The city's peculiar name is apparently taken from an incident which occurred between the Cree and Blackfoot Indians who were fighting on the banks of the river when the hat of the Cree medicine man fell into the river. This was such a bad omen the Cree fled and the Blackfoot were victorious. The site was known as "ford-where-the-medicine-man-lost-his-hat," later condensed to Medicine Hat. Medicine Hat was incorporated as a town in 1899 and as a city in 1907.

LEGEND

⌂ CHURCHES

1. Church of Jesus Christ of
   Latter-Day Saints
2. Evangelical Free Church of Medicine Hat
3. Crescent Heights Church of Christ
4. Heights Baptist Church
5. Christian Reformed Church
6. Kingdom Hall United Church
7. Riverside Presbyterian Church
8. St. Patrick's Roman Catholic Church
9. Salvation Army
10. St. John's Presbyterian Church
11. First Church of Christian Scientists
12. Fifth Avenue United Church
13. St. Barnabas Anglican Church
14. Memorial Evangelical Church
15. Full Gospel Church
16. Sons of Abraham Synagogue
17. Grace Baptist Church
18. Holy Trinity Anglican Church
19. Memorial Salem United Church
20. Christ The King Roman Catholic Church
21. Grace Lutheran Church
22. St. Paul's Lutheran Church
23. Westminster United Church
24. Temple Baptist Church
25. Medicine Hat Gospel Hall Assembly
26. St. Peter's Lutheran Church
27. Hillcrest Evangelical Church
28. First Assembly of God
29. Division Avenue Church of God
30. All Saints Anglican Church
31. St. Mary's Roman Catholic Church
32. Bible Baptist Church
33. Alliance Church
34. Crestwood Mennonite Brethren Church
35. Southview Church of God
36. Norwood Christian Life Assembly
37. Seventh-Day Adventist Church
38. Medicine Hat Southside Church of Christ
39. Lutheran Victory Church
40. St. Paul's Roman Catholic Chapel
    (Meetings in Mother Teresa School)

☐ HOTELS

1. Michael's Motel
2. Rancho Motel
3. El Bronco Motel
4. Royal Hotel
5. Assiniboia Inn
6. Medicine Hat Inn
7. Cecil Hotel
8. Alta Motel
9. Corona Hotel
10. Continental Inn

11. Park Lane Motor Inn
12. Silver Buckle Inn
13. Best Western Flamingo Terrace Motel
14. Searra Motel
15. Cloverleaf Court
16. Trans-Canada Motel
17. Cloverleaf Motel
18. Hat Motel
19. Travel Lodge Motor Inn
20. Circle T. Lodge
21. Sun-Dek Motel
22. Frontier Motel
23. Bel-Aire Motel
24. Ranchmen Motel
25. Satellite Motel
26. Westlander Inn
27. Imperial Motor Inn
28. Holiday Motel

✳ POINTS OF INTEREST

1. Riverside Waterslide
2. Medicine Hat and District Centennial
   and Historic Museum
3. Altaglass Manufacturer

⌂ SCHOOLS

1. Crescent Heights Junior and Senior High
   School
2. Webster Niblock Elementary School
3. Vincent Massey Elementary School
4. McCoy Catholic High School
5. St. Francis Xavier Catholic Elementary
   School
6. St. Michael's Catholic Elementary School
7. St. Patrick's Catholic Elementary School
8. Riverside Elementary School
9. Montreal Street Elementary School
10. St. Louis Catholic Elementary School
11. River Heights Elementary School
12. Earl Kitchener Elementary School
13. Herald Elementary School
14. Medicine Hat High School
15. Alexandra Junior High School
16. Elm Street Elementary School
17. Connaught Elementary School
18. Central Park Elementary School
19. St. Mary's Catholic Elementary and
    Junior High School
20. George P. Vanier School
21. St. Thomas Aquinas Catholic Elementary
    School
22. Cornerstone Academy (Located in
    Alliance Church)
23. Crestwood Elementary School
24. Southview Elementary School
25. Mother Teresa Catholic Elementary
    School
26. Ross Glen Elementary School
27. George Davidson Elementary School

For explanation of symbols, see General Legend on page 5

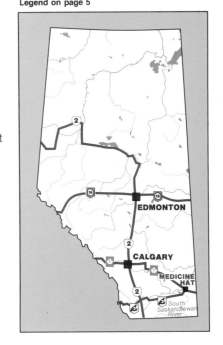

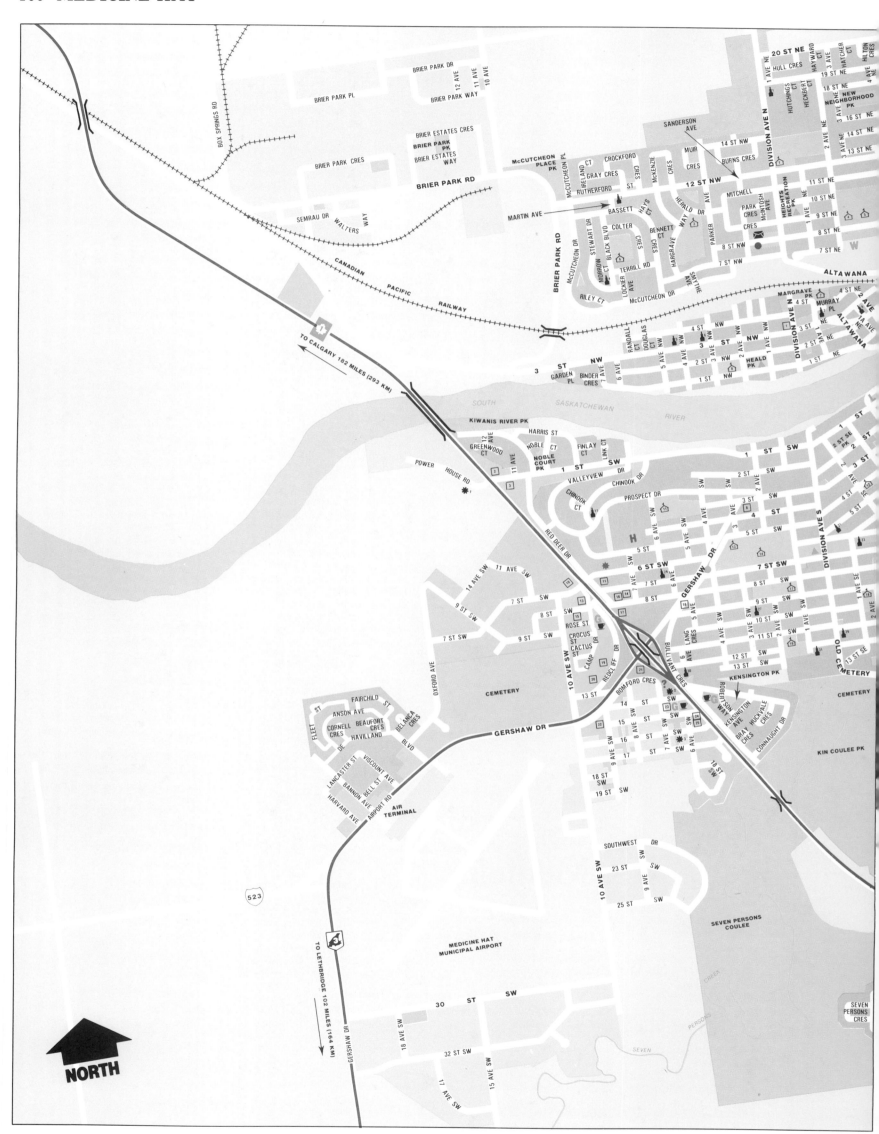

NORTH

Legend for Medicine Hat appears on page 105

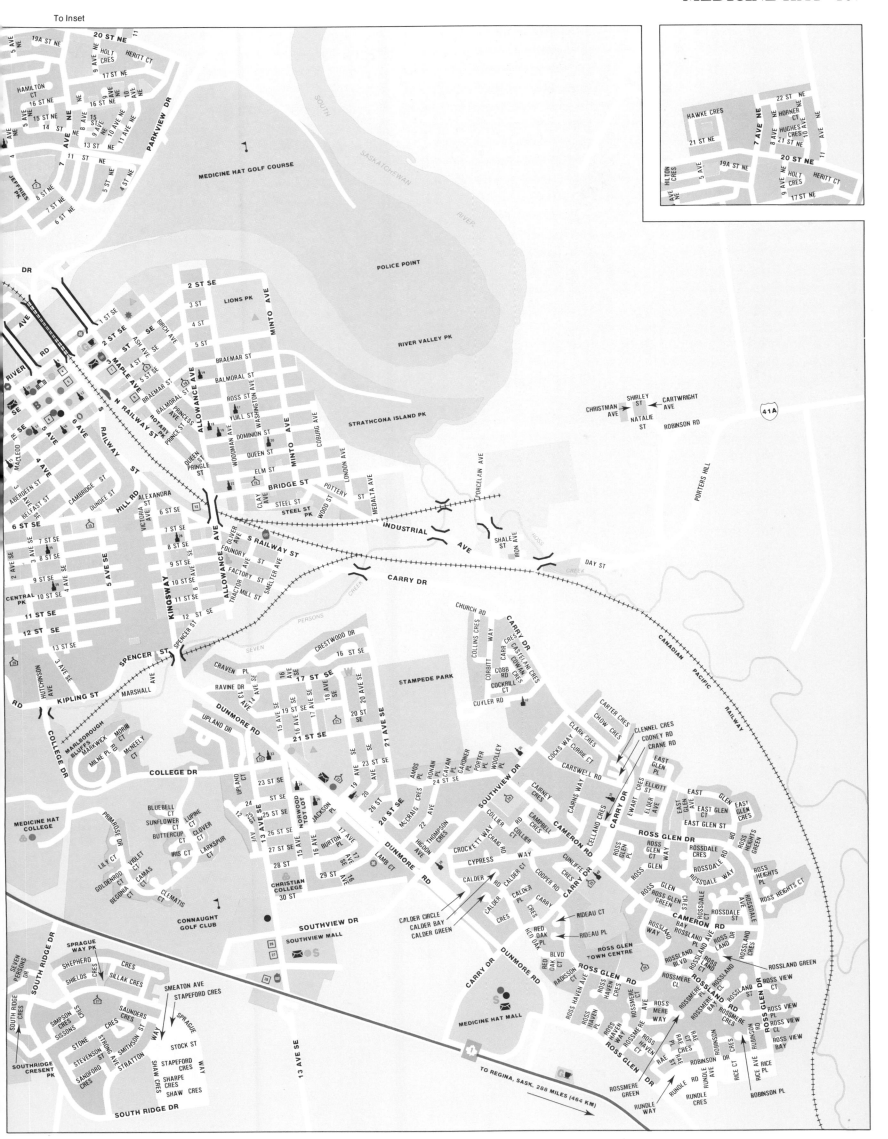

Red Deer

Population: 50,257.

Location: On the north bend of the Red Deer River and on Highway 2, 92 miles (148 km.) south of Edmonton and 90 miles (145 km.) north of Calgary.

Street System: Avenues run north and south from 30 Avenue in the east to 67 Avenue in the west with odd numbers on the east side of the avenues. Streets run east and west, from 28 Street in the south to 81 Street in the north, with odd numbers on the south side of the streets.

Transportation Facilities: Red Deer is on the CP Rail line between Calgary and Edmonton and has VIA Rail service twice a day to and from each. Greyhound and Pacific Western buses run eight times a day each way to Calgary and Edmonton. There is no scheduled air service but the city has an industrial airport capable of accommodating jets. Inter- and intra-city courier services are available.

History: The first homesteader and land title holder was Dr. Leonard Gaetz, who arrived in the area from eastern Canada in 1884. He gave part of his land to the Calgary and Edmonton Railway Company to build a station beside his farm. The name Red Deer was mentioned on maps by David Thompson in the early 1800s. The Cree name for the river was Waskasoo, which means elk, and it is believed that the explorer translated the word incorrectly. Red Deer was incorporated as a village in 1898, as a town in 1901 and as a city in 1913.

LEGEND

▲ CHURCHES

1. Community Baptist Church
2. Northside Church of God
3. Fairview United Church
4. Sacred Heart Roman Catholic Church
5. Woodlea Pentecostal Tabernacle
6. St. Luke's Church
7. Seventh-Day Adventist Church
8. Gaetz United Church
9. Knox Presbyterian Church
10. Church of God Michener Hill
11. Bethany Baptist Church
12. Anglican Church of St. Leonard's on The Hill
13. Parkland Christian Church
14. West Park Church of The Nazarene
15. Trinity Lutheran Church
16. First Baptist Church
17. St. Andrew's West Park Presbyterian Church
18. First Church of The Nazarene
19. Christian Reformed Church (Meetings in Red Deer Christian School)
20. St. Mary's Catholic Church
21. Mount Calvary Lutheran Church
22. Sunnybrook United Church
23. Church of Jesus Christ of Latter-Day Saints
24. Jehovah's Witnesses Kingdom Hall
25. Red Deer Alliance Church

☐ HOTELS

1. Sleepy's Inn North
2. Parkland Inn
3. Northhill Inn
4. Quality Inn Great West
5. Western Inn
6. Buffalo Hotel
7. Arlington Inn
8. Granada Motor Inn
9. Windsor Hotel
10. Valley Hotel
11. Red Deer Lodge
12. Red Deer Inn
13. Gemini Inn
14. Capri Centre
15. Black Knight Inn
16. Sleepy's Inn South
17. Plainsman Hotel

✳ POINTS OF INTEREST

1. Cronquist House
2. Red Deer Museum

⌂ SCHOOLS

1. Normandeau Elementary and Junior High School
2. Aspen Heights Elementary School
3. Pine Community Elementary School
4. St. Patrick's Catholic Community School

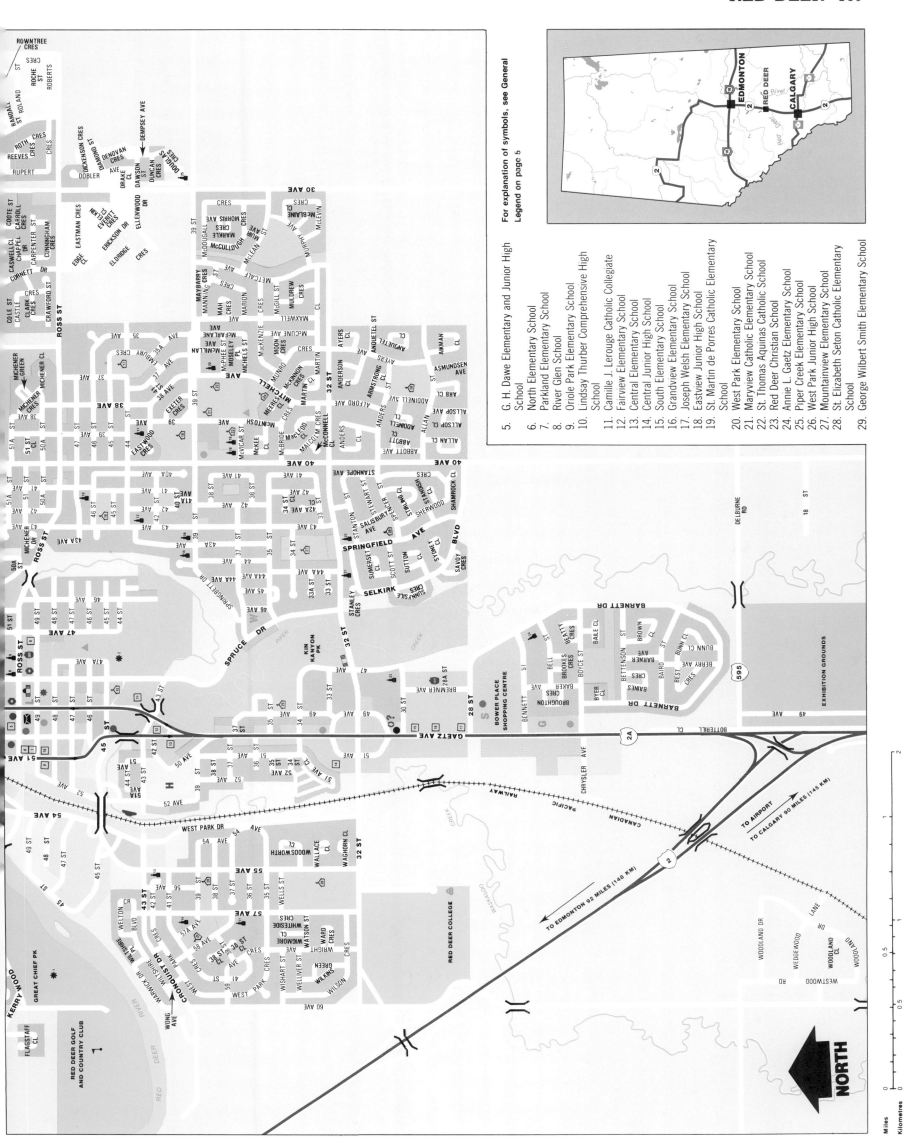

For explanation of symbols, see General
Legend on page 5

5. G. H. Dawe Elementary and Junior High School
6. North Elementary School
7. Parkland Elementary School
8. River Glen School
9. Oriole Park Elementary School
10. Lindsay Thurber Comprehensive High School
11. Camille J. Lerouge Catholic Collegiate
12. Fairview Elementary School
13. Central Elementary School
14. Central Junior High School
15. South Elementary School
16. Grandview Elementary School
17. Joseph Welsh Elementary School
18. Eastview Junior High School
19. St. Martin de Porres Catholic Elementary School
20. West Park Elementary School
21. Maryview Catholic Elementary School
22. St. Thomas Aquinas Catholic School
23. Red Deer Christian School
24. Annie L. Gaetz Elementary School
25. Piper Creek Elementary School
26. West Park Junior High School
27. Mountainview Elementary School
28. St. Elizabeth Seton Catholic Elementary School
29. George Wilbert Smith Elementary School

NORTH

Banff

Population: 3,410.

Location: On the Trans-Canada Highway (Hwy. 1) 80 miles (128 km.) west of Calgary and 179 miles (288 km.) south of Jasper. The town is inside Banff National Park and is administered by the federal government.

Street System: Streets are named not numbered.

Transportation Facilities: Banff is on the CP main line and VIA Rail provides service once a day to and from Calgary and Vancouver. Buses run between Calgary and Banff daily. There is no scheduled air service. Inter-city courier service is available.

History: Frank McCabe and William McCardell, CPR employees, found the hot springs at Cave End Basin around 1883. The park, originally called Rocky Mountains Park, was the first national park in Canada and extended for about 10 square miles around the townsite. Banff, Scotland, was the birthplace of Donald Smith, a founder and promoter of the CPR.

LEGEND

♦ CHURCHES
1. Full Gospel Church
2. Banff Park Church
3. Church of Jesus Christ of Latter-Day Saints
4. St. Mary's Roman Catholic Church
5. St. Paul's Presbyterian Church
6. Rundle Memorial United Church
7. St. George's Anglican Church

☐ HOTELS
1. Hidden Ridge Motor Inn
2. Douglas Fir Chalets
3. Mountview Village
4. Tunnel Mountain Chalets
5. Timberline Lodge
6. Big Horn Motel
7. Inn of Banff Park
8. Swiss Village Lodge
9. Voyager Inn Motor Hotel
10. Spruce Grove Motel
11. Banffshire Inn
12. Alpine Motel
13. Banff Motel
14. Charlton's Cedar Court
15. Aspen Lodge
16. Charlton's Evergreen Court
17. Pinewoods Motel And Chalets
18. Woodland Village Inn
19. Siding 29 Lodge
20. Irwin's Motor Inn
21. Red Carpet Inn
22. Traveller's Inn
23. High Country Inn
24. Rundle Manor Motel
25. Driftwood Motor Inn
26. Y Mountain Lodge
27. Ptarmigan Inn
28. Bow View Motor Lodge
29. Banff Park Lodge
30. The Homestead Inn
31. King Edward Hotel
32. Mount Royal Hotel
33. Cascade Inn
34. Banff Springs Hotel

✷ POINTS OF INTEREST
1. The Natural History Museum
2. Peter And Catharine Whyte Gallery
3. Banff National Parks Museum
4. Luxton Museum
5. Bow Falls

⌂ SCHOOLS
1. Banff Elementary School
2. Banff Composite High School

For explanation of symbols, see General Legend on page 5

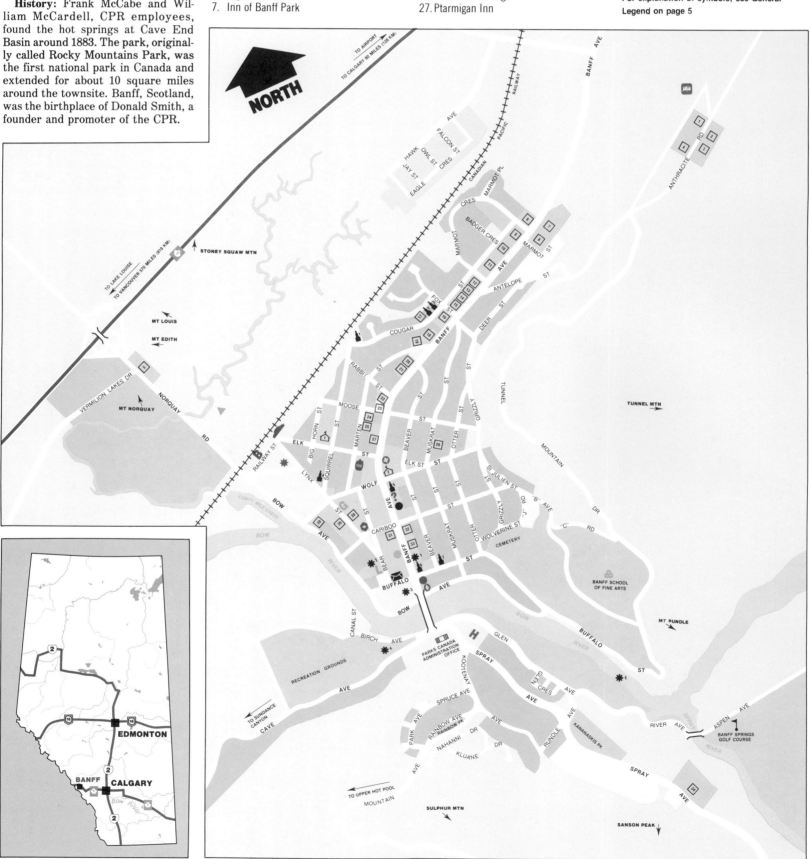

Brooks

Population: 9,421.

Location: On the Trans-Canada Highway (Hwy. 1) 115 miles (185 km.) southeast of Calgary, and 69 miles (111 km.) west of Medicine Hat.

Street System: Streets run north and south, from Centre Street to 9 Street in the east and from Centre Street to 11 Street in the west. Even numbers are on the west side. Avenues run east and west, from 1 Avenue in the south to 13 Avenue in the north, with even numbers on the north side.

Transportation Facilities: Brooks is situated on the CP main line and has VIA Rail passenger service to and from Calgary once a day. Greyhound buses run four times a day to Calgary and five times daily from Calgary. There is no scheduled air service. Inter-city courier service is available.

History: The Crooker family, ranchers from Winnipeg, settled in Brooks in 1904, setting up a grocery store near the stockyard. They later added a hotel and cafe. The village was incorporated in 1910 and became a town the following year. Brooks was named after Noel Edgell Brooks, a divisional engineer for the CPR.

LEGEND

🛉 **CHURCHES**
1. Christian Reformed Church
2. Brooks Baptist Church
3. Trinity Lutheran Church
4. Church of Jesus Christ of Latter-Day Saints
5. St. Mary's Catholic Church
6. Jehovah's Witnesses Kingdom Hall
7. Immanuel Assembly
8. Evangelical Free Church
9. Brooks United Church
10. St. Alban's Anglican Church

☐ **HOTELS**
1. Pheasant Motel
2. Heritage Inn
3. Plainsman Motor Inn
4. Plains Motel
5. Westbrook Motel
6. Tel Star Motor Inn
7. Circle-A-Motel
8. Bluebird Motel
9. Hotel Newell
10. Brook Hotel
11. Oxford Hotel
12. Eastbrook Motel

✳ **POINTS OF INTEREST**
1. Brooks and District Museum

⌂ **SCHOOLS**
1. Griffin Park Elementary School
2. Primary School A
3. Primary School B
4. Central Elementary School
5. Brooks Junior High School
6. Brooks Composite High School
7. Eastbrook Elementary School

For explanation of symbols, see General Legend on page 5

Camrose

Population: 12,809.

Location: On Highway 13, 58 miles (94 km.) southeast of Edmonton and 171 miles (275 km.) northeast of Calgary.

Street System: Streets run north and south, from 37 Street in the east to 75 Street in the west, with odd numbers on the west side. Avenues run east and west, from 34 Avenue in the south to 55 Avenue in the north, with odd numbers on the south side.

Transportation Facilities: Camrose is on the Camrose subdivision of the CN rail line and the Wetaskiwin subdivision of the CP line but has no passenger rail service. Buses to Edmonton and Calgary run three times daily. Inter-city courier service is available. There is no scheduled air service.

History: Camrose was first settled by Norwegian homesteaders in 1903, one of the first being a bachelor named Ole Bakken who farmed near the present-day courthouse. The village was originally called Sparling, but the name was changed to Camrose to avoid confusion with several other towns of the same name. The name "Camrose" is taken from a community of the same name in Britain and means "Valley of the Roses." Camrose was incorporated as a village in 1905, a town in 1906, and a city in 1955 for its 50th anniversary.

LEGEND

♠ CHURCHES
1. Ukrainian Greek Orthodox Church of All Saints
2. Church of The Nazarene
3. Jehovah's Witnesses Kingdom Hall
4. Deeper Life Chapel
5. Grace Lutheran Church
6. Truth Tabernacle
7. Ukrainian Catholic Church
8. Calvary Pentecostal Tabernacle
9. Bethel Lutheran Church
10. St. Francis Xavier Roman Catholic Church
11. Camrose United Church
12. Messiah Lutheran Church
13. Evangelical Covenant Church
14. St. Andrew's Anglican Church
15. Church of God
16. Camrose Alliance Church
17. First Baptist Church
18. Century Meadows Baptist Church

☐ HOTELS
1. Alice Hotel
2. Windsor Motel
3. Cam-Rest Motel
4. Johnson Motel
5. Crystal Springs Motor Hotel
6. Camrose Motel
7. Hacienda Motor Inn
8. Norsemen Flag Inn Hotel

✻ POINTS OF INTEREST
1. Camrose and District Centennial Museum

⌂ SCHOOLS
1. St. Patrick's Catholic Elementary and Junior High School
2. Sparling Elementary School
3. Charlie Killam Elementary and Junior High School
4. County of Camrose Sifton School
5. Lutheran Bible Institute
6. Camrose Composite High School
7. Our Lady of Mount Pleasant Elementary School
8. Burgess School for the Mentally Retarded
9. Chester Ronning Elementary and Junior High School
10. Jack Stuart Elementary and Junior High School (Open September 1984)

For explanation of symbols, see General Legend on page 5

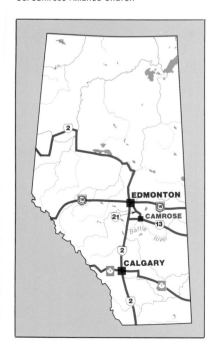

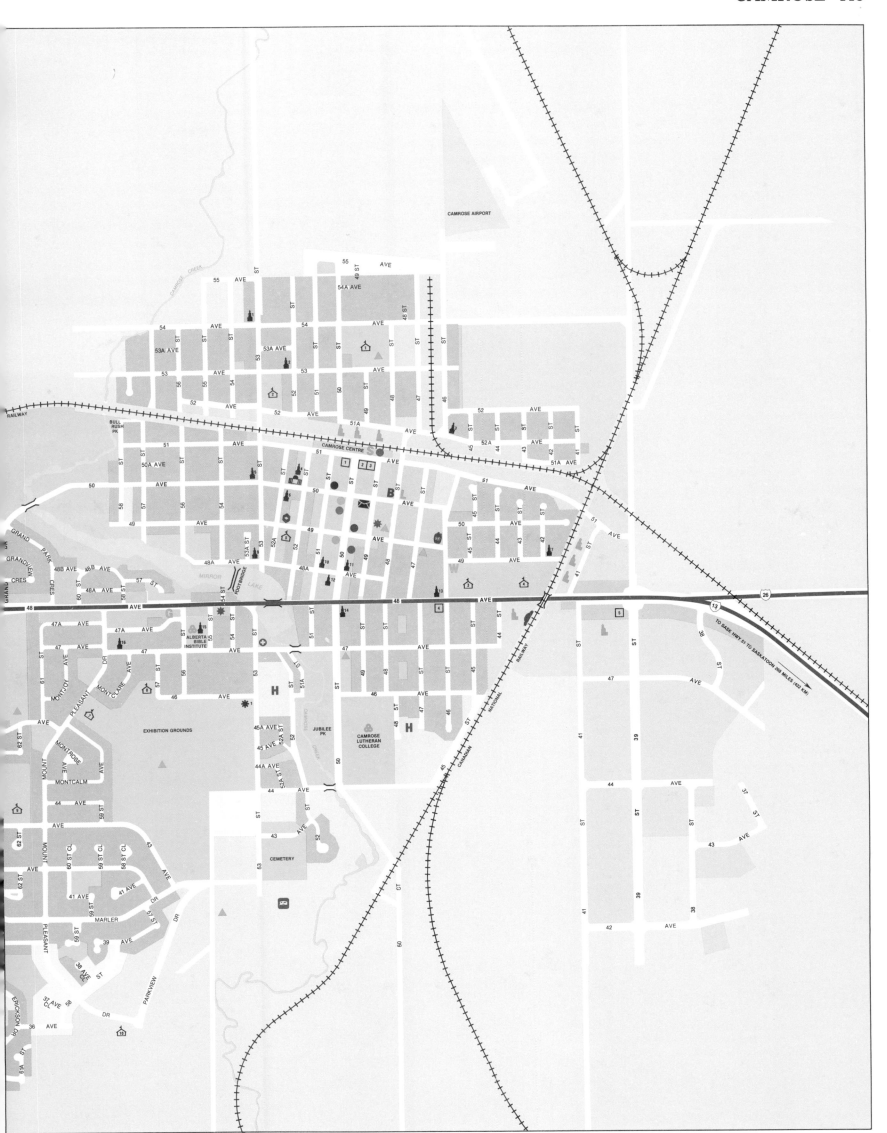

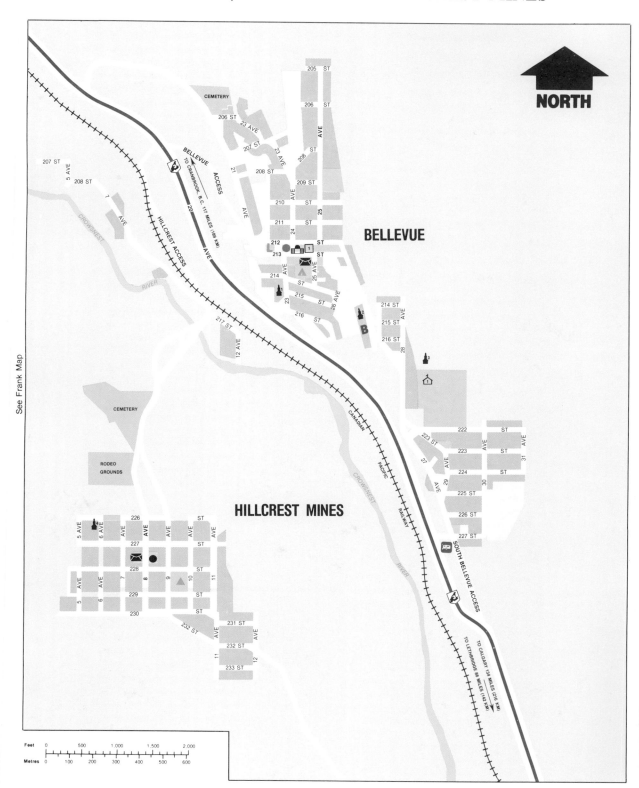

Municipality of Crowsnest Pass

Population: 7,577.

Location: On Highway 3 in the Crowsnest Pass through the Rocky Mountains, 134 miles (216 km.) south of Calgary.

Street System: In all communities except Bellevue and Hillcrest Mines, streets run north and south, from 56 Street in the west to 153 Street in the east. Avenues run east and west from 4 Avenue in the south to 29 Avenue in the north. Odd numbers are on the north side of avenues and the east side of the streets.

In Bellevue and Hillcrest Mines streets run east and west, from 205 Street in the north to 233 Street in the south. Avenues run north and south from 4 Avenue in the west to 31 Avenue in the east. Odd numbers are on the south side of the streets and the east side of avenues.

Transportation Facilities: The municipality is located on the CP Crowsnest line, but has no passenger rail service. Buses run between Calgary and Crowsnest Pass twice daily. There is no scheduled air service. Inter-city courier service is available.

History: In 1979 the communities of Bellevue, Hillcrest Mines, Blairmore, Frank and Coleman were amalgamated to form the Municipality of Crowsnest Pass. The history of each is given with its map.

Bellevue

Bellevue (population 1,231) was established by a French engineer, J.J. Fleutot, who came to Canada in the early 1900s to look for coal. He formed the Western Canadian Collieries in 1903 and set up a mine and townsite. The town was named by his daughter Elise who upon first seeing the site exclaimed, "Quelle belle vue." (What a beautiful scene!) Much of the town was destroyed by fire in 1917.

Hillcrest Mines

Hillcrest Mines (population 789) was built in 1905 by Hillcrest Coal and Coke, an American company owned by Charles Plummer Hill. The company town had a main street 80 feet wide. A railway owned by the Hillcrest Collieries ran through town. The Hillcrest mine explosion in 1914 killed 189 men. Another explosion in 1926 rocked the community but no one was killed. The mine shut down in 1939.

LEGEND

🏛 **CHURCHES**
1. St. Cyril's Catholic Church
2. Christian Reformed Church
3. Church of Jesus Christ of Latter-Day Saints
4. Hillcrest United Church

☐ **HOTELS**
1. Bellevue Inn

⌂ **SCHOOLS**
1. M. D. McEachern Elementary School

For explanation of symbols, see General Legend on page 5

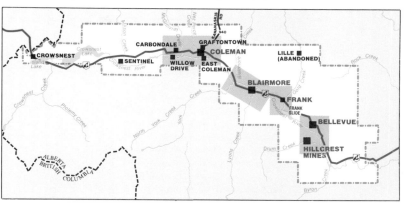

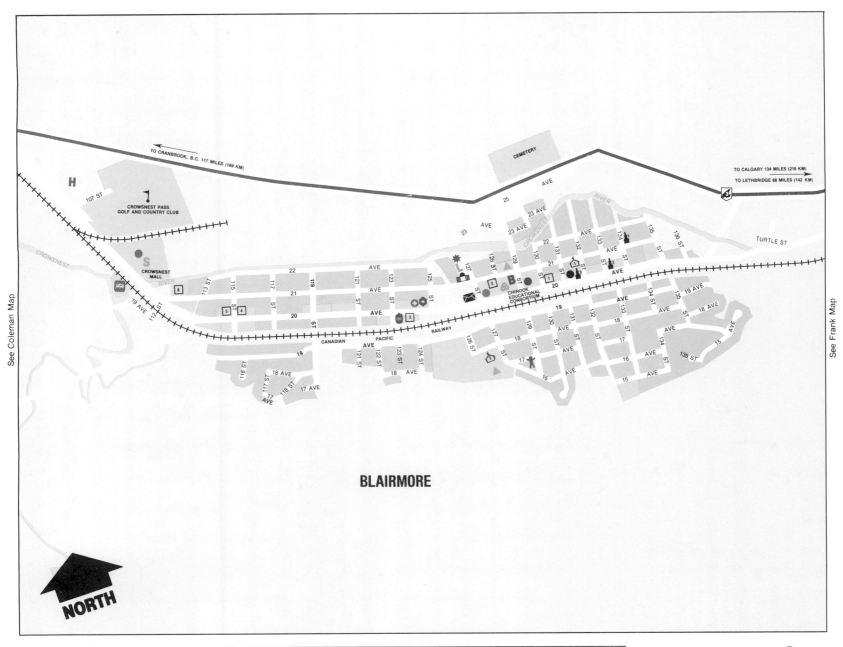

BLAIRMORE

Blairmore

Blairmore (population 2,476) was the first settlement in the Crowsnest Pass. The community was the Tenth Siding of the Canadian Pacific Railway when the line was built through the Pass in 1898. The first two settlers were H.E. Lyon, the CPR station agent, and Felix Monalbetti, a section foreman. The community was named Blairmore after A.G. Blair, the federal minister of highways at the time. Blairmore was incorporated as a village in 1901.

LEGEND

🛐 CHURCHES
1. St. Luke's Anglican Church
2. Blairmore United Church
3. St. Anne's Roman Catholic Church

☐ HOTELS
1. Pass Hotel
2. Blairmore Motel
3. Greenhill Hotel
4. Sleepee Teepee Motel
5. Highwood Motel
6. Cedar Inn Motel

⌂ SCHOOLS
1. Kids College School
2. Isabelle Sellon School

For explanation of symbols, see General Legend on page 5

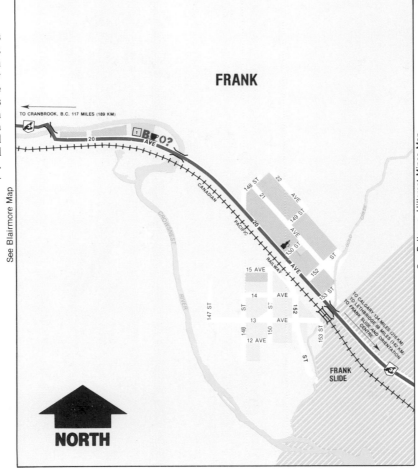

FRANK

Frank

One of the first settlers in what is now Frank (population 188) was S.W. Gebo, who arrived about 1900 to look for coal property. He met up with one A.L. Frank from Montana who bought land from Gebo and set up a coal mine. The town opened in 1901. Disaster struck two years later when the great Frank Slide buried the south side of the town, killing about 70 people. The mine continued to produce until 1917 when it was shut down. Frank is now a residential community.

LEGEND

🛐 CHURCHES
1. Jehovah's Witnesses Kingdom Hall

☐ HOTELS
1. Turtle Mountain Motor Inn

For explanation of symbols, see General Legend on page 5

Feet	0	500	1,000	1,500	2,000
Metres	0	100 200 300 400 500			600

See Blairmore Map

Coleman

Coleman (population 2,893) was set up in 1903 by the International Coal and Coke Co. which began selling lots to prospective miners in 1903. The deeds restricted the sale of liquor for 15 years. The town was named after Coleman Flummerfelt, daughter of the president of the International Coal and Coke Co. Coleman was incorporated as a village in 1904 and as a town in 1910. In the past 50 years the town's two mines have produced 25 million tons of coal and almost 2 million tons of metallurgical coke.

LEGEND

♠ CHURCHES
1. Holy Spirit Roman Catholic Church
2. Crowsnest Bible Chapel

☐ HOTELS
1. Stop Inn Motel
2. Grand Union Motel

✳ POINTS OF INTEREST
1. Crowsnest Historical Museum

⌂ SCHOOLS
1. Horace Allen Elementary School
2. Crowsnest Consolidated High School

For explanation of symbols, see General Legend on page 5

NORTH

TO CRANBROOK, B.C. 117 MILES (189 KM)

TO CALGARY 134 MILES (216 KM)
TO LETHBRIDGE 88 MILES (142 KM)

KANNASKIS RD

FLUMERFELT PK.

CANADIAN PACIFIC RAILWAY

CROWSNEST RIVER

EDMONTON

CALGARY

MUNICIPALITY OF CROWSNEST PASS

NORTH

Drayton Valley

Population: 4,867.

Location: On Highway 39, 86 miles (138 km.) southwest of Edmonton and 188 miles (303 km.) northwest of Calgary.

Street System: Streets run north and south, from 37 Street in the east to 80 Street in the west. Odd numbers are on the east side of the street. Avenues run east and west, from 41 Avenue in the south to 56 Avenue in the north with odd numbers on the north side.

Transportation Facilities: The town is not on a rail line and has no scheduled air service. Buses run once daily to Calgary and Edmonton. Inter-city courier service is available.

History: Drayton Valley is primarily an oil service centre. Before 1911, the site was called Power House because of a proposed project (never built) to dam the North Saskatchewan River. In 1911, the name was changed to Drayton Valley, after the British home town of the Drake family who ran the local post office. With the Alberta oil boom, population in the tiny community soared from 75 people in 1953 to 2,000 in 1954.

LEGEND

⚱ CHURCHES

1. Drayton Valley United Church
2. All Saints Anglican Church
3. Church of God
4. St. Anthony's Roman Catholic Church
5. Emmaus Lutheran Church
6. Pentecostal Tabernacle
7. Calvary Baptist Church
8. Jehovah's Witnesses Kingdom Hall
9. St. Peter's and St. Paul's Ukrainian Catholic Church
10. Church of Jesus Christ of Latter-Day Saints

▢ HOTELS

1. Twin Pines Motor Inn
2. Ceasar's Inn
3. Drayton Valley Hotel
4. Coach Motel
5. Matador Motel
6. Aspen Motor Inn
7. Blackgold Inn
8. Westwind Motor Inn

⌂ SCHOOLS

1. Eldorado Elementary School
2. St. Anthony's Catholic School
3. Frank Maddock High School
4. H. W. Pickup Junior High School
5. Elementary (B) School

For explanation of symbols, see General Legend on page 5

Drumheller

Population: 6,671.

Location: Beside the Red Deer River on Highway 9 in Alberta's Badlands, 86 miles (138 km.) northeast of Calgary and 176 miles (283 km.) southeast of Edmonton.

Street System: Streets run north and south, from Centre Street to 19 Street in the east and from Centre Street to 25 Street in the west. Odd numbers are on the west side of the streets. Avenues run east and west, from 4 Avenue in the north to 12 Avenue in the south, with odd numbers on the south side of the avenues.

Transportation Facilities: Drumheller is on the CN rail line but has no passenger rail service. Buses run twice daily each way between Drumheller and Calgary and once daily between Drumheller and Edmonton. There is no scheduled air service. Inter-city courier service is available.

History: One of the first settlers in the area was Thomas Greentree, a rancher. The city took its name from one Samuel Drumheller, who came to the Alberta coalfields and opened a mine in Drumheller in 1918. Drumheller was incorporated as a city in 1930.

LEGEND

⚑ CHURCHES
1. Church of Jesus Christ of Latter-Day Saints
2. Grace Lutheran Church
3. St. Anthony's Roman Catholic Church
4. St. Magloire's Anglican Church
5. Fellowship Baptist Church
6. Pentecostal Church
7. Knox United Church
8. Church of The Nazarene
9. Alliance Church
10. Parkdale Baptist Church

☐ HOTELS
1. Western Gem Hotel
2. Badlands Motel
3. Rockhound Motor Inn
4. Dinosaur Motel
5. Dinosaur Hotel
6. Hotel Waldorf
7. Alexandra Hotel
8. Travelodge
9. Drumheller Inn
10. Hoo-Doo Motel

✳ POINTS OF INTEREST
1. Future Home of Tyrell Museum of Palaeontology (Scheduled Opening 1985)
2. Homestead Museum
3. Dinosaur Monument
4. Drumheller Fossil Museum
5. Prehistoric Parks

⌂ SCHOOLS
1. Central Elementary School
2. Greentree Junior High School
3. St. Anthony's Catholic Elementary and Junior High School
4. Drumheller Composite High School

For explanation of symbols, see General Legend on page 5

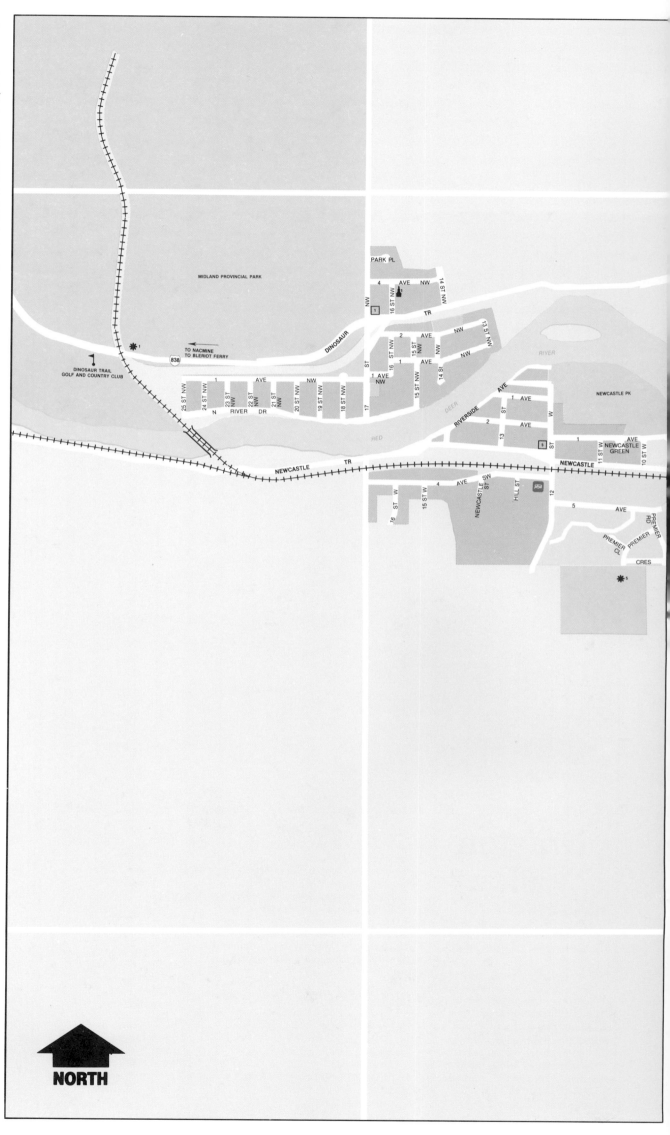

NORTH

Feet 0 500 1,000 1,500 2,000
Metres 0 100 200 300 400 500 600

Edson

Population: 7,329.

Location: On Highway 16, 124 miles (199 km.) west of Edmonton, and 102 miles (164 km.) east of Jasper.

Street System: Streets run north and south, from 40 Street in the east to 59 Street in the west. Avenues run east and west, from 1 Avenue (Railway Avenue) in the south to 18 Avenue in the north. Odd numbers are on the east side of the streets and south side of the avenues.

Transportation Facilities: Edson is on the CN rail line and has VIA Rail service from Edmonton and Jasper three times a week. Greyhound buses run three times a day between Edson and Edmonton. There is no scheduled air service but there is a private heliport which serves the coal and petroleum industry. Inter-city courier service is available.

History: The Edson site came about in the race between the Grand Trunk Pacific and Canadian Northern Railways for construction of a line through the Yellowhead Pass. In 1909, the GTP beat CN and planned to establish its mountain divisional point 18 miles east of what is now Edson. Speculators had driven up the price of land at that spot, however, so the flag was planted instead in muskeg at a site called Heatherwood. The town was renamed Edson after Edson J. Chamberlain, general manager of the GTP. Edson was incorporated as a village in January 1911, and as a town in September of 1911.

LEGEND

CHURCHES

1. Church of Jesus Christ of Latter-Day Saints
2. Edson United Church
3. Bethel Pentecostal Church
4. Seventh-Day Adventist Church
5. Edson Baptist Church
6. Russian Orthodox Church
7. St. Catherine's Anglican Church of Canada
8. Christian Reformed Church
9. Grace Lutheran Church
10. Sacred Heart Roman Catholic Church
11. Ukrainian Catholic Church

HOTELS

1. Cedars Motel
2. Castle Motel
3. Blackstrap Motor Inn
4. Yellowhead Motel
5. Sundowner Inn
6. Edson Motor Hotel
7. Hotel Commodore
8. Black Gold Inn
9. Summit Motel
10. Pick and Lantern Inn
11. Plainsman Motor Inn
12. Totem Motel
13. Pine Motel
14. Park Avenue Motel

POINTS OF INTEREST

1. Historic Station House

SCHOOLS

1. Evergreen Elementary School
2. Vanier Catholic Elementary and Junior High School
3. West Haven Elementary School
4. Jubilee Junior High School
5. Parkland Composite High School
6. Pine Grove Elementary School
7. Central Elementary School
8. A. H. Dakin Elementary School

For explanation of symbols, see General Legend on page 5

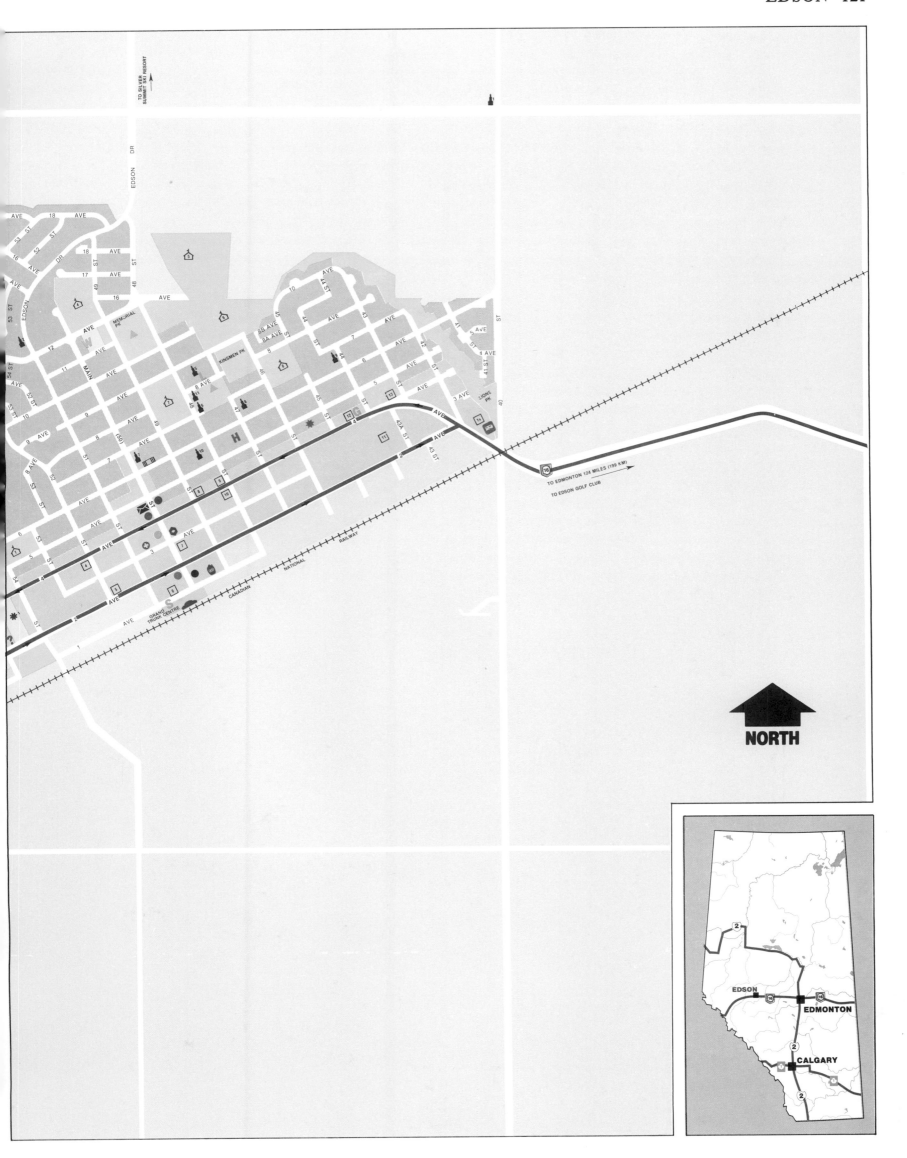

TO SILVER
SUMMIT SKI RESORT

EDSON   DR

NORTH

TO EDMONTON 124 MILES (199 KM)
TO EDSON GOLF CLUB

EDSON
EDMONTON

CALGARY

Hinton

Population: 8,825.

Location: On Highway 16, the Yellowhead Highway, 178 miles (286 km.) west of Edmonton.

Street System: Streets in the town are named, with odd numbers on the south and west sides of the streets and even numbers on the north and east sides of streets.

Transportation Facilities: The town is located on the CN main line. Via Rail passenger service runs three times a week to Edmonton eastward and Jasper and Prince Rupert westward. There are three buses daily from Hinton to Edmonton and four from Edmonton to Hinton. There is no scheduled air service. Inter-city courier service is available.

History: One of the first white men to see the site of present-day Hinton was the explorer David Thompson, who ascended the Athabasca River past Hinton in 1810. A century later, in 1911, the Grand Trunk Pacific Railway was completed to Hinton and the town was named after W.D. Hinton, one of the railway company's general managers. In 1956, the province's first pulp mill, operated by St. Regis Paper Company, was opened in Hinton. Hinton was incorporated as a town in 1958.

LEGEND

⌖ CHURCHES
1. Hinton Christian Centre
2. Hinton United Church
3. Grace Lutheran Church
4. Anglican Church of St. Francis of Assisi
5. Bethany Baptist Church
6. Our Lady of the Foothills Roman Catholic Church
7. Jehovah's Witnesses Kingdom Hall
8. Church of Jesus Christ of Latter-Day Saints (Meetings in Hinton Recreation Complex)

☐ HOTELS
1. Johnson's Motel
2. Pines Motel

3. Inn West
4. Twin Pines Motel
5. Big Horn Motel
6. Tara Vista Motel
7. Greentree Travel Lodge
8. Hotel Timberland
9. Hinton Hotel
10. Downtowner Motel
11. Rocking Star Motel
12. Athabasca Valley Hotel

⌂ **SCHOOLS**

1. Mountain View Elementary School
2. Overlander Junior High School
3. Harry Collinge High School
4. Crescent Valley Elementary School

For explanation of symbols, see General Legend on page 5

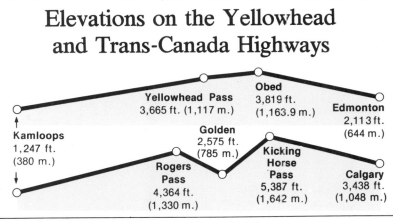

Elevations on the Yellowhead and Trans-Canada Highways

Kamloops 1,247 ft. (380 m.)

Yellowhead Pass 3,665 ft. (1,117 m.)

Obed 3,819 ft. (1,163.9 m.)

Edmonton 2,113 ft. (644 m.)

Golden 2,575 ft. (785 m.)

Rogers Pass 4,364 ft. (1,330 m.)

Kicking Horse Pass 5,387 ft. (1,642 m.)

Calgary 3,438 ft. (1,048 m.)

The Yellowhead Highway extends from Winnipeg to Prince Rupert, B.C., with a southern arm to Kamloops, a total of 1,998 miles (3,216 km.). The highest point of the highway occurs, not in the mountains, but between Hinton and Edson at Obed.

The Trans-Canada Highway which takes the southern route through the mountains has considerably higher elevations. In a 268-mile (431 km.) stretch from Kamloops to Kicking-Horse Pass, the highway rises 4,140 ft. (1,262 m.). In the Selkirk range, the Rogers Pass section of the highway rises 2,992 ft. (912 m.) in approximately 30 miles (48 km.).

High River

Population: 5,049.

Location: The town of High River is located 35 miles (56 km.) south of Calgary on Highway 2A.

Street System: Streets run north and south from 1 Street E. to 24 Street E., east of the railway tracks, and from 1 Street W. to 12 Street W., west of the railway tracks. Odd numbers are on the west side of the streets. Avenues run east and west, from 1 Avenue S. to 12 Avenue S. on the south side of the river and from

1 Avenue to 4 Avenue north of the river. Odd numbers are on the south side of the avenues.

Transportation Facilities: The town is located on the CP Rail line but has no passenger rail service. There are five buses daily to Calgary and four a day from Calgary to High River. Inter-city courier service is available. There is no scheduled air service.

History: High River was originally called "The Crossing" because it was a convenient spot to cross the Highwood River. The first couple to settle there were Katy and John Quirk who drove their herd of cattle from Montana in

1882, built a log cabin and settled at High River. High River was incorporated as a village in 1901 and as a town in 1906. Former Prime Minister Joseph Clark was born in High River.

LEGEND

⚑ CHURCHES

1. High River United Church
2. Full Gospel Tabernacle
3. Salvation Army
4. Church of the Nazarene
5. High River Baptist Church
6. St. Benedict Anglican Church
7. Christian Reformed Church
8. St. Francis de Sales Catholic Church
9. Church of Jesus Christ of Latter-Day Saints
10. Good Shepherd Lutheran Church

☐ HOTELS

1. Gateway Hotel
2. High River Motor Hotel
3. Foothills Motel
4. Heritage Inn

✳ POINTS OF INTEREST

1. Museum of the Highwood

⌂ SCHOOLS

1. Senator Riley High School
2. Joe Clark School
3. Spitzee Elementary School

For explanation of symbols, see General Legend on page 5

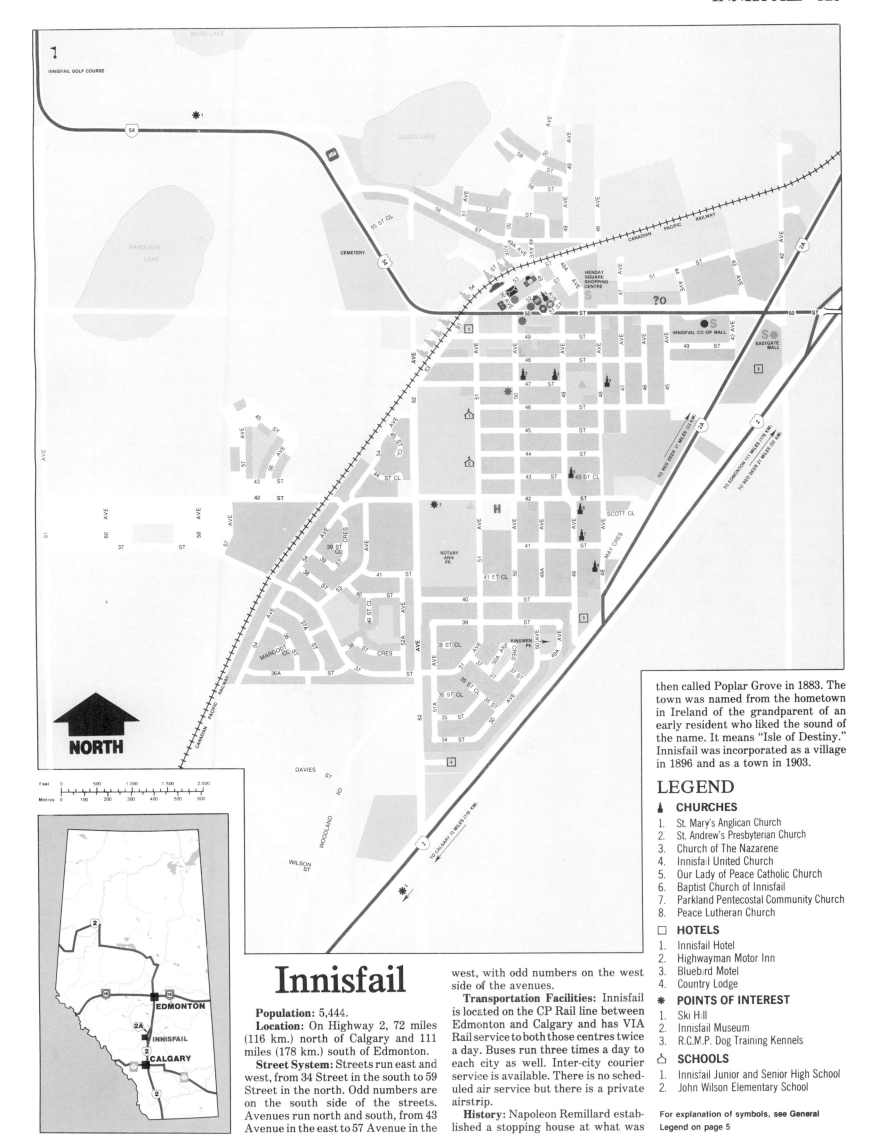

then called Poplar Grove in 1883. The town was named from the hometown in Ireland of the grandparent of an early resident who liked the sound of the name. It means "Isle of Destiny." Innisfail was incorporated as a village in 1896 and as a town in 1903.

LEGEND

🛆 CHURCHES

1. St. Mary's Anglican Church
2. St. Andrew's Presbyterian Church
3. Church of The Nazarene
4. Innisfail United Church
5. Our Lady of Peace Catholic Church
6. Baptist Church of Innisfail
7. Parkland Pentecostal Community Church
8. Peace Lutheran Church

☐ HOTELS

1. Innisfail Hotel
2. Highwayman Motor Inn
3. Bluebird Motel
4. Country Lodge

✳ POINTS OF INTEREST

1. Ski Hill
2. Innisfail Museum
3. R.C.M.P. Dog Training Kennels

⌂ SCHOOLS

1. Innisfail Junior and Senior High School
2. John Wilson Elementary School

For explanation of symbols, see General Legend on page 5

Innisfail

Population: 5,444.

Location: On Highway 2, 72 miles (116 km.) north of Calgary and 111 miles (178 km.) south of Edmonton.

Street System: Streets run east and west, from 34 Street in the south to 59 Street in the north. Odd numbers are on the south side of the streets. Avenues run north and south, from 43 Avenue in the east to 57 Avenue in the west, with odd numbers on the west side of the avenues.

Transportation Facilities: Innisfail is located on the CP Rail line between Edmonton and Calgary and has VIA Rail service to both those centres twice a day. Buses run three times a day to each city as well. Inter-city courier service is available. There is no scheduled air service but there is a private airstrip.

History: Napoleon Remillard established a stopping house at what was

Jasper

Population: 3,404.

Location: Beside the Athabasca River in Jasper National Park on Highways 16 and 93, 225 miles (362 km.) west of Edmonton and 256 miles (412 km.) northwest of Calgary.

Transportation Facilities: This resort centre has VIA Rail service three times a week to and from Edmonton and Prince Rupert. There are three buses daily between Edmonton and Jasper and during the summer there is daily bus service to Banff. There is no scheduled air service. Inter-city courier service is available.

History: The area around Jasper was declared a federal preserve in 1907, when both the Grand Trunk Pacific and the Canadian Northern Railways were planning lines to the west coast through the Yellowhead Pass for which Jasper is the eastern access. The GTP line came through in 1911 followed two years later by the CN. In 1913 the townsite was surveyed. One early settler to the area, Lewis John Swift, a farmer located outside the town but in the park, refused to sell to the government and his land remained freehold until 1962 when the rights reverted to the federal government. Jasper was named after Jasper Hawes who set up a fur trading post in the area about 1817. The town is not incorporated and is administered by the federal government under Parks Canada.

LEGEND

🛉 CHURCHES
1. Jasper Park Baptist Church
2. Jasper Lutheran Church
3. Our Lady of Lourdes Catholic Church
4. Anglican Church of St. Mary and St. George
5. Jasper United Church
6. Jasper Assembly of God

☐ HOTELS
1. Jasper Park Lodge
2. Sawridge Hotel Jasper
3. Marmot Motor Lodge
4. Tonquin Motor Inn
5. Lobstick Lodge
6. Chateau Jasper
7. Jasper Inn
8. Roche Bonhomme Bungalows
9. Andrew Motor Lodge
10. Astoria Motor Inn
11. Athabasca Hotel
12. Whistlers Motor Hotel
13. Mount Robson Motor Inn
14. Diamond Motel

✱ POINTS OF INTEREST
1. Jasper The Bear
2. Historic Train Station
3. The Den (Wildlife Display in Whistlers Motor Hotel)

⌂ SCHOOLS
1. Jasper Junior and Senior High School
2. Jasper Elementary School

For explanation of symbols, see General Legend on page 5

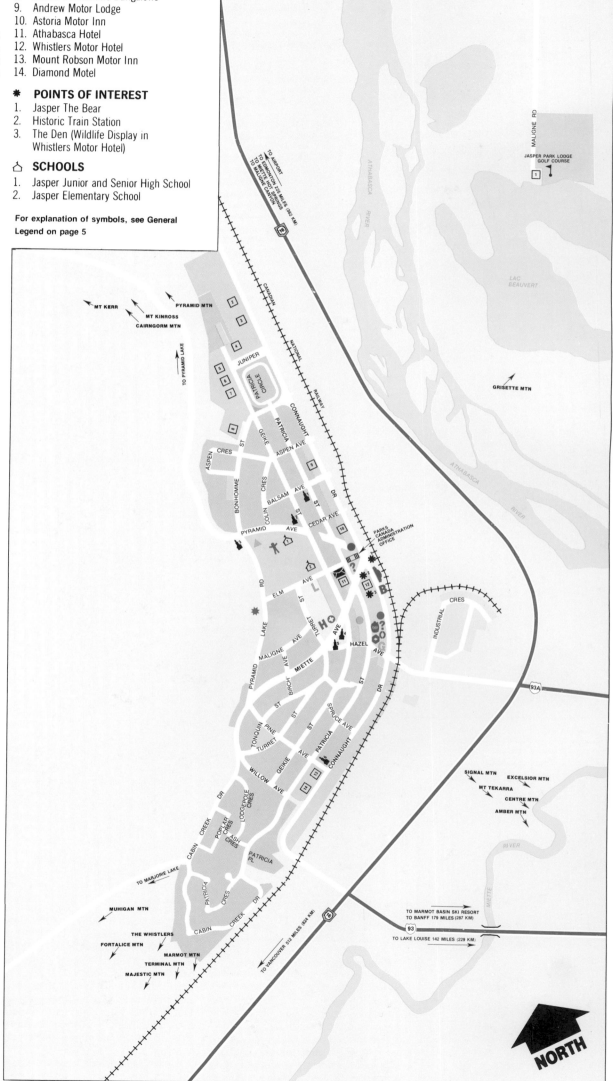

Lacombe

Population: 5,723.

Location: On Highway 2A, 79 miles (128 km.) south of Edmonton and 103 miles (166 km.) north of Calgary.

Street System: Streets run north and south, from 47 Street in the east to 64 Street in the west with odd numbers on the east side. Avenues run east and west from 43 Avenue in the south to 55 Avenue in the north with odd numbers on the south side.

Transportation Facilities: Greyhound buses run four times daily between Edmonton and Lacombe and five times a day to and from Calgary. Lacombe is on the CP Calgary-Edmonton line but has no passenger rail service. Inter-city courier service is available.

History: Lacombe was first settled in 1883 by Ed Barnett, an ex-Northwest Mounted Police officer, who set up a stopping house between Edmonton and Calgary. Officials of the CPR renamed siding 17 Lacombe in memory of Father Albert Lacombe who worked with the Indians to allow the railway to be built. Lacombe was incorporated as a village in 1896 and as a town in 1902.

LEGEND

⛪ CHURCHES

1. Seventh-Day Adventist Church
2. Trinity Lutheran Church
3. Church of The Nazarene
4. First Baptist Church
5. St. Stephen's Catholic Church
6. Bethel Christian Reformed Church
7. St. Andrew's United Church
8. Pentecostal Tabernacle
9. St. Cyprian's Anglican Church
10. Grace Chapel
11. Calvary Evangelical Free Church
12. Jehovah's Witnesses Kingdom Hall

☐ HOTELS

1. Lacombe Motor Inn
2. Lacombe Hotel
3. Empress Hotel
4. Empress Motel

⌂ SCHOOLS

1. Lacombe Composite High School
2. James S. McCormack Elementary School
3. Lacombe Junior High School
4. Lacombe Christian Elementary and Junior High School (Private)

For explanation of symbols, see General Legend on page 5

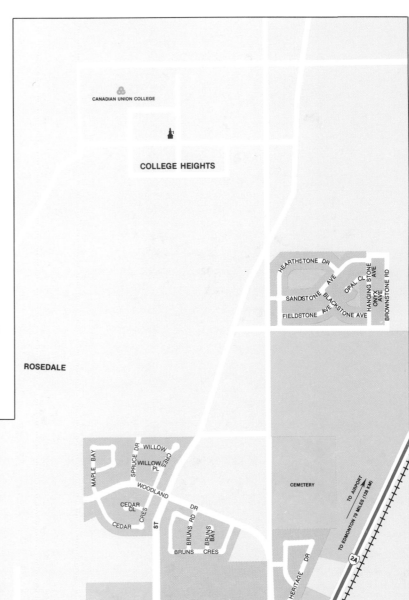

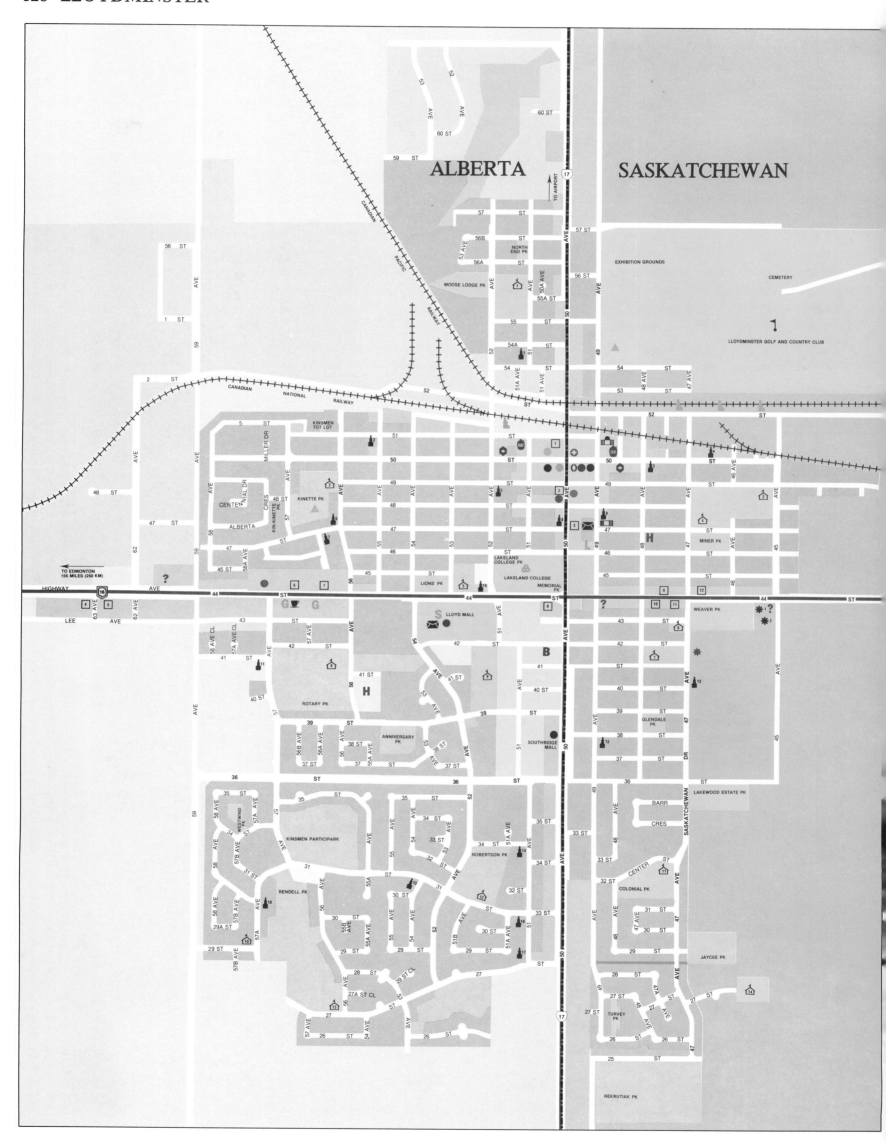

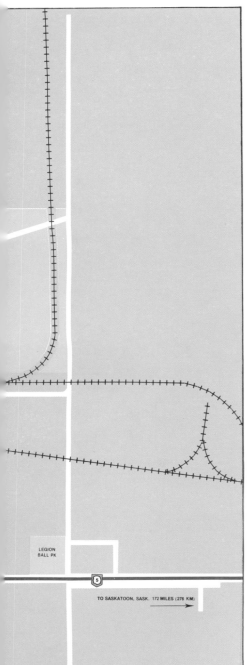

LEGION BALL PK

TO SASKATOON, SASK. 172 MILES (276 KM)

NORTH

Lloydminster

Population: 15,232.

Location: On Highway 16, 155 miles (250 km.) east of Edmonton, straddling the border between Alberta and Saskatchewan.

Street System: Streets run east and west, from 25th in the south to 60th in the north with odd numbers on the south side of the streets. Avenues run north and south, from 45th in the east to 63rd in the west with odd numbers on the east side. The main north-south road is 50th Avenue or Meridian which is also the provincial boundary.

Transportation Facilities: Located on both the CN and CP rail lines, but has no passenger rail service. Buses between Lloydminster and Edmonton run five times daily. There is no scheduled air service. Inter- and intra-city couriers are available.

History: Lloydminster was settled in 1903 by a group of British settlers led by the Reverend Isaac Barr and his English Missionary Society. Two thousand people left Great Britain for Canada with Barr. The group split up in Saskatchewan with 500 following the Reverend George Lloyd to the site of Lloydminster. In 1905 the provinces of Alberta and Saskatchewan were created, with the boundary established at the 4th Meridian which cut through the centre of the community. The two halves operated as separate municipalities with their own councils and police forces until 1930, when they were incorporated as one city.

LEGEND

🔥 CHURCHES

1. Holy Ghost Ukrainian Catholic Church
2. Salvation Army
3. Church of God
4. Maranatha Christian Centre
5. Knox Presbyterian Church
6. Church of Christ
7. Ukrainian Orthodox Church
8. Grace United Church
9. St. John's Anglican Church
10. St. Anthony's Roman Catholic Church
11. Southridge Community Church
12. First Baptist Church
13. Mennonite Brethren Church

14. Church of Jesus Christ of Latter-Day Saints
15. Seventh-Day Adventist Church
16. Pentecostal Tabernacle
17. Jehovah's Witnesses Kingdom Hall
18. First Lutheran Church

☐ HOTELS

1. Alberta Hotel
2. Prince Charles Motor Inn
3. Capri Motor Inn
4. Lodge Motel
5. Ivanhoe Motel
6. Esquire Motor Inn
7. Thunderbird Motel
8. Lloydminster Motel
9. Voyageur Motel
10. Good Knight Motel
11. Trailside Inn
12. Cedar Inn

✳ POINTS OF INTEREST

1. Barr Colony Museum
2. Fuchs Wildlife Display

⌂ SCHOOLS

1. Queen Elizabeth Elementary School
2. Martin Browne Elementary School
3. E. S. Laird Junior High School
4. Neville Goss Elementary School
5. St. Thomas Elementary School
6. Parkland School (For the Handicapped)
7. Avery Elementary School
8. Comprehensive High School
9. St. Mary's Catholic Junior High School
10. St. Joseph's Catholic Elementary School
11. Father Gorman's Catholic Elementary School
12. Barr Colony Elementary School
13. Bishop Lloyd Junior High School
14. Winston Churchill Elementary School

For explanation of symbols, see General Legend on page 5

Lloydminster
Canada's bi-provincial city

The city of Lloydminster is unique in North America because it in effect exists legally in two provinces at the same time. There are many examples of "twin cities" (Ottawa and Hull, Minneapolis and St. Paul), but in those cases two separate corporate bodies exist. What's unique about Lloydminster is that there's only one and it's recognized by both provinces.

When the provinces of Saskatchewan and Alberta were created out of the Northwest Territories in 1905, most of the settlement at Lloydminster was on the east side of the fourth meridian, in Saskatchewan. The new provincial boundary thus created the Town of Lloydminster, Saskatchewan, and a village of Lloydminster, Alberta. The two had separate elections for mayor and councillors and separate police and fire departments with no jurisdiction outside their own municipal borders.

They remained separate for 25 years when the awkwardness and additional expense of duplication led officials in each community to request the provincial governments to amalgamate the communities into one city. In 1930 both legislatures passed laws incorporating the city of Lloydminster, Saskatchewan-Alberta.

For city administrators, however, such a hybrid creature means four times the paperwork as they fill out and file forms and keep records for two masters. Programs which apply in one province do not necessarily apply in the other and officials run back and forth trying to work out schemes to serve all the residents. There is no blanket policy between the two provinces on how to deal with Lloydminster so each new program unveiled by either results in meetings, negotiations and pleadings with the governments.

For residents of Lloydminster life can be confusing. About 60% of them now live on the Alberta side of the border. The Alberta liquor store outsells its Saskatchewan counterpart because of cheaper prices, except during Alberta's frequent beer strikes. Hotels on the Alberta side of town serve 18 year olds. In Saskatchewan one has to be 19 to drink legally.

People who work in Saskatchewan are eligible for a minimum wage of $4.35 an hour and three weeks vacation after one year. Albertans aren't so fortunate. Their minimum is $3.85 with two weeks holidays after one year. The trick, say some locals, is to live in Alberta, where income tax is lower, but to work in Saskatchewan where the benefits are better.

Sales tax is another confusion. Technically, Saskatchewan retailers are obliged to charge a 5% health and education tax on all goods purchased and consumed in Saskatchewan. The administrative nightmare and higher prices mean that most don't do it—except on high-priced goods like cars and major appliances. Instead they estimate what they owe the province and send a cheque to Regina or they just don't pay.

All telephones are serviced by Alberta Government Telephones but power is provided by both Alberta Power and Saskatchewan Power. However, Alberta residents get a rebate on power bills from Alberta Power so that rates vary wildly throughout the city.

Housing prices are higher on the Alberta side since more people want to live there. During the boom years in the late '70s, prices varied by as much as one-third. The province of Alberta charges a monthly fee for health care while Saskatchewan does not, but the city's hospital is located in Saskatchewan.

With all the confusion and additional expense of operating (estimated by one city official at almost double the cost of other cities) one wonders why the city wouldn't be declared the property of one province or the other. Never, says a local resident. Citizens of Saskatchewan do not want to give up their status nor do Albertans. They like it this way.

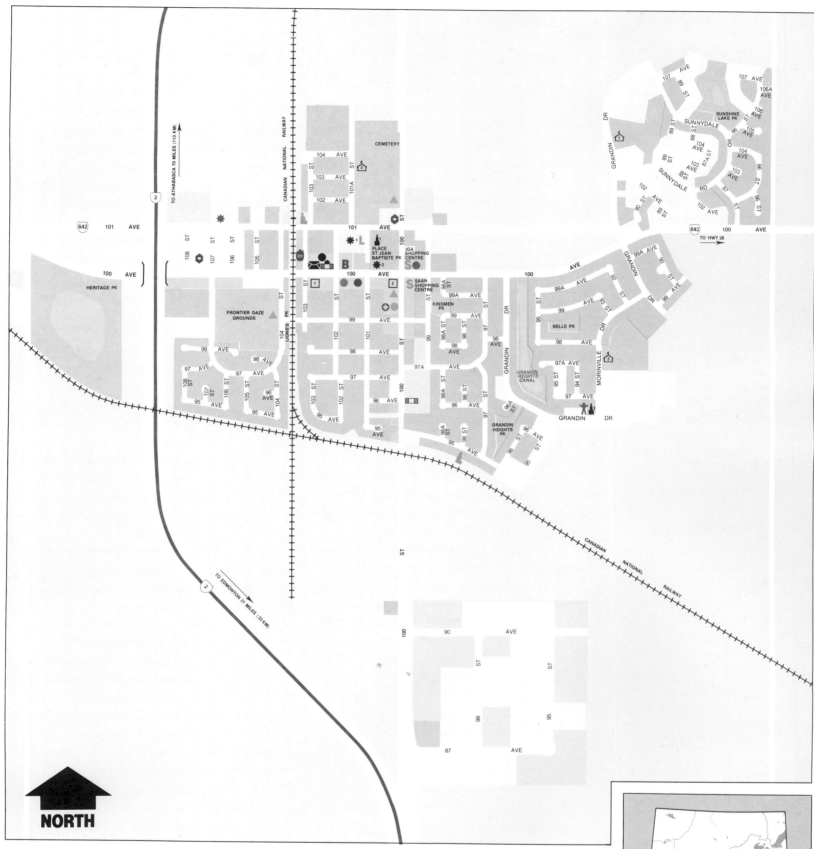

NORTH

Morinville

Population: 5,109.

Location: 21 miles (33 km.) north of Edmonton on Highway 2.

Street System: Streets run north and south, from 86th in the east to 108th in the west with odd numbers on the east side of the streets. Avenues run east and west, from 87th in the south to 107th in the north, with odd numbers on the south side of the avenues.

Transportation Facilities: On the CN rail line but has no passenger rail service. There is no scheduled air service. Buses run three times daily to and from Edmonton. Inter-city courier service is available.

History: The first settlers to the Morinville area were French Canadians from Quebec brought to Alberta by Abbe Jean-Baptiste Morin, an Oblate missionary, who convinced them that a better life was to be had in the West. Named after the abbe, Morinville was incorporated as a village in 1905 and as a town in 1911.

LEGEND

CHURCHES
1. St. Jean Baptiste Roman Catholic Church
2. Morinville United Church

HOTELS
1. Frontiersman Hotel
2. Morinville Hotel

POINTS OF INTEREST
1. Notre Dame Convent
2. St. Jean Baptiste Rectory

SCHOOLS
1. Georges Primeau Junior and Senior High School
2. Georges P. Vanier Elementary School
3. Notre Dame Elementary School

For explanation of symbols, see General Legend on page 5

| Feet | 0 | 500 | 1,000 | 1,500 | 2,000 |
| Metres | 0 | 100 | 200 | 300 | 400 | 500 | 600 |

Indian bands, reserves and treaty areas

The Canadian government bought Rupert's Land from the Hudson's Bay Company in 1870. The government needed title to the land in order to build the Pacific railway, which necessitated treaties with the Indians. They signed three treaties in Alberta: Treaty 6 covering central Alberta in 1876, Treaty 7 covering southern Alberta in 1877, and Treaty 8 covering northern Alberta in 1899. In exchange for surrendering their rights to the land, the Indians were given reserves on a location of their own choice on the basis of five people per square mile and certain other privileges. The reserves were surveyed and more or less permanent boundaries were established. However, the government did have the right to expropriate land for roads and the Indians themselves could vote to surrender land, which they were often pressured to do between 1907 and 1920.

The original reserves were established on the basis of the existing Indian population. Since that time growth of some bands has led to overcrowding and disputes with the federal government over the treaties. In addition, there are arguments over whether the existence of the treaties quashes aboriginal rights, particularly since many of the band chiefs who signed the agreements did not understand what they were doing.

As of November 1983, there are 42,256 treaty Indians in the province of Alberta. They are divided into 41 bands occupying 1.62 million acres on 92 reserves. The largest band in the province is the Blood band in southern Alberta with a population of 6,015. The smallest is the Sawridge, located near the town of Slave Lake, with 41 members. Most bands are governed by a chief and council elected by the band members every two years. However, there are three bands in the province, the Dene Tha' in the northwest, the Heart Lake band near Cold Lake and the Grouard band in the Peace River area, which are run by chiefs elected for life. In the case of the Dene Tha', Chief Harry Chonkolay has been in charge since 1938.

Twenty-three reserves in the province obtain revenue from resources which amount to about $200 million annually. The four bands at Hobbema, the Ermineskin, Louis Bull, Montana and Samson, are the wealthiest in the province. The money obtained from resources is held in trust by the federal government and can be used for a variety of projects with government approval. For example, the Hobbema group has built a furniture factory and owns a semi-professional hockey team. The Sarcee Indians near Calgary have built a housing development and golf course at Bragg Creek called Redwood Meadows. The project is located on the reserve and the properties are available for lease or rental to non-band members. The Blackfoot Indians have also built a summer housing development and golf course called Siksika Vacation Resort just south of Cluny on the Bow River.

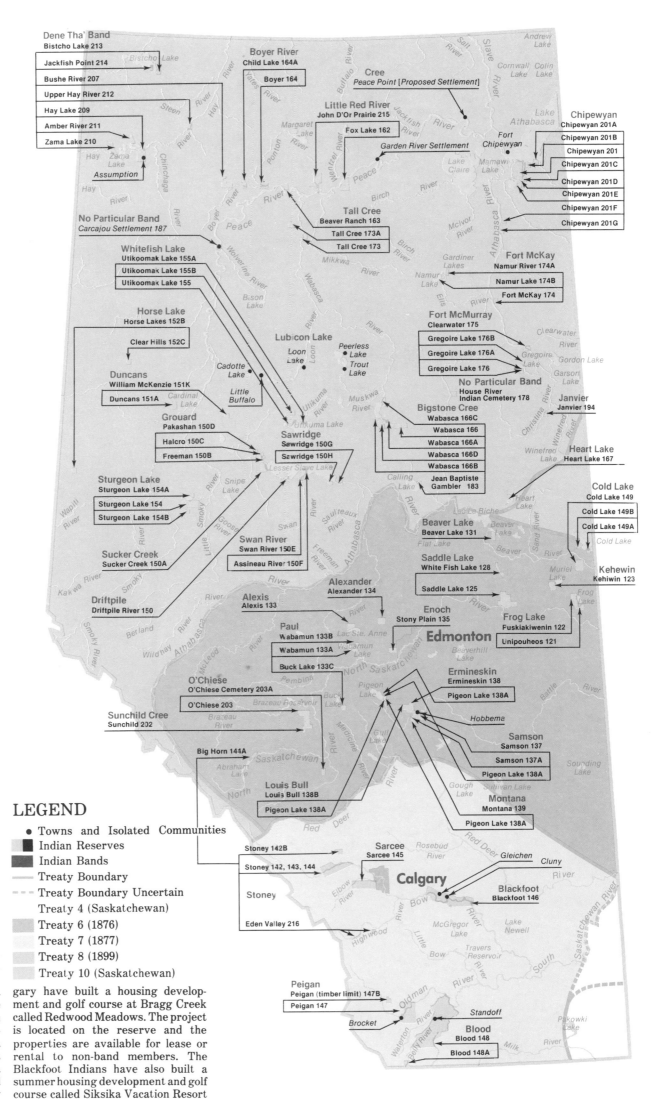

LEGEND

- • Towns and Isolated Communities
- ▪ Indian Reserves
- ▪ Indian Bands
- — Treaty Boundary
- --- Treaty Boundary Uncertain
- Treaty 4 (Saskatchewan)
- Treaty 6 (1876)
- Treaty 7 (1877)
- Treaty 8 (1899)
- Treaty 10 (Saskatchewan)

Peace River

Population: 6,043.

Location: 301 miles (485 km.) north-west of Edmonton on Highway 2.

Street System: Streets run north and south, from 73rd in the west to 103rd in the east with even numbers on the west side of the streets. Avenues run east and west, from 70th in the north to 116th in the south with even numbers on the north side of the avenues.

Transportation Facilities: The town is situated on the CN rail line but has no passenger rail service. Pacific Western Airlines and Time Air provide scheduled air service to Edmonton daily except Saturday. Inter-city courier service is available.

History: In 1793, Sir Alexander Mackenzie passed through the Peace River area on his trek to the Pacific, the first European to do so. Before 1900 the area was a centre for the fur trade and missionaries; then a publicity campaign across North America attracted homesteaders to the area, many from the United States. Peace River was incorporated as a village in 1914 and as a town in 1919.

LEGEND

CHURCHES
1. Salvation Army
2. Prince of Peace Lutheran Church
3. Jehovah's Witnesses Kingdom Hall
4. Church of Jesus Christ
   of Latter-Day Saints
5. First Baptist Church
6. Pentecostal Tabernacle
7. Anglican Cathedral of St. James
8. St. Paul's United Church
9. Our Lady of Peace
   Roman Catholic Church

HOTELS
1. Travellers Motor Hotel
2. Peace Valley Hotel
3. Crescent Motel
4. McNamara Hotel

POINTS OF INTEREST
1. Twelve Foot Davis Statue
2. Peace River Centennial Museum

SCHOOLS
1. McGrath Elementary School
2. Springfield Elementary School
3. T. A. Norris Junior High School
4. Glenmary Catholic School
5. Peace River High School
6. Immaculate Conception Catholic School

For explanation of symbols, see General Legend on page 5.

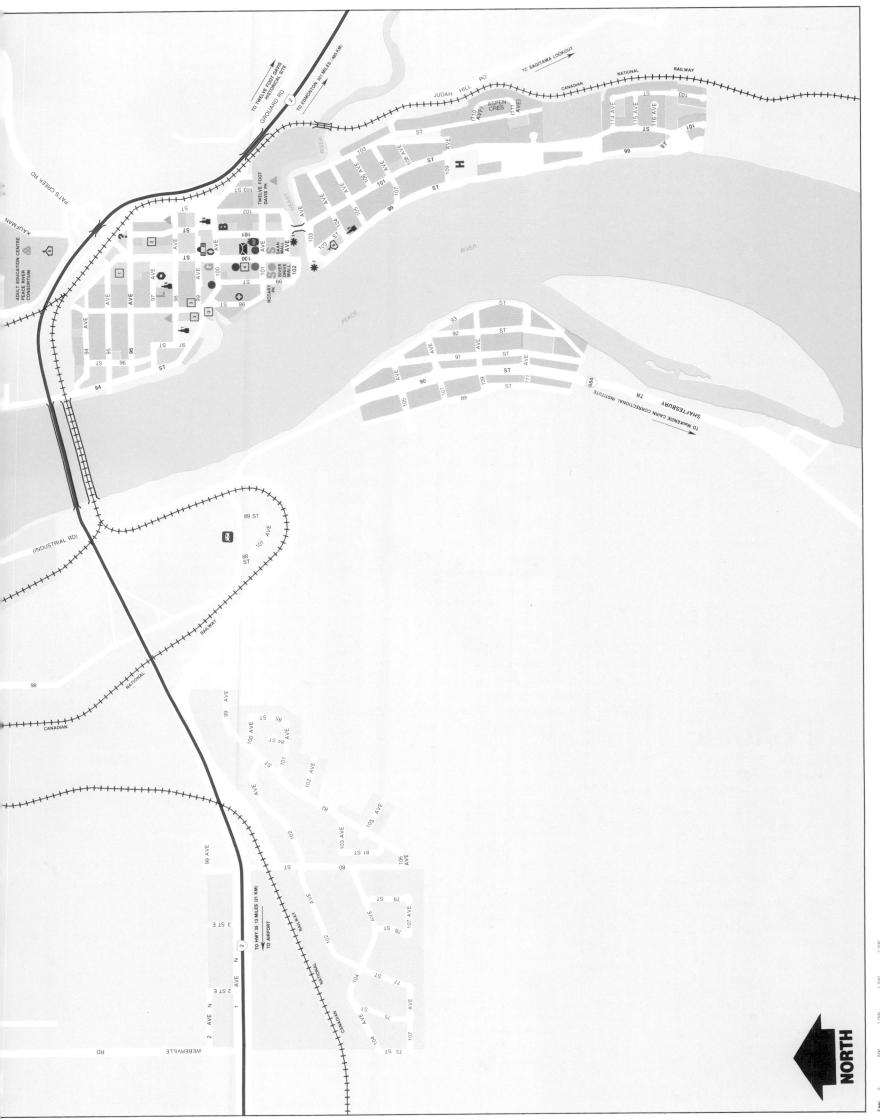

NORTH

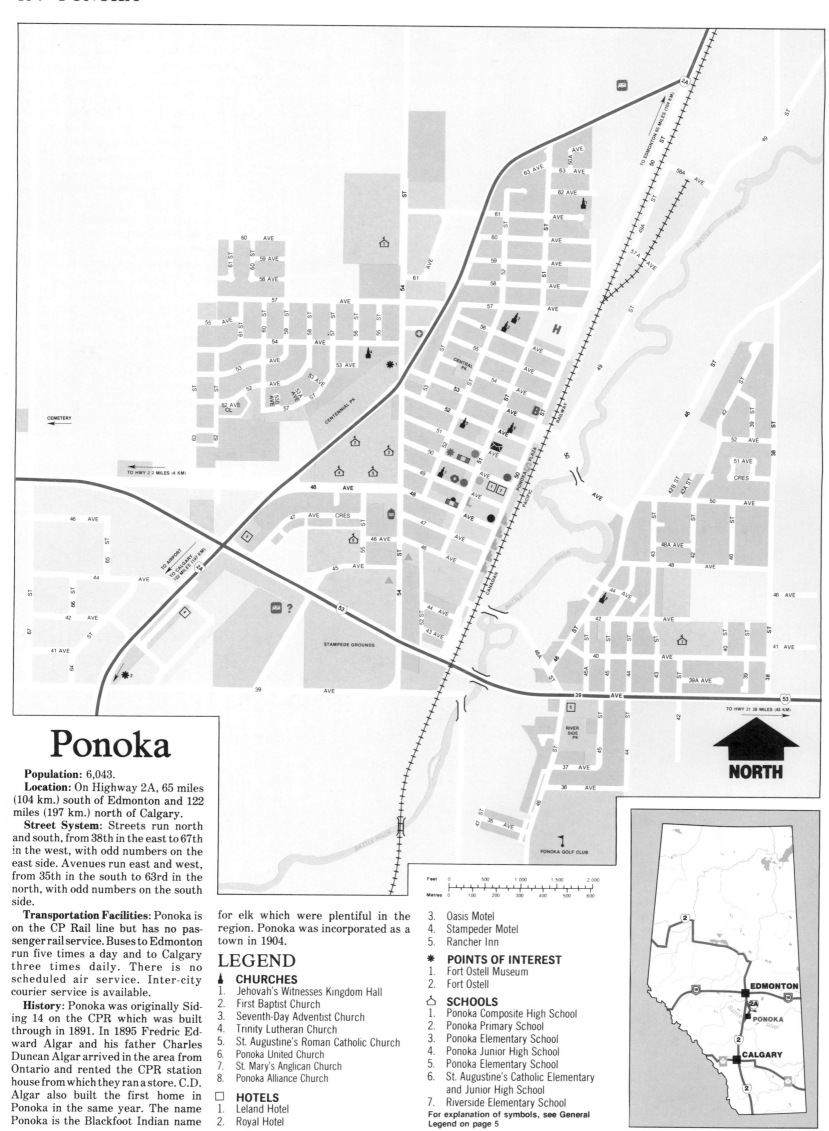

Ponoka

Population: 6,043.

Location: On Highway 2A, 65 miles (104 km.) south of Edmonton and 122 miles (197 km.) north of Calgary.

Street System: Streets run north and south, from 38th in the east to 67th in the west, with odd numbers on the east side. Avenues run east and west, from 35th in the south to 63rd in the north, with odd numbers on the south side.

Transportation Facilities: Ponoka is on the CP Rail line but has no passenger rail service. Buses to Edmonton run five times a day and to Calgary three times daily. There is no scheduled air service. Inter-city courier service is available.

History: Ponoka was originally Siding 14 on the CPR which was built through in 1891. In 1895 Fredric Edward Algar and his father Charles Duncan Algar arrived in the area from Ontario and rented the CPR station house from which they ran a store. C.D. Algar also built the first home in Ponoka in the same year. The name Ponoka is the Blackfoot Indian name for elk which were plentiful in the region. Ponoka was incorporated as a town in 1904.

LEGEND

CHURCHES
1. Jehovah's Witnesses Kingdom Hall
2. First Baptist Church
3. Seventh-Day Adventist Church
4. Trinity Lutheran Church
5. St. Augustine's Roman Catholic Church
6. Ponoka United Church
7. St. Mary's Anglican Church
8. Ponoka Alliance Church

HOTELS
1. Leland Hotel
2. Royal Hotel
3. Oasis Motel
4. Stampeder Motel
5. Rancher Inn

POINTS OF INTEREST
1. Fort Ostell Museum
2. Fort Ostell

SCHOOLS
1. Ponoka Composite High School
2. Ponoka Primary School
3. Ponoka Elementary School
4. Ponoka Junior High School
5. Ponoka Elementary School
6. St. Augustine's Catholic Elementary and Junior High School
7. Riverside Elementary School

For explanation of symbols, see General Legend on page 5

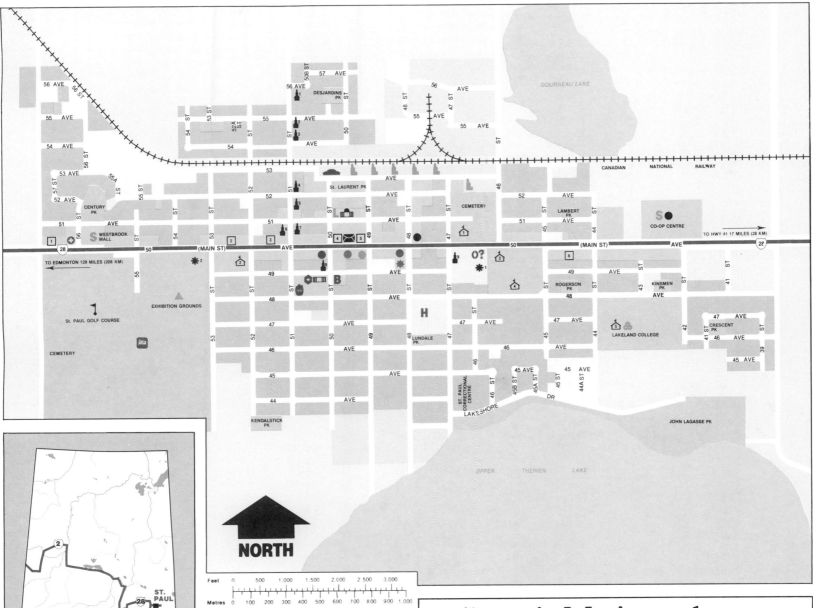

NORTH

Feet 0 500 1,000 1,500 2,000 2,500 3,000

Metres 0 100 200 300 400 500 600 700 800 900 1,000

St. Paul

Population: 4,963.

Location: On Highway 28, 129 miles (208 km.) northeast of Edmonton.

Street System: Streets run north and south, from 39th in the east to 57th in the west, with odd numbers on the east side of the streets. Avenues run east and west, from 44th in the south to 57th in the north, with odd numbers on the south side.

Transportation Facilities: On the CN rail line but has no passenger rail service. Buses travel to and from Edmonton twice daily. There is no scheduled air service. Inter-city courier service is available.

History: St. Paul des Metis was established in 1896 as a Metis settlement and mission by the Oblate fathers of Quebec after an earlier Metis colony was wiped out by disease. In 1909 it was opened to white settlers and 500 people stood in line at the Edmonton land office to apply for homesteads. St. Paul des Metis acquired village status in 1912; it was incorporated as a town in 1936, and the name was changed to St. Paul.

LEGEND

⚑ **CHURCHES**
1. Church of Jesus Christ of Latter-Day Saints
2. Greek Orthodox Church
3. St. Paul Mission Church
4. Ukrainian Catholic Church
5. St. Paul United Church
6. St. Paul Pentecostal Church
7. Anglican Parish of St. Joan
8. St. Paul Alliance Church
9. St. Paul's Roman Catholic Cathedral

☐ **HOTELS**
1. King's Motel
2. Lakeland Motel
3. Galaxy Motel
4. Donald Hotel
5. Habitat Inn
6. Apollo Motel

✳ **POINTS OF INTEREST**
1. Cultural Centre
2. U.F.O. Landing Pad

⌂ **SCHOOLS**
1. Racette Junior High School
2. Glen Avon Protestant Elementary and Junior High School
3. New Hope Catholic Elementary School
4. St. Paul Elementary School
5. St. Paul Regional High School

For explanation of symbols, see General Legend on page 5

Alberta's Metis settlements

In 1885 a Metis rebellion in Saskatchewan was crushed by central Canadian troops. With their capital Batoche captured and their leader Louis Riel executed, many Metis drifted west into Alberta.

The Ottawa government found an inexpensive measure to placate their need for land. Scrip was issued to all Metis entitling each individual to a quarter section homestead. Some did become successful settlers but far more did not. Most Metis lacked the training, equipment and motivation required to transform raw bush and prairie into profitable farms.

In 1896 the Roman Catholic Church tried to remedy this situation. Receiving a federal lease on four townships in northeast Alberta, the church drew 50 families to its settlement, St. Paul des Metis. Again some individuals prospered but the majority did not. In 1910 the Ottawa administration opened unoccupied lands in the settlement to all comers.

Metis poverty during the 1930s shocked the provincial government into action. After heavy lobbying by what was then called the "Half-Breed Association of Alberta," the province in 1939 set aside substantial tracts of land for their use.

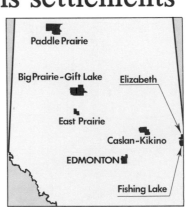

Each of the nine parcels was placed in the jurisdiction of a settlement association. Membership in these associations is open to adults with at least one Indian grandparent and five years' residence in Alberta. Settlement land cannot be sold to outsiders. These settlements are governed by elected councils with powers similar in many respects to those of municipalities.

One settlement, Wolf Lake, was revoked by government order in 1960, the area being transformed into the Cold Lake Air Weapons Range. The lands of the remaining eight total 1.25 million acres. Approximately 4,000 Metis form the total population in these settlements.

Stettler

Population: 5,136.

Location: On Highways 12 and 56, 115 miles (185 km.) southeast of Edmonton and 143 miles (230 km.) northeast of Calgary.

Street System: Streets run north and south, from 40th in the east to 74th in the west, with odd numbers on the east side. Avenues run east and west, from 35th in the south to 53rd in the north, with odd numbers on the south side.

Transportation Facilities: Stettler is on both the CN and CP rail lines but has no passenger rail service. Buses run once daily to Edmonton and Calgary. There is no scheduled air service. Inter-city courier service is available.

History: Stettler was originally a Swiss farming settlement called Blumenau, established around the turn of the century. A pause in construction of the CPR in 1905 encouraged growth there. Carl Stettler, the Blumenau postmaster who built a hotel and store there, gave his name to the village which was incorporated in 1905. It became a town in 1906.

LEGEND

⛪ CHURCHES
1. Jehovah's Witnesses Kingdom Hall
2. Christ-King Catholic Church
3. Church of The Nazarene
4. Stettler United Church
5. St. George's Anglican Church
6. St. Peter's Evangelical Lutheran Church
7. Pentecostal Assembly Church
8. Seventh-Day Adventist Church
9. Stettler Baptist Church
10. Church of Jesus Christ of Latter-Day Saints

☐ HOTELS
1. Stettler Hotel
2. Royal Hotel
3. Crusader Motel
4. Stettler Motel
5. Plainsman Motor Inn
6. Heartlander Motel
7. Grandview Motel

✳ POINTS OF INTEREST
1. Stettler Town and Country Museum

⌂ SCHOOLS
1. William E. Hay Composite High School
2. Stettler Junior High School
3. Stettler Elementary School
4. Waverly County Elementary and Junior High School

For explanation of symbols, see General Legend on page 5

NORTH

Taber

Population: 5,988.

Location: On Highways 3 and 36, 165 miles (266 km.) southeast of Calgary.

Street System: Streets run north and south, from 46 Street in the west to 64 Street in the east, with odd numbers on the east side. Avenues run east and west, from 36 Avenue in the south to 64 Avenue in the north, with odd numbers on the north side of the avenues.

Transportation: Taber is on the CP Rail line but has no passenger rail service. Buses run twice daily to Calgary and twice daily to Medicine Hat. There is no scheduled air service. Inter-city couriers are available.

History: Taber was originally Watertank No. 77 on the CPR line. In 1901 the area was opened up to homesteaders and attracted settlers from the U.S. and eastern Canada, many of them Mormons. James Hull, who arrived from the U.S. in 1902 with his brothers, built the first homestead in 1903. The name "Taber" was taken from "tabernacle" reflecting the religious influence of the Mormons. The original spelling when the village was incorporated in 1905 was "Tabor" after Mount Tabor. This was changed to the current spelling when Taber was incorporated as a city in 1906.

LEGEND

▲ CHURCHES
1. Taber Mennonite Brethren Church
2. Jehovah's Witnesses Kingdom Hall
3. Peace Lutheran Church
4. Christian Reformed Church
5. Church of Jesus Christ of Latter-Day Saints
6. Knox United Church
7. St. Augustine's Roman Catholic Church
8. St. Theodore's Anglican Church
9. Japanese United Church
10. Evangelical Free Church
11. Taber Buddhist Church

☐ HOTELS
1. Royal Hotel
2. Palace Hotel
3. Heritage Motor Hotel
4. Lodge Motel
5. Taber Motel

⌂ SCHOOLS
1. St. Mary's Catholic Junior and Senior High
2. Central Secondary School
3. Taber Junior High School
4. W.R. Meyers High School
5. Taber Christian School
6. Dr. Hammond Elementary School
7. St. Patrick's Catholic Elementary School
8. L.T. Westlake Elementary School

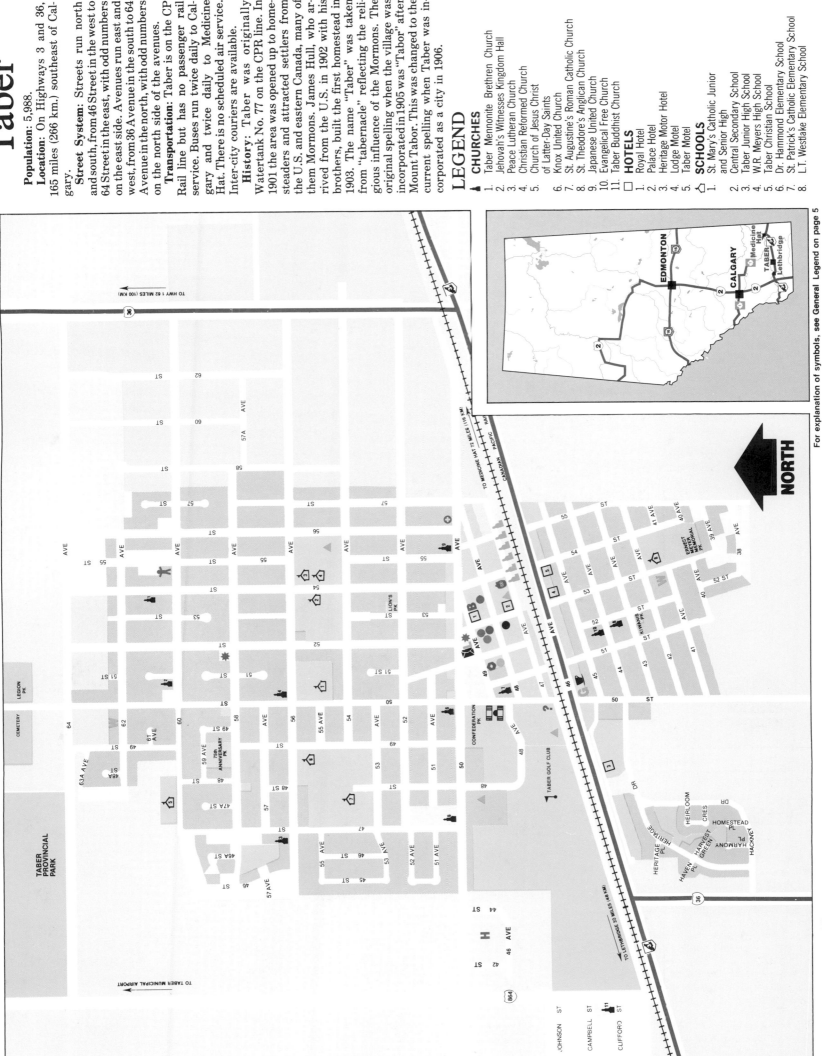

For explanation of symbols, see General Legend on page 5

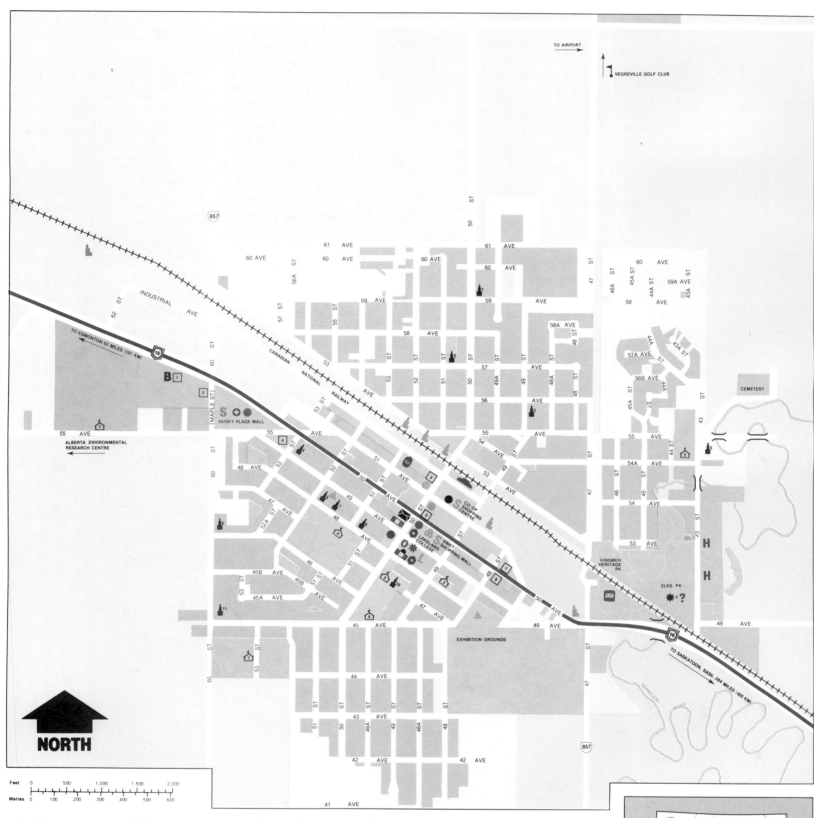

Vegreville

Population: 5,251.

Location: On Highway 16, 63 miles (101 km.) east of Edmonton.

Street System: Streets run north and south, from 43rd in the east to 75th in the west, with odd numbers on the east side. Avenues run east and west, from 41st in the south to 61st in the north, with odd numbers on the south side.

Transportation Facilities: Vegreville is situated on the CN rail line and has no passenger rail service. There are buses three times a day each way between Vegreville and Edmonton. There is no scheduled air service. Inter-city courier service is available.

History: Vegreville was established in 1895 by a group of French settlers from Kansas. They named their community after Father Valentin Vegreville, the Roman Catholic Oblate missionary who brought them to Alberta. Vegreville was incorporated as a village in 1906, and attracted a large number of Ukrainian settlers between 1910 and 1930.

LEGEND

CHURCHES

1. Jehovah's Witnesses Kingdom Hall
2. Holy Trinity Ukrainian Catholic Church
3. St. John the Baptist Russo Greek Orthodox Church
4. Vegreville Alliance Church
5. St. Martin's Roman Catholic Church
6. St. Vladimir's Ukrainian Greek Orthodox Church
7. Vegreville United Church of Canada
8. St. Mary's Anglican Church
9. Seventh-Day Adventist Church
10. Vegreville Pentecostal Church (Meetings in Queen Elizabeth School)
11. St. John's Lutheran Church

HOTELS

1. Homestead Inn
2. Wild Rose Inn
3. Alberta Hotel
4. Twi-Lite Motel
5. Prince Edward Hotel
6. Vista Motel
7. Town Centre Motel

POINTS OF INTEREST

1. Vegreville Easter Egg

SCHOOLS

1. Vegreville Composite High School
2. St. Martin's Catholic Elementary and Junior High School
3. Dr. R. R. Cairns School for the Mentally Handicapped
4. A. L. Horton Junior High School
5. Queen Elizabeth Elementary School
6. Peter Svarich Elementary School
7. Saint Mary's Catholic Elementary School

For explanation of symbols, see General Legend on page 5

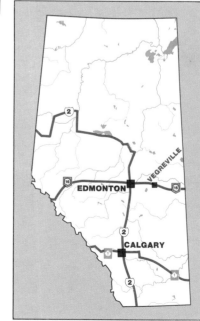

Wetaskiwin

Population: 10,022.

Location: Wetaskiwin is on Highway 2A, 43 miles (69 km.) southeast of Edmonton and 144 miles (232 km.) from Calgary.

Street System: Streets run north and south from 45 Street in the east to 57 Street in the west with even numbers on the west side. Avenues run east and west, from 36 Avenue in the south to 64 Avenue in the north with even numbers on the north side.

Transportation Facilities: Wetaskiwin is situated on the CP Rail line with VIA Rail passenger service to Edmonton and Calgary twice daily. Greyhound bus service runs seven times daily to Edmonton, four times daily to Calgary. Inter-city courier service is available.

History: Wetaskiwin was the sixteenth siding on the CP line when the railroad was built in 1891. Father Albert Lacombe, an Oblate priest, suggested the name Wetaskiwin, which means Hills of Peace in Cree. Incorporated as a village in 1902, a town in 1904 and proclaimed a city in 1906, Wetaskiwin was for many years the smallest city in the British Empire.

LEGEND

▲ CHURCHES
1. Jehovah's Witnesses Kingdom Hall
2. St. John's Evangelical Lutheran Church
3. First United Church
4. Salvation Army
5. Ebenezer Baptist Church
6. Wetaskiwin Mission Church
7. Sacred Heart Roman Catholic Church
8. Church of God
9. Calvary Baptist Church
10. Bethel Lutheran Church
11. Immanuel Anglican Church
12. Seventh-Day Adventist Church
13. German Church of God
14. Zion Lutheran Church
15. Church of Jesus Christ
    of Latter-Day Saints

□ HOTELS
1. Driard Hotel
2. Wales Hotel
3. Westakiwin Motel
4. Wayside Inn
5. Southwyn Motel
6. Fort Ethier Lodge

✳ POINTS OF INTEREST
1. Hills of Peace Monument
2. Old Court House
3. Sacred Heart Roman Catholic Church
    (Heritage Site)
4. Reynold's Museum

⌂ SCHOOLS
1. Centennial Elementary School
2. Lynn Lauren School
    (For the Mentally Retarded)
3. Norwood Elementary School
4. St. Joseph's Catholic Junior High School
5. Wetaskiwin Composite High School
6. Sacred Heart Catholic
    Elementary School
7. Queen Elizabeth Junior High School
8. C. B. McMurdo Elementary School
9. Clear Vista County Elementary
    and Junior High School
10. Parkdale Elementary School

For explanation of symbols, see General Legend on page 5

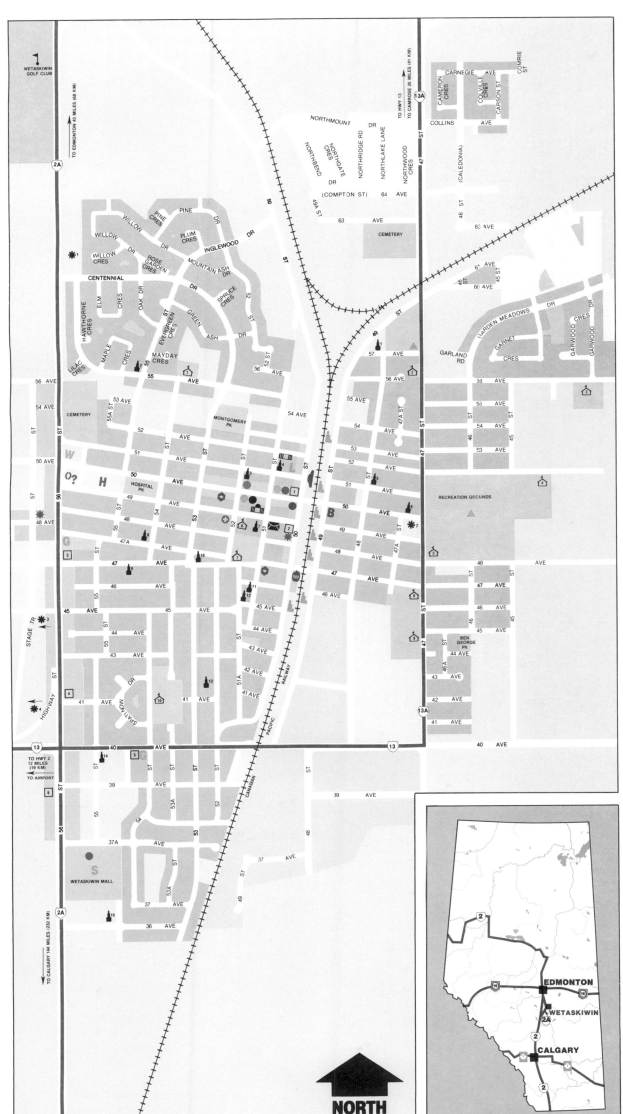

Whitecourt

Population: 5,408.

Location: On Highway 43, 111 miles (178 km.) northwest of Edmonton.

Street System: Streets run north and south, from 35th in the east to 52nd in the west, with even numbers on the west side. Avenues run east and west, from 34 Ave. in the south to 57th in the north, with odd numbers on the north side.

Transportation Facilities: On the CN rail line but has no passenger rail service. Buses run three times a day to and from Edmonton. There is no scheduled air service. Inter-city courier service is available.

History: The Hudson's Bay Company established a substation at this site in 1897; the subsequent settlement was named after local postmaster Walter White. In 1959 it was incorporated as a village and was declared a new town by the province in 1961. Ten years later it acquired town status.

LEGEND

⚱ CHURCHES

1. Whitecourt Baptist Church (Meetings in St. Mary's Catholic Elementary School)
2. St. Joseph's Roman Catholic Church
3. Whitecourt United Church
4. Pentecostal Tabernacle
5. St. James Lutheran Church
6. St. Patrick's Anglican Church (Meetings in St. James Lutheran Church)
7. St. Joseph's Roman Catholic Chapel
8. Evangelical Free Church

☐ HOTELS

1. Gateway Motel
2. Northwoods Inn
3. Rivers Motor Inn
4. Freddy's Motor Inn
5. Whitecourt Motor Inn
6. Blue Grass Motel
7. White-Kaps Motel
8. Jack Pine Motel
9. Plainsman Motor Inn
10. Glenview Motel
11. Alaska Highway Motel
12. Cascade Motor Inn
13. Royal Oak Inn

⌂ SCHOOLS

1. St. Mary's Catholic Elementary School
2. Whitecourt Central Elementary School

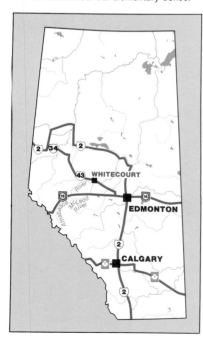

3. Pat Hardy Elementary School
4. St. Joseph's Catholic School
5. Whitecourt Hilltop High School

For explanation of symbols, see General Legend on page 5

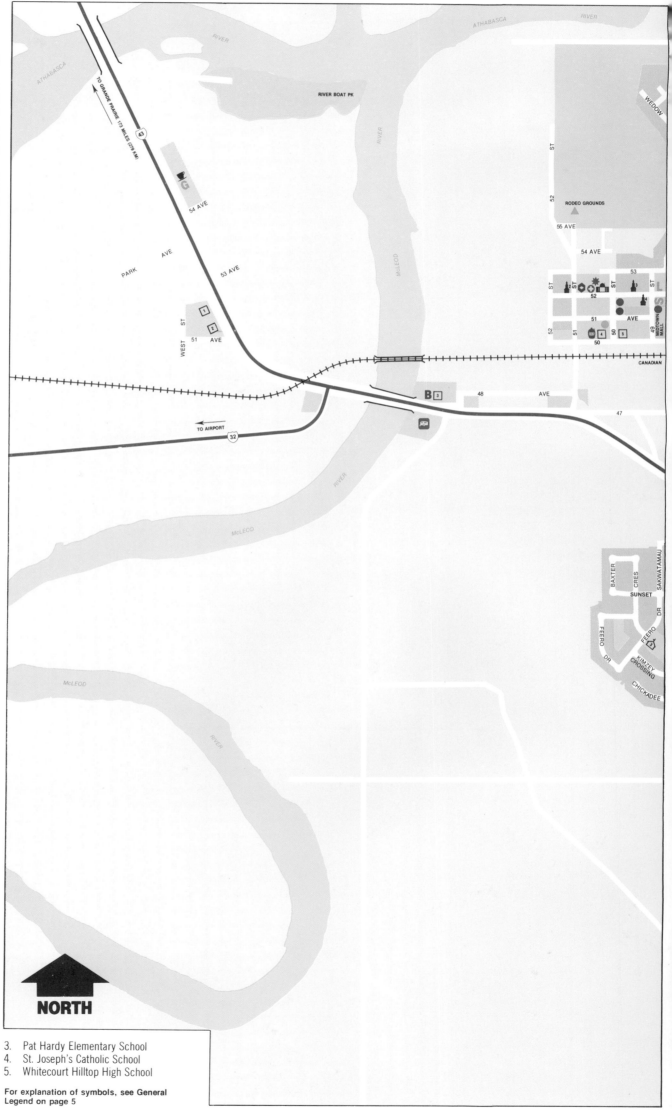

NORTH

The Resources
of Alberta

Virtually all Albertans depend on the land for survival, very directly. This dependence is nearly as total today as it was in the prehistoric hunting era. Petroleum and wheat, cattle and coal, all derive from the land, and these provide the means by which Albertans eat and live. Without them the commercial and industrial sectors would collapse.

Alberta's resource development, however, has always faced two great obstacles. The province is a long way from the sea and far removed from the world's strategic trading routes. Second, though Albertans are blessed with a vast quantity of raw material, the variety of their resources is limited. Therefore the provincial economy has always tended to be unstable, booming or busting with the price fluctuations of a few commodities, particularly oil and grain.

PETROLEUM

Early in 1947 a probing drill bit chewed into oil-soaked limestone near the small town of Leduc, 21 miles (34 km.) south of Edmonton. Conventional liquid petroleum roared up the oil rig's hollow drillstem, carrying Alberta into the era of vigorous oil development. As additional discoveries accumulated rapidly, the province's population and development surged ahead. Until 1970, the known reserves of conventional oil continued to grow. Alberta was the only major source of oil in Canada.

However since 1970 the province's known oil reserves have fallen steadily. More oil was pumped out of the ground each year than was found. Most experts expect conventional oil production to taper off drastically in Alberta by the end of the 1980s.

HEAVY OIL AND OIL SANDS

Though Alberta's conventional oil production may well keep on shrinking, the province could continue to supply all Canada's oil needs for centuries. This is not theory but fact. Alberta contains enormous known reserves of non-conventional oil; estimates run in the range of a trillion barrels.

This oil is thicker than conventional crude, ranging from a molasses-like sludge to actual tar. Whereas conventional oil, soaked in the ground like water in a sponge, can squeeze through the pores between the grains of rock to a well bore, 'heavy' oil can at best ooze very slowly. The oil sands 'tar' will not budge at all on its own. These oils can be strip-mined or flushed out with underground injections of steam and chemicals. Either way, non-conventional production is more expensive than conventional oil.

Alberta has two major oil-sands operations near Fort McMurray, Suncor and Syncrude, both of which work by mining. Experimental injection projects, especially in the heavy oilfields of the province's northeastern region, are well underway. Should the world price of energy rise sufficiently, non-conventional sources may be able to lessen Albertans' dangerous dependence on revenues from rapidly disappearing conventional oil.

NATURAL GAS

The Alberta gas industry is considerably older than its oil counterpart. A CPR crew drilling for water near Medicine Hat in 1883 ignited a gas deposit that burned down their rig. By the First World War Calgary and other southern centres were hooked into a gas pipeline network, supplying heat and street lighting.

Alberta's wildcat drillers have always been able to find gas faster than the market would absorb it. In the early decades of the century, when a well produced both liquid petroleum and gas, more often than not the gas was flared, that is, burned off, representing millions of dollars at today's prices. At that time it couldn't be given away. Today the province's proven reserves stand close to two trillion cubic feet, better than a 30-year supply at the 1982 rate of production.

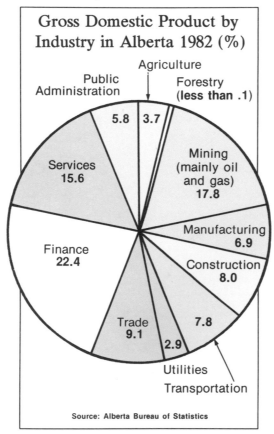

Gross Domestic Product by Industry in Alberta 1982 (%)

Agriculture

Public Administration
Forestry (less than .1)

5.8   3.7

Mining (mainly oil and gas) 17.8

Services 15.6

Finance 22.4

Manufacturing 6.9

Construction 8.0

Trade 9.1

7.8

2.9

Utilities
Transportation

Source: Alberta Bureau of Statistics

COAL

From earliest times, coal was reported in many areas of Alberta. As the coal-burning steam engines pushed west, deposits in the Lethbridge and Drumheller regions were mined on a large scale. During its peak year, 1947, the Drumheller operations alone produced two million tonnes and employed more than 2,000 men. The coal miners' long fight for better pay and less dangerous working conditions made them a driving force in the province's early labour movement.

When the railways and other traditional customers switched to oil during the 1950s, coal fell on hard times. The industry revived in Alberta with the building of coal-fired electrical generating plants, both in the province and elsewhere. Alberta mines produce almost half the Canadian total; the province's reserves of both high- and low-grade coal constitute the bulk of the national supply.

FORESTS

About 60% of Alberta is forest. At the beginning of this decade, the provincial government calculated that a complete regrowth cycle could be maintained with an annual harvest of 28 million cubic metres of timber. The actual cut in 1980 was four million cubic metres.

Traditionally Alberta's forest industries have been dominated by hundreds of small plants, and that remains the case still. A recent count showed 325 manufacturing units, of which 300 were sawmills. Besides dressed lumber, the province produces paper, bleached kraft pulp, plywood, fibreboard, flakeboard and veneer.

AGRICULTURE

Canada's total rural population in 1981 amounted to just over a million people, of whom one in five was Albertan. Of the 50 million acres used for crops and livestock in the province, approximately 28 million were classed as cultivated. Albertans produce about 20% of Canada's total agricultural output.

The provincial farm income for the year 1981 was $3.9 billion, of which cattle accounted for $1.2 billion, wheat for $1.1 billion, and barley almost half a billion. Canola earned better than a quarter billion dollars, hogs a fifth of a billion.

The primary agricultural challenge to southern Alberta's pioneers was drought. During the 1920s and 1930s, many southerners re-emigrated northward, settling much of the Peace River country. Current dryland farming methods place a heavy emphasis on summer fallowing. Typically half the land is left fallow every year while the soil's moisture replenishes itself.

In the north three generations of spine-wrenching work was often necessary before the thick brush could be completely cleared from a farm.

Every year Alberta's ranchers and farmers cope with a formidable combination of unpredictable prices for their products, rising costs, increasingly larger scale operations, complex equipment, political interference, and ever more sophisticated agricultural techniques. As a rule, even the best need a little luck to make the grade.

OTHER RESOURCES

Northern Alberta's abundant water may one day transform the south; visionaries have persistently dreamt of a time when higher food prices and new technology combine to make possible a massive north-to-south irrigation of the southern plain.

Some other Alberta assets are more tangible. The province is a world-scale supplier of sulphur. The Canadian Rockies' global reputation is the solid basis of an expanding tourist industry. Should the western Arctic develop strongly, Alberta's strategic position as a jumping-off point for the North could emerge as an important advantage.

Despite these alternatives, one fact is inescapable: the massive new structure of post-Second World War Alberta rests on a foundation of fossil fuels. No alternate economic resource now visible is of sufficient scale to alter that basic dependency. Whether oil sands, heavy oils, coal, the more difficult reserves of conventional oil and gas—the development of its resources remains Alberta's most probable, though problematic, source of future prosperity.

Oil fields of Alberta

The information for each field listed below is in the following order: field/pool, total recoverable reserves, year of discovery, name of discovery well.

b. - billion
bbl - barrels
mm - million
cu.m. - cubic metres

1. Pembina Cardium, 1.5 b. bbl. (239 mm. cu. m.), 1953, Mobil Oil Seabord 1
2. Redwater D-3, 805 mm. bbl. (128 mm. cu. m.), 1948, Imperial Redwater 1
3. Swan Hills Beaverhill Lake A and B, 798 mm. bbl. (127 mm. cu. m.), 1957, Home Oil et al Regent Edith
4. Bonnie Glen D-3A, 507.6 mm. bbl. (80.7 mm. cu. m.), 1951, Texaco Bonnie Glen CPR A-1
5. Swan Hills South Beaverhill Lake A and B, 4.78 mm. bbl. (76 mm. cu. m.), 1959, BA Pan Am Sarah Lake
6. Judy Creek Beaverhill Lake A, 4.06 mm. bbl. (64.6 mm. cu. m.), 1959, Imperial Judy Creek
7. Mitsue Gilwood A, 348.5 mm. bbl. (55.4 mm. cu. m.), 1964, Home Alminex Mitsue
8. Wizard Lake D-3A, 323.3 mm. bbl. (51.4 mm. cu. m.), 1951, Texaco B1 Wizard
9. Nipisi Gilwood A, 269.2 mm. bbl. (42.8 mm. cu. m.), 1965, Hamilton Unotex E Utik
10. Fenn Big Valley D-2A, 283 mm. bbl. (45 mm. cu. m.), 1950, Big Valley 9
11. Leduc Woodbend D-3A, 242.1 mm. bbl. (38.5 mm. cu. m.), 1947, Imperial Leduc 2
12. Willesden Green Cardium A, 231.5 mm. bbl. (36.8 mm. cu. m.), 1954, Imperial Leslieville
13. Golden Spike D-3A, 210.7 mm. bbl. (33.5 mm. cu. m.), 1949, Imperial Schoepp 1
14. Swan Hills Beaverhill Lake C, 204.4 mm. bbl. (32.5 mm. cu. m.), 1959, Teca Micrn Code Deer Mountain
15. Virginia Hills Beaverhill Lake, 158.5 mm. bbl. (25.2 mm. cu. m.), 1957, HB Union Virginia Hills
16. Sturgeon Lake South D-3, 156.6 mm. bbl. (24.9 mm. cu. m.), 1953, Amerada HB Unior Crown
17. Turner Valley Rundle, 136.5 mm. bbl. (21.7 mm. cu. m.), 1936, Turner Valley Royalters 1
18. Rainbow Keg River B, 132.1 mm. bbl. (21.7 mm. cu. m.), 1965, Aquit Mobil Rainbow
19. Carson Creek North Beaverhill Lake, 126.4 mm. bbl. (20.1 mm. cu. m.), 1958, Mobil PR Carson N
20. Kaybob Beaverhill Lake A, 125.8 mm. bbl. (20.0 mm. cu. m.), 1957, Phillips Kaybob
21. Judy Creek Beaverhill Lake B, 125.2 mm. bbl. (19.9 mm. cu. m.), 1959, Imperial Virginia Hills
22. Rainbow Keg River F, 120.1 mm. bbl. (19.1 mm. cu. m.), 1966, Aquit Mobil Rainbow
23. Acheson D-3A, 108.8 mm. bbl. (17.3 mm. cu. m.), 1950, Cal Std. Acheson Province 1
24. Joarcam Viking, 108.2 mm. bbl. (17.2 mm. cu. m.), 1949, Med Joarcam
25. Westerose D-3, 106.9 mm. bbl. (17.0 mm. cu. m.), 1952, BA CPR Fiverland Westerose
26. Leduc Woodbend D-2A, 92.4 mm. bbl. (14.7 mm. cu. m.), 1947, Imperial Leduc 1
27. Kaybob South Triassic A, 87.4 mm. bbl. (13.9 mm. cu. m.), 1963, HB Union Kaybob South
28. Harmattan East Rundle, 82.4 mm. bbl. (13.1 mm. cu. m.), 1957, Shell Canada Sup. Harmattan East
29. Rainbow Keg River A, 79.3 mm. bbl. (12.6 mm. cu. m.), 1965, Aquit Mobil Rainbow
30. Snipe Lake Beaverhill Lake, 78 mm. bbl. (12.4 mm. cu. m.), 1962, Atlantic Snipe Lake

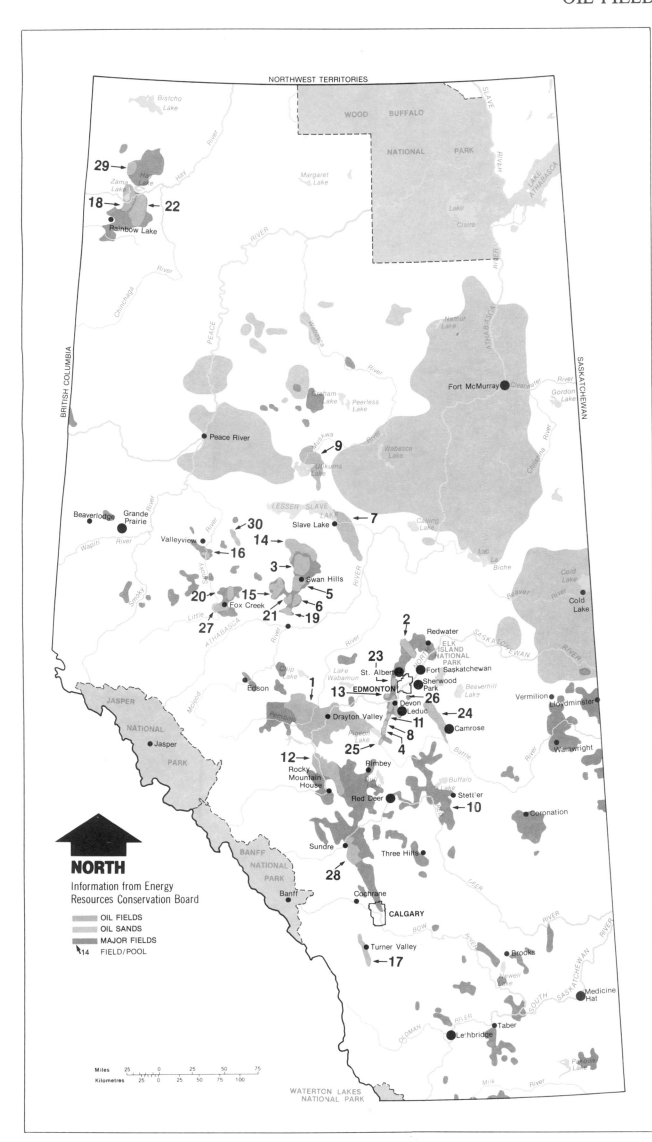

Information from Energy Resources Conservation Board

NORTH

OIL FIELDS
OIL SANDS
MAJOR FIELDS
14 FIELD/POOL

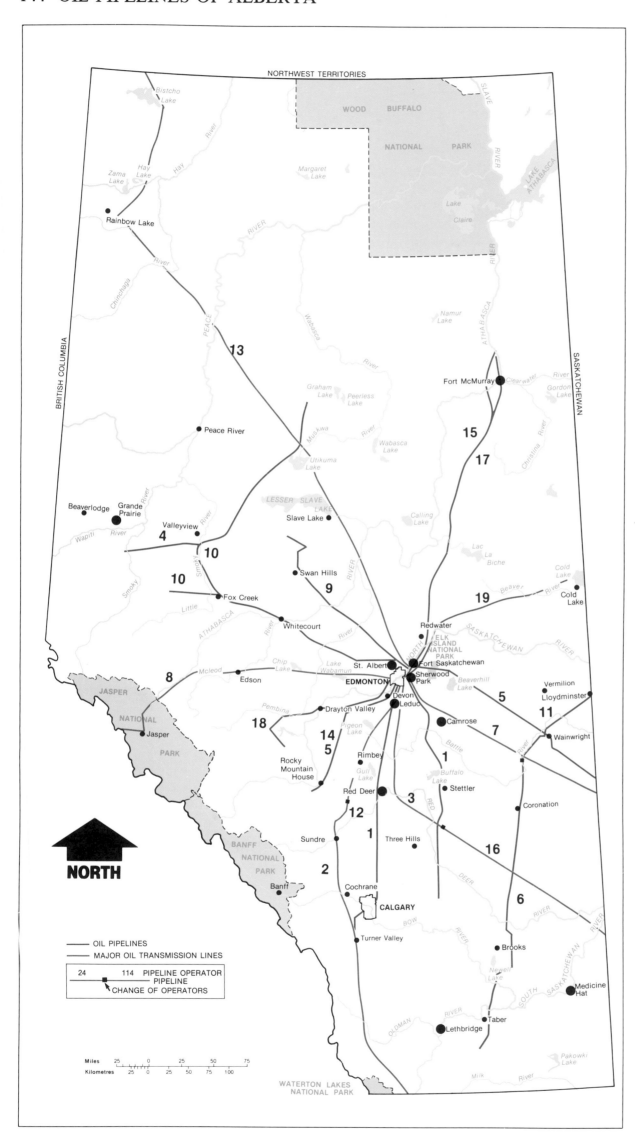

Oil pipelines of Alberta

There are 26,298 miles (42,313 km.) of oil pipelines in the province of Alberta regulated by the provincial Energy Resources Conservation Board. In addition, the National Energy Board regulates 972 miles (1,564 km.) of oil pipeline in the province. These include the Interprovincial Pipeline, the Trans Mountain Pipeline and the Cochin Pipeline. Lines which cross provincial boundaries fall under federal jurisdiction. There are several types of oil lines. Flow lines gather production at the wells and move it to a battery which separates the oil into component products. From the battery, the oil is moved through secondary pipelines to a pipeline terminal for refining or shipment through a major pipeline.

The first major oil line in Alberta was built by the Royalite Oil Co. in 1925. The four-inch line ran approximately 30 miles from Turner Valley to Calgary carrying condensate to an Imperial Oil refinery.

OPERATORS

1. Gulf Canada Resources Ltd.
2. Hudson's Bay Oil and Gas Company Limited
3. Apache Oil Corporation
4. Koch Pipelines Ltd.
5. Dome Petroleum Limited
6. Bow River Pipe Lines Ltd.
7. Interprovincial Pipe Line Limited
8. Trans Mountain Oil Pipe Line Co.
9. Federated Pipe Lines Ltd.
10. Peace Pipe Lines Ltd.
11. Husky Pipeline Ltd.
12. Rimbey Pipe Line Co. Ltd.
13. Rainbow Pipe Line Company Ltd.
14. Pancanadian Petroleum Limited
15. Alberta Oil Sands Pipeline Ltd.
16. Alberta Ethane Development Co. Ltd.
17. Great Canadian Oil Sands Ltd.
18. Pembina Pipe Line Ltd.
19. Alberta Energy Corp.

Information from Energy Resources Conservation Board

Natural gas pipelines of Alberta

There are 102,537 miles (165,012 km.) of gas pipelines in Alberta. Most of that is regulated by the provincial Energy Resources Conservation Board, with the exception of approximately 15 miles (24 km.) of line near the provincial border and the 312 miles (502 km.) of the Alaska Highway Gas Pipeline. Construction of an additional 494 miles (795 km.) on that line has been suspended pending a decision on gas sales in the United States.

Natural gas is gathered in secondary gas lines and shipped to gas plants where hydrogen sulphide is removed and in some cases, liquids like propane, butane and ethane are extracted. The sweet gas is then gathered by Nova An Alberta Corporation's pipeline system and delivered to export points. The extracted liquids move in different lines under extremely high pressure.

The first major gas line in the province was a 16-inch line built in 1912 by Canadian Western Natural Gas. The line was 167 miles (269 km.) long and ran from Bow Island to Calgary.

OPERATORS

1. Nova, An Alberta Corporation
2. Northwestern Utilities Limited
3. Canadian Western Natural Gas Company Limited
4. Albersun Oil and Gas Limited
5. Inter-City Gathering Systems Limited
6. North Canadian Oils Limited
7. Mid-Western Industrial Pipelines Limited
   Mid-Western Industrial Pipelines (Redwater) Limited
   Mid-Western Industrial Pipelines (Wabamun) Limited
8. South Alberta Pipe Lines Limited
9. Canadian-Montana Gas Company Limited

Information from Energy Resources Conservation Board

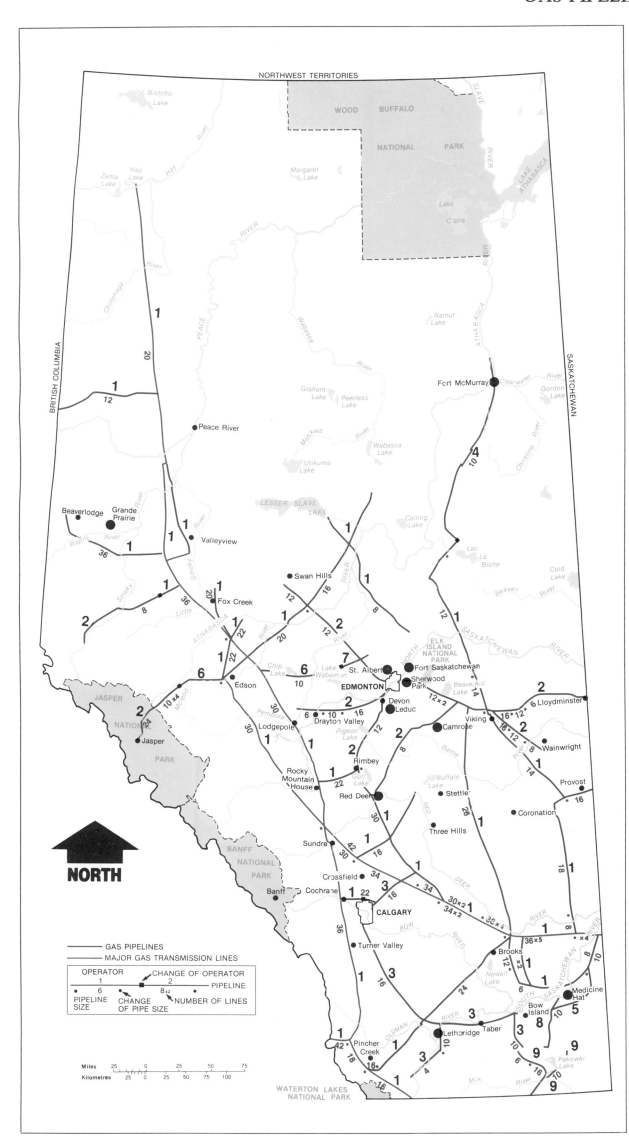

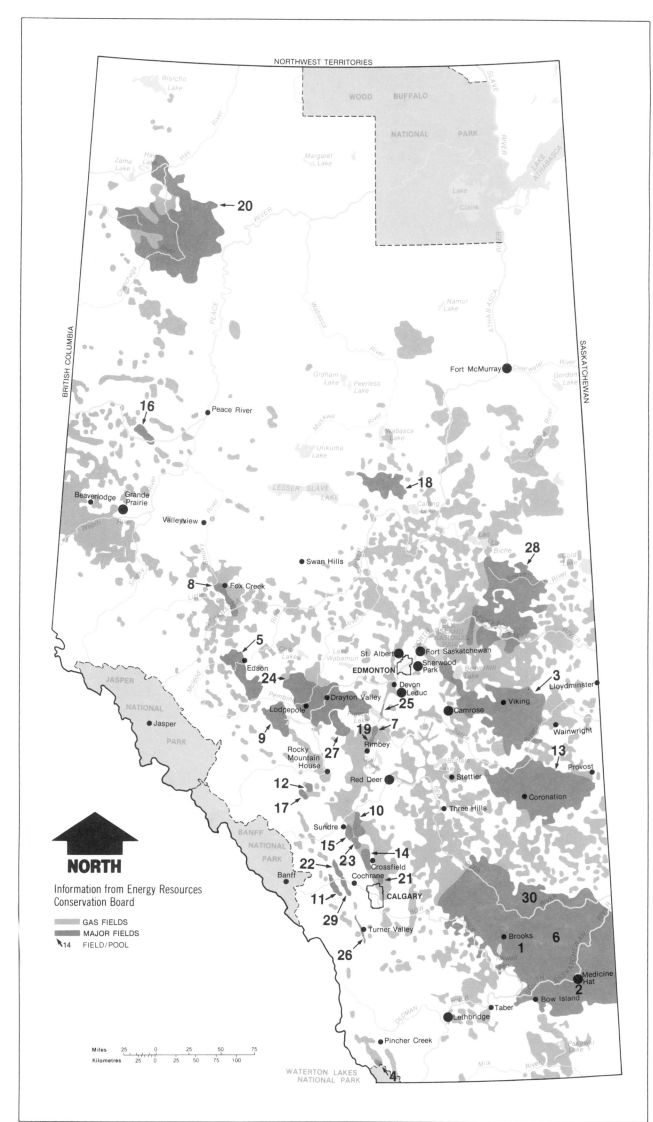

Gas fields of Alberta

The information for each field listed below is in the following order: field/pool, total recoverable reserves, year of discovery, name of discovery well.

tcf - trillion cubic feet
bcf - billion cubic feet
b.cu.m.—billion cubic metres

1. Multi-Field Pool (Includes the following fields: Medicine Hat, Suffield, Bindloss, Atlee-Buffalo, Bow Island, Anderson, Jenner, Cessford, Wintering Hills, Connorsville, Matziwin, Verger, Princess, Baltry) Milk River Pool 1, 5.0 tcf (141.7 b. cu. m.), 1910, CPR Brooks 1
2. Multi-Field Pool (Includes the following fields: Rosedale, Hussar, Medicine Hat, Suffield, Bindloss, Anderson, Jenner, Cessford, Wintering Hills, Connorsville, Matziwin, Verger, Princess, Baltry, Atlee-Buffalo) Medicine Hat Pool 1, 3.80 tcf (107.6 b. cu. m.), 1904, Medicine Hat 2
3. Multi-Field Pool (Includes the following fields: Sugden, Craigend, Ashmont, Clay, Cache, Duvernay, Canard) Viking Pool 2, 1.76 tcf (49.8 b. cu. m.), 1917, NUL Viking 6
4. Waterton Rundle-Wabamun A, 1.72 tcf (48.9 b. cu. m.), 1959, Shell 7 Waterton
5. Edson Elkton A-Shunda A and B, 1.52 tcf (43.2 b. cu. m.), 1962, HB Hamilton Edson
6. Multi-Field Pool (Includes the following fields: Suffield, Medicine Hat, Anderson, Jenner, Cessford, Princess) Second White Specks Pool 1, 1.37 tcf (38.9 b. cu. m.), 1939, Anglo-Canadian Steveville 2
7. Westerose South D-3A, 1.35 tcf (38.2 b. cu. m.), 1954, CPR Stevens 12
8. Kaybob South Beaverhill Lake A, 1.28 tcf (36.4 b. cu. m.), 1961, HB BL Gas Unit 1 Kaybobs
9. Brazeau River Elkton-Shunda B, 1.28 tcf (36.4 b. cu. m.), 1959, Imperial et al Brazeau River
10. Harmattan East Rundle, 1.12 tcf (31.6 b. cu. m.), 1954, Shell West Olds A-16-15
11. Jumping Pound West Rundle A and B, 1.07 tcf (30.3 b. cu. m.), 1961, Shell Jumping Pound West
12. Strachan D-3A, 1.06 tcf (30.1 b. cu. m.), 1967, Stampede BA Strachan
13. Provost Viking A, C, K and Mannville E, 999.0 bcf, (28.3 b. cu. m.) 1946, Provo Provost 4
14. Crossfield Rundle A, 914.3 bcf (25.9 b. cu. m.), 1956, Shell Crossfield
15. Harmattan Elkton Rundle C, 889.9 bcf (25.2 b. cu. m.), 1954, Norcen CDN Sup. Harm. In.
16. Dunvegan Debolt A, B, C and D, 889.1 bcf (25.19 b. cu. m.), 1963, Anderson et al Dunvegan
17. Ricinus West D-3A, 843.7 bcf (23.9 b. cu. m.), 1969, Aquit et al , Ricinus West
18. Marten Hills, Wabiskaw A and Wabamun A 829.6 bcf (23.5 b. cu. m.) 1961, Pan Am A-1 Marten Hills
19. Homeglen Rimbey D-3 816.8 bcf (23.14 b. cu. m.) 1953, Chevron Gulf Rimbey
20. Multi-Field Pool Bluesky Pool 1, 812.4 bcf (23.01 b. cu. m.) 1972, Ranger Arco Keg R
21. Crossfield Rundle B 804.8 bcf (22.8 b. cu. m.) 1957, Jefferson Lake CPR N Calgary 27-6
22. Wildcat Hills Rundle A, 770.5 bcf (21.7 b. cu. m.) 1958, Fina Imperial Wildcat Hills
23. Carstairs Elkton A, 734.2 bcf (20.8 b. cu. m.) 1958, Home et al Carstairs
24. Pembina Cardium, 720.1 bcf (20.4 b. cu. m.) 1953, Mobil Oil-Seaboard-Pembina 1
25. Bonnie Glen D-3A 707.4 bcf (20.0 b. cu. m.) 1952, Texaco Bonnie Glen A1
26. Turner Valley Rundle, 695.4 bcf (19.7 b. cu. m.) 1924, Royalite 4
27. Minnehik-Buck Lake Pekisko A, 695.4 bcf (19.7 b. cu. m.) 1952, Canadian Delhi et al Minnehik 1
28. Multi-Field Pool Viking Pool 6, 617.8 bcf (17.5 b. cu. m.), 1949, Syracuse Ashmont
29. Jumping Pound Mississippian, 617.7 bcf (17.48 b. cu. m.), 1944, Shell Jumping Pound Unit Well 1
30. Cessford Basal Colorado A, 596.6 bcf (16.9 b. cu. m.), 1950, HB Gas Unit 1 Cessford

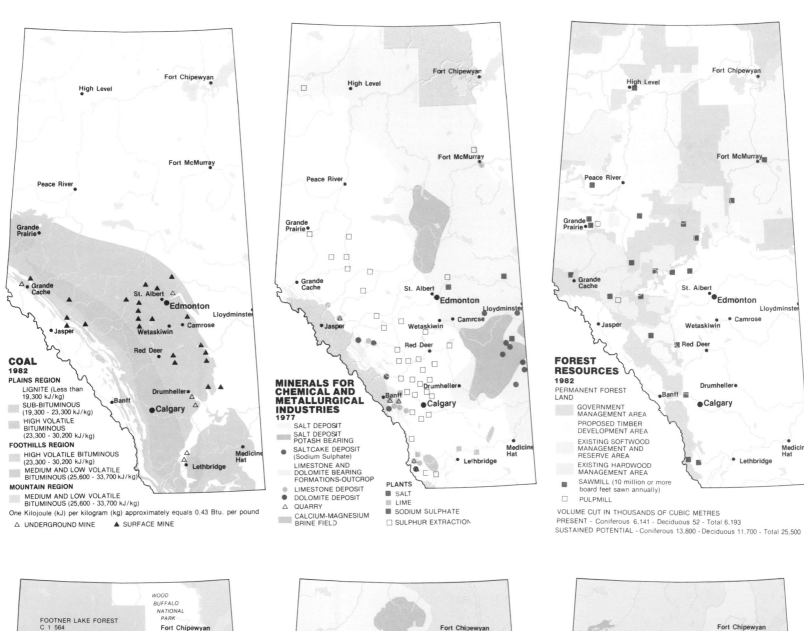

COAL
1982

PLAINS REGION

LIGNITE (Less than 19,300 kJ/kg)

SUB-BITUMINOUS (19,300 - 23,300 kJ/kg)

HIGH VOLATILE BITUMINOUS (23,300 - 30,200 kJ/kg)

FOOTHILLS REGION

HIGH VOLATILE BITUMINOUS (23,300 - 30,200 kJ/kg)

MEDIUM AND LOW VOLATILE BITUMINOUS (25,600 - 33,700 kJ/kg)

MOUNTAIN REGION

MEDIUM AND LOW VOLATILE BITUMINOUS (25,600 - 33,700 kJ/kg)

One Kilojoule (kJ) per kilogram (kg) approximately equals 0.43 Btu. per pound

△ UNDERGROUND MINE   ▲ SURFACE MINE

MINERALS FOR CHEMICAL AND METALLURGICAL INDUSTRIES
1977

SALT DEPOSIT

SALT DEPOSIT POTASH BEARING

● SALTCAKE DEPOSIT (Sodium Sulphate)

LIMESTONE AND DOLOMITE BEARING FORMATIONS-OUTCROP

● LIMESTONE DEPOSIT

● DOLOMITE DEPOSIT

△ QUARRY

CALCIUM-MAGNESIUM BRINE FIELD

PLANTS

■ SALT

■ LIME

■ SODIUM SULPHATE

□ SULPHUR EXTRACTION

FOREST RESOURCES
1982

PERMANENT FOREST LAND

GOVERNMENT MANAGEMENT AREA

PROPOSED TIMBER DEVELOPMENT AREA

EXISTING SOFTWOOD MANAGEMENT AND RESERVE AREA

EXISTING HARDWOOD MANAGEMENT AREA

■ SAWMILL (10 million or more board feet sawn annually)

□ PULPMILL

VOLUME CUT IN THOUSANDS OF CUBIC METRES
PRESENT - Coniferous 6,141 - Deciduous 52 - Total 6,193
SUSTAINED POTENTIAL - Coniferous 13,800 - Deciduous 11,700 - Total 25,500

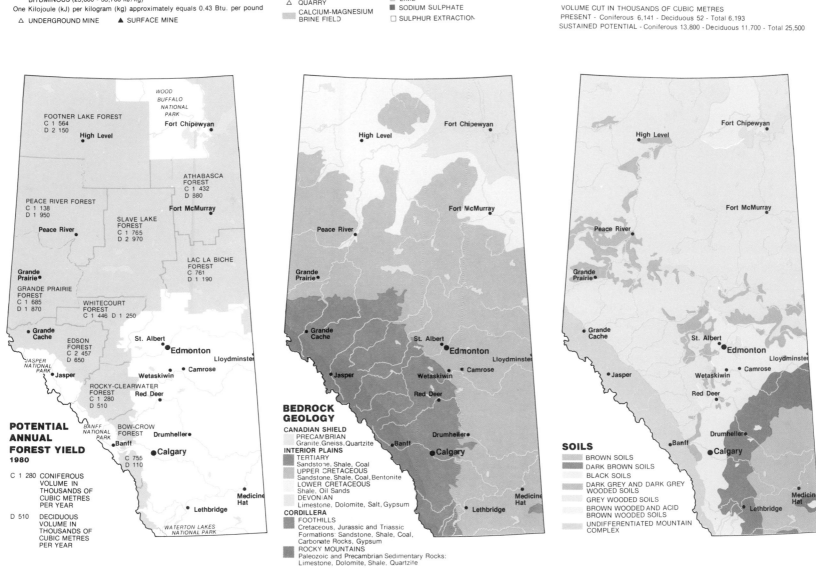

POTENTIAL ANNUAL FOREST YIELD
1980

C 1 280 CONIFEROUS VOLUME IN THOUSANDS OF CUBIC METRES PER YEAR

D 510 DECIDUOUS VOLUME IN THOUSANDS OF CUBIC METRES PER YEAR

FOOTNER LAKE FOREST C 1 564 D 2 150

ATHABASCA FOREST C 1 432 D 880

PEACE RIVER FOREST C 1 138 D 1 950

SLAVE LAKE FOREST C 1 765 D 2 970

LAC LA BICHE FOREST C 761 D 1 190

GRANDE PRAIRIE FOREST C 1 685 D 1 870

WHITECOURT FOREST C 1 446 D 1 250

EDSON FOREST C 2 457 D 650

ROCKY-CLEARWATER FOREST C 1 280 D 510

BOW-CROW FOREST C 755 D 110

BEDROCK GEOLOGY

CANADIAN SHIELD

PRECAMBRIAN
Granite,Gneiss,Quartzite

INTERIOR PLAINS

TERTIARY
Sandstone, Shale, Coal

UPPER CRETACEOUS
Sandstone, Shale, Coal, Bentonite

LOWER CRETACEOUS
Shale, Oil Sands

DEVONIAN
Limestone, Dolomite, Salt, Gypsum

CORDILLERA

FOOTHILLS
Cretaceous, Jurassic and Triassic Formations: Sandstone, Shale, Coal, Carbonate Rocks, Gypsum

ROCKY MOUNTAINS
Paleozoic and Precambrian Sedimentary Rocks: Limestone, Dolomite, Shale, Quartzite

SOILS

BROWN SOILS

DARK BROWN SOILS

BLACK SOILS

DARK GREY AND DARK GREY WOODED SOILS

GREY WOODED SOILS

BROWN WOODED AND ACID BROWN WOODED SOILS

UNDIFFERENTIATED MOUNTAIN COMPLEX

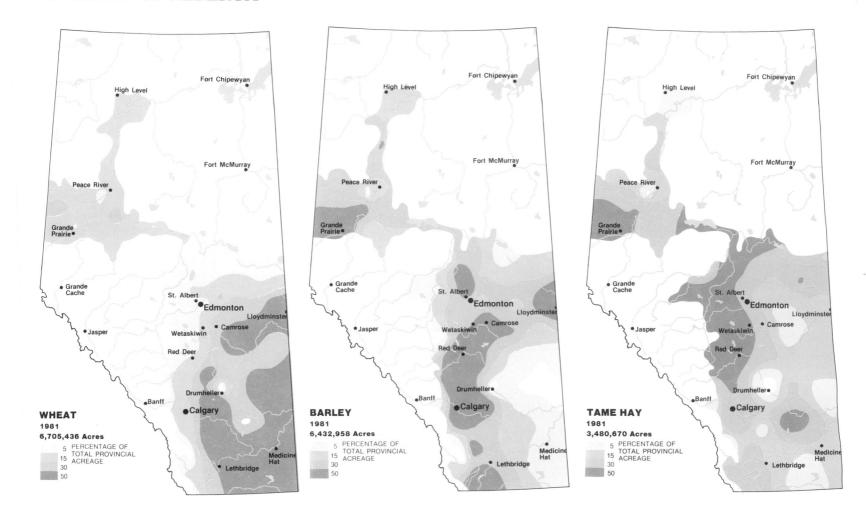

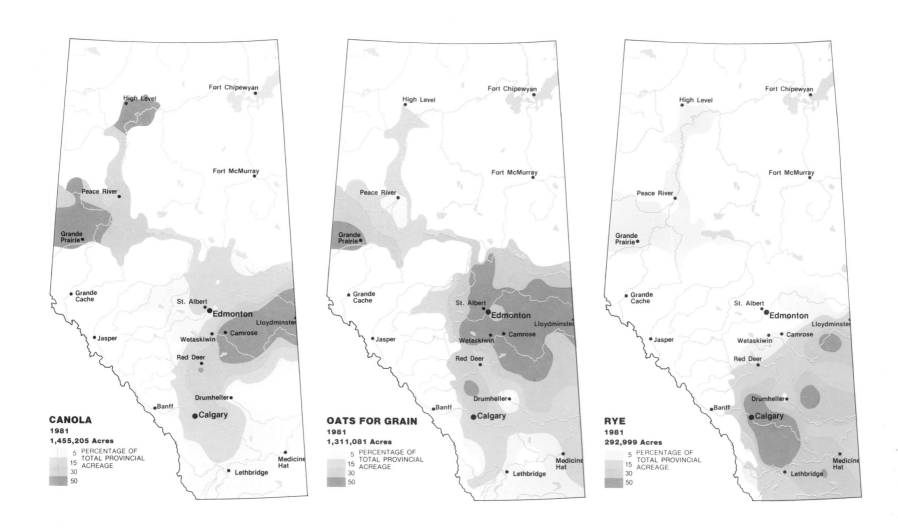

WHEAT
1981
6,705,436 Acres

PERCENTAGE OF
TOTAL PROVINCIAL
ACREAGE
5
15
30
50

BARLEY
1981
6,432,958 Acres

PERCENTAGE OF
TOTAL PROVINCIAL
ACREAGE
5
15
30
50

TAME HAY
1981
3,480,670 Acres

PERCENTAGE OF
TOTAL PROVINCIAL
ACREAGE
5
15
30
50

CANOLA
1981
1,455,205 Acres

PERCENTAGE OF
TOTAL PROVINCIAL
ACREAGE
5
15
30
50

OATS FOR GRAIN
1981
1,311,081 Acres

PERCENTAGE OF
TOTAL PROVINCIAL
ACREAGE
5
15
30
50

RYE
1981
292,999 Acres

PERCENTAGE OF
TOTAL PROVINCIAL
ACREAGE
5
15
30
50

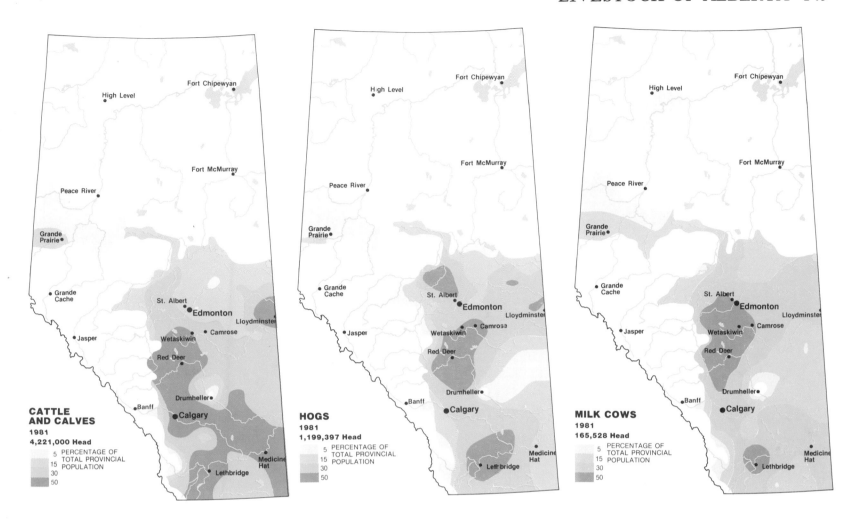

CATTLE AND CALVES
1981
4,221,000 Head

PERCENTAGE OF
TOTAL PROVINCIAL
POPULATION
5
15
30
50

HOGS
1981
1,199,397 Head

PERCENTAGE OF
TOTAL PROVINCIAL
POPULATION
5
15
30
50

MILK COWS
1981
165,528 Head

PERCENTAGE OF
TOTAL PROVINCIAL
POPULATION
5
15
30
50

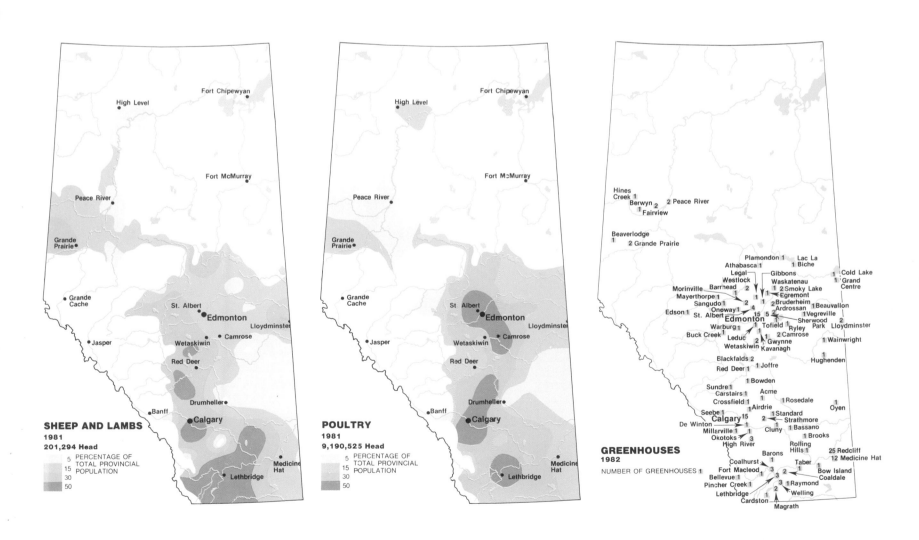

SHEEP AND LAMBS
1981
201,294 Head

PERCENTAGE OF
TOTAL PROVINCIAL
POPULATION
5
15
30
50

POULTRY
1981
9,190,525 Head

PERCENTAGE OF
TOTAL PROVINCIAL
POPULATION
5
15
30
50

GREENHOUSES
1982

NUMBER OF GREENHOUSES 1

The Rocky Mountain Passes

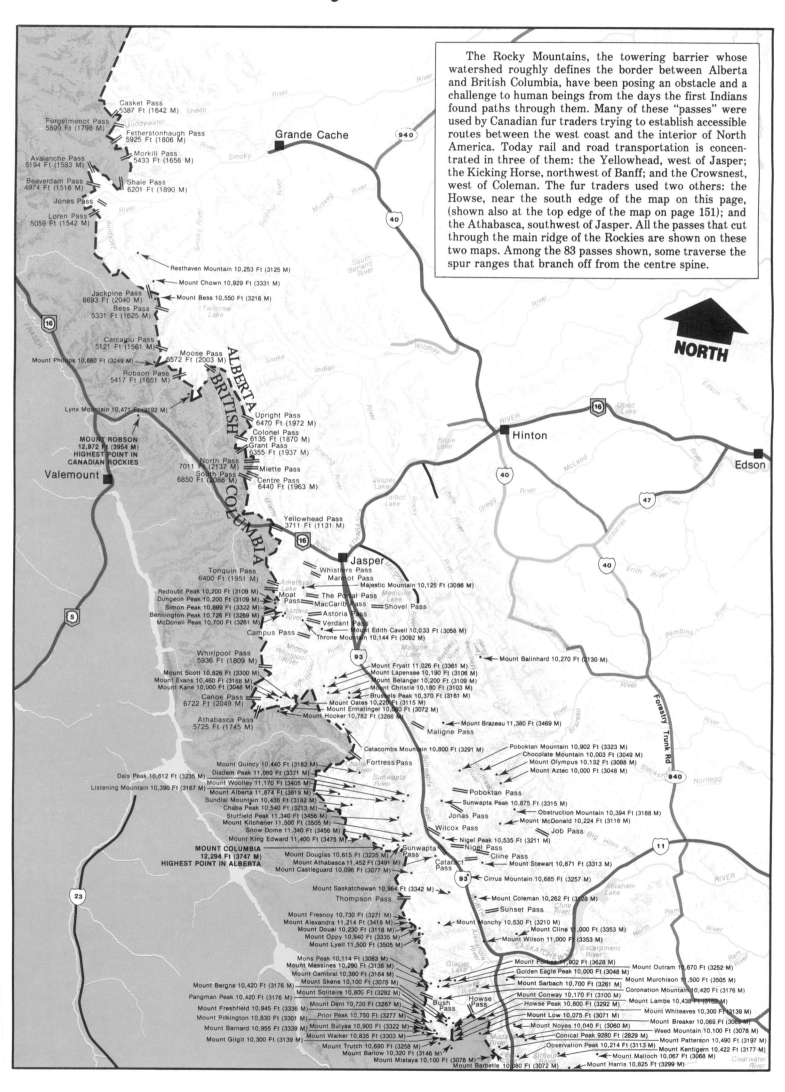

The Rocky Mountains, the towering barrier whose watershed roughly defines the border between Alberta and British Columbia, have been posing an obstacle and a challenge to human beings from the days the first Indians found paths through them. Many of these "passes" were used by Canadian fur traders trying to establish accessible routes between the west coast and the interior of North America. Today rail and road transportation is concentrated in three of them: the Yellowhead, west of Jasper; the Kicking Horse, northwest of Banff; and the Crowsnest, west of Coleman. The fur traders used two others: the Howse, near the south edge of the map on this page, (shown also at the top edge of the map on page 151); and the Athabasca, southwest of Jasper. All the passes that cut through the main ridge of the Rockies are shown on these two maps. Among the 83 passes shown, some traverse the spur ranges that branch off from the centre spine.

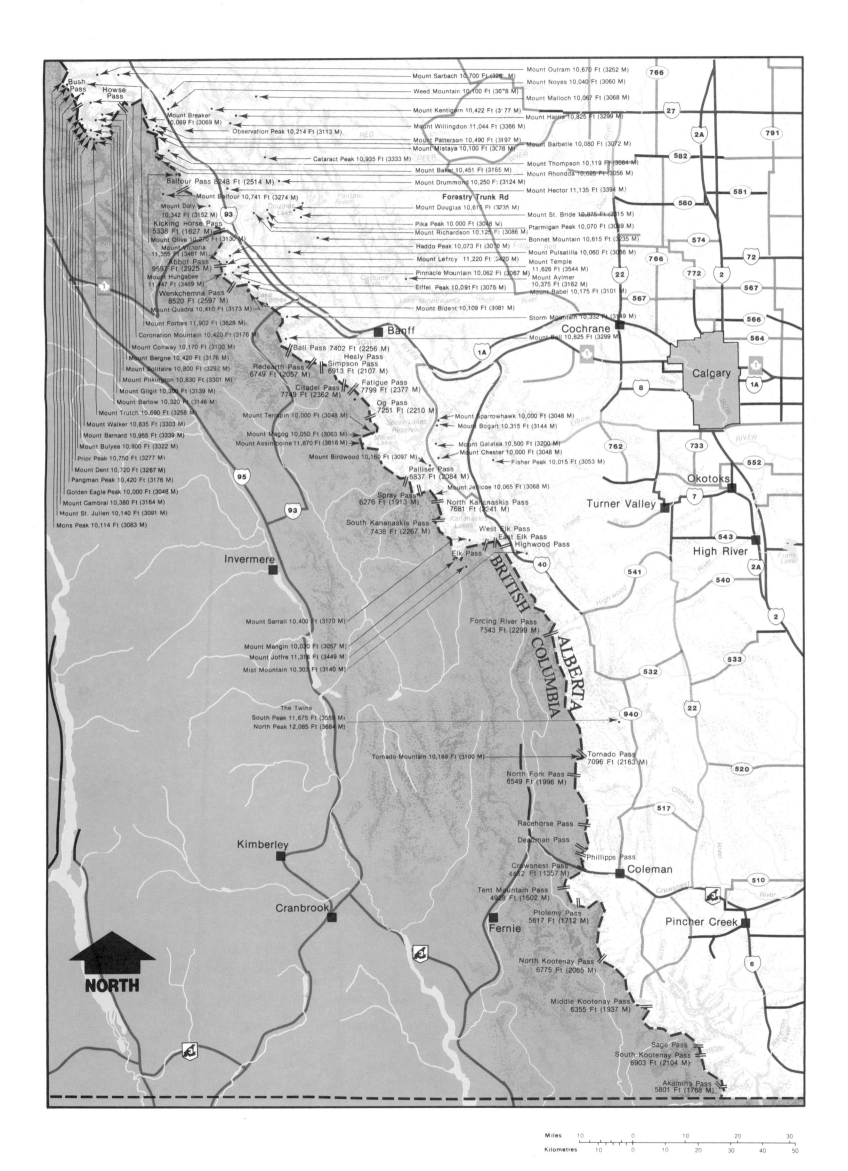

Bush Pass

Howse Pass

Mount Breaker 10,069 Ft (3069 M)

Observation Peak 10,214 Ft (3113 M)

Mount Sarbach 10,700 Ft (326..M)
Weed Mountain 10,100 Ft (30?8 M)
Mount Kentigern 10,422 Ft (3?.77 M)
Mount Willingdon 11,044 Ft (3366 M)
Mount Patterson 10,490 Ft (3197 M)
Mount Mistaya 10,100 Ft (3C78 M)
Cataract Peak 10,935 Ft (3333 M)

Mount Outram 10,670 Ft (3252 M)
Mount Noyes 10,040 Ft (3060 M)
Mount Malloch 10,067 Ft (3068 M)
Mount Harris 10,825 Ft (3299 M)
Mount Barbetle 10,080 Ft (3072 M)
Mount Thompson 10,119 Ft (3084 M)
Mount Rhondda 10,025 Ft (3056 M)
Mount Hector 11,135 Ft (3394 M)

Balfour Pass 8248 Ft (2514 M)
Mount Balfour 10,741 Ft (3274 M)
Mount Daly 10,342 Ft (3152 M)
Kicking Horse Pass 5338 Ft (1627 M)
Mount Olive 10,270 Ft (3130 M)
Mount Victoria 11,355 Ft (3461 M)
Abbot Pass 9597 Ft (2925 M)
Mount Hungabee 11,447 Ft (3489 M)
Wenkchemna Pass 8520 Ft (2597 M)
Mount Quadra 10,410 Ft (3173 M)

Forestry Trunk Rd

Mount Douglas 10,615 Ft (3235 M)
Pika Peak 10 000 Ft (3048 M)
Mount Richardson 10,125 Ft (3086 M)
Haddo Peak 10,073 Ft (3070 M)
Mount Lefroy 11,220 Ft (3420 M)
Pinnacle Mountain 10,062 Ft (3067 M)
Eiffel Peak 10,091 Ft (3075 M)
Mount Bident 10,109 Ft (3081 M)

Mount St. Bride 10,875 Ft (3315 M)
Ptarmigan Peak 10,070 Ft (3069 M)
Bonnet Mountain 10,615 Ft (3235 M)
Mount Pulsatilla 10,060 Ft (3056 M)
Mount Temple 11,626 Ft (3544 M)
Mount Aylmer 10,375 Ft (3162 M)
Mount Babel 10,175 Ft (3101 M)
Storm Mountain 10,332 Ft (3149 M)

Banff

Cochrane

Mount Ball 10,825 Ft (3299 M)

Calgary

Mount Forbes 11,902 Ft (3628 M)
Coronation Mountain 10,420 Ft (3176 M)
Mount Conway 10,170 Ft (3100 M)
Mount Bergne 10,420 Ft (3176 M)
Mount Solitaire 10,800 Ft (3292 M)
Mount Pilkington 10,830 Ft (3301 M)
Mount Gilgit 10,300 Ft (3139 M)
Mount Barlow 10,320 Ft (3146 M)
Mount Trutch 10,690 Ft (3258 M)
Mount Walker 10,835 Ft (3303 M)
Mount Barnard 10,955 Ft (3339 M)
Mount Bulyea 10,900 Ft (3322 M)
Prior Peak 10,750 Ft (3277 M)
Mount Dent 10,720 Ft (3267 M)
Pangman Peak 10,420 Ft (3176 M)
Golden Eagle Peak 10,000 Ft (3048 M)
Mount Cambrai 10,380 Ft (3164 M)
Mount St. Julien 10,140 Ft (3091 M)
Mons Peak 10,114 Ft (3083 M)

Ball Pass 7402 Ft (2256 M)
Healy Pass
Simpson Pass 6913 Ft (2107 M)
Redearth Pass 6749 Ft (2057 M)
Fatigue Pass 7799 Ft (2377 M)
Citadel Pass 7749 Ft (2362 M)
Og Pass 7251 Ft (2210 M)
Mount Terrapin 10,000 Ft (3048 M)
Mount Magog 10,050 Ft (3063 M)
Mount Assiniboine 11,870 Ft (3618 M)
Mount Birdwood 10,160 Ft (3097 M)

Mount Sparrowhawk 10,000 Ft (3048 M)
Mount Bogart 10,315 Ft (3144 M)
Mount Galatea 10,500 Ft (3200 M)
Mount Chester 10,000 Ft (3048 M)
Fisher Peak 10,015 Ft (3053 M)

Palliser Pass 6837 Ft (2084 M)
Mount Jellicoe 10,065 Ft (3068 M)
Spray Pass 6276 Ft (1913 M)
North Kananaskis Pass 7681 Ft (2341 M)
South Kananaskis Pass 7438 Ft (2267 M)
West Elk Pass
East Elk Pass
Highwood Pass
Elk Pass

Okotoks
Turner Valley
High River

Invermere

BRITISH COLUMBIA
ALBERTA

Mount Sarrail 10,400 Ft (3170 M)
Mount Mangin 10,030 Ft (3057 M)
Mount Joffre 11,316 Ft (3449 M)
Mist Mountain 10,303 Ft (3140 M)

Forcing River Pass 7543 Ft (2299 M)

The Twins
South Peak 11,675 Ft (3559 M)
North Peak 12,085 Ft (3684 M)

Tornado Mountain 10,169 Ft (3100 M)

Tornado Pass 7096 Ft (2163 M)
North Fork Pass 6549 Ft (1996 M)

Kimberley

Racehorse Pass
Deadman Pass
Phillipps Pass
Crowsnest Pass 4452 Ft (1357 M)
Tent Mountain Pass 4928 Ft (1502 M)
Ptolemy Pass 5617 Ft (1712 M)
North Kootenay Pass 6775 Ft (2065 M)
Middle Kootenay Pass 6355 Ft (1937 M)
Sage Pass
South Kootenay Pass 6903 Ft (2104 M)
Akamina Pass 5801 Ft (1768 M)

Coleman
Cranbrook
Fernie
Pincher Creek

NORTH

Miles   10   0   10   20   30
Kilometres   10   0   10   20   30   40   50

Parks in Alberta

There are in Alberta five national parks under the jurisdiction of Parks Canada, and 61 provincial parks operated by Alberta Recreation and Parks. Together, national and provincial parks occupy almost 24,900 square miles (64,296 square kilometres).

National Parks

Banff was Canada's first national park, though then it was part of the Northwest Territories. In 1885, the federal government set aside 10 square miles (26 sq. km.) in the Rocky Mountains after conflicting claims arose over the rights to hot springs at Sulphur Mountain. Sir John A. Macdonald's cabinet realized the potential of the springs and decided to preserve the site in its natural state for all Canadians. At that time there was no official parks policy, but politicians wanted to protect the area from private developers. Two years later the federal government passed the Rocky Mountains Park Act, creating the first national park and expanding it to 260 square miles (673 square kilometres).

Alberta now has more national parks than any other province. Three are in the Rockies: Jasper National Park west of Edmonton, Banff National Park west of Calgary, and Waterton Lakes National Park in the province's southwest corner, part of the Glacier-Waterton International Peace Park. Elk Island National Park east of Edmonton is the smallest of the five, and Wood Buffalo National Park, which straddles the border between Alberta and the Northwest Territories, ranks as Canada's largest.

Each is under the administrative governance of a superintendent, who reports to the regional director of Parks Canada; ultimate political responsibility rests with the federal minister of the environment. The superintendents of Jasper, Banff and Waterton, each of which includes a town, run civic affairs through townsite managers. There is no elected municipal government and no local taxation. This has led to periodic complaints from residents that they have no voice in the way their communities are run, and a continuing demand for elected government.

All national parks regulations reflect a single overall purpose: to reserve places of natural beauty and scenic value for the benefit of this and future generations; their officials urge all visitors to treat them as such.

Wood Buffalo

For location, see Alberta: The Province map, pages 27 and 29

This enormous 17,301 square-mile (44,807 sq. km.) tract straddles the border between Alberta and the Northwest Territories. It is a massive subarctic wilderness, teeming with wildlife. Originally 10,500 square miles (27,193 sq. km.), the park was set aside in 1922 primarily to preserve a dwindling herd of woodland bison which still roamed wild in the territory. Today it numbers 5,000 to 6,000 buffalo, the largest free-roaming herd in the world. In 1954, biologists discovered that the park also contained the last nesting grounds for the whooping crane, which remains a rare and endangered species.

In addition to its wildlife, Wood Buffalo National Park boasts the most extensive gypsum karst terrain in the world, consisting of sinkholes, underground rivers, caves and deep valleys.

The only road into Wood Buffalo is via Highway 5 from Fort Smith in the Northwest Territories. It is an undeveloped wilderness park for the most part, though there are some fixtures in place to assist camping, picnicking and swimming. The surrounding country is almost entirely uninhabited, and only a few hundred tourists visit Wood Buffalo each year.

Elk Island

(For location, see Alberta: The Province map, pages 29 and 31)

Elk Island National Park was the first large federally controlled area to be enclosed as a big game sanctuary. In 1913, a 16-square-mile (41 sq. km.) area, 21 miles (34 km.) east of Edmonton, was declared a national park, though it had been set aside since 1906 to protect an overhunted elk herd. The park now contains 75 square miles (194 sq. km.) and shelters a herd of bison.

The park is not in fact an island, except in that it is located in the Beaver Hills, which rise out of the surrounding prairie. It consists of large outcroppings of rock, aspen forests and numerous spruce bogs.

Waterton Lakes

In 1895 the federal government, at the request of nearby residents, reserved 54 square miles (140 sq. km.) around Waterton Lake. Sixteen years later it founded Waterton Lakes Dominion Park, within a tiny area of 13.5 square miles (35 square kilometres). In 1914, however, local pressure led to an expansion of the park to 423 square miles (1,095 square kilometres), and in 1932, the U.S. and Canadian governments passed complementary legislation to create the Waterton-Glacier International Peace Park between Montana and Alberta. This was the first such park in the world.

It lies 160 miles (257 km.) south of Calgary on Highways 2, 5 and 6. The area encompasses both prairie and mountain landscapes and boasts the largest lake in the Rockies, Upper Waterton Lake, 485 feet (148 metres) deep. Waterton Park has 109 miles (175 km.) of trails through a wide variety of terrains. Cruise boats operate on Upper Waterton Lake to provide a view of the park's interior.

Waterton Park is rich in minerals as well. In 1902, western Canada's first oil well was drilled on Cameron Creek in the southwest corner of the present-day park. The activity surrounding that find created a town called Oil City. The excitement died quickly, however, and the town has long since vanished. A decade later the town of Pocahontas was established to exploit coal deposits. That lasted for about 10 years, as did the town. Since then national parks policy has precluded any resource exploitation.

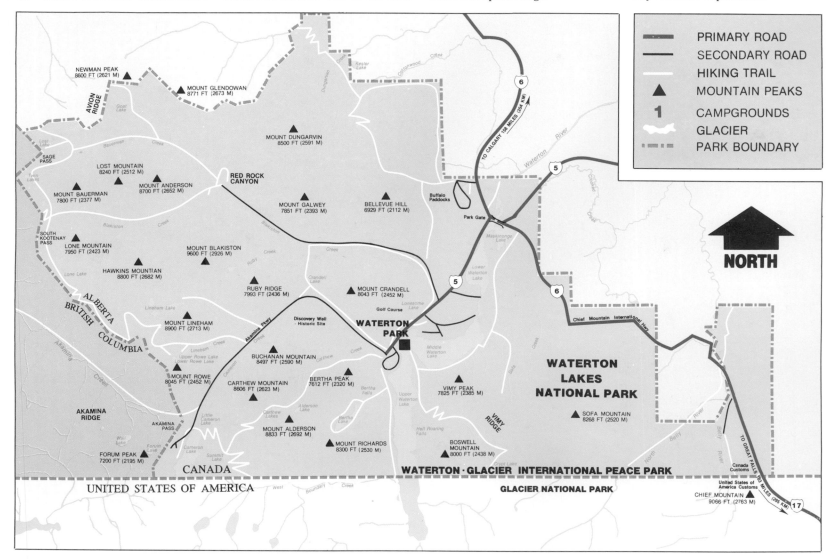

Banff National Park

In 1883, Frank McCabe and William McCardell, workers on the Canadian Pacific Railway, came upon a pool fed by hot springs from Sulphur Mountain. They put up shacks, as did other railway workers, and applied to the federal government for permission to develop the area. The Minister of the Interior, Thomas White, received claims from several people, however, and after examining the area his government decided that it should be reserved for public use. In 1887 Rocky Mountains Park was officially created with an area of 260 square miles (673 square kilometres). That same year, the CPR began construction of the Banff Springs Hotel on a spot chosen by CPR vice-president W.C. Van Horne.

In the first year, there was some confusion over whether lots surrounding the hotel should be leased or sold. The acting park superintendent, George Stewart, thought they should be sold, and accepted options to that end. The government later decided upon leasing only. A scandal soon erupted which eventually led to the removal of Mr. Stewart as park superintendent.

In 1887, the new park attracted 3,000 visitors. By 1891, that had increased to 7,250. In 1892, 51 square miles (132 sq. km.) around Emerald Lake, now Lake Louise, were reserved by the government, and were added to Rocky Mountains Park in 1902. Until after the First World War, access to the parks was by railway only. In 1912, the CPR built a tram line from the Lake Louise station to Chateau Lake Louise, to shuttle passengers to its hotel on the remote, picturesque lake. The line was in service for 20 years.

A unique aspect of this park is the presence of the Banff Centre, a fine arts and management school. It began in 1948 as the Banff School of Fine Art, then an extension of the University of Alberta. The school's Summer Festival of the Arts now attracts visitors and acclaim from around the world each year, and has made Banff an international cultural centre.

Campgrounds

1. Cirrus Mountain
2. Rampart Creek
3. Waterfowl Lakes
4. Mosquito Creek
5. Lake Louise
6. Protection Mountain
7. Castle Mountain
8. Johnston Canyon
9. Two Jack
10. Tunnel Mountain

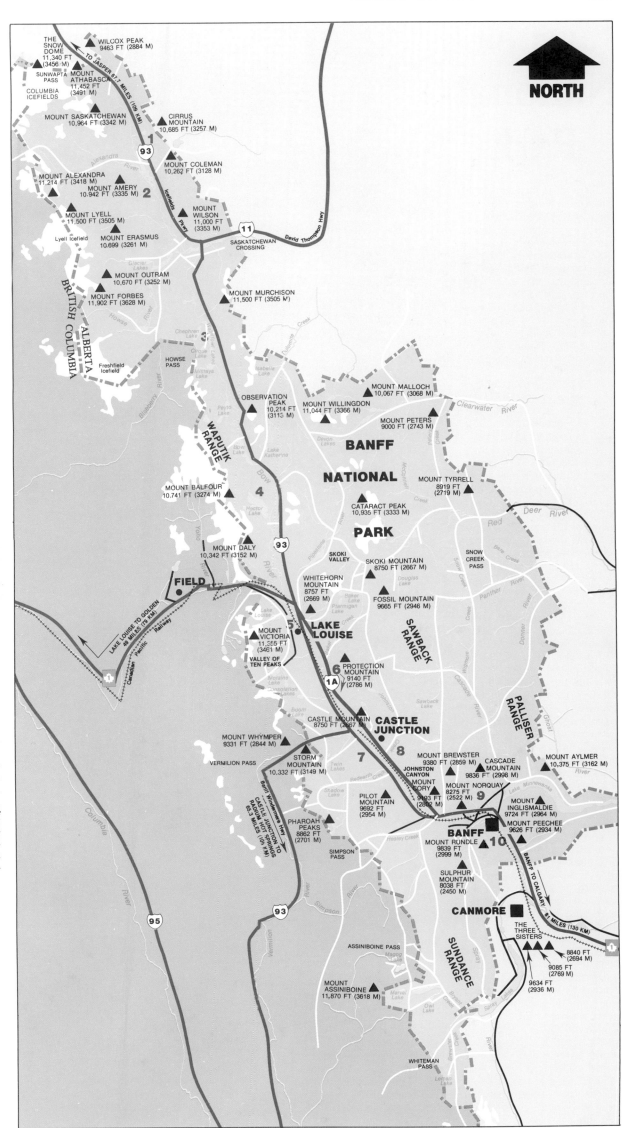

Jasper National Park

The area around Jasper figured prominently in Alberta's early history. The Athabasca, Whirlpool and Miette Rivers were routes for early explorers and fur traders. As early as 1811 explorer David Thompson crossed the Athabasca Pass, opening up the area for fur traders and missionaries. The North West Company built a post at Brule Lake in 1813 called Jasper House, named for the man who ran it, Jasper Hawes.

In 1907, with plans underway for two northern transcontinental railways, the federal government set aside 5,000 square miles (12,945 sq. km.), incorporating the watershed of the Upper Athabasca River, as Jasper Forest Park. As planned, the Grand Trunk Pacific Railway ran right through it. The railway, completed in 1912, and its competitor, the Canadian Northern, provided the only access to the park until after the Second World War. In 1913, the Jasper townsite was surveyed to provide for tourists.

When the park was established, the government had to persuade a few settlers, who had already staked homesteads in the area, to leave. Only one refused. Lewis Swift, the first in the vicinity, was eventually given title to his claim, a gesture for which the government would pay dearly. In 1926, Swift refused the government's $6,000 offer for his land. During the Depression he offered to sell but the government wouldn't buy. Instead, he sold to a private developer, who set up a dude ranch within the park. The property changed hands several times and in the late 1950s, Ottawa finally purchased the property for over a quarter of a million dollars.

The first downhill ski runs at Jasper were developed in 1937 at Whistler. In 1949 Marmot Basin began to attract skiers as well. With no road access to the mountain, visitors had to be carried by snowmobile from the highway. Active development of the ski hills did not begin until the mid-1960s, and the first major highway with access to the slopes was completed in 1970.

Residents in the townsite of Jasper lease their property from the federal government and pay other fees for community maintenance.

Motorists can drive along the Icefields Parkway between Jasper and Lake Louise past scenic waterfalls, the Athabasca Glacier and the Columbia Icefield. Jasper is also the site of the Miette Hot Springs.

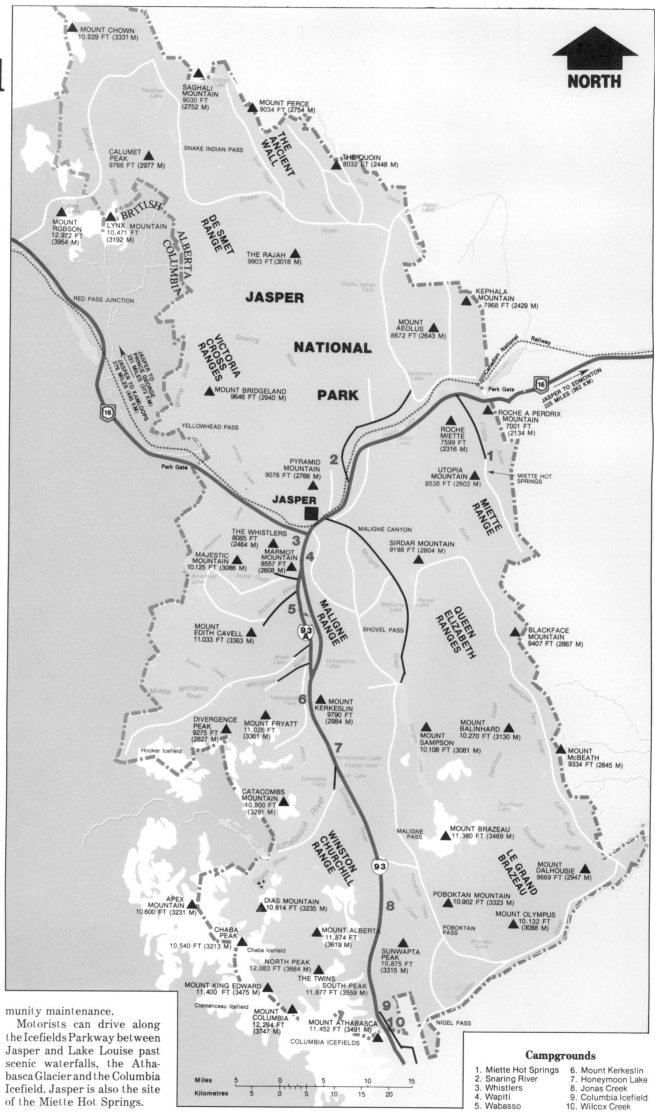

Campgrounds

1. Miette Hot Springs
2. Snaring River
3. Whistlers
4. Wapiti
5. Wabasso
6. Mount Kerkeslin
7. Honeymoon Lake
8. Jonas Creek
9. Columbia Icefield
10. Wilcox Creek

Kananaskis Country

Kananaskis Country was set up in 1978 as a "multi-use recreation area," funded by the Alberta Heritage Savings Trust Fund. Kananaskis covers 1,600 square miles (4,143 sq. km.) and encompasses three provincial parks: Kananaskis, Bragg Creek and Bow Valley. They lie 56 miles (90 km.) southwest of Calgary.

The vicinity has long been popular with Albertans for everything from skiing, hiking and camping to off-road drives and wildlife watching. Part of the rationale for creating Kananaskis Country was to accommodate and control conflicting uses.

Kananaskis Country is not considered a provincial park, and is run by its own managing director. As well, a citizens' advisory committee appointed by the government represents the public's interest to the minister of recreation and parks. Over 300,000 persons visited Kananaskis Country during 1982. In addition to summer and winter camping, fishing, skiing and a variety of other activities, Kananaskis boasts two world-class 18-hole golf courses, and designated trails for off-road and all-terrain vehicles.

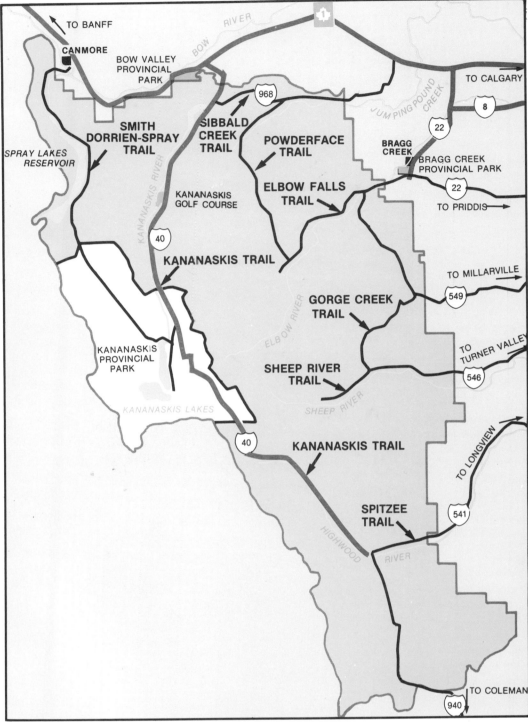

KANANASKIS PROVINCIAL PARK

Campgrounds and picnic areas

1. Grizzly Creek Picnic Area
2. King Creek Picnic Area
3. King Creek Interpretive Trail
4. Elpoca Viewpoint Picnic Area
5. Lakeview Picnic Area
6. Little Highwood Pass Picnic Area
7. Elbow Lake Backcountry Campground
8. Elbow Pass Junction Picnic Area and Elbow Lake Hiking Area
9. Ptarmigan Cirque Interpretive Trail
10. Highwood Meadows Hiking Trail
11. Chester Lake Hiking Trail
12. Burstall Pass Hiking Trail
13. Mount Murray (Ranger Creek) Picnic Area
14. Sawmill Picnic Area
15. Black Prince Cirque Interpretive Trail
16. Smith-Dorrien Picnic Area
17. Black Prince Picnic Area
18. Peninsula Picnic Area
19. Turbine Canyon Backcountry
20. Maude-Lawson Lakes Hiking Trails
21. Three Isle Backcountry Campground
22. Three Isle Hiking Trail
23. Forks Backcountry Campground
24. Point Backcountry Campground
25. Upper Lake Hiking Trail
26. Elk Pass Hiking Trail
27. Elk Pass Picnic Area
28. Canyon Campground, Picnic Area and Boat Launch
29. Visitor Centre
30. William Watson Lodge (Disabled Facility)
31. Elkwood Campground and Amphitheatre
32. Boulton Campground, Concession and Picnic Area
33. Upper Lake Picnic Area and Boat Launch
34. Interlakes Campground and Interpretive Trail
35. Indefatigable Hiking Trail

Provincial Parks

Alberta has 61 provincial parks and one multi-use recreation area called Kananaskis Country, which itself contains three more. These all told comprise some 483 square miles (1,251 sq. km.), and drew over five million visitors in 1982.

The provincial government entered park development relatively late, considering that Alberta's national parks began in 1887. Not until 1932 did Alberta create its first provincial park, which was at Aspen Beach, northwest of Red Deer. This stemmed from the fact that before 1930, the federal government retained control over all natural resources and crown land in Alberta. Shortly after land jurisdiction was handed over to the province, the Alberta government created eight parks.

Until the early 1950s, provincial parks were small waterside areas set aside to serve local, mainly rural, residents. For this reason, much of the work and materials required to develop and maintain them was donated, and Alberta's parks budget was fairly modest. As urbanization and prosperity increased, so too did the need for different sorts of parks. Their management was gradually taken away from local advisory boards to become a full-time government responsibility.

The province's parks now reflect a variety of interests and uses. Many are used primarily for swimming, fishing and camping. But others, like Dinosaur Park near Drumheller and Writing-on-Stone near the Montana border, help preserve the province's geological, historical and archaeological heritage. Still others, like Strathcona Science Park in Edmonton and Fish Creek in Calgary, cater to urban hikers, cyclists and picnickers. Provincial parks present a full range of Alberta's topography, from mountains and foothills to flat prairie, parkland forest and deep coulees.

Regulations and facilities vary considerably from one to the next. In general, admission is free but some levy a fee for camping, and accommodation may be reserved at some. Fishing in any of the parks requires only a provincial permit.

NAME OF PARK	LOCATION
Aspen Beach	9 miles (14 km) west of Lacombe
Beauvais Lake	7 miles (11 km) west; 5 miles (8 km) south of Pincher Creek
Big Hill Springs	5 miles (8 km) north; 3 miles (5 km) east of Cochrane
Big Knife	5 miles (8 km) west; 8 miles (13 km) south of Forestburg
Bow Valley	10 miles (16 km) east of Canmore
Bragg Creek	11 miles (18 km) west; 13 miles (21 km) south of Calgary
Calling Lake	30 miles (48 km) north of Athabasca
Carson-Pegasus	4 miles (6 km) west; 7 miles (11 km) north of Whitecourt
Chain Lakes	24 miles (39 km) southwest of Nanton
Cold Lake	2 miles (3 km) east of Cold Lake
Crimson Lake	5 miles (8 km) west; 4 miles (6 km) north of Rocky Mountain House
Cross Lake	30 miles (48 km) north; 12 miles (19 km) northeast of Westlock
Cypress Hills	18 miles (30 km) east; 21 miles (34 km) south of Medicine Hat
Dillberry Lake	32 miles (52 km) east; 13 miles (21 km) south of Wainwright
Dinosaur	5 miles (8 km) north; 21 miles (33 km) northeast of Brooks
Dry Island Buffalo Jump	8 miles (13 km) north; 12 miles (19 km) east of Trochu
Fish Creek	Calgary southern limit
Garner Lake	30 miles (48 km) east; 3 miles (5 km) north of Smoky Lake
Gooseberry Lake	1 mile (2 km) east; 8 miles (13 km) north of Consort
Gregoire Lake	12 miles (19 km) south; 6 miles (10 km) east of Fort McMurray
Hasse Lake	7 miles (11 km) west; 4 miles (6 km) south of Stony Plain
Hilliard's Bay	10 miles (16 km) east; 12 miles (19 km) northeast of High Prairie
Jarvis Bay	4 miles (7 km) north of Sylvan Lake
Kananaskis	17 miles (27 km) east; 31 miles (50 km) south of Canmore
Kinbrook Island	8 miles (13 km) south; 1 mile (2 km) west of Brooks
Lesser Slave Lake	6 miles (10 km) north of Slave Lake
Little Bow	12 miles (19 km) south; 12 miles (19 km) east of Vulcan
Little Fish Lake	11 miles (18 km) south; 14 miles (22 km) east of Drumheller
Long Lake	4 miles (6 km) east; 24 miles (37 km) northeast of Thorhild
Ma-Me-O Beach	Summer Village of Ma-Me-O Beach; 25 miles (40 km) west of Wetaskiwin
Midland	1 mile (2 km) west of Drumheller
Miquelon Lake	2 miles (3 km) west; 16 miles (26 km) north of Camrose
Moonshine Lake	18 miles (29 km) west; 3 miles (5 km) north of Spirit River
Moose Lake	2 miles (3 km) north; 7 miles (11 km) west of Bonnyville
Notikewin	23 miles (37 km) north; 18 miles (29 km) east of Manning
O'Brien	7 miles (11 km) south of Grande Prairie
Park Lake	9 miles (14 km) north; 1 mile (2 km) west of Lethbridge
Pembina River	2 miles (3 km) east of Evansburg
Pigeon Lake	30 miles (48 km) west; 6 miles (10 km) north of Wetaskiwin
Police Outpost	10 miles (16 km) west; 11 miles (18 km) south of Cardston
Queen Elizabeth-Lac Cardinal	2 miles (3 km) north; 3 miles (5 km) west of Grimshaw
Red Lodge	8 miles (13 km) south; 8 miles (13 km) west of Innisfail
Rochon Sands	7 miles (11 km) west; 10 miles (16 km) north of Stettler
Saskatoon Island	12 miles (19 km) west; 2 miles (3 km) north of Grande Prairie
Sir Winston Churchill	6 miles (10 km) northeast of Lac La Biche
Strathcona Science	Edmonton eastern limit
Sylvan Lake	11 miles (17 km) west of Red Deer
Taber	1 mile (2 km) west; 2 miles (3 km) north of Taber
Thunder Lake	13 miles (21 km) west of Barrhead
Tillebrook	5 miles (8 km) east of Brooks
Vermilion	1 mile (2 km) northwest of Vermilion
Wabamun Lake	18 miles (29 km) west; 1 mile (2 km) south of Stony Plain
Whitney Lakes	16 miles (26 km) east of Elk Point
William A. Switzer	2 miles (3 km) west; 9 miles (15 km) north of Hinton
Williamson	11 miles (18 km) west; 1 mile (2 km) north of Valleyview
Willow Creek	4 miles (6 km) west; 5 miles (8 km) south of Stavely
Winagami Lake	10 miles (16 km) south; 7 miles (11 km) east of McLennon
Woolford	2 miles (3 km) northeast; 8 miles (13 km) southeast of Cardston
Writing-on-Stone	20 miles (32 km) east; 6 miles (10 km) south of Milk River
Wyndham-Carseland	15 miles (24 km) south of Strathmore
Young's Point	16 miles (26 km) west; 6 miles (9 km) northeast of Valleyview

Alberta
RECREATION AND PARKS

0   50   100 km

▲ PROVINCIAL PARKS

PRODUCED 1983

Prepared by Graphics, Design and Implementation Division.

How to read the legal description of an Alberta property

The Dominion Land Survey, initiated during the 1870s, divided the fertile Canadian prairies into a mammoth grid of 160-acre parcels. These "quarter-section" homestead lots, available virtually free at one per family, lured a tidal wave of settlers to the West. The DLS system forms the basis of Alberta land titles to this day.

To create the grid, the surveyors required reference lines running both north/south and east/west. The north/south requirement was met by choosing five lines of longitude, known as meridians. The first DLS meridian passes west of Winnipeg. The fourth meridian today forms the border between Saskatchewan and Alberta. The fifth runs through the community of Stony Plain; in Calgary the Barlow Trail in part follows the course of this meridian. The sixth and last of the Alberta meridians cuts east of Grande Prairie, west of Edson and winds up in Jasper National Park. Meridians are shown on the map this way ——.

East/west "base lines" were also established, numbering 32 in Alberta, the first being the U.S.-Canadian border along the 49th parallel. Edmonton's 101st Avenue follows the 14th base line; the seventh slices through north Calgary. They're shown on the map thus ——.

Meridians and base lines, therefore, formed a large-scale grid. Using these as reference, surveyors laid out hundreds of additional parallel lines, blanketing the province with 36-square-mile units known as "townships."

The accompanying map illustrates the township system. Moving south to north, "township" lines are numbered. (Note that township row 29 is also the eighth base line.) Cutting across the township rows are "ranges," parallelling the meridians. Ranges move numerically from east to west, with the sequence beginning again at 1 as each meridian is crossed. Every individual township is bounded by two range lines and two township lines. Range and township lines are shown——.

Between the base lines, the ranges jog westward a little along correction lines. This compensates for the error inherent in laying out a grid on the earth's curvature. (This error factor is due to the meridians' drawing closer as they move towards the North Pole, where all lines of longitude converge.) Along the U.S. border, 30 ranges lie between the fourth and fifth meridians. In the north, that figure has been stepped down to 24.

An individual township is divided into 36 "sections," each a square mile (see below). The other diagram below shows the pattern of subdivision identification, within any section. Note that the numbers increase east to west, south to north like the township rows and ranges.

A section in turn is made up of quarter sections, identified as northeast, southeast, northwest and southwest. Alternatively a section may be carved into 16 legal subdivisions, with the numbers running back and forth from the southeast corner. The finer legal subdivision grid was useful to surveyors in need of a rough, quick method of identifying bodies of

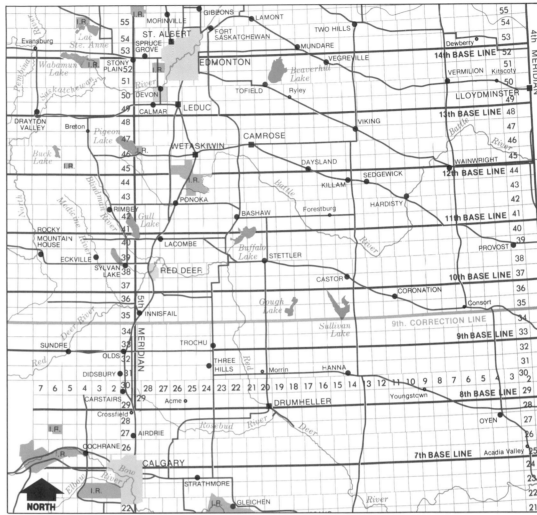

water. Instead of delineating the water's actual boundary, the surveyor would simply identify a legal subdivision or approximate fraction as being water.

The DLS ensured access by providing road allowances. An Alberta motorist driving east or west will encounter a "section road" every mile. Moving north or south, road allowances appear every second mile. Occasionally local geography will force the second pattern to skip a beat and a "forced road" has been built along the "blind line" where normally no route would exist. Old section roads were often incorporated into the urban network, as with Calgary's 17th Avenue S.W.

In areas settled before the DLS, such as St. Albert, Fort McMurray and Edmonton, the township grid ran up to existing property lines. Typically these earlier boundaries reflect the long, narrow riverfront lots popular with the Metis.

Later towns were often laid out by a railway company; names like Grand Trunk Pacific are still preserved in Alberta legal titles. The urban system of land identification did not replace the DLS

usages but rather built on top of the earlier pattern with the quarter-section grid being formed into convenient subdivisions. Developers file legal "plans" with municipal and provincial agencies. On a plan, a subdivision is split into clearly defined "blocks" and blocks into numbered "lots."

The following example illustrates the system:

LOT TWELVE (12)
IN BLOCK TWENTY-FOUR (24)
PLAN 720 H.W.
DEVON   (N.W. 34-50-26-W.4TH)

This title identifies the property as lot 12 in block 24 as laid out on a permanent plan filed and numbered by the North Alberta Land Registration District. Devon is an incorporated town southwest of Edmonton. The land is further identified under the DLS system as situated in the northwest quarter of section 34, north of township line 50 and west of range 26, a range lying west of the fourth meridian. It is shown on the map in green.

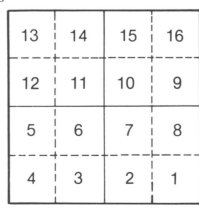

How sections are numbered within a township

How subdivisions are numbered within a section

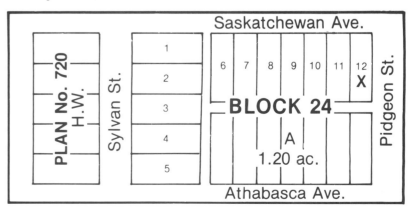

A typical urban plan

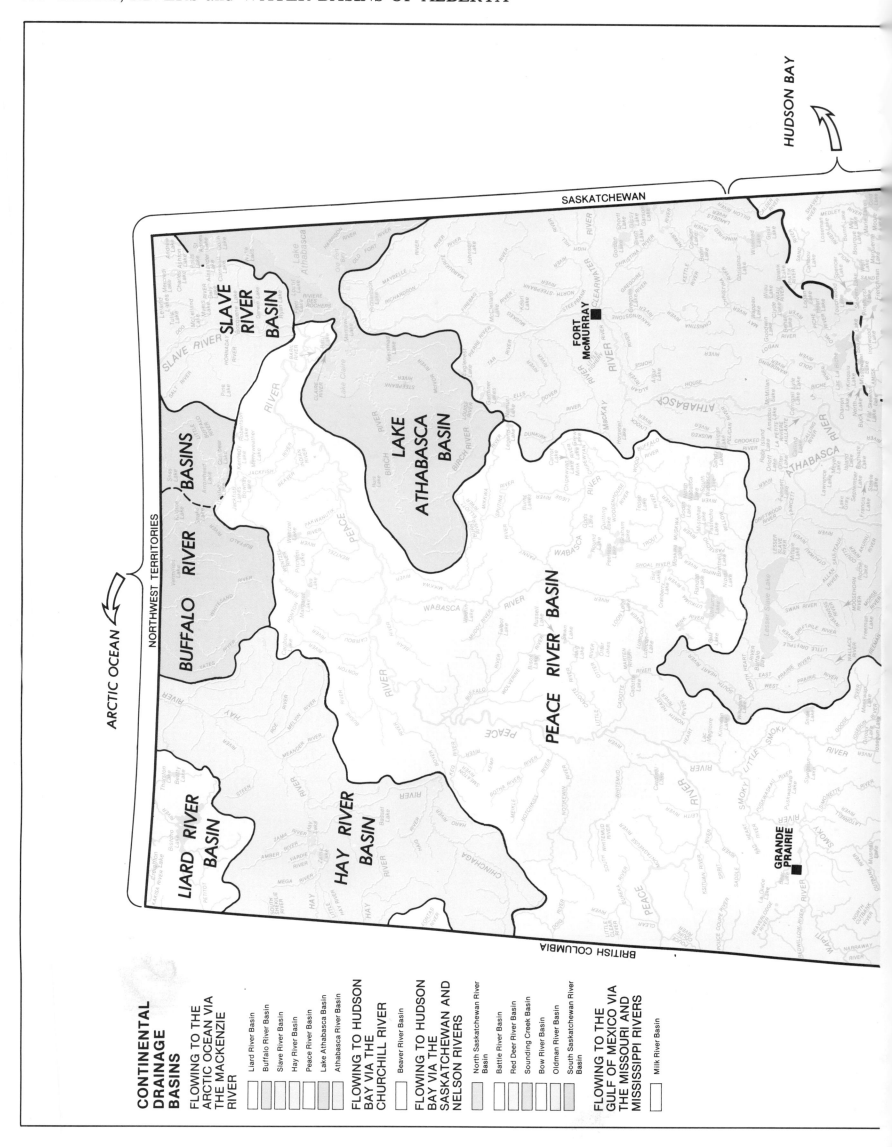

CONTINENTAL DRAINAGE BASINS

FLOWING TO THE ARCTIC OCEAN VIA THE MACKENZIE RIVER

Liard River Basin
Buffalo River Basin
Slave River Basin
Hay River Basin
Peace River Basin
Lake Athabasca Basin
Athabasca River Basin

FLOWING TO HUDSON BAY VIA THE CHURCHILL RIVER

Beaver River Basin

FLOWING TO HUDSON BAY VIA THE SASKATCHEWAN AND NELSON RIVERS

North Saskatchewan River Basin
Battle River Basin
Red Deer River Basin
Sounding Creek Basin
Bow River Basin
Oldman River Basin
South Saskatchewan River Basin

FLOWING TO THE GULF OF MEXICO VIA THE MISSOURI AND MISSISSIPPI RIVERS

Milk River Basin